Women and Asian Religions

Women and Asian Religions

ZAYN R. KASSAM, EDITOR

Women and Religion in the World
Cheryl A. Kirk-Duggan, Lillian Ashcraft-Eason,
and Karen Jo Torjesen, Series Editors

 PRAEGER ™

An Imprint of ABC-CLIO, LLC
Santa Barbara, California • Denver, Colorado

Library of Congress Cataloging-in-Publication Data

Names: Kassam, Zayn, editor.
Title: Women and Asian religions / Zayn R. Kassam, editor.
Description: Santa Barbara : Praeger, 2017. | Series: Women and religion in
  the world | Includes bibliographical references and index.
Identifiers: LCCN 2017004205 (print) | LCCN 2017011737 (ebook) |
  ISBN 9780313082757 (ebook) | ISBN 9780275991593 (alk. paper : alk. paper)
Subjects: LCSH: Women and religion—Asia.
Classification: LCC BL458 (ebook) | LCC BL458 .W5623 2017 (print) |
  DDC 200.82/095—dc23
LC record available at https://lccn.loc.gov/2017004205

ISBN: 978-0-275-99159-3
EISBN: 978-0-313-08275-7

21 20 19 18 17   1 2 3 4 5

This book is also available as an eBook.

Praeger
An Imprint of ABC-CLIO, LLC

ABC-CLIO, LLC
130 Cremona Drive, P.O. Box 1911
Santa Barbara, California 93116-1911
www.abc-clio.com

This book is printed on acid-free paper (∞)

Manufactured in the United States of America

To all who work for gender justice
in honor of Kathleen M. Mirante, M.D.
(April 8, 1940–April 10, 2017)

Contents

Part V. WOMEN, WORLDVIEW, AND RELIGIOUS PRACTICE

Acknowledgments

This volume would not have been possible without the vision of Cheryl Kirk-Duggan, Lillian Ashcraft-Eason, and Karen J. Torjesen, who envisaged a series of works that would bring together the way in which women were addressing contemporary and local issues through a globalized, and often religious, consciousness. I would like to thank each of the contributors to this volume for generously responding to my request to share their thinking and research with a broader readership. Working with Bridget Austiguy-Preschel, Gordon Hammy Matchado and Ezhil RK, the editors at ABC-CLIO, has been a pleasure and I thank each one for attending to the myriad details involved in bringing a project such as this to light. My profound gratitude for Kathleen Mirante, who so kindly offered a place in which to read, reflect, and write. Her generosity was boundless, and for that I am deeply grateful. To my parents, children, siblings, and close friends, I owe a debt of gratitude for their unqualified love and support. And finally, as with all such work, any blemishes are mine alone.

Zayn R. Kassam
Claremont, California, 2017

Introduction

Zayn R. Kassam

This volume was conceived as the volume on Asian Religions in a series titled *Women and Religion in the World*. Its intent is to focus on contemporary selected experiences of women and how their lives interface with religion. Each volume is organized according to five themes: (1) women, family, and environment; (2) socioeconomics, politics, and authority; (3) mind, body, and spirit; (4) sexuality, power, and vulnerability; and (5) women, worldview, and religious practice. Although the boundaries between each of the themes are permeable, the chapters under each theme illumine different lenses through which the theme may be engaged.

Contrary to popular perception, religions in Asia comprise not only the traditions of Hinduism, Islam, and Buddhism, but also Christianity, Judaism, Jain, Bahai, and indigenous traditions. As the chapters reveal, the challenges and opportunities Asian women face arise both from within and outside, whether in relation to developments within their countries or in relation to international political and economic regimes. The issues they face have as much to do with cultural and religious codes as with politics, economics, education, and the law. Thus, the various chapters under each theme take on many important arenas of investigation. The overarching question for the volume might be: How do women draw upon and/or negotiate their faith identities to address the issues they face in the changing contexts of politics, globalization, religion/spirituality, and feminism? Each of the chapters is reviewed under the relevant theme.

WOMEN, FAMILY, AND ENVIRONMENT

Maria Talamantes examines the narratives of M. Switri and N. Suastini, two women dancers who, as part of touring *gamelan* or music and dance ensembles, performed throughout Indonesia, Japan, and the United States during the late New Order period (1995–1998). These performers recreated their identities as mothers, family providers, and independent women by embodying and performing the intersecting discourses of the Indonesian national agenda of gendered tourism and local Hindu-Balinese religion and *adat* or customary practice, which extolls motherhood and restricts traveling. Faced with the challenges of a country fast-tracking itself into a globalized economy, Balinese women found themselves in the midst of Indonesia's state campaign to construct them as wives and mothers within their families and the family of the state. Positioned at the juncture of modernity and tradition, Balinese women dancers were mobilized by the state to participate in performances associated with the 18-month traveling Festival of Indonesia, through which the state sought to export an exotic representation of its culture in order to attract tourism to Bali and Yogyakarta. Thus, they were caught between the national agenda of women as workers traveling abroad for the nation and the conventional cultural/religious framework of women as wives and mothers. The chapter examines the ways in which women performers, mindful of the social consequences that could be borne by their families if they were perceived as challenging conventional male authority and religious and culturally assigned roles to women, frame and negotiate their performance-related travels abroad. The chapter compellingly shows how forces of modernity are mediated through religious frameworks that allow for integration between the competing pulls of Balinese religious tradition and Indonesian national development, which permit women simultaneously to participate in both arenas.

Narasingha P. Sil examines another situation in which a woman had to negotiate not state power or the agenda of the state for Indian women, but the power of a husband-turned-godman, whose decision to leave his wife childless yet the mother of many sons entailed his wife's divinization after his death. The process by which Sriramakrishna *Paramahaṁsa's* wife Saradamani Chattopadhyay (1853–1920) became a living goddess after her husband's death is examined by Sil in a departure from the usual theological explanations for this turn; rather, he examines conversations and exquisitely detailed eye-witness accounts to argue for a middle way between patriarchal and feminist readings of religion so as to focus on each seeker's realization of the divine. Denied the joys of physical motherhood, as Divine Mother, Saradamani becomes the conduit for others to attain spiritual realization, thereby fulfilling her husband's prophecy that she would become the mother of many sons.

Visisya Pinthongvijayakul explores a female medium's marital tension within the context of labor migration and social changes in northeast Thailand. The chapter seeks to address the following questions: What impact does labor mobility have on the mediums' conjugal and familial relationships? How does spirit possession work in such transnational contexts? And in what ways do the mediums reinterpret and operate spirit possession to negotiate the struggles experienced by the family in crisis? Anthropological study of female mediums has sought to understand why women are preponderant in spirit possession and mediumship, and how mediums construct their identity and mediate domestic issues, suggesting that such a role allows them to overturn or negotiate with social power structures in addition to serving the spirits. Utilizing a life histories approach, Pinthongvijayakul examines the specific familial and social context of a medium whose husband works abroad for long periods of time to ask: "To what extent does her hardship of child-raising and tension of husband's long-term absence shape the logic of the spirits and of mediumship practice? Likewise, how do other mediums' experiences of parental and connubial desertion influence the logic of their ritualized enactments? In what ways do they privatize communal deities and local spirits into their own family's problematic concerns? And in the context of transnational migration, how does possession by the spirits mediate a resolution of critical situations in the domestic domain?" Theoretically grounded, this chapter argues that spirit possession practices can enable the rehabilitation of the social self and moral restitution in the domestic domain, while simultaneously paying attention to the dislocations caused by economic globalization and labor migration.

Lavanya Vemsani's illuminating chapter examines concepts of motherhood in premodern and contemporary India. Her examination of a mother's rights, practices of motherhood within social and cultural norms, and its economic aspects alongside health care facilities for mother and child reveal a deeply disturbing picture to show that the valorization of motherhood has not translated into greater access to health care for mothers and children, nor to better protections in the face of newer technological developments such as artificial reproductive therapy or surrogacy. Such deficits hamper the development of women and children in one of the most highly populated countries in the world, and one of the world's largest democracies, despite the economic and educational strides made in the country since gaining independence from the British in 1947.

SOCIOECONOMICS, POLITICS, AUTHORITY

Vivienne SM Angeles examines Muslim women's movements in the Philippines in the context of struggles for statehood. Her study of Muslim women's activism from the 1970s to the present day reveals the multivalency and multiple foci of such activism, evolving from involvement in the secessionist movement to participating in transnational discourses such as the CEDAW (Convention on the Elimination of all forms of Discrimination against Women), DEVAW (Declaration on the Elimination of Violence against Women), and women's rights legislations more locally. Interviews with women involved in the Moro National Liberation Front (MNLF) established in 1969 and consisting largely of men reveal how the political struggle for better treatment of Muslims became intensely personal for women losing kin on the battlefield while also raising political consciousness among women and in time creating a women's committee to support the secessionist effort. The slowing down of the war in the 1980s and the creation of the Autonomous Region of Muslim Mindanao ultimately led to Muslim women's roles in creating and sustaining nongovernmental organizations through international and national funding to address the deleterious effects of war on families and children. In the 1990s, struggles for gender justice represented in Islamic terms became the focus of Muslim women's organizational efforts, which extended to ensuring just and fair participation in political matters, peace making, religious instruction, and the right to wear the hijab.

Antoinette E. DeNapoli tells the story of a powerful *sādhu,* the late Ganga Giri Mahārāj, whose rhetorical practices instruct her disciples in moral lessons that speak particularly to the plight of women. Drawing attention to the shadow story, that is, stories that reveal the harsh and hidden side of everyday reality, DeNapoli explores Ganga Giri's shadow stories as a form of protest against the marginalization of vulnerable populations such as the aged, the poor, women, and *sādhus.* However, the stories are not just a form of protest drawing attention to the vulnerable but also open up the possibility to construct a meaningful life negotiating the gap between the ideal and the real. The chapter highlights the tension between a *sādhu's* commitment voluntarily to choose poverty and live independently of others, and life's exigencies positioned around issues of gender, ageism, and violence that demand interdependence and a source of livelihood.

William Harman, in his chapter on Sri Lankan Tamil female martyr bombers, examines the power of women to address injustice and violence utilized in a manner in which the female protagonist herself becomes an instrument of death and vilified in the media. This chapter argues that simply dismissing such women as insane hampers our understanding of the reasons behind the high percentage of the occurrence of women martyr bombers in the Sri Lankan conflict. Considering that South Asian culture views a woman as having "both special powers as well as special responsibilities when it comes to constructing and influencing a society in which justice and prosperity prevail," the chapter explores antecedents in human beings-turned-goddesses to explore the deeper cultural and religious underpinnings of the phenomenon of the Sri Lankan female who is willing to give up her life in acting out of commitment to her principles.

Jae Woo Jang examines the social, political, and economic empowerment of indigenous women in the Cordillera region of the Philippines. The culture is arguably structured in a manner that allows human beings to live in a symbiotic relationship with the natural environment while valuing the contributions of both genders to societal well-being in a manner that is neither patriarchal nor matriarchal. Rather, its religious tradition is a combination of polytheism, mythology, superstition, and animism through which members of the community view women not as subordinate but as complementary to men, and which values women's status and authority as orators, landowners, artists, artisans, mothers, and leaders. This chapter examines the worldview of indigenous peoples and the struggles and challenges indigenous women face brought about by the changes wrought by colonization, modernization, and Christianization.

BODY, MIND, AND SPIRIT

Anru Lee and Wen-hui Anna Tang take us to Taiwan to examine the renovation of the Twenty-Five Ladies' Tomb, so named in commemoration of 25 unmarried female workers who drowned in a ferry on their way to an export-processing zone in Kaohsiung, southern Taiwan. The Taiwanese taboo on unmarried female ghosts made the site a place to be avoided and the subject of unkind banter, raising the ire of feminists at how these unfortunate female laborers were memorialized and treated. The city's increasing tourism sparked an urban revitalization project that brought to the forefront the politics of memory as the site was renovated, relocated, reconceptualized, and renamed to signal the incident as a pivotal point in female labor history in Taiwan. Delving into issues pertaining to the unmarried status of the women who died so tragically, the compensation given to families on their deaths, reports of miraculous visitations and healings, and contributions made by Taiwanese women to the globalizing economy of Taiwan, this chapter weaves together these discrete strands to show how larger feminist concerns were "subsumed under the government's economically minded urban revitalization effort."

Angela Rudert goes to Punjab, India, to chart the transformational journey of Gurpreet Grover into the celebrated spiritual guide Anandmurti Gurumaa. Charting this journey to show the awakening of *śakti* (feminine power) within Gurumaa, and the establishment of her nongovernmental organization Shakti, aimed at addressing the needs of young women, Rudert reveals Gurumaa to have transformed her religious tradition while simultaneously remaining deeply rooted within it. As an exemplar of women's empowerment, Gurumaa's spiritual teachings challenge all forms of oppression, especially masculinist domination of religion and women's disempowerment, through critiquing such use of tradition, on the one hand, and awakening the *shakti* or power, within, usually conceptualized as a feminine force, on the other. The latter is most powerfully expressed in her song titled *"Suno, Suno"* (Listen!), a call for women to unleash the power of transformation from within, which Rudert explores to show its deep roots within the tradition.

Kristen Rudisill leads us to Hyderabad, India, to examine the role of intentionality in the transformative work theater activist Pritham Chakravarthy undertakes with regard to the politics of representation and issues of the body. Intended to benefit the communities Chakravarthy features in her work, she employs storytelling to introduce progressive topics that connect the storyteller to the person/woman being represented and the audience, thereby allowing for silent/silenced voices to be heard and their situations better understood. Drawing on Martin Ganz's observation that stories motivate us to act, Rudisill explores how Chakravarthy's performance "motivates and inspires people," especially those for whom Chakravarthy bears witness. A powerful example of the potential of stories to bear witness is found in the request made by transgendered female subjects that their stories be told to show how much more their lives convey than the stereotypical stigmatized victims they are often depicted as being.

Leesa Davis looks at narratives of Buddhist women in Australia and France, countries that fall under the Western orbit, to ask how "traditional boundaries of institutional organization and gender are traversed in cross-cultural encounters." How do they address the contentious issues that surround Buddhist women with respect to salvation, for instance, given that the sacred texts themselves give differing views on whether gender is irrelevant, whether being born female is due to past negative karma, or whether only a male can attain Buddhahood, thus necessitating rebirth as a male in order to attain salvation. Arguing with Bernard Faure that although misogynistic tendencies are well represented in Buddhism—as in other world faiths—its openness to "multiplicity and contradiction" allows practitioners the space to negotiate more equitable gender roles in Western Buddhist institutional hierarchies as well as in practice. In viewing themselves as independent agents who are not only practicing self-transformation but also reorienting institutional practice, the women practitioners interviewed here continue the trend in evidence in Asian societies explored in the final chapter of this volume—the two chapters could fruitfully be read together—of Buddhist women as agents of personal and institutional transformation, in both Asian and cross-cultural contexts, whether these women are lay or ordained. While this chapter argues that such transformations draw upon the Western emphasis on egalitarianism, the final chapter argues that similar transformations are under way in Asian countries due to the institutionalization of meditation schools in which women have been able to assume greater leadership roles. It is quite possible to conceive of increasing gender parity coming about in societies throughout the world due to their engagement with modernity (rather than Westernization, per se) at the same time as the democratization of spiritual practice aimed at self-transformation has led to institutional changes globally, making it possible for women to reinvent their traditional religious roles.

SEXUALITY, POWER, AND VULNERABILITY

Nicole Aaron examines the ambiguous figure of the *devadasi* ("sacred servant"), popularly considered to be a sex worker, in the South Indian state of Karnataka in relation to their multiple and changing identities due to reform and rehabilitation schemes. The Karnataka *devadasis* tend to be Dalit women who were once considered empowered temple dancers devoted to the service of Hindu deities. Building on historical associations of sex work undertaken by *devadasis*, the colonial gaze transformed them into exploited prostitutes, thus blurring the religious aspects of their identity and conflating the godservant, the dancing girl, and the prostitute into the figure of the devadasi, who was then subjected to colonial reforms. Emerging nationalism and feminist movements conceptualized an idealized female representative of the nascent postcolonial Indian nation, and the *devadasi* was further condemned by these middle class women's movements which saw them as a threat to their own ideals of marriage, respectability, and domesticity. Ironically, such condemnation enacted subordination of lower class women rather than establishing solidarity with women across classes. The chapter traces the disenfranchisement of *devadasis* from their traditional occupations and dedication to the temple, the criminalization of their sexual practices, the hijacking of their dance traditions, and the wresting of their control over their sexual relations with men into the more "respectable" institution of marriage. The larger feminist question of whether sex work can be empowering for women within the context of the shifting marital, economic, and religious identities of *devadasis* remains an intriguing question explored by the rich ethnographic research presented in this chapter.

Keun-Joo Christine Pae turns the volume's attention to Christianity and women's peace activism in Korea, in consideration of the 60th anniversary (2013) of the devastating three-year war between North and South Korea. The continued military presence of U.S. armed forces and the powerlessness thereby invoked have resulted in the silencing of the voices of the over a million Korean women who have sold sex to G.I.s in "comfort sta-tions" and "camptowns." As Pae notes, "In a society where the interweaving of anti-communism with patriarchal militarism is real, women can hardly speak about their particular experiences related to military violence, mil-itarized imperialism, and patriarchal nationalism." However, through eth-nographic and textual research, this chapter lays out the tireless efforts of Korean women to work for gender equality, women's rights, and protection of women and girls from sexual violence, especially in the context of militarized prostitution. In developing the frame of "a politics of empathy," Pae lays out how Christian Korean faith-based activists in conjunction with the global feminist antiwar movement have responded to domestic and international military issues in their peace activism, thereby modeling "important praxis for antiwar global feminism." The chapter raises critical issues regarding the importance of global solidarity in peace praxis; the mainstreaming of gen-der as an analytical category for examining transnationalized militarism and global politics; and, finally, the role that a politics of empathy could play in overcoming fear, healing, and peacefully resisting militarization.

Khani Begum ponders cinematic responses to the trauma of the 9/11 attacks. She sees the initial silence after the 9/11 attacks as respecting the nation's need to mourn, while also reflecting confusion over how to repre-sent this national trauma. In turning to South Asian cinema, she shows how filmic responses to 9/11 built on the deeply ingrained memories of Partition trauma, "through their engagement with discourses of terrorism, religion, gender, and nation." Theoretically rooted in Sarkar's evocation of "the return of the repressed," Begum suggests that in films depicting Partition, women are conceptually seen as symbol for the nation, for whom men are willing to perform the ultimate sacrifice. In the case of South Asian films depicting post-9/11 realities, Begum contends that they are located within the larger global discourse of terrorism and offer as-yet unexamined perspectives on the angst of diasporan South Asians caught in the "crossfire of the rhetoric on the war on terror." Taking the Pakistani film *Khuda ke Liye* (2007), popularly translated as *In the Name of God,* as her point of focus, Begum notes that the film takes on the form and function of national mourning. Simultaneously, she appeals to the concept of transvergence to argue that "non-linear and trans-linear 'derailments' of idealized conceptions of nationhood, patriotism, religion, gender, and cultural heritage in this, as in other post-9/11 South Asian films, question current ideologies that drive these discourses today." The film depicts post-9/11 realities in a manner that allows it to address Pakistan's own nationalist struggles, its recollection of Partition trauma, and the discord wrought by fundamentalism. The female character in the film is unwittingly caught in these conflicts, and her character points to creative spaces through which some of these complexities may be engaged.

WOMEN, WORLDVIEW, AND RELIGIOUS PRACTICE

Petcharat Lovichakorntikul, Phramaha Min Putthithanasombat, and John Walsh in their chapter relate the life and teachings of the Thai Buddhist nun Khun Yai Chand Khonnokyoong (1909–2000) from the traditional perspective in order to show why devotees turn to her as a model for advancement in their own worldly and spiritual lives. This remarkable figure with little formal education was able to amass sufficient spiritual authority under the tutelage of Phramongkolthepmuni (1885–1959), the Abbot of Wat Paknam Bhasicharoen, Bangkok. She was able to raise the funding and resources required to build her temple, Wat Phra Dhammakaya. The temple has become one of the major global centers of Buddhism today, attracting visitors from around the globe to observe Buddhist holy days as well as receive instruction in meditation and *dhamma* (dharma). Her teachings and methods for attaining self-realization are explored in this chapter and continued, implemented, and built upon by her students, who have since become abbots in their own right.

Paola Cavaliere turns her attention to women's engagement in contemporary Japanese faith-based volunteer organizations to examine the role of such women in eliciting social change including democratization supporting women's social participation and the inclusion of women in the formal and informal Japanese economy. Based on data collected in a survey conducted in 2009–2010, the chapter lays out the scope and nature of the work undertaken by volunteers from religious organizations including Buddhist-related new religious movements and the Roman Catholic Church. Departing from established paradigms and polarities (such as secular/religious) seeking to explain religious women's participation in volunteer organizations through the lenses of "internalized social norms, internalization of doctrinal conservative views, or responses to externalized constraints," this chapter seeks instead "to elucidate the extent to which women's everyday interaction and agency in grassroots faith-based volunteering helps in cultivating social stewardship and articulating new trajectories of self in contemporary Japanese society." It draws upon actor network theory and utilizes narrative and network analysis as tools through which to view the volunteer as an actor able to tell his or her own stories and to map out the social space and its effect on volunteers. The actor's stories show that despite "structural, ideological, and socioeconomic components channeling women into social roles providing volunteer attitudes and practices, women are able to create new orientations and new customs and develop an enterprising approach that gives them the opportunity of social entrepreneurship."

June McDaniel examines the role played by religion in women's lives in West Bengali Shaktism or goddess worship through both textual and ethnographic material. She focuses on four groups: tribal or *adivasi* women, such as those belonging to the Santal and Oraon tribes; rural Hindu women; urban Hindu women who are *tantrikas* (followers of Tantra Hinduism); and urban women who observe Shakta bhakti (devotion to Shakti). A consideration of the rituals accompanying the worship of the Old Lady goddess, in contrast to the worship of youthful Hindu goddesses, highlights the respect given to older women for the wisdom earned through a lifetime of experience, while also showing how the possession of both younger and older women by the Old Lady goddess builds a sense of shared experience and community. Among rural Hindu women, the performance of vows or *bratas* entailing observance of certain restrictions in return for a divine boon instantiates within the girls and women keeping a *brata* the resilience to deal with life's tribulations through virtuousness. The urban renunciant women examined in this chapter comprise female *tantrikas*, who take on roles beyond those usually prescribed for women in Tantric texts, namely, ritual incarnation of the goddess, ritual consort for sexual *sadhana*, and female gurus. As the ethnographic evidence shows, female *tantrikas* comprise "holy women" of various types ranging from renunciant to teacher to wife, such as explored in this chapter. The final section of the chapter deals with devotion to the goddess, or emotional Shakta bhakti, in which four major relationships with the goddess are examined: the Great Goddess, the Daughter, the Lover, and Ocean of Consciousness. The conclusion considers the question of whether worshipping the goddess has any effect on the social location of the women who do so.

Brooke Schedneck's chapter on the rise of Theravada Buddhist *vipassanā* (or insight meditation) teachers in Southeast Asia culminates the volume. Focusing primarily on Thai and Burmese women, and to a lesser extent on Laotian and Cambodian women due to the disparities in scholarship, this chapter argues that emergent educational and training opportunities for women have contributed significantly toward "increasing the respect and prestige directed toward Buddhist women in Southeast Asia, especially precept nuns." In addition to the role of educational institutions in creating legitimation for Buddhist women, social engagement projects undertaken by some notable Buddhist women are explored in this chapter to show the pathways to leadership roles that are being opened up by women for women. Not to be overlooked is the role of spiritual power, or *iddhi,* in establishing noteworthy women as healers and religious teachers, who attract a following that is often drawn to the teacher/healer for her supernatural powers.

Schedneck then explores an unexpected avenue that has opened up for female meditators and teachers in *vipassanā* meditation schools. Traditionally taught by monks to their students, meditation underwent a process of laicization that "has reconfigured Buddhist practice in Theravāda Southeast

Asia, as well as created openings for female meditators and teachers." The *vipassanā* reform movements that emerged against a backdrop of colonization and modernization centered on making mediation available to all and were accompanied by the rise of meditation centers that offered classes in scripture and practice in meditation to monks and laity alike, regardless of gender. The success and extent of these centers have created national movements in the Theravāda Buddhist countries of Southeast Asia and, with them, leadership opportunities for women, as explored in the remainder of the chapter.

PART I

Woman, Family, and Environment

CHAPTER 1

Balinese Dancers on the Global Stage: Negotiating Motherhood, Religion, and Politics during the Suharto Regime

Maria Talamantes

Indonesian artists, particularly Balinese women dancers and their performances became a unique cultural product of the Indonesian New Order
government policies of development and gender during the 1966–1998
period. Impelled by the national agenda, the dancers performed locally
and internationally, negotiated their roles as mothers and housewives, and
reimagined their identities in ways that addressed their local system of religion. This chapter examines the narratives of M. Switri and N. Suastini,[1] two
women dancers who, as part of touring *gamelan* (music and dance ensembles), performed throughout Indonesia, Japan, and the United States during
1995–1998. These performers recreated their identities as mothers, family
providers, and independent women by embodying and performing the intersecting discourses of the Indonesian national agenda of gendered tourism,
which promoted an "idealized femininity,"[2] and the local Hindu-Balinese
religion and *adat* (customary practice), which extolled motherhood and
restricted traveling.

3

To analyze and contextualize the women's practices, it is necessary to look beyond Eurocentric notions of agency (individual power, personal autonomy and free will), which are incompatible with Balinese culture.[3] Thus, my broad framework brings together the women's proactive behaviors, aspirations, and ability to plan and enact them as acts of intentional agency,[4] changes in states of consciousness (e.g., spirit possession), transnational alliances with traveling deities,[5] and identification with mythological icons of femininity such as Sita.[6] This framework incorporates the fluid Balinese cosmological worldview, which is populated by humans, spirits, and gods capable of possessing humans,[7] as shown in Balinese magic-religious dance performances.[8] The ethnographic aspect of this chapter is based on field-work conducted in the villages of Ketewel and Peliatan in Bali, Indonesia, during 1999, 2001, and 2002. The following section briefly introduces the sociopolitical and religious matrix during this period.

INTRODUCTION

Like other women in Southeast Asia, Balinese women faced complex dilemmas as their countries began to incorporate globalized development agendas. As Eastern and Southeast Asian countries benefited from eco-nomic global trends, they became a hub for female migratory labor force. Women from Cambodia, Indonesia, Malaysia, the Philippines, Myanmar, Thailand, and Sri Lanka traveled abroad to engage in lowly paid jobs as domestic workers, caretakers, entertainers, and sex workers while they were expected to remain their family's primary caretakers.[9] At the close of the 20th century, Balinese women—and dancers in particular—were at the center of contending discursive practices operating within the local, national, and transnational contexts. This event was an outcome of the family, gender, and tourism development policies established during the Dutch colonial period (1908–1945),[10] changed during the Sukarno era of Independence (1945–1967),[11] and reconfigured during the Suharto's New Order govern-ment (1966–1998).[12]

The Dutch colonial policies reconstructed Indonesian women's identity and roles to fit a modernized notion of motherhood and the family.[13] During the Independence phase, the politically active "Manipol"[14] family replaced the colonial notion. Thereafter, the New Order regime changed the concept of the "Manipol" to a subordinate one, led by *Bapak* ("Father") Suharto and *Ibu* ("Mother").[15] Based on the concept of *kodrat*[16] (intrinsic nature) and "state *ibuism*,"[17] Suharto's gender and family policies and organizations rede-fined the identity, behavior, work, and morality of Indonesian people and in particular of civil servants and their wives. "State *ibuism*" portrayed women as "appendages and companions to their husbands, procreators of the nation, mothers and educators of children, housekeepers, and as members of Indonesian society—in that order."[18] While this approach affixed women and their identities to the domestic roles of wives and mothers within their family and the family of the state,[19] the national organizations enlisted the voluntary work of both female civil servants and civil servants' wives to embody and disseminate the official agenda across urban and rural communities.[20]

The Festival of Indonesia (1990–1992) crowned the wave of national development sweeping Indonesia during the 1990s. The festival toured for 18 months across the United States exporting a refined yet exotic image of Indonesia to lure tourists to Bali and Yogyakarta, the designated sites of classical arts production. This type of events reenergized the colonial image of Balinese women (particularly dancers) as alluring and exotic cultural icons[21] and placed them at the juncture of tradition and modernity. In short, the women operated within a matrix of development, religion, and gender. The cultural policy indirectly endorsed international traveling for performance as a "safe and acceptable" occupation for women, adults, and children alike. Female dancers of all ages traveled abroad and away from their parents, spouses, and children to perform an official form of "idealized femininity" while exploring a new sense of agency as travelers.[22] The new policy brought a sense of conflict to women's lives. The traveling requirements conflicted with state *ibuism* and with Hindu–Balinese tradition–Balinese religious dogma and Hindu-Balinese *adat* practices circumscribed women's authority. The notion of women's *peran ganda* (dual/multiple roles) gained official support and entailed a reaffirmation of their role as both homemakers and workers outside the home.[23] The dominant national agenda mandated a modern Muslim-Javanese worldview, which the Balinese perspective[24] contradicted by limiting women's upbringing and reinforcing their roles as mothers and wives.

The fertility of women and the land are exalted themes in Balinese culture, and both men and women are expected to marry and procreate. However, women's ability to give birth makes them solely accountable for reproduction.[25] First and foremost, the portrayal of "the ideal woman" has been as a mother and, "secondarily [as] a faithful wife and hard worker at home, in the fields and in the performance of ritual offerings."[26] The Hindu-Balinese holy book, *Manawa Dharma Sastra*, states that "principally, a female child, adult or old woman is not free to act even in her own house."[27] This dogma is reinforced by Hindu-Bali *adat*. As *kepala keluarga* (heads of households), men occupy a "higher and critical" position of authority within the family and the community, while wives must "respect and honor their husband as the master of the family and household."[28] Balinese women, often state, "*saya tidak berani*" ("I don't have the courage") when they may have to speak out or act against the status quo. Fearing social chastisement for attracting attention away from their husbands, women prefer to claim "weakness."

Hindu-Balinese religion encompasses the whole spectrum of Balinese people's spiritual, familial, and public life, affecting the realms of the divine, ancestral, and physical by means of the individual's daily behaviors. Cultur-ally, the Balinese people's identity and roles have been constructed on the basis of the Hindu-Balinese religious tenets of the *Tri Hita Karana*[29] ("Three Sources of Happiness"), and the *Panca Srada*,[30] ("Five Principal Beliefs"), which emphasize harmony. For the Balinese, adherence to these precepts ensures their own and their descendants' well-being through the mainte-nance of harmonious relationships to the spiritual, human, and natural worlds. Within this social code, wives' and mothers' decision to work abroad is a courageous one, considering that their family's physical, social, and spir-itual well-being rests on their deeds. It defies conventional social codes and acknowledges their husband's failure to provide for the family. The women addressed in this chapter decided to travel abroad in full awareness of the social consequences their actions might bring upon them and their families. They did not consider themselves *courageous* or feminist; instead, they were striving to fulfill their duty as mothers and wives. The following discussion examines their narratives and their reliance on religious and cultural tradi-tions to negotiate their stay abroad.

TRAVELING GODS

M. Switri, her husband, and their two children resided in his family's compound in the village of Ketewel, a subdistrict of Sukawati, Gianyar dis-trict. During 1999–2001, the hamlet had approximately 9,000 residents who belonged to 15 *banjar* (family associations). In addition to managing the multiple responsibilities of motherhood, household chores, and ritual obli-gations typical of Balinese women, M. Switri worked outside the home. She was keenly aware of the fact that, despite the demands of her various jobs and her financial contributions to the family, she had to fulfill her domes-tic and ritual obligations, with which she struggled to comply.[31] M. Switri held two part-time jobs at the Art Center in Denpasar. In the mornings, she worked as a cultural host and as a clerk in the afternoons. Additionally, she performed with the center's music and dance ensemble in local touristic venues and nearby islands. Her work at the site typified the cultural issue of low-wage gendered labor.[32] The anticipated transformation of cultural tradi-tions (e.g., gender roles and ideology) brought by development had not taken place given that the tourism development policy reinforced the local ideology of gender. In fact, women's work in Bali continues to be considered comple-mentary to men's and, as such, comprises part of their lot and is perceived as the women's source of pride.[33]

Ni Made Switri and her daughter. (Photograph supplied by Ni Made Switri)

In 1997, toward the end of the New Order regime, M. Switri joined another music and dance touring ensemble coordinated by the Kanwil Pendidikan dan Kebudayaan Propinsi Bali (Regional Office of Education and Culture of Bali). The ensemble planned to tour six Japanese cities during a six-week span, and M. Switri would have to leave her two children, an eleven-year-old girl and a five-year-old boy, in the care of her husband. Her husband, an accomplished artist who suffered from a chronic illness, also held two part-time jobs. He worked at home carving wooden sculptures and as a clerk at the village's government office. His earnings were insufficient to provide for the family.

M. Switri's decision to go abroad would give her the opportunity to supplement her family's income while she traveled on her own, and her children would be safely cared for by her husband and his extended family. She made arrangements with the latter, expecting that the change would not be detrimental to family stability.[34] However, as part of the family team, she still faced the problematic position of having multiple roles, which presented the dilemma of transgressing *adat* or failing to contribute to family welfare. In both cases and regardless of the decision she took, M. Switri remained responsible for familial stability.

While the Suharto era's dominant national ideology of development exerted a significant influence on contemporary Balinese women, the Hindu-Balinese tradition still maintained its powerful hold on women's lives by delimiting and shaping their roles as mothers and housewives and, above all, subservient beings. Added to the weight imposed on Balinese women by colonial rule as the keepers of "traditional" custom, whose behavior was judged "from the vantage of whether they can produce good quality children, and can work as part of a family team,"[35] the *Tri Hita Karana* and *Panca Srada* further burdened them by not only making them responsible for the moral guidance and physical well-being of their children, but also for the retributions that their daily decisions and actions might bring on their nuclear, extended, and blood families and their ancestors. Women must be continually aware, self-vigilant, and fearful of their actions, which could shame or damage their relationships with the spiritual, familial, and communal worlds.

M. Switri's choice combined her sense of family responsibility and her own personal desires and manifested a deliberate intention to fulfill both. Her thinking and framing of the situation expressed a sense of intentional agency configured by her own desires and purposes instead of an imposition of power entailing both domination and resistance.[36] Rather than resign herself to remain home and endure financial hardship, M. Switri's personal wish to travel strengthened her deliberate decision to go abroad. If she had taken this self-fulfilling course of action openly, her community and her extended family would have considered it a woman's selfish transgression and it would have made her the target of gossip, envy, or even witchcraft.

The touring ensemble M. Switri joined sought to introduce the Japanese people to the arts and culture of Bali and foster tourism to the island. As they traveled from one city to the next, the ensemble members were aware of their identity as "cultural emissaries." In her own words, "*Seperti duta budaya, kita, ya?*" ([We were] like cultural emissaries, right?).[37] Highly impressed with her touring experience, M. Switri stated that the ensemble was very well received by the host country. She felt reciprocated in her role as a "cultural emissary" because the tour provided her with the unique opportunity to expand her knowledge about the culture and customs of the host country, as well as establish friendships with some of her audience members. The ensemble performed inside a theme park or "foreign village"[38] that was built according to Balinese standards. Members of the ensemble were taken daily from their hotel to the "Balinese village" where they simulated Balinese culture by displaying daily life activities (e.g., preparing offerings, weaving, pounding rice, carving masks, etc.). M. Switri's schedule was demanding although it excluded these activities. For M. Switri, the construction of the village's replica symbolized the deep interest the Japanese had for Balinese culture, and she derived a sense of pride from the event.

In comparison with this visit, M. Switri felt that her previous trip to Lombok was extremely uncomfortable. She recalled the extreme fear she felt while performing the Barong and Rangda magic-religious dance drama because numerous spectators fell into an uncontrollable trance and the priest intervened to pacify them. This behavior is culturally expected in local Balinese performances, but M. Switri apparently felt it was inappropriate in Lombok despite the large Balinese population of the island. In Java, she was greatly disappointed by the audience's response. She sensed aloofness and felt that the ensembles' performance went unappreciated because the spectators exited as soon as the performance was completed. Unlike the Japanese, the Javanese spectators did not make any effort to meet and greet the performers or take photographs.

M. Switri attributed the Japanese audience's positive response to the efforts of the Balinese ensemble, her own feelings of well-being and, most importantly, to the protection of Japanese gods that had accompanied her from Bali to Japan. Through the intervention of these gods, M. Switri and a friend were granted to experience *kerauhan* (spirit possession) during their stay in Japan. The Balinese consider the experience of this phenomenon a favorable event in a ritual context, although it may occur during theatrical performances. They customarily visit the temple to *mepamit* (take leave and present offerings to the gods) before departing on a journey. M. Switri and some of her fellow dancers followed this tradition before departing for Japan and, upon their safe arrival, thanked the deities by making a modest altar and giving offerings. It was then that, to her surprise, M. Switri was possessed by a spirit, following the trance of one of her colleagues. With great certainty, she recounted,

> It is this way. [According] to our belief here in Bali if we want to leave, we ask permission first, here at the temple. Soon after, [we] asked permission and prayed [because] we wanted to go to Japan. Once we arrived in Japan, we prayed at the place there . . . while my friend prayed, she fell into trance and I also followed her [into] trance. It is said in Japan that there are Japanese gods here [in Bali] that stay in [the] temples [in Bali]. When we took leave for Japan they [the Japanese gods] followed us. They accompanied us over there [and] we [were] safe.[39]

The dancer further clarified that these Japanese gods protected Japanese tourists when they traveled to Bali, and when the tourists returned home, the gods remained in the Balinese temples visited by the tourists during their stay. M. Switri was unsure about the identity of the Japanese gods or spirits, but she knew that they were auspicious.

Protective entities that attend to their local and transnational congregations are a "symptom" and an "inscrutable agent" of global ideologies.[40] For example, Japanese and Latin Americans travel and migrate globally trusting in the protection of their traveling deities. Tobi-Fudo, the Japanese Flying God, is a manifestation of Fudo Myo-o, a Japanese Buddhist god of Hindu origin that traverses space to answer prayers and accompanies travelers in their journeys regardless of their destination. This deity's worship dates to 1530 with the construction of its temple by a Buddhist priest in Ryusen, Japan.[41] Nowadays, travelers leave *ema* (votive amulets) at the shrine(s), which depict the god framed by red flames and a cloud with an airplane zooming across. According to Bond, the Tobi Fudo of Shoboin Temple in Tokyo (which belongs to a network of 36 sacred Fudo temples in the Kanto region) is the most famous of its temples.[42] Bond clarifies that Fudo "was a composite creation of time and place" alluding to the Buddhist principle of *ensho* ("codependent origination").[43] The Mexican virgin of Zapopan, who unfolds into three identities—the original (*la original*), the pilgrim (*la peregrina*), and the traveler (*la viajera*)—to accompany and protect her local, national, and transnational constituency, is another example of travelers' adapting deities according to their needs and contexts. Narratives of wandering deities' apparitions are an active response of those who strive to achieve consistency and cultural meaning and establish a sense of community while living in a global, often alien context.[44] Spirit visitation and possession in transnational contexts and multinational sites may also be partially viewed as a "complex negotiation of reality by an emergent female industrial workforce" that experiences a "sense of ambiguity and dislocation."[45]

Notwithstanding M. Switri's excitement of being abroad, performing Balinese practices such as dancing at a Balinese village replica called for a kind of divine intervention that was appropriately recontextualized and attributed to Japanese wandering deities. The competing pull of the Balinese religious traditions and the demands of Indonesian national development on Balinese society—and certainly on this woman, who confidently viewed herself as "cultural emissary" and "motor of development"—is framed within religious beliefs that, according to Suryani, have held and continue to hold Bali together in spite of foreign intrusion.[46] M. Switri's belief in divine intervention, foreign or not, is rooted in her community's complex tradition of numinous mediation that restores harmony to life and eases misfortune.

The tour offered her the opportunity to be on her own and away from her domestic routine. Nonetheless, with a nervous smile softened by a "shiny face" (a Balinese moral obligation regulating interpersonal conduct[47]) she confided that she did not have time to miss her family because the tour was brief and her schedule busy. As if apologizing to her then 14-year-old daughter for what she was about to say, M. Switri embraced her and explained that, if the opportunity presented itself, she would tour again because of the economic advantage and the opportunity to travel abroad.[48] With this statement, she defined herself as a capable family provider and a decisive woman willing to explore the world at large—a modern woman. On the other hand, she simultaneously complied with the ambivalent national discourse of the working woman/home-bound wife, appropriating and transgressing it in equal measure. While she conformed to the official touristic agenda, she also used it to expand her personal possibilities for action and breached the boundaries of the local Hindu-Balinese ideology of *adat*. Throughout her undertaking, M. Switri reclaimed and retained the control of her narrative by bringing into play her alliance with the wandering Japanese gods and her Hindu-Balinese spirit possession tradition. This way, she recreated a meaningful world that was situated within her traditional religious network and enabled her own and her friend's spiritual communion.

I suggest that, in this manner, and even though she acted and incorporated herself into the objectifying discourse of tourism, M. Switri remained both the author and the player in her own narrative.

FOLLOWING SITA

N. Suastini, a 28-year-old dancer, lived in Peliatan, a hamlet located northeast of Denpasar in the Gianyar district, a modest tourist destination bordering the internationally famous village of Ubud. She was married to an architect, and they lived in his family's compound with their then two-year-old son and four-year-old daughter. N. Suastini grew up in the midst of her village's emerging tourist activity. As a child, she would imitate adults at the tourist stands. She would try to sell imaginary objects to tourists, shouting, "Satu dolar! Turis. Satu dolar!" ("One dollar! Tourist. One dollar!"), while her embarrassed relatives tried to stop her.[49] N. Suastini began her dancing career at the age of nine and went on to perform with the renowned Tirta Sari and Gunung Sari[50] local ensembles, which served as cultural ambassadors during the New Order's apogee. At the time we met, 1999, she danced weekly with Semara Madya, her *banjar*'s ensemble, in her community's benefit.

In 1995, at the age of 22, N. Suastini had rejoined the Gunung Sari group to dance in a 10-week cultural tour through the United States. With her first child only six months old and her husband unemployed, she decided to accept the contract and leave her baby and family behind in order to earn an income that could easily solve her family's financial difficulties. Being fully aware of her obligations as a mother and a wife and like M. Switri,

N. Suastini engaged her extended family (particularly her mother-in-law) to attend to her baby's needs. Upon her return home, she was able to cover the mounting debts that her husband had incurred in order to survive during her absence. Her salary in the United States was roughly a hundred times higher than in Bali.[51] Once the tour was over, she continued to work in order to make ends meet. Four years after her return, she taught private dance lessons to Japanese students, both at home and at the ARMA (Agung Rai Museum of Art) weekend workshops.

Unlike M. Switri, N. Suastini performed in concert settings during her tour, and although her dance repertoire was vast, she primarily performed the Pendet and the Balinese Kecak dances. Kecak is based on two episodes of the Balinese *Ramayana* Kakawin and depicts the abduction of Sita, the wife of Rama, Vishnu's seventh avatar, by the demon king Rawana. In this rendition, Sita is taken to Alengka for a number of years during which she refuses the demon's romantic advances and remains loyal to her husband.

Ni Nyoman Suastini pregnant with her second child. (Photograph taken by the author)

During her captivity, she desperately longs to return to Rama, which she does after a series of battles that culminate in Rawana's defeat and her liberation by Rama's allies.

The following stanzas are an excerpt from the only letter ascribed to Sita during her captivity. While her words express deep feelings of familial love, loyalty, and devotion, they also depict her remorse and feelings of responsibility regarding the precarious situation in which she placed herself.[52]

> My respectful salutations, Prince, may come to your feet, King.
> Here is a letter! Read its contents; they are a token of my longing,
> And the crest jewel is as it were myself coming to you, to pay obeisance
>   to you.
> Look! The ring you sent me, is your touch to me. (22)
> For all that used to be tasty when tasted, the one to give it taste was not
>   around.
> Flowers filling the garden were by no means a cure for my longing.
> All that sounded sweet and everything that spread fragrance,
> Were useless and worthless, water not passing one's throat. (25)
> What makes me even sadder is that I was the origin of all this misfortune.
> We were separated because you carried out my orders, out of love for me.
> If my lord should find me, I shall not behave like that again.
> Whatever should be done by one who is enslaved I shall do, being just a
>   slave;
> To that as a slave I shall keep. (31)
> I shall obey all that my lord orders, I shall oppose nothing my lord says.
> Thus is my wish, nothing else, because of my great debt.
> If you do not look at me, what can I say; I really don't know.
> Therefore come my lord, soon, because of my longing.

The character of Sita provided a flexible, multilayered, parallel space for reinscription, reappropriation, and negotiation that allowed N. Suastini to incorporate local, national, and transnational expectations through her performance. Notwithstanding her extraordinary economic reward from the tour, N. Suastini endured deep stress and guilt due to the separation from her young daughter and family. N. Suastini stated:

> . . . I was two and a half months over there and I was forced to stop breast-feeding. My child was six months old [when I left] and she needed her mother's milk. While I was in the United States, I had plenty of milk still. I could not sleep over there.
>
> I was sleepless. I cried throughout [my stay]. I thought and thought and counted the days left until I could return home.

> [During a performance], in the section of Sita's dance in Kecak, when she cries, I followed her and started crying, right?
>
> I just cried and cried; Oh! Oh! It was very difficult.[53]
>
> The American hotels and the bedrooms were nice but empty, right?
>
> While [I was] over there, I could not eat [although] the food was delicious, I could not [eat].[54]

At a height of about 5'4", N. Suastini's weight dropped to a low 100 lb. during the first month of touring. Her emotional outpour during her performance of Sita exemplifies this female heroine's cultural and personal significance for the Balinese people. The emotional breakdown and the intensity of the moment may have erased N. Suastini's recollection of the particular dance section she enacted, radically disrupting her performance. Still, she ascertained that her representation of other characters did not elicit or provoke this kind of reaction. Customarily in this section, a somber sound from the Kecak male chorus and a haunting woman's chant accompany Sita's expressions of heartache. The dancer embodies Sita's mourning through swaying of her body right-left-right, as if suspended in motion until she sinks into the ground while simultaneously wiping the tears off her face by gesturing with the flowing scarf hanging from her waist. Her motions are languid, weighted, and deliberate, meant to project the burden of her sorrow. N. Suastini's emotions empathetically resonated with her kinesthetic rendition of Sita's pain, and she subjectively aligned herself with the mythological character's grief and perhaps regret over familial separation.

Upon her return, the dancer experienced more sadness and confusion: her daughter felt estranged from her and rejected her embrace. Her distress increased when she observed her mother-in-law feeding the infant milk from a plate instead of a bottle. Feeling both angry and guilty upon witnessing this event, she wondered if her baby had been properly attended to throughout her absence. She questioned her mother-in-law's motivation and suspected her touring may have angered her. With time and patience, N. Suastini regained her daughter's love, and resolutely decided she would not leave her young children behind again. She expressed a desire to tour in the future, either accompanied by her children or once they were old enough to stay behind.

The Hindu-Balinese principles of the *Tri Hita Karana*, by which the Balinese seek to attain peace and harmony, involve the suppression or control of emotional expression, a Balinese virtue. Public expressions of sadness and anger, for example, are viewed as inappropriate while laughter, joking, and gaiety are accepted within family interactions, theatrical performances, and ceremonies such as cremation.[55] N. Suastini's emotional outburst occurred outside of these social conventions, and therefore, she felt it was contextually inappropriate and a social breach. Nonetheless, she released her emotions through the dance, an occupation that entwined her with discourses of both modernity and tradition. Her desolation may have been caused by guilt, regret, shame, longing, postpartum stress, or a combination of these factors. But whether she initially assumed the identity of the national mother (*ibu*), the sacrificing Hindu-Bali mother, or realigned with the mythological Sita, her lived experience of motherhood as expressed in the dance performance redefined her identity as a "working woman," "cultural emissary," and performer, repositioning her back into her local identity and maternal role.

Her inability to eat and sleep also constituted a rupture with the discursive practices of Balinese acceptable behavior by attracting attention to her person and causing other members of the group to worry about her well-being. In short, by reestablishing her identity as a mother, N. Suastini disrupted other subject positions, including that of the compliant, well-balanced woman who is ready to present the required "shiny face." While she initially and courageously adopted the identity of the modern working woman in order to help her family, her satisfaction was brief and overshadowed by longing for her daughter. Not once did she mention having obtained a sense of personal pleasure or achievement through her venture. Instead, as she spoke to me, her sadness and regret managed to show through her smile.

CONCLUSIONS

The complex narratives of the two dancers addressed in this chapter entail particular reasons for performing abroad, distinct affective experiences, and, most significantly, the ways in which they reappropriated, negotiated, and reimagined their identities. Whereas the women have some points in common, such as their marital and motherly status and financial motives for touring, their stories contain remarkably distinct explanations and reimaginings of identity based on individual circumstance. Their actions are heterogeneous, and the identities they shape reflect their individual subjectivities and local contexts. Both performers considered themselves *orang biasa* (everyday folks); they graduated from high school, and their spouses had professional careers. In both cases and for different reasons, the women's husbands were unable to support the family and the women assumed the responsibility even though it would entail temporary familial separation. Considering that cultural, religious, and educational practices circumscribe the activities and behaviors of Balinese women, the dancers' decision to travel could not have been made lightly; it contradicted, then and now, Hindu-Balinese ideals of feminine behavior.

My goal throughout this chapter has been to draw attention to M. Switri's and N. Suastini's subjective experiences and intentions as expressed and enacted within the particularities of their historical moment and show that their actions and intentions were not subversive, reactive, or defiant but, rather, creative and transformative. Economic hardship compelled these women to negotiate their positions as mothers and wives, performers, and "motors of development." As participants of touring ensembles, they both belonged to groups that offered emotional support and allowed them to reenact cultural practices and actions while abroad (e.g., observe traditional ceremonies, speak in their native language, and socialize with fellow Balinese). Their position as "cultural emissaries" provided them with an acceptable, "safe and honorable" occupation that allowed them to leave their homes and families and venture into foreign contexts. It was in this setting that the performers summoned the protection of traveling gods and mythological heroines and reimagined and recreated their own subjectivities, recasting known meanings and interpreting and experiencing the separation from their families and communal networks. Their affective experiences and reactions were both diverse and complex, and yet the two remained attached to their local value systems and placed great emphasis on religion and kinship.

Both M. Switri and N. Suastini largely reinscribed and revalidated their experiences through the tenets of Hindu-Balinese *adat* rather than the liberal, modernized perspective of Indonesian nationalism. Their complex negotiations reaffirmed the local view on women's societal priorities: "In the midst of all the changes, Balinese women's sense of identity continues to be rooted in their traditional roles."[56] Significantly, the women explained their actual transgressions of *adat* through a manipulation of its principles of harmony, belief, and religious practice in order to keep their traditional link intact. Instead of the new, foreign context, a deeply rooted Balinese perspective guided their individual interpretations. They managed the transnational context's inevitable crisis of conflicting paradigms (national policies of gender and tourism, and local Balinese system) by defining their identity in terms of their most familiar system of values. Their transformative cultural resilience may indicate how Balinese women are managing the strict traditionalist approaches of the post-Suharto era of *reformasi* (reformation), which are currently attempting to reshape regional female roles and identity in Indonesia as well as other parts of Asia.[57]

The women's experiences were constituted and shaped by outside pressures transforming their local communities. Their narratives conveyed both partial adherence to the Indonesian State's discourse and its rejection; they were also characterized by wavering feelings of satisfaction, independence, guilt, and the desire to comply with institutional and societal expectations. Their narratives are better understood in terms of a struggle that implies agency in processes of adjustment and negotiation, as well as a reimagining of belonging through the meanings of the "traditional" and "modern" self. In the end, religion became the crux of these two women's negotiations, as they defined themselves via their relationship to traveling gods and cultural heroines that embody religious principles.

NOTES

1. The informants preferred to use their names instead of pseudonyms.

2. Williams 2007.

3. Parker 2005, 13.

4. Ortner (2001) establishes two kinds of agency: inclusive (as power, domination and resistance) and intentional (projects, purposes and desires).

5. Pratt 2006.

6. A *Ramayana* character portrayed in Javanese and Balinese performances.

7. The Balinese term *kerauhan* refers to the coming down or arriving (*rauh*) of a high spirit, god or ancestor. It expresses the experience of "being entered" or possessed by a spirit or god Parker 2005, 12. Also, Connor et al. 1986, 268.

8. Kecak, Rangda and Barong are popular magic-religious dances performed in tourist venues. Topeng Ratudari and Pelegongan Andir are performed at the temples.

9. Brooks and Devasahayam 2011.

10. Gouda 1995.

11. Wieringa 1992.

12. Sears 1996.

13. Blackburn 2004, 144.

14. It combined Sukarno(ist) and socialist discourses. Women became men's "comrades" in the fight for a socialist future (Wieringa 2003, 73).

15. Suryakusuma 1996.

16. Jennaway 2003; Wieringa 2003.

17. "*Ibuism*" combined *priyayi* (aristocratic Javanese) and middle class Dutch values (Blackburn 2004, 148).

18. Suryakusuma 1996, 101.

19. Aripurnami 2000, 55.

20. Ibid., 57.

21. See Gregor Krause and Karl With (1920); Hickman Powell, Alexander King, and Andre Roosevelt (1930); Miguel Covarrubias (1936); Henri Cartier-Bresson (1954).

22. "Idealized femininity" refers to employment associated with "feminine qualities although it entails travel (Williams 2007, 6, 122).

23. Blackburn 2004, 185–187; Oey-Gardiner 2002, 104.

24. It includes syncretic practices from Balinese aboriginal culture, pre-Hindu animistic and ancestral cults, Hindu-Javanese religion and Buddhism (Suryani, 1993, 225).

25. Parker 2003, 183.

26. Parker 2003, 262.

27. Ariani and Kindon 1995, 507–519, 514.

28. Ibid., 514.

29. "Tri" (three), "Hita" (happiness) and "Karana" (the cause). The concept refers to creating harmony through the relationship with: *buana alit* (microcosm) humans' realm; *buana agung* (macrocosm or universe); and *Sang Hyang Widi Wasa* (Supreme God). Personal communication with Ni Luh (Noni) Estiti Anda-rawati, May 15, 2006.

30. The Five Principal Beliefs: *Sang Hyang Widi Wasa* (one Supreme God); *atman* (spirit, eternal soul); *hukum karma* or *karma pala* (the retribution from past life deeds, foundation of future lives, and their application to one's self and one's descendants); *punarbawa* (reincarnation), and *moksha* (unity with God) (Suryani 2004, 215, 224).

31. Cukier et al. 1996, 268.

32. Ariani 1992, 9.

33. Suryani 2004, 222.

34. Cukier 2002, 180.

35. Suryani 2004, 213.

36. Ortner's inclusive agency (Ortner 2001, 78–79).

37. M. Switri, Ketewel, Bali, interview by M. Talamantes, July 2001.

38. Hendry 2000.

39. Talamantes 2004, 229–230, 298–300.

40. Pratt 2006, 33.

41. Bond 2009. See also http://tobifudo.jp/engi/eengi.html (accessed December 2011).

42. Personal communication with Kevin Bond on June 13, 2015.

43. Bond explains "codependent origination" as being a product of local causes and conditions (2009, 32).

44. Pratt 2006, 27–33.

45. Ong 1987, 28.

46. L. Ketut Suryani, Denpasar, Bali, interview by Maria Talamantes, August 1999.

47. Wikan 1990, 44.

48. She earned about US$530 monthly (about Rp. 3,180,000) plus covered expenses. Her salary in Bali was US$20 (Rp. 120,000) monthly. M. Switri, Ketewel, Bali, interview by M. Talamantes, July 2001.

49. Talamantes 2004, 300.

50. Gunung Sari was founded in 1926 under the royal auspices of Anak Agung Gede Mandera. It appeared in the Paris Exposition in 1931, and it toured Europe and the United States under John Coast in 1952.

51. She earned about US$800 monthly (Rp. 4,800,000), expenses included, while in Bali, about US$8 (Rp. 48,000). N. Suastini, Peliatan, Bali, interview by Talamantes, July 2002.

52. Excerpt from Van Der Molen (2003, 341).

53. N. Suastini, Peliatan, Bali, interview by Talamantes, July 2002.

54. Ibid.

55. Suryani 1993, 110.

56. Suryani 2004, 222.

57. Creese 2004.

CHAPTER 2

The Holy "Mother Who Is Not a Mother": Saradamani Chattopadhyay[1]

Narasingha P. Sil

I

Śrīmatī Saradamani Chattopadhyay (1853–1920), wife of Sri Rama-krishna *Paramahaṁsa* (monastic name of Gadadhar Chattopadhyay, the celebrated priest of the Kālī temple of Dakshineshwar), became the central figure of the Ramakrishna Order after her husband's death. This chapter argues that Saradamani's apotheosis owed to her being the widow of a celebrated godman as well as to her personal qualities. Her recorded conversations and the eyewitness accounts of several devotees together with her biographies by the scholar monks provide enough data for an explanation of her popular accolade as the Holy Mother who often became an incarnation of the Goddess Annapurna of Hindu mythology and folk imagination.

Sarada's achievements contribute immensely to the current feminist response to the male-dominated theology that Elizabeth Davis celebrates as the antithesis of "masculist materialism."[2] But wholesale "feminist religion" is likely to create new myths equally pernicious as patriarchal spiritualism while attempting to demolish the old ones. A more wholesome option for our world would be to adopt a "universal religion" that conduces the develop-ment of a "perfect personality" of the individual seeking to realize the "divine principle" in everybody.[3] As this chapter seeks to demonstrate, Sarada's life illustrates this balanced approach wonderfully.

II

Saradamani (1853–1921) was the eldest child of Ramchandra Muk-hopadhyay, a petty farmer and a priest of Jayrambati village in the present district of Bankura, West Bengal, and his wife, Shyamasundari. The typical 19th-century Bengali village was marked by religious rites, folklore, and legends. The child Sarada grew up in this milieu, playing with idols of gods and goddesses; one of her monastic biographers believed she was "going through her lessons in the kindergarten of religion."[4]

Like most Bengali girls of her days, Sarada loved to wear gold ornaments and wished to become a mother. The five-year-old bride of the 23-year-old Gadadhar, reportedly refused to part with her bridal jewelry borrowed by her mother-in-law.[5] Even in her adult years, Sarada continued to be fascinated by gold ironically when her husband, by now a popular *paramahaṁsa*, was preaching the merits of giving up *kāminī-kāncana* (woman and wealth [gold]). He, however, encouraged his wife to wear gold armlets by declaring her Goddess Sarasvatī, as her name "Sarada" happened to be another name of the deity. He also presented her with a pair of gold bracelets following his vision of Sītā, wife of the folk God Rāma.[6] Sarada was, in fact, admonished by a devotee for her habit of wearing ornaments, which were deemed unsuitable for an ascetic's spouse.[7]

Even after Ramakrishna's death on August 16, 1886, the 33-year-old Sarada dreamed her late husband commanding her to go on wearing gold ornaments like a *sadhavā* (married woman whose husband is alive) as, he being an incarnation, she remained "forever a married woman."[8] Thus, back in her in-laws' home at Kamarpukur (close to her paternal village of Jayrambati), the young widow continued her unusual practice of wearing "bangles and red-bordered *sārī*" as well as "a necklace of *rudrākṣa* beads held by a gold wire."[9] With a view to preempting further objections of neighbors and relations, she performed the fire ritual of *Pañcatapā* for seven days, during which she sat within a circle of lighted mounds of cow dung cakes (*ghuṇṭé*) doing *japa* (silent repetition of sacred words).[10]

Sarada's other feminine desire, after she came of age, was to become a mother. Married in infancy, the child-bride returned to her parents' home following the nuptial ceremony, while her adult groom left for his work at Dakshineshwar. When she turned a teenager by 1867, she was alarmed at the rumors of her husband's *tantra sādhanā* with a mysterious *bhairavī* (a female practitioner of *tantra*) named Yogeshvari. She rushed to Kamarpukur, where Ramakrishna had taken the *bhairavī* to practice *tāntrika* rituals.[11]

Here, as a young pubertal girl, she came close to her husband for the first time. Ramakrishna, on the other hand, avoided any husbandly relationship with his wife and instead instructed her on proper social behavior and on domestic religious rituals. He taught her about the unreality of the phenomenal world, and the merits of "detachment and devotion," and the futility of beastly procreation.[12] He even tried to frighten her about the agony of motherhood should the children die. When after repeated references to deaths of children, Sarada protested "Will all of them really die?" the exasperated husband yelled: "My, my! Here indeed have I trampled on the tail of a deadly snake. Wow! I thought she was good-natured and innocent of everything, but she seems to know a lot!"[13]

III

The *Paramahaṁsa*, who never had sex with his wife, quite expectedly harbored a deep anxiety about her chastity and fidelity. Reportedly, he shared the same bed with her and passed his nights conversing but never lovemaking. One night Ramakrishna made her repeat the statement three times (by way of swearing an oath) that she knew no other man and that her avowed goal in life was to serve her husband.[14] He was, of course, convinced that women are generally untrustworthy and hence they ought to be kept busy with cooking all the time. He told his nephew Hridayram Mukhopadhyay that "only cooking helps them [women] to become good." The target of this *obiter dicta* was his wife, Sarada, and his cousin sister Lakṣmimani Devi, who he feared would stare at men whenever they were free.[15] In fact, Sarada was constantly reminded by her husband to remain "mild and weak . . . meek and sober" because he believed that "modesty is . . . [a woman's] forte; otherwise there will be public scandal."[16]

Back to Dakshineshwar in the latter part of 1867, Ramakrishna began practicing various *sādhanas* for the next four years. His tantric and *vedantist* phase (with the *bhairavī* Yogeshvari and the Vedantist Totapuri) was followed by *vātsalya bhāva*, that is, the mood of a child, dallying with the doll *Rāmlālā* he had received as a gift from a roving monk. The *vātsalya* state was followed by his ecstatic state, the so-called *madhura bhāva*, the "sweet mood" of Rādhā, Lord Kṛṣṇa's lover. This is the period of Ramakrishna's *divyonmāda*—the state of divine madness—when he dressed and behaved like Rādhā mad in love with the lusty Lord Kṛṣṇa.

When rumors that the young priest had lost his head due to self-inflicted continence reached Jayrambati in March 1872, Sarada, by now in her late teens, hastened to Dakshineshwar in sheer panic.[17] Her unannounced arrival at the Kālī temple seemed to upset her husband as he had now to deal with his pubertal wife when he himself had chosen to behave like a romantic cow girl of mythology. Ramakrishna solved his personal problem by transforming his unsuspecting wife into a goddess. He told her that he always looked upon her as the Blissful Mother, *Mā Ānandamayī*.[18] At another time he proclaimed her to be his *Śakti* and, as noted earlier, Sarasvatī.[19] Thus, he successfully deified and desexualized his young wife. As he deposed later: "After marriage I anxiously prayed to the Divine Mother to root out all sense of physical enjoyment from her mind. That my prayer had been granted I knew from my contact with her during this period [March 1872–October 1873]."[20]

Sarada's divine status was legitimized through a number of painful and powerful experiences. Nikhilananda documents a number of events in her life from 1872 through 1886 and concludes that "all this time the chrysalis was being transformed into a butterfly."[21] The most celebrated of these events is, of course, the *Ṣoḍaśī Pujā* ("virgin worship," supposedly a *tāntrika* ritual) celebrated by her husband, who, imitating the example of his tantric devotee Gauri Paṇḍit (Gaurikanta Tarkabhūṣṇṇa), actually worshipped her as a goddess on May 25, 1872.[22]

Sarada's ritual deification was further affirmed by her experiences during moments of personal extinction. Sometime in 1875 she was stricken with life-threatening dysentery at Dakshineshwar. Ramakrishna was alarmed and lamented to Hriday that if she just came to the world and departed, she would not be able to "fulfill the purpose of her human embodiment" and, reportedly, was prescribed an effective cure in a dream. Later, in another dream the Lionborne (appellation of the Goddess Jagaddhātrī) noted her special intimacy with Sarada. This divine liaison must have toughened her to endure the ordeals of other pathological experiences such as malaria and the enlargement of the spleen. She even patiently went through the painful treatment of having her abdomen branded with a lighted palm tree branch to be cured![23]

Sarada's intimacy with the goddess was later transmuted into her identity with the divine. In February 1877, on the way from Jayrambati to Dakshineshwar, Sarada encountered a low-caste (*bāgdī*) brigand who recognized her as the Goddess Kālī, and she fondly addressed him as her "robber-father" (*ḍākāt bābā*).[24] Then we have the Master's stern admonition to Hriday, who had been rude to her, that if she was provoked, even the Trinity of Brahmā, Viṣṇu, and Maheśvara could not save him from her wrath.[25]

IV

Initially, her divine reputation functioned as a strategy for the rehabilitation of the childless and penniless widow following her husband's death. Ramakrishna had been able to command a large following among the Calcutta *bābus*, some of whom became his eager *rasaddārs* (suppliers of victuals).

During his lifetime, Sarada had remained in the background as the Master's wife who cooked for his flock. Her secondary role was perhaps echoed in the words of Ramakrishna's great householder disciple Ramchandra Datta, who openly declared at the Master's demise: "We knew *Paramahaṁsamaśāi* [Mr. *Paramahaṁsa*], but who's his wife? We do not know anything about her."[26]

In the decade following her husband's death (1886–1898), the young widow was shuffled back and forth from Kashipur in the northern suburb of Calcutta, where during the last months of his illness, Ramakrishna had been relocated by his devotees from Dakshineshwar for regular medical attention. Thereafter, probably at the behest of his wealthy householder devotee Balaram Basu, Sarada undertook a pilgrimage to Vrindavan accompanied by a few disciples of the Master. Upon her return, she went back to Kamarpukur to live largely on her own. Ramakrishna's employers at Dakshineshwar had initially arranged for a paltry monthly allowance for the widow but discontinued it during her prolonged pilgrimage. The news of her penurious subsistence at Kamarpukur moved her mother at Jayrambati to send for help from Calcutta. It was then decided by most of Ramakrishna's disciples, including the influential Narendranath and Girish, the flamboyant actor and socialite of Calcutta, to relocate her to the city to live in a rented home together with the renouncer disciples of her late husband.[27]

Sarada's village elders were uneasy about her living with her late husband's devotees and advised her to stay with her mother or with her nephew-in-law Ramlal Chattopadhyay. However, on the insistence of Prasannamayi, the widowed daughter of the Laha family of Kamarpukur and childhood friend of Gadai, Sarada was able to come to Calcutta to live with the young monks. Prasannamayi very thoughtfully counseled Sarada: "Why, Gadai's disciples are also like your disciple children. Who would care for you except they? Your village people won't come to your succor in times of trouble."[28] Indeed the young widow had been concerned about her future. In her first rented residence at Belur, she jestingly albeit sincerely responded to her visitor Narendranath, who confessed to his growing world-weariness by adding "that everything is blown off" from his life: "Take care that you do not blow me away, too!"[29]

It was through the construction of the young widow as a goddess that Sarada was reconciled with her society's misgivings about her association and living with young men. Her divine status also ensured her lifelong care by her late husband's followers and admirers. According to *Svāmī* Gambhirananda, the Jagaddhātrī *Pūjā* held at Jayrambati on November 10, 1891, showed beyond doubt that "the Mother had then been fully established in her Motherhood, and that her divinity, too, had become acknowledged among intimate acquaintances."[30] In particular, her divinity was popularized by *Svāmī* Niranjanananda (Nityaniranjan Ghosh), Durgacharan Nag (Nāg *Mahāśay*), and most notably Girishchandra Ghosh and *Svāmī* Vivekananda (Naren-dranath Datta). A fiercely outspoken and powerfully built young man, Niran-janananda "preached her divinity among the devotees without any reserve."[31] When Durgacharan came to visit Sarada at Belur sometime in 1893, he kept on crying "Mā, Mā" and banged his head so hard on the steps while bowing down to his late *guru's* widow that her maidservant on attendance feared that it would bleed. He calmed down after Sarada affectionately wiped his eyes, patted his pate, and fed him some fruits and sweets like a child.[32] Sarada had become the quintessential mother figure, the blissful Holy Mother—*Śrīmā*.

In the remainder of the 1890s, Sarada continued to gain public con-firmation of her divinity. Girish Ghosh, a habitual drinker and smoker of hemp, who had turned a "born again" Hindu following his acquaintance with Ramakrishna, confessed that he could not look at the Holy Mother because he thought of himself to be a great sinner. However, in 1891, following the death of his infant son and on the suggestion of Niranjanananda, he went to Jayrambati in search of consolation. When he looked at Saradamani, he saw in her the exact resemblance of the face of a "radiantly motherly figure" he had seen in a dream during his early youth when suffering from chol-era. During his stay at Jayrambati, Girish one day argued vehemently with Sarada's skeptical brother Kalikumar Mukhopadhyay, who refused to regard her as a goddess. Girish called him an ignorant bucolic Brahmin and com-manded him to "take refuge at the Mother's feet at once."[33] Several years later, in 1896, Girish created another scene at Sarada's temporary residence in Calcutta by proclaiming her as "the Mother of the Universe—Mahā-māyā, Mahā-Śakti" publicly.[34] His dramatic behavior—he was a popular playwright and a stage director—highlighting Sarada's divinity chimed very well with the image of a benevolent goddess of popular imagination.

Sarada's internationally recognized Holy Mother image was fabricated by Vivekananda, who was also responsible for the universally revered image of Ramakrishna.[35] Most probably, the *Svāmī* admired Sarada's selfless devo-tion to her husband, felt sorry for her austere life,[36] and was grateful for her generosity to him among all other disciples of the late Master. He declared to his *gurubhai* (brother monk) *Svāmī* Shivananda (Taraknath Ghosal): "Of Ramakrishna, you may claim, my brother, that he was an incarnation or whatever else you may like, but shame on those who have no devotion for Mā."[37] He also became aware of female power and leadership in the United States, where, on his own admission, he saw how much India lagged behind the Western world in recognizing the worth of women. He had found the American women to be "the goddess Lakshmi in beauty and the goddess Sar-asvati in talents and accomplishments."[38] Now back home he declared that "Mother is the incarnation of Bagalā in the guise of Saraswatī" and more of "*Jyānta* [Live] *Durgā*"[39] He concurred with *Svami* Yogananda's (Yogindranath

Raychaudhuri) remark made as early as April 23, 1890, that if Ramakrishna was *Īśvara* (god), "she must be the *Īśvarī* [Goddess]."[40]

Vivekananda also wished to publicize the image of the Holy Mother as the inspiration, not necessarily the leader, behind his projected Ramakrishna Movement in India and abroad. Thus, Vivekananda conceived of the *Shakti* (*Śakti*) motif with an eye on the world at large. As he wrote to Shivananda from the United States: "Mother has come to awaken that great *Śakti* in India, and following her, once again will the Gargīs and the Maitreyīs be born into the world."[41] Often, the ebullient *Svāmī* would go to the length of glorifying Sarada at the expense of her godman husband and his acknowledged *guru* with such remarks as "in fact the Master was nothing"[42] or "to me, Mā's grace is a hundred thousand times greater than Father's."[43] With a view to demonstrating his utter devotion and ultimate loyalty to the Holy Mother, the flamboyant *Svāmī* drank dirty pond water in order to purify himself before coming into her presence. When he was prevented by his companion Hari *Mahārāj* (*Svāmī* Turiyananda) from drinking the foul liquid, Vivekananda replied: "No, brother, I am afraid. We are going to the Mother, I am not sure if I am pure enough."[44] Following Vivekananda' death, she emerged as the sole inheritor of the *Paramahaṁsa's* spiritual empire, attracting numerous visitors who rushed to her home in Calcutta, Kamarpukur, or Jayrambati seeking her grace and guidance. A few select cases are appended below.

V

In 1906 at Kamarpukur, Surendranath Sen fell into a coma during his initiation by the Holy Mother because he found an uncanny resemblance between her and the Goddess Sarasvatī of his dream.[45] Nishikanta Majumdar dreamt the Mother Kālī of Kalighat, Calcutta, lifted him, like a child, with her four hands. A month later, when he saw the Mother at Jayrambati carrying a vegetable and a fish cutter (*baṇṭi*) in her hand, he beheld the goddess of his dream materialize in real life.[46] A certain orphaned boy came across the Holy Mother's name while reading Akshaykumar Sen's *Śrīśrīrāmakrṣṇapuṁthi*.[47] He hastened to the ailing Sarada's home in Calcutta, and "on seeing Mother inclined in bed he had a vision, in turn, of Rādhā-Krṣṇa, the Master, Mother Kālī, and Śrīrādhā and he was so overwhelmed by the Kālī vision that Sarada had to calm him down by touching him with her blessed hand." Kusumkumari Devi had a vision during her initiation that Sarada was seated naked inside a halo, giving birth to worm-like tiny human beings and gorging them immediately—a vision of *prakṛti*, as explained by the Mother. Nagendranath Chakrabarti saw in Sarada, with her long locks of hair, a brilliantly fair woman with a large third eye in between the eyebrows.[48]

Svāmī Abjajananda maintains that she deliberately concealed her true identity (*svarūpa*). Even her veil (*ghomṭā*), a common enough practice with Hindu married women or widows in Bengal, has been interpreted as her *yogamāyā*, that is, divine illusion.[49] Abjajananda finds a strong confirmation of his belief in her divine identity in the conversation of a visitor. This man, referred to as a distinguished monastic son of the Holy Mother (*Śrīśrīmār janaika viśiṣṭa santān*), once told Sarada that she must be the Mother of the Universe (*Jagadambā*) because she had herself admitted that her husband, Ramakrishna, was the eternal Brahman in its fullness (*Pūrṇabrahma Sanātana*).[50] *Svāmī* Satsvarupananda could not realize that Mother was divine when he first met her in 1919. Her stature and countenance reminded him of his own grandmother. Later, the *Svāmī* reflected on the reasons for his inability to detect her divinity. He came to realize that Mother had hidden her *svarūpa* behind her *māyā*, which also blocked his vision and stunned his intelligence. "Perhaps I was not ready then," he cogitated.[51]

Saradamani became adept at assuming the divine role and posture popular in folk mind in the long run. Once she wore a white *sārī*; with the locks of her hair falling on the back and with a grave but serene countenance, she raised her right hand (*abhayamudrā*) and bade her young devotee Nareshchandra to fetch some white and yellow flowers. Awestruck at her visage, Naresh promptly procured the flowers, and with trembling hands offered them to her feet. She then asked him to adorn her right foot with white flowers and the left foot with yellow ones. The reporter of this scene wonders if "Mother is a representation of all goddesses [*sarvadevīsvarūpiṇī*]."[52] Ashutos Mitra describes Sarada's worship as the living Durgā along with the ritual worship of the Durgā effigy around 1903:

> On the same pavilion, in one corner flowers and leaves have been heaped at the feet of the image and on the other end various flowers smeared with sandal-paste were gathered at the feet of the living image, the Holy Mother. It was an unprecedented and unimaginable spectacle![53]

It should be recalled that years ago, Sarada overpowered her late husband's young devotee Harish Mustafi, who had chased her in a sudden fit of insanity, by squatting on his chest and pulling his tongue out with her own hand, thereby assuming the iconography of the Goddess Bagalā.[54] At times Sarada would impersonate the terrible Kālī (*bhīm bhavānī karālī*). When a devotee jestingly wondered what would happen if the temple of the goddess of Kamarpukur (meaning Ramakrishna's home) were gutted in fire, she yelled: "Fine—fine! That would then be a cremation ground [*śmaśān*] just as the Master would have preferred." She then burst into a peal of laughter (*attahāsi*): "Hah, hah, hah!" The unsuspecting devotee stared at her dumbstruck.[55]

On another occasion, at Kothar, Orissa, Sarada calmly allowed Surendranath Sarkar and two fellow devotees to worship her feet with flowers. She even arranged to have the flowers brought for the purpose and accepted the oblations standing. When her young devotees confessed to their innocence of Sanskrit *mantras* for the ritual, she advised them to offer flowers only, cautioning them to avoid offering *dhuturā* (datura) flowers as the latter were meant for Śiva worship only.[56] Similarly, she instructed her devotee Sarayu Roy, who considered the Holy Mother as Jagajjananī, on how to worship her with flowers.[57] When the child Shivaram (Ramakrishna's nephew) insisted on knowing his aunt's divine identity on pain of refusing to enter her home, the importuned Sarada told the child that she was considered *Kālī* by the people, and thereupon, Shivaram cavorted merrily inside the courtyard.[58]

Sarada, in fact, came to be convinced that she really was a goddess in human form as she genuinely felt that her divinity was derived primarily from her relationship with a godman. She told a devotee that "the Master is really God who assumed a human body to remove the sufferings of people."[59] When a devotee had the temerity to query whether she, as the wife of the *Brahman*, was aware of her own status, Sarada responded calmly and casually that she actually was the wife of the God Nārāyaṇa, but her human state was caused by *māyā*.[60] She even claimed confidently, "I am Bhagavati, the Divine Mother of the Universe."[61] Her devotee Chandramohan Datta of Dhaka reports how she transformed herself into the Goddess Jagaddhātrī in a blaze of light.

VI

Often Sarada had to pay the price for her widely acknowledged exalted status. Once a young man visited her at her Calcutta home, Udbodhana, for the purpose of worshipping her with flowers. On sighting the stranger, she covered herself with a thick wrapper and sat on the bed with her feet dangling, to which the stranger visitor offered flowers and his salutation (*praṇām*) and sat down "like a log of wood" to practice *yoga*. Sarada under her wrapper perspired profusely. Mercifully she was rescued by her attendant Golap-*mā* (Golapsundari Devi), who virtually kicked out the heedless troublemaker.[62] Once a middle-aged *paṇḍit* placed his head on her feet and grasping her both legs began to sob loudly beseeching her to awaken his *caitanya*. Sarada sat covering herself from head to toe with a thick sheet and perspired heavily. She managed to maintain her composure nevertheless.[63] Gambhirananda describes Sarada's predicament when some of her devotees even inflicted acute physical pain on her by literally biting or hurting her limbs considering they would be remembered by their Holy Mother.[64]

She, however, endured such torments of love (*bhālobāsār atyācar*) with perfect equanimity.[65] When a devotee suggested that people should not touch Mother's feet because it causes her suffering, she responded:

> No, my child, we're here for this purpose only. If we do not accept others' sins and sorrows and digest them, who else will? Who else will bear the responsibility for sinners and sufferers?[66]

She used to be harassed by an intrepid and alcoholic devotee Padmavinod (Vinodbihari Som), who habitually visited her late in the night. Unable to enter her home at that unearthly hour, he would start singing from across the street: "Awake my merciful Mother, open the door. . . . You've left your son out. How could you still sleep while I cry 'Mā, Mā'?" Som would leave only after she responded by lifting up the blinds of her room. Yet Sarada told her disciple Durgapuri Devi that she did not mind the disturbance at all, as she could not help responding to his piteous call.[67] Such emotional hassles constituted the daily fare of the Holy Mother's public life. As Satyendranath Majumdar writes:

> There was no end to the merciful Mother's sufferings. . . . She was endowed with the qualities of forbearance and forgiveness. . . . Some of them [devotees] were real troublemakers. Middle-aged men sobbing loudly [*bheu bheu kare kāṅdcche*], their heads [on the ground]. . . . One day one of them just lay on his back and began to entreat her to place her feet on his chest to impart [divine] consciousness.

Majumdar once made fun of this lachrymose lunacy, but she told him: "When you grow up you'll understand the sufferings of unfortunate people. The fact is you're not a mother."[68] She even quipped in a conversation with a skeptic who was hesitant to acknowledge her unique status: "Would you find anyone like me anywhere? Would you like to search for someone as myself?"[69]

VII

However, the secret of Saradamani's ubiquitous popularity with her devotees, disciples, and admirers lay not in her divinity claimed or earned but in her unlearnt but inherent maternity. "Why do you worry?" Ramakrishna had assured his wife: "I shall leave you . . . jewels of children. . . . You will find in the end so many children calling you 'mother', that you will be unable to manage them all." Later after his death when she despaired alone at Kamarpukur, "I've no son and nothing else; what will be my lot?," she had a vision of the Master in a dream saying: "You want one son—I have left for you all these jewels of sons. In time many will call you mother."[70] Ramakrishna prophesied with uncanny accuracy. Within a short time after his death, Sarada's thwarted human motherhood was sublimated into a compensatory divine motherhood. Saradamani became *Śrīmā*, Blessed Mother or Holy Mother—mother as if by divine right.

She became a mother to her husband's devotees, followers, and admirers, who enjoyed her affectionate attention to their physical and emotional comforts. Sarada remained throughout her life a loving, nurturing, and compassionate maternal figure—never a matriarch—of the Ramakrishna Order. She truly was, as Vivekananda said, the *sanghajananī*, that is, "mother of the Order."[71] As *Brahmacārī* Akshaychaitanya has written:

> [She] prayed for the material as well as spiritual welfare of her children day and night . . . cooked food for them at all times for days and years sacrificing rest which she severely needed. . . . [She] absorbed [others' worries] and inspired them with the ideals of sacrifice and forbearance [and] . . . sheltered them . . . so that they were delivered from ignorance. . . . These, in short, are the manifestations of *Śrī* Saradadevi's motherhood in the world.[72]

Svāmī Virajananda (Kalikrishna Basu) recalls his first meeting with the Holy Mother:

> How happy she was with us! She could not decide where to lodge us, what to cook for us! She toiled day and night for all this. She got busy cooking a variety of dishes for the two [major] meals of the day and watched us eat and forced us to take second helpings. We have never tasted such nectar-like meals.

About his spiritual experience or enlightenment, Virajananda writes: "We had nothing to do but meditate occasionally, gossip, gorge, snooze, or go for a walk along the banks of the Amodar River."[73] Spiritual gain, if any, consisted in personal feelings of satisfaction. To quote the *Svāmī* once more:

> While staying there we used to be filled with a powerful holiness, happiness, and well-being and felt that "we are treading on holy ground . . . vibrant with spirituality." It seemed as if the place was out of this world![74]

Svāmī Vishuddhananda (Jitendranath Singha Roy) and Nilkanta Chakravarti, recipients of Sarada's maternal care and affection, commented that her best identity was that of a mother.[75] Her compassion touched everyone from an obscure Muslim vendor or a Muslim bandit named Ajad and, as we have noted a low-caste robber—her *ḍākāt bābā*—to her devotees from the genteel society. Instances testifying to her motherly affection and care may be multiplied manifold.

Sarada's principal concern for food preparation and distribution that made her appear as the grace-and-grub bestowing Goddess Annapūrṇā (literally, "stuffed with foods") was an eloquent testimony to her femininity even from a cross-cultural perspective. A mother's passion, writes Elias Canetti, "is to give food."[76] She, in fact, gives her own body to be consumed by her children from the womb down to their breast-feeding stage and subsequently looks after their creature comforts till they grow to be independent adults. This maternal sacrifice transmutes itself into an unconscious (and often unintended) strategy for control and domination. Caroline Bynum observes in the context of the society of medieval Europe that for women food is the easiest thing to give away in a male-dominated and controlled society. This observation is equally valid for Hindu society even to this day.[77]

VIII

It should be noted that Saradamani was neither an ascetic nor a saint in conventional Hindu terms. Unlike a *brahmacāriṇī*, who is usually initiated into a tradition of asceticism by a recognized *guru*, she remained very much of this world and in this world.[78] She, in fact, lived a comfortable life surrounded with maids, cooks, and numerous devotees who were always eager to lend a hand in any chore.[79] Sarada was also not a typical married Hindu female saint. Her *prapattibhakti* (single-minded devotion to God) did not replace her *pati* (husband) with an *iṣṭadevatā* (chosen ideal).[80] Thus, Sarada the Holy Mother does not quite fit the profile of some female ascetics and *gurus* of Varanasi discussed by Catherine Ojha.[81] Instead, her life exemplifies a peculiar reaffirmation of conventional womanhood, while providing a creative and unorthodox path for spiritual leadership.

Yet Sarada remained far from a passive recipient of the dictates of her culture and society. On the contrary, she was resourceful enough to discover sources of empowerment or everyday resistance within the conformity and compromises linked to Hindu tradition.[82] Through Sarada's position and community action, her life suggests an important dimension of women's struggle for identity and leadership in the colonial society of late-19th-century Bengal. Her example stands as an affirmation of the visions and values of the urban middle class mediated through the rhetoric of religion. She was so convinced of the propriety of covering women's bodies (unlike her ecstatic spouse, who danced stark naked in public) that she would consider a woman virtually naked if she lifted her *sārī* up to the knees. She even defied her husband's counsel to women to be rid of the three impediments to realizing God—shame, hate, and fear (*lajjā, ghṛṇā, bhay, tin thākte nai*), arguing that the Master's dicta were not meant for laypeople but for those who were experiencing divine madness.[83]

Sarada possessed neither her husband's charm and charisma nor the skill of his dances, trances, songs, and wacky mischievousness that accounted for his phenomenal popularity as a performer *par excellence*. She, on the other hand, endeared herself to her followers through her maternal compassion expressed through the hard work of cooking and catering. She neither sang nor danced and preached; she, in fact, considered lecturing a preeminently male prerogative. She simply delighted in mothering her devotees and disciples.[84] As she was not a member of the educated *bhadralok* class, she was not a *bhadramahilā* (lady) in the strict sense of the term. Sarada, thus, never fully acquired the ideal of class distinctions or the proper role of a caste-conscious genteel woman. She had little difficulty socializing with low-caste or lower class people, the so-called *chotalok* or *itarjan*.[85] As such, she was able to move quite freely between classes and castes.

Sarada's world was dominated by monks whose spiritual *élan* consisted in renouncing women and sex but who exhibited an unusual fondness, even sheer cravings, for food. Her role as a preparer and server of food together with her relentless striving to keep her visitors, disciples, and devotees satisfied brought her the reputation of a renouncer of sorts—that of a selfless and tireless mother to all her children. In the final analysis, it is her exemplary humanity that accounts for her apotheosis. "What can I say about Mother? We have not yet realized who she is," *Svāmī* Keshavananda (Kedarnath Datta), head of Koalpara Math, observed. The *Svāmī* related the story of Sarada's inflexible stand in support of her cook whom he tried to fire because of incompetence. Sarada said to Keshavananda, "You may leave if you like but if I leave him, where will he go?" Whereupon the chastised *Svāmī* readily realized who she was. As he confided to Amulyavandhu Mukhopadhyay: "Can you figure out who *Śrīmā* is? Who could pronounce such a word of sincerity and assurance [*abhayavāṇī*]?" Amulyavandhu concludes his memoir: "Bless you *Mā*, ... Only a mother like you is the refuge for people in the *Kaliyuga* [Kali Age]."[86]

Saradamani's devotees and disciples delighted in seeing a veritable maternal figure in someone they genuinely loved and adored. In fact, one of her disciples from eastern Bengal, Surendranath Bandyopadhyay, asserted categorically that she was truly a mother to him and never a goddess.[87] Even Sarada herself was aware of her primordial identity as a human mother. "I am your true mother," she reminded Girish Ghosh, "a mother not by virtue of being your *guru's* wife, nor because of any assumed relationship, nor by way of empty talk, but your own true mother."[88] When Ashutosh Mitra clasped her feet and insisted on knowing her true identity, she told him calmly and firmly: "What will you do with that [knowledge]? I am your mother."[89]

Saradamani thus remained a quintessential mother of the household possessing an affectionate disposition and quiet authority. Her mother–Holy Mother interface owed significantly to the constructions of her devotees and admirers. They saw in her a demure Jagajjananī, a dashing Jagad-dhātrī, or the terrible Kālī. Svāmī Purnatmananda reports how an unlettered rickshaw-puller of Calcutta, a simple tea vendor of Bangladesh, and an educated woman from Hollywood found in Sarada's photograph a compelling reminder of their own mothers.[90] It is perhaps best to let Sarada's "devotee-children" have the final say on her humanity and divinity:

> The Holy Mother stands out as a unique example . . . whose heart held all humanity in its maternal embrace, and who considered it a privilege to labour and to suffer for even the least of them. If we cannot see here the face of the all-loving Universal Mother, of God the Redeemer, where else [could] we?[91]

NOTES

1. This study is adapted from and is an elaboration of my article titled "Saradamani's Holy Motherhood: A Reappraisal," *Asian Journal of Women's Studies*, IV, 1 (1998), 33–76. Copyright © Asian Center for Women's Studies, reprinted by permission of Taylor & Francis Ltd, www.tandfonline.com, on behalf of Asian Center for Women's Studies. All citations from Bengali sources appear in my translation.

2. Sepaniants 1992, 239; Davis 1971, 338–339.

3. Sepaniants 1992, 245.

4. *Svāmī* Ghanananda, "Sarada Devi the Holy Mother," in Ghanananda and Stewart-Wallace 1972, 95.

5. Gambhirananda 1977, 27.

6. Ibid., 114–115.

7. Ibid., 92.

8. Akṣaycaitanya 1396, 52 n. 3.

9. Ibid., 52: deposition of Bibhutibhusan Ghosh reproduced by Akshaychaitanya.

10. Gambhirananda 1977, 173. *Pañcatapā* is the *vrata* or penance with "five fires" of the Hindu widows.

11. Datta 1995, 31.

12. Gambhirananda 1977, 33.

13. Ibid., 34.

14. Akṣaycaitanya 1396, 17: excerpts from the deposition of Nikunjadevi, a female devotee of Sarada.

15. Jagadishvarananda 1398, 191–92.

16. Gambhirananda 1977, 111.

17. Between 1873 and 1886, Sarada shuffled from Jayrambati and Kamarpukur to Dakshineshwar several times until she returned to her husband in 1885. See Nikhilananda 1982, 42–53.

18. *Śrīśrīrāmakṛṣṇalīlāprasaṅga* 1398, 362; *Śrīśrīrāmakṛṣṇakathāmṛta* 1394, II, 155 (diary of October 11, 1884).

19. See Gambhirananda 1977.

20. *Life of Sri Ramakrishna Compiled from Various Authentic Sources* 1928, 252; no author.

21. Nikhilananda 1982, 46.

22. *Śrīśrīrāmakṛṣṇakathāmṛta* 1394, IV, 74 (diary of February 24, 1884).

23. Nikhilananda 1982, 47–48.

24. Ibid., 51.

25. Gambhirananda 1977, 66.

26. Bhumananda 1986, 102. Despite several references to Sarada's presence and activities, she has no voice in the *Śrīśrīrāmakṛṣṇakathāmṛta* 1934.

27. Bhumananda 1986, 98–104. In 1888 Sarada first stayed at the home of Nilambar Mukhopadhyay of Baranagar and thereafter at various places in the northern part of the city until she moved into her newly built home at 1 Udbodhana Lane, Calcutta, in 1909. This home is presently the site of Udbodhana Kāryālaya.

28. Devi n.d., 169. For a succinct account of Sarada's predicament as to where to stay after her husband's death in 1886 through 1920, see Tapasyananda 1982, 37–47.

29. Bhumananda 1986, 107.

30. Gambhirananda 1977, 168.

31. Ibid., 213.

32. Ibid., 175.

33. Ibid., 218.

34. Ibid., 220.

35. Sil 2009, ch. 9.

36. Sil 1993, 71–81; 76–78.

37. Vivekananda 1394, 257: letter of 1894.

38. Vivekananda 1990, VII, 475: letter to Manmathanath Bhattacharya (September 5, 1894).

39. Prabhananda 1984, 18. Bagalā is the eighth of the 10 *Mahāvidyās* of the *Śākta* pantheon. See Kinsley 1988, ch. 11.

40. Ibid., 10.

41. Vivekananda 1394, 256–257: letter to Shivananda (1894).

42. Gambhirananda 1977, 183.

43. Vivekananda 1394, 257: letter to Shivananda (1894).

44. Prabhananda 1984, 18.

45. Akṣaycaitanya 1396, 108.

46. Ibid., 117.

47. Sen was Vivekananda's close and a devotee of Ramakrishna. He published the Master's biography in verse, the *Puṅthi* in 1901.

48. Akṣaycaitanya 1396, 140 and notes 7 and 8.

49. Abjajananda 1397, I, 1,2,5. See also 1–157 for a detailed canonical explanation of Sarada's Kālī identity.

50. Ibid., I, 5.

51. "Karuṇāmayī" in *Śrīśrīmāyer Padaprānté* 1994–1997, I, 63.

52. Archanapuri 1989.

53. Mitra 1994–1997, II, 346.

54. Abjajananda 1397, I, 170–171; Tapasyananda 1982, 209–211. This episode seems to be a garbled account of Sarada's attempted rape. Reportedly a married young man of character and devotion, Harish lost his head when his in-laws forced him to consume some aphrodisiac with a view to turning his mind from hyper-asceticism to his wife. The improbable story of the widow defending herself by assuming her *svarūpa* as the Goddess Bagalā was started by Sarada herself and further colored by her devotees and hagiographers. See *Śrīśrīmāyer Kathā* 1398, 174; Her Devotee-Children 1984, 78 note.

55. Archanapuri 1989, 172–173.

56. *Śrīśrīmāyer Kathā* 1398, 98.

57. Roy, "Kalkātāy Māyer Bāḍīté Māké Pratham Dekhi," in *Śrīśrīmāyer Padaprānté* 1994–1997, I, 86.

58. *Śrīśrīmāyer Kathā* 1398, 170 note.

59. Her Devotee-Children 1984, 301.

60. Gambhirananda 1977, 465.

61. Nikhilananda 1982, 187. See also Akṣaycaitanya 1396, 114.

62. Ishanananda 1396, 165–166.

63. Akṣaycaitanya 1396, 111–112.

64. Gambhirananda 1977, 381–382.

65. Ishanananda 1396, 166.

66. Her Devotee-Children 1984, 343: reminiscences of *Swāmī* Maheshvarananda.

67. Devi n.d., 212–213.

68. *Mātṛdarśan* [A View of the Mother] 1397, 157–158.

69. Prabhananda 1403, 91.

70. Gambhirananda 1977, 127.

71. Cited in Prabhananda 1984, 12.

72. Akṣaycaitanya 1396, 77 (also 78–106).

73. *Mātṛdarśan* [A View of the Mother] 1397, 6–7. The English words in quotes are Virajananda's own.

74. Ibid., 10. The English words in quotes are Virajananda's own.

75. Ibid., 23, 231.

76. Canetti 1962, 221.

77. Bynum 1987, 191.

78. Denton 1991, 214; McDaniel 1989, 230–231.

79. *Śrīśrīmāyer Kathā* 1398, 154–155.

80. Gupta, "Women in Shiva/Shakta Ethos," Leslie, ed. *Roles and Rituals*, 194.

81. Ojha 1981, 254–285.

82. Leslie, "Introduction" and "Sri and Jyestha," idem., ed., *Roles and Rituals*, 107–127.

83. Ishanananda 1396, 162.

84. *Mātṛdarśan* [A View of the Mother] 1397, 65.

85. Banerjee 1989, 131.

86. *Mātṛdarśan* [A View of the Mother] 1397, 214–215.

87. Personal interview with Surendra's son Ranendranath Banerjee and his wife Rina, Calcutta (September 7, 1997). I thank Ranjana Mukherjee for introducing me to the Banerjees.

88. Hiranmayananda, "Sve Mahimni" ["Unto Her Own Glory"], *Śatarūpé Sāradā* 1989, 110.

89. Mitra 1994–1997, II, 343.

90. Purnatmananda 1997, 2–6.

91. Her Devotee-Children 1984, xxxix.

CHAPTER 3

Crisis of Transnational Families and Restoration of a Medium's Marriage Life in Northeast Thailand[1]

Visisya Pinthongvijayakul

This chapter intends to explore a female medium's marital tension in line with social changes in northeast Thailand and the transnational economy. In her locality, villagers from almost every household have engaged in labor migration to Taiwan. Husbands, wives, and children are separated from each other for years. This transformation brings about socioeconomic issues such as adultery, children's use of drugs and liquor, and shortage of domestic labor, among others. Regarding my informant's life experience, I would like to highlight the mediumistic practice as the rehabilitating operation that enables her to negotiate her marital crisis. The analysis is based on an ethnographic study in a village of Chaiyaphum province in northeast Thailand.

Anthropologists have examined spirit possession in diverse cultures. The main focus deals with mediumistic practices in the ritualized domain. A small number of works pay attention to the practitioners' everyday life and their relations with other family members. This chapter intends to address the unattended issues of personal life experience and domestic relations of spirit mediums. It suggests that ritualized actions can be better understood by exploring the mediums' everyday life situations. It treats spirit possession as the domestic religion where the deification of gods and the operation of spiritual power are refashioned according to changes in the mediums' conjugal and familial circumstances.

After the end of Cold War, Thailand has been intensively engaged in globalized industrialized processes and has undergone massive socioeconomic transformations in terms of social and labor mobility, demographic change, and shifting marriage and divorce patterns. These trends inevitably have an effect on the socially constructed unit of the family.[2] With respect to labor migration, the number of northeasterners who work overseas surpasses those from other regions.[3] In the village where I conducted my research project, men and women from almost every household were gone to Taiwan for a long time. Husbands, wives, and children were separated from each other for many years. Among them are some mediums whom I study in my project. Such a phenomenon brings about interesting questions concerning their everyday life and religious practices. How does labor mobility impact the mediums' conjugal and familial relationships? How does spirit possession work in such a transnational context? And in what ways do the mediums reinterpret and operate spirit possession to negotiate the struggles experienced by the family in crisis?

This chapter centers on a female medium and her network in a village in Chaiyaphum province, northeast Thailand. Busaba (not her real name) is now 37 years old and lives with her two daughters, aged 17 and 8. Her husband has been working in Taiwan for 15 years. He comes back for brief visits of a month every three years. In the village, a number of family crises result from labor migration: many cases of adultery, children's use of drug and liquor, and shortage of domestic labor. Drawing on Busaba's life experience narrative and other mediums' accounts, I argue that, apart from being a venue for healing and fertility rituals, mediumistic practice becomes a rehabilitating operation that enables Busaba to negotiate marital crisis. Her tutelary god and goddess are transformed into conjugal protectors and nurture familial relationship during the long-term absences of her husband.

MEDIUMSHIP, WOMEN, AND THEIR LIFE EXPERIENCE IN FAMILY

A certain number of works identify women as the central actors in spirit possession. They try to understand how the mediums construct their identity and how they mediate a resolution of critical situations in the domestic domain. For Bruce Kapferer,[4] the major factor that brings women more regularly than men into the orbit of exorcism are "the typifications or cultural constructs" related to Sinhalese understanding that women are more vulnerable to the attack of demons and ghosts. I. M. Lewis[5] proposes that women's spirit possession provides them with an effective means to call attention to their needs and to protest against their husbands. Barley Norton[6] indicates Vietnamese female mediums who claim the importance of their duty to serve the spirits and challenge their husbands' patriarchal authority. Laurel Kendall looks at the shamanic practice of Korean society. She argues that gods and ghosts are integral elements of Korean family and village religion. "Within this religious system, women and shamans perform essential ritual tasks that complement men's ritual tasks."[7] She verifies elsewhere that the Korean afflicted shamans construct the logic of their story from a history of family crisis and fortune and then the story is enacted in mediumistic performance.[8]

Anthropologists have long made use of the method of life history collection in ethnographic research. As my ethnographic questions aim to understand female experiences concerning conjugal and familial relationships, life history research offers a way of exploring both individual lives and collective cultural constructs. Anthropologists maintain that the life history method should be employed in identity research depending upon circumstances of the society.[9] Regarding female agency in ethnographic studies, Susan N. G. Geiger[10] considers women's life histories as primary sources for the database of women's lives and life history research as a feminist method for the broader and deeper understanding of women's consciousness, historically and in the present. The life history method can be used to give expression to female hidden or silenced lives. It opens onto the pluralist stories and selves of the local women.

Review of the existing literature and methodology gives an insight into the life history accounts of Busaba and her network and brings about interesting questions about their ritualized actions and religious practices. Mediumship can be identified as household religion with females as central agents. Busaba and her female consociates play a crucial role in possession practices in both household shrine worship rituals and annual pilgrimages to sacred sites. The purpose of these activities is to achieve prosperity and well-being. Two main reasons that initially brought these women into the orbit of spirit possession are female cultural constructs and illness. Here, I would like to address some questions arising from the literature and the particularities of Busaba's cultural and environmental situation. To what extent does her hardship of child-raising and the tension of her husband's long-term absence shape the logic of the spirits and of mediumistic practice? Likewise, how do other mediums' experiences of parental and connubial desertion influence the logic of their ritualized enactments? In what ways do they privatize communal deities and local spirits into their own family's problematic concerns? And in the context of transnational migration, how does possession by the spirits mediate a resolution of critical situations in the domestic domain?

LIFE IN DESERTION: COMMUNAL SOCIAL SUFFERING

On October 23, 2012, Thai TV Channel 7 reported that there are about 70,000 Thai labor workers in Taiwan who work in construction, industry, and caretaking businesses. They send USD27 million back each month. However, they encounter physical and emotional deprivation and cannot come back home until the end of their three-year contract. Labor migration to Taiwan brings about single-parent families in the village. This socioeconomic transformation causes social suffering among the left-behind family members. In the introduction of *Social Suffering*, Arthur Kleinman and his colleagues argue that "social suffering results from what political, economic, and institutional power does to people, reciprocally, from how these forms of power themselves influence responses to social problems. Included under the category of social suffering are conditions that are usually divided among separated fields, conditions that simultaneously involve health, welfare, legal, moral, and religious issues."[11] Kleinman clarifies elsewhere that suffering is a transpersonal engagement with pain and misery in social relationships.[12] Given that labor migration might inflict traumas on social relationships, I will demonstrate how the left-behind household members, especially mediums, in transnational families experience social suffering in terms of psychological well-being and gender relations.

Busaba has brought up her first daughter like a boy and reads her non-normative gender as virginity protection. During the long-term absence of her husband, Busaba has constituted her gender role as both father and mother. By nature, she has a strong personality and works in the field like a man. Busaba has tried to raise her children to be strong so that they can take care of themselves without paternal care and protection. Now, Busaba's first daughter is 17 years old and has become a *tom*, the Thai term referring to masculine women. She is a school player of *sepak takraw*, a ball game mostly played by men. For some time, the daughter's girlfriend came to stay at Busaba's house. The girl's mother put the blame on Busaba, but Busaba told me it was not problematic since none of them would be pregnant. Busaba stated that being a *tom* protected her daughter from premature sexual intercourse with the opposite sex and the daughter would quit being a *tom* when she finished high school.

"The second daughter is unfamiliar with her father. She was born after my husband left for Taiwan" is how Busaba described the weak relationship in her family after her husband made the decision to work overseas. He went to Taiwan when their first child was about two years old and came back to visit his family for a one-month period every three years owing to his work contract and the high cost of travel. Busaba became pregnant at the last visitation and gave birth to the second child when her husband was away. Even though he regularly sends a good deal of remittance, his long-term absence during Busaba's child-raising phase and hard work alone in a cassava plantation has caused emotional disturbance and physical deterioration. "She works hard like a man," one medium in the network told me. It should be noted here that Busaba has had health problems since she was young. She had a right ear and brain operations in the early years of marriage life. And recently, she has been repudiated by her own mother because of a financial conflict. Here, I read Busaba's unpleasant experiences in her struggle with the effects of local and transnational changes as an example of social suffering.

Malai (not her real name), Busaba's elder sister, has also undergone traumatic family life crises connected to labor mobility. After her marriage with her first husband failed, Malai decided to marry a man introduced to her by Busaba. Her second husband left a few years ago for Taiwan with Busaba's husband. Malai has been left with a teenage daughter and a small son. Malai's husband occasionally sends back remittances so she is financially insecure. Nowadays, she has to take care of two children alone and be careful of household expenses. Busaba allocates labor jobs to Malai and helps her on an everyday basis.

Keng (not his real name), 18, is a young medium in Busaba's network. His mother has been working in Taiwan for nine years. She sends back a remittance each month. A few years ago, Keng's mother came back to visit her family and bought a piece of land in the village for Keng and promised him that she would build a house for him when she came back in the next two years. There was a rumor in the village that Keng had an affair with a woman who was older than his mother. Busaba confirmed this to me and told that this woman lived with a younger man whom she called "beloved brother" while her husband and children worked and stayed in Bangkok. Rhacel Salazar Parrenas[13] indicates that children experience more emotional troubles when their mothers migrate compared to when their fathers migrate because of traditional gender norms related to care and attention. The lack of maternal care and attention in teenage years might cause Keng's emotional responsiveness to the older woman's approaches. Busaba said that Keng aspired to hedonistic delight dressing and hanging around the village. The woman's skill of fine cooking and nurturing her partner attracted Keng. The "beloved brother" learned what was going on and threatened to kill Keng. Keng had to stay at his relative's house in another village during the daytime and came back to his house when his father returned from the field in the evening.

Jib (not her real name) is another medium who encounters social suffering of postmigration life traumas. She has experienced domestic violence at the hands of her husband, who returned from working abroad many years ago. At the shrine worship ritual organized by a medium in the network,

I met Yut (not his real name), Jib's husband. He was in his late fifties but looked very old and weary. Yut was sitting on the separate area out of the shrine and drinking liquor with his friend. He was very drunk and disclosing his everyday distresses. I asked Yut whether he had worked overseas. He revealed that he had worked in Taiwan in the late 1990s. Then he went to Singapore for four years. In the meantime, both his father and mother died but he could not return to Thailand for the funerals. Then, he went to work in Taiwan again for four years before coming home permanently. Now, Jib's and Yut's children are working in Taiwan. Yut revealed that at many of the working sites to which he moved, he paired off with women. Each time his partners were pregnant, he took them to obtain an illegal abortion. The life experiences of adultery and risky sexual health care in the working site abroad to some extent psychosomatically affect both workers and their partners when returning to the home country. What Jib has experienced after her husband returned home is psychosomatic abuses. Yut becomes particularly violent when he is drunk, beating his wife and children. Villagers become aware of the situations. They criticize Yut as a troublemaker and drug user.

Transnational labor migration unavoidably inflicts disturbing experiences on household relationships. The left-behind family members struggle with the difficulties of psychosomatic health and challenging legal and moral modes of gender relations. Kleinman[14] suggests that suffering is a societal construction that enacts as a cultural model, a moral guide of and for experience. The chapter aims to investigate further how these life experiences of the mediums are construed and enacted in the ritualized realm with specific cultural meanings.

THE PERFORMANCE OF SUFFERING AND NEGOTIATING REHABILITATION

I began my fieldwork with Busaba and her network by participating in their annual shrine worship rituals during April to June 2012. While they were conducting the rituals, all offerings were presented in front of the shrines and all mediums sang, danced, and drank. Most of them hysterically sang and cried as if they tried to disgorge their sufferings out of their bodies. With the traditional music pattern of bamboo mouth organ, the lyrics narrated life difficulties and the crisis of social relationships. Erika Bourguignon[15] identifies possession trance as "dissociation in the service of the self." I was curious as to what ways these performances serve and connect to their social lives. Thus, I started to explore the mediums' everyday life and their personal experiences.

I propose that to understand ritualized actions and religious practices, not limited only to spirit possession, the everyday life experiences of human agents should be seriously taken into consideration. Extraordinary behaviors of singing, dance, and ecstasy intertwine with everyday social and gender relationships and are enacted to deliver specific cultural meanings. For the cases in the village where I conducted my research project, I argue that ritualized gatherings and actions become an outlet where mediums render their experiences of marital and familial suffering that arise in the context of transnational labor migration in the locality.

When the spirits possessed Busaba, she sang out how she had suffered life difficulties. The content did not specify the particular problems of her familial relationship but generally addressed the idioms of loneliness from social exclusion and friendship she received from fellow mediums in the network. Even though Busaba always closed her eyes in the time of being possessed, that could not obstruct the lengthy flow of tears. She told me her tutelary spirit was very sad that local politicians were corrupted and that the villagers were involved in gambling, drug, and adultery. Thongdam, one of her possessing spirits, was the community's guardian god who protected the village and chased away wickedness.

However, once Busaba recounted her relationship with her husband, the deity Thongdam was significantly brought up into our conversations. On one occasion, she revealed that the psychosomatic problems resulting from her ear and brain operations affected her livelihood. Sometimes she wanted to leave her family behind and go away. But she confessed that Thongdam pulled her back to the social world. She said, "The other half of me is Thongdam. Nowadays, he never leaves me in five minutes. If he leaves me, I will chase my sister away from my house. I will be mad and cannot control myself." I came to realize the way she privatized the communal deity and brought him into play in her familial relationship. Furthermore, she described Thongdam as the connubial tie between her husband and herself. "My husband stays with me because of Thongdam Without him, my husband must leave me for so long. Thongdam is inside me."

I argue that spirit possession practices have rehabilitated Busaba's social self and moral restitution in the domestic domain during the phase of child-raising and marital desertion. Intriguingly, Thongdam came to Busaba in the same year her husband left for Taiwan. The god has become the conjugal protector and the proxy of her husband. Her two daughters recognized the god's existence in their mother's everyday life. Outside the rituals, the god usually appeared when Busaba drank liquor with her fellow mediums after finishing their long hours of labor in the field. He came down and gave didactic messages to the mediums in the network. The issues I often heard were about national politics and the transnational economy. Thongdam exposed that no matter who the Thai prime minister or politicians might be, they brought unsustainable livelihoods to local people. They brought loans and debts to poor people. The god also predicted that Thailand would be commercially colonized by other countries in the next 10 years. How the local god became interested in these beyond-border movements and predicted Thailand's future can be understood by considering the god as the communicative channel of Busaba's husband. He called her every evening and had conversations with her over the telephone for a long time. His transnational experiences and messages were transferred through the telephone and the spirit's voices.

Ethnographic works on spirit possession discuss female mediums' identity as the brides of their possessing spirits.[16] They expose the working processes of spiritual ties and gender relationships of the cases examined. The initiation rituals from these works significantly become the rite of passage for those female mediums to transform their personhood to be "women" or "professional practitioners" in their religious world. In Chaiyaphum, however, it is not apparent that the initiation or healing rituals project the concept of spiritual marriage. There is only one case in which two female mediums organized a marriage following their gods' will. The event was fully arranged and villagers were invited to participate. Nevertheless, the idioms of "spiritual marriage" and "god's wife" might illuminate the working processes of Busaba's spirit mediumship as the operation to revitalize familial relationship and marriage life.

I suggest that Busaba associated Thongdam's position as her protector and the proxy of her absent husband. Even though Busaba's initiation process to accept Thongdam did not explicitly signify a marriage to the spirit, the male god, it has to a great extent helped to formulate Busaba's social self as a good wife and mother. When Busaba had conversations and interacted with male villagers, she performed like a man with power and charisma. Her voices were strongly projected. Kunimitsu Kawamura[17] examines a type of initiation processes for female shamans in the Japanese context. Kawamura illustrates that *kamisama* deals with a middle-aged, married woman who encounters a crisis situation in domestic life. To maintain her family life, she has to overcome the crisis situation by entering into an initiation rite. She applies the possessing spirit to legitimate her religious authority in everyday life along with maintaining her role as a good housewife. Busaba's spirit mediumship exposes, in some ways, the socially constructed female gender and power in her context that addresses legal and moral relations. The existence of Thongdam confirms Busaba's social self as a good wife and mother in the locality where adultery has been increasing as the result of labor mobility.

Busaba's life crisis culminated in her early years of marriage. She had encountered severe health conditions since her childhood. In the first year of her marriage, Busaba had visited clinics and hospitals. Thereafter, she went through ear and brain operations and spent some precarious time before recovery. The family decided to have a child when Busaba was in a good condition. However, Busaba's husband made the decision to work in Taiwan and left his wife and his two-year-old daughter. Busaba has suffered from states of dissociation and grief of bereavement for 15 years. Now, she is in her middle age, entering her forties. This transitional phase is critical for a woman's life cycle in villages. Remarkably, I observe in the field that middle-aged women in the late thirties to forties tend to remarry if they divorce or if their husbands die, or commit adultery when their husbands migrate to other places and leave them for so long. Thus, during such a period of threat to social norms and taboos, Busaba might settle her male god as a contribution to a certain form of moral restoration to underscore her marital responsibilities and cultural expectations of the good wife and mother.

Busaba's mediumship rearranges and regulates relationships with her parents and family. Anthropologists have shown that female spirit possession establishes a means for the gratification of desires ordinarily denied to them.[18] Thongdam has prioritized Busaba's everyday life activities and the way to spend money. Recently, Busaba has become isolated from her parents and relatives because of financial conflict. Busaba's mother criticized her costly expenditure on monastic and mediumistic domains. The mother was angry with her daughter that instead of paying off the mother and brother's debts, Busaba spent a great amount of money to renovate the village temple and the local spirit shrine. Busaba took me to see the constructions of the temple gate and restrooms where her name was inscribed as the money donor. Kawamura[19] mentions cases of shamans who implore protective deities and buddhas for their household and family, but their husbands, mothers-in-law, and neighbors consider them afflicted by "devotion dizziness." The shamans then think nobody understands them and become isolated from society and increasingly absorbed in their own world of belief and intense devotion. However, I read Busaba's "devotion dizziness" and aspiration for spirit mediumship as the means through which to attain self-control, emotional purification, and social integration to revitalize her social self during marital desertion.

Apart from Thongdam, the protective god, Busaba has another possessing female spirit. Yomara is her husband's lineage goddess who has come to her recently. Busaba went to her husband's family shrine worship during the three years preceding my interviews with her. On that occasion, the new medium of Yomara would be selected after the elder medium died. Yomara chose Busaba among other contestants. Busaba told me that the goddess did not choose other daughters-in-law because they committed adultery and wrong deeds. From then on, Yomara has come to stay at her shrine and possessed her in special occasions. Roger Gomm[20] illustrates how marriage life in Kenya threatens women's emotional security. A girl in Digo tribe who marries a young man may find herself the most insignificant member of her husband's residential group. She may also face the prospect of having to accept a co-wife or her husband's financial meanness. Thus, Gomm argues that the manifestation of spirit possession symptoms by women offers an essential alternative to marital crisis for coping with the tensions of Digo marriage.

The transference of the goddess from the shrine of the husband's clan to Busaba's own shrine reveals the operation of calling attention to, drawing divine ties with, and empowering her status. The possession of her husband's lineage goddess positions her to initiate and strengthen the building of ties and to create respect, kinship, and power. It is also the strategy that provides Busaba's social reintegration of her intimate selfhood in her husband's family during the long-term absence of the husband. While Thongdam is a hot-tempered male spirit, Yomara is soft and temperate. However, this conciliatory goddess enables Busaba to move to occupying a central position in her husband's family. Once a year, the family of Busaba's husband has to participate in her annual shrine worship. They come and pay respect to the goddess. On June 19, 2012, I had a chance to observe the occasion when a group of people from the husband's family came to visit the ritual. When they arrived, Busaba changed her clothes to pink, the color of Yomara. Even though most of them were older than Busaba, they bowed their heads and put their palms together to show respect to the goddess. Busaba began singing and crying. The content of the song narrated that the goddess still kept an eye on her children even though she had moved to Busaba's shrine. Busaba then blessed and tied sacred threads on their wrists.

Busaba's mediumistic rituals are the avenues of restoring her social self as a good wife and mother during the state of martial separation. The operation of spirit possession accounts for the communicative scheme that reestablishes her personhood at the central attention of her husband's family. Thongdam and Yomara are the god and goddess that Busaba employs to achieve her aspirations. Kirsten W. Endres[21] examines a spirit medium's life and hardship through different periods of Vietnam's restless history, from the last years of French colonization through the Vietnam/American War to the present market-oriented renovation era. The concept of several "spirit roots" connected to a various range of spirit personalities gives the medium the opportunity to deal with her unconventional character in terms different from the mainstream Vietnamese social context. With the contradictions between self-perceptions and the perceptions of others, spirit mediumship provides the medium with a stage in which she can perform her unruly self and unconventional identity in a culturally meaningful way. Busaba's "spirit roots" provide the possibility to enact different personalities in particular situations. Thongdam functions as Busaba's marital and familial protector, while Yomara plays the role as a linkage between herself and her husband's family.

Spirit mediumship resolves the issues of marital and familial crisis for both Busaba and her elder sister. Malai has experienced traumatizing family livelihood from her husband's migration to Taiwan. Interestingly, it is Busaba who actively directed Malai to the orbit of spirit possession. Malai told me that Thongdam determined that she should be the medium of Ong Tue, the Buddha image at Sila-Ard Temple, one of the pilgrimage destinations of Chai-yaphum mediums. Malai looked up to Thongdam and her younger sister. She told me that Thongdam taught her and other mediums in the network how to live well without debts and stay away from gambling. Her life had been getting better since she came to stay close to Busaba and Thongdam. The god even predicted who in the village would commit adultery and it turned out to be true. Here, I read Malai's spirit mediumship as the self-control operation in line with her financial demands and moral threats. Adeline Masquelier[22] shows that spirit possession opens up a space of self-awareness for a female medium in Niger. The interaction between the host and the possessing spirit reveals their negotiation of social, financial, and moral demands. Possession plays a role as an indirect means of inducing Malai's behaviors. Ong Tue is the well-known Buddha image; the interaction between Malai and her possessing spirit leads to her mindfulness to stay close to the monastic domain and to be a good wife and mother while her husband is absent.

In trance, Keng's ritualized actions communicate his life crisis of being left behind by his mother and his aspirations for well-being. Keng's mother is a friend of Busaba. After his mother left for Taiwan, Keng has kept company with Busaba and her network. His association with the group of mediums attracted him to mediumistic practices. His lack of maternal care and attention has been, to some extent, compensated by Busaba's presence and watchfulness. Busaba treated him as one of her children and Keng called her "mother." She realized that Keng was in need of maternal care. When Busaba talked about Keng's affair with the woman in the same village, she emphasized that the woman had what Keng desired: nurturing and caretaking skills. Another ambition that Keng strived for was to work in Taiwan and to be rich. He told me that when his mother returns from Taiwan in the next two years, it will be his turn to go. The family would arrange Keng's departure to Taiwan after he completed his informal education and a period of monkhood.

Keng's aspirations were expressively enacted in the ritualized trance. James Dow[23] argues that entrancement is the therapeutic stage of the spirit medium. While in trance, the medium is being healed. In this self-healing mechanism, Dow makes an interesting note that the catharsis is the medium's, and not the patient's. When I attended annual shrine worship rituals, I observed Keng's repetitive verbal and physical communications. After Keng drank liquor, he joined the group of mediums. While other mediums were singing and crying along with the music from bamboo mouth organ, Keng wildly danced, jumped, and repeated, "I will ride on the plane." He talked to the others and invited them to jump with him "you see friends, I will fly, I will fly." Many times Keng took a wood stick and drew a sketchy picture of a plane on the floor. Then, he stepped on the picture and jumped up and down. He screamed, "I'm riding on the plane!" I read Keng's ritualized actions as the visionary route connecting him with his absent mother and the village dream for good fortunes.

Jib's experience of post-transnational family and domestic violence brings about aggressive ritualized actions. After Jib's husband returned from working abroad, villagers have observed their habitual quarrels. Jib and her daughter have often been beaten. Jib's husband has been addicted to liquor and drugs. His guilt of past traumatic experiences overseas and psychological disturbances might impose violence upon marital and familial relationships. Consequently, Jib became very aggressive when she was in the state of being entranced. Jib drank a lot every time before performing possession. On June 29, 2012, I participated in the annual shrine worship of a medium in Busaba's network. At 7.30 A.M., about 10 mediums were present in front of the shrine located outdoor at the left side of the house. They changed their clothes and started drinking liquor. The musician blew his bamboo mouth organ and the mediums sang and danced. I saw Jib cry and sway her thin and tall body back and forth. Her eyes were half-closed. Her face was red and full of sweat.

About an hour later while I was talking to Jib's husband, I heard a noise from the shrine area. There was a brawl between Jib and Malai. Jib smashed all offerings down on the floor. Then they started hitting each other. The music was propulsive and continuous as if it provided the sound backing for the scene. Shortly after, the other mediums settled the fight. Jib's husband took her home. At lunch, we discussed Jib's stories. The mediums criticized Jib's ritualized actions that she went mad and could not adjust herself to the spirit community. Jib wanted to be superior. She never paid respect to other mediums. Busaba revealed that Jib drank too much. Good mediums would not be boastful and challenge others. Many times when Jib was possessed, she became hot tempered. She pointed her finger and sword to people and swore at them. She always thought people wanted to challenge her power. I witnessed this fact a few times. Many mediums and villagers who attended shrine worship rituals left the scene when Jib was drunk and picked a fight with them.

Busaba suggested that Jib's aggressive behavior had begun two years ago when she was experiencing financial problems and facing her husband's domestic violence. Busaba criticized Jib for never going to the temple and doing meditation. Jib had entangled her familial trouble with spirit possession. So, her possession became wild and aggressive. Busaba emphasized that gods liked entertainment—singing, dancing, and greeting each other. The way Jib performed destroyed the spiritual ambience and chased away the gods. Unlike Busaba, Jib could not operate her mediumship to rehabilitate her social self in the family. Her domestic violence and financial crisis in everyday life cause long-term trauma. The traumatic experiences cannot avoid entanglement with ritualized times, and they have been enacted in violent and threatening manners, as can be seen from Jib's example.

PROSPECTIVE REPOSITIONING OF TRANSNATIONAL FAMILIES AND MEDIUMISTIC PRACTICES

In this chapter, I have examined the mediums' social sufferings resulting from transnational labor migration. Valentina Mazzucato and Djamila Schans[24] contest that to understand transnational families' modalities and the effects they experience, we should take cultural norms around the family into consideration and realize that the family might not be bound only by the nation-state. In the village where I conducted my field research, the mediums' family members had gone to Taiwan for a long time and left them behind. These mediums' life experiences of parental and marital dissociations inflict social, moral, and economic threats. I have explored further the logic of mediumistic practices as the culturally meaningful enactments of such experiences and the rehabilitation negotiated.

My examination provides the arena for potential issues on future mediumistic formation in these transnational families. It would be interesting to explore further how social and gender relations in the domestic realm change and to what extent such changes refashion spirit mediumship after the migrants return home. Jib's mediumship demonstrates her traumas in a post-transnational family and the failure to revitalize her marriage and resolve marital tensions with her husband. For Keng, I am curious whether he will continue mediumistic practice when his mother comes home. His mother's permanent homecoming might reintegrate his social self from the lack of maternal care and attention. Or he might pursue his desire of good fortunes by engaging in labor migration to Taiwan.

My central interest focuses on Busaba's familial and gender relations in her domestic domain. It is crucial to note the prospective question regarding the ways in which Busaba's relationship with Thongdam and Yomara will transform when her husband returns from working overseas and permanently remains at home. Busaba told me that when her husband permanently returns home, Yomara would be with him. The female spirit is related to the husband's unresolved gender. Busaba revealed that when her husband visited home, he usually put lipstick on his mouth and powder on his face. Villagers teased him as being *kathoey*, the Thai term referring to effeminate men. In Taiwan, the husband's colleagues at his workplace reported to Busaba that they called her husband *kathoey* because he usually put cosmetics on his face. Keng affirmed to me that Busaba's husband was "well-mannered." His latent message signified deviant sexual orientation. Nevertheless, Busaba construed her husband's nonnormative gender as the "spirit root" preparing him to be the medium of the goddess of his lineage. The husband's identity might be worth exploring in local gender relations. It even raises a crucial issue to me if working overseas provides Busaba's husband a comfort zone for his nonnormative gender aspirations. In closing, I attest that spirit mediumship is still a vital avenue to understanding villagers' social and gender relations and religious practices in 21st-century Thai society. However, such an examination should not only address ritualized behaviors per se but also thoroughly investigate the practitioners' everyday experiences.

NOTES

1. Fieldwork for this study has been supported by the Field Research Grant, Department of Anthropology, the Australian National University, and the Thai Studies Field Research Grants 2011, Asia Institute, at the University of Melbourne.

2. Hayami 2012, 1–25.

3. Statistical Report for 2011 Overseas Employment 2012.

4. Kapferer 1983, 100–110.

5. Lewis [1975] 2003.

6. Norton 2006.

7. Kendall 1985, 25.

8. Kendall 1996, 17–58.

9. Goodson 2001, 129; Peacock and Holland 1993, 374.

10. Geiger 1986, 335.

11. Kleinman et al. 1997, ix.

12. Kleinman 1997, 315–336.

13. Parrenas 2005.

14. Kleinman 1997

15. Bourguignon 1994, 181–212.

16. Spiro 1978; Bacigalupo 2004, 203–229; de la Perrière 2009, 283–305; Kawamura 2003, 257–289.

17. Kawamura 2003, 257–289.

18. Bourguignon 2004, 557–574.

19. Kawamura 2003.

20. Gomm 1975, 530–543.
21. Endres 2008, 34–65.
22. Masquelier 2002, 49–76.
23. Dow 1986, 56–69.
24. Mazzucato and Schans 2011, 704–712.

CHAPTER 4

Indian Women Through the Ages: Mother's Roles in Mythology, Current Practices, and Future Prospects

Lavanya Vemsani

INTRODUCTION

"Who wants to have a baby girl when the attitude of the police and society will be to deny her justice?" questioned the mother of "Nirbhaya" (name changed), who was brutally raped, assaulted, and left to die on the streets of New Delhi in December 2012.[1] Her question aptly illustrates the reality of a woman's life in modern India. There exists an apparent dichotomy in the case of women's development in India. On the one hand, India has opened up educational and employment opportunities for women including political representation since its independence in 1947. As an example of such openness and development, it should be noted that India is the world's second nation to elect a female prime minister (Indira Gandhi, 1966).[2] On the other hand, the cultural and administrative systems still lag far behind in providing adequate health care, basic sanitation facilities, safety, and security to women in all walks of life. A woman is urged and encouraged to achieve her goals of life and take advantage of educational and political opportunities a modern society offers, and yet, the cultural norms, social expectations, and government services rooted in cultural views pull her down.[3] An illustration of this dichotomy: While education or female literacy in 1950 averaged at less than 10 percent, it was 68–86 percent in 2011, almost equaling or surpassing male literacy levels in certain regions of India. However, the representation of women in employment is less than half when compared to men (in 2008, male employment was 85%, while female employment was 35%[4]) and their role in fields such as finance and industry is still miniscule, due to the lack of health care facilities and safety and security concerns. Unless the cultural norms are adjusted to reflect the basic safety, security, and rights of women immediately, women's contribution to society and their role in public will not change. Education without employment will bring no consequential changes in the life of millions of women of India. I will address the life of women as a mother in relation to her fertility, that is, her children, in order to understand the life of women in India, and how cultural and social limitations still control a major part of the life of women. Women's rights and quality of life are closely connected. If a woman's status is low in a society, and her fertility rights and feminine care are not secure, her civil rights become severely limited and she cannot take advantage of modern education or employment.

According to the Millennium Development Goals (MDGs) adopted by the United Nations, in the year 2000 women's development was a major constituent of progress, which includes three major benchmarks that incidentally concern women, namely, promoting gender equality, reducing child mortality, and improving maternal health.[5] These three Millennial Development Goals (MDGs) are an innate part of the mother's rights in India, where the contradiction between goals and practice is clearly apparent. Even though a number of legislations have been enacted with good intentions, with some fiduciary support allotted each year from the annual budget of India, the government could not implement or design a successful program due to the prevailing cultural attitudes ingrained in the cultural system of India.

Women's rights and status in India have a complex, and varied, history,[6] which could be understood from a broad examination of religious traditions and practices. Whatever her upbringing and childhood might have been, a woman's marriage and motherhood place an enormous amount of stress on her with few legal or social protections.[7] Any examination of women of India also needs to include an examination of fertility rights, and motherhood, in order to understand the status of women, socially and legally.[8] Therefore, in this chapter, I begin my examination of the topic with some ancient Indian mythology, such as the epics *Mahabharata* and *Ramayana*, and continue with colonial and postcolonial legislations in order to understand the current status of women with regard to social, political, economic, religious, and legal precedents. At each stage of historical evolution, the law is closely connected to the cultural understanding of women as a mother or daughter, but not as an individual. Her status is closely tied to her family, especially her fertility. In this chapter, I will track the progress of women's fertility rights in India during the past 1,000 years in the purview of social and cultural norms.

This chapter is divided into two sections in addition to the introduction and conclusion. The first section discusses the premodern concepts of fertility, motherhood, and a mother's rights as a precursor to understanding the present-day concerns on a mother's rights through an analysis of myths from the *Mahabharata* and the classical *puranas*. The second section discusses fertility rights of women, in addition to the current issues brought forth due to scientific development, such as surrogacy and artificial reproduction therapies (ART), which lack any type of legal precedents in India and which completely negate women's rights in this area in favor of commercial interests. The conclusions provide summary provisions of the traditional understandings, past legislations, as well as offer suggestions for future programs.

Mythology suggests limited social and economic rights for women in a highly centralized patriarchal ancient society, although the women's fertility rights are fully fledged in classical India (which is an advantage and disadvantage at the same time, discussed in detail below) and stand in stark contrast to her overall image and social status. This contrasting position is also partly reflected in the traditional mythology and classical image of women, which treat her as the sole proprietor of her own fertility (pregnancy and childbearing), but do not confer to her any rights over the resulting children or consequences. A woman's role in childbearing and child rearing is noted only as superficial with male contribution centrally placed. The current practice is not much different from this classical image. This creates concern and a considerable gray area in the areas of pregnancy and infant, and child care. A woman's rights with regard to her fertility and her overall status and rights in society stand in stark contrast. It appears that this contrast is not only visible in practice, but is also ingrained in the traditional image of women depicted in the classical mythology of India. Services for maternal health and well-being are limited, as are pregnancy/fertility services noted above, which result in wider repercussions for Indian society at large. We cannot ignore, along with inadequate healthcare facilities, the appallingly low levels of sanitation available to women.

Fertility and Motherhood in Ancient India: An Examination of Classical Literature

The mother and her child are treated as a single unit for legal, socioeconomic as well as health-planning purposes in India. This has been supported by a long-established traditional Indian culture.[9] Both have some rights together, but not rights that could be considered individual rights, with the exception of fertility rights, discussed in detail in the second section on reproductive rights of women. The main reason for this is that motherhood is entrenched as secondary to marriage based on the interlaced notions of family traditions of India. Motherhood outside of marriage may exist in present-day society, but it is not an accepted or recognized norm of the society, and hence the rights of mothers in India are limited. Likewise, female health issues related to fertility, child bearing, and child rearing do not receive the attention that they rightfully deserve. Whatever may be the notions of pregnancy and childbirth in Indian religions,[10] as far as traditional law is concerned, the identity of the child begins only at birth, and the child belongs to the father as the primary guardian, and not the mother, who is considered a secondary guardian, although she is the primary care giver of the child. Recently, into this already confusing mix of the mother's rights come two new issues concerning motherhood and fertility, due to advances in medical science, namely, egg donation, and surrogate motherhood (bearing a child for another couple, who would be recognized as the parents of the child). This pushes the issue of the mother and her child into an area where no comprehensive law exists currently. Therefore, it is pertinent to address the rights of a woman as a mother in order to ascertain the well-being of the child, mother, and thereby women's status and rights in the society. Therefore, in this chapter, I will examine important issues concerning the concepts of motherhood and the rights of the mother in premodern India, as well as the present practices of motherhood, social and cultural norms, economic aspects of motherhood, and health care facilities for the mother and her child in connection with the mother's rights in India.

To be fruitful and multiply is innate to Indian culture. The common blessing that a woman receives upon her marriage, "be the mother of a hundred sons," echoes this innate desire, although it may appear a bit skewed in terms of gender ratio.[11]

NARRATIVES OF FERTILITY AND MOTHERHOOD IN HINDUISM AND JAINISM

This section examines Hindu as well as Jain birth stories. Each story set is again divided into three parts depending on the concept of pregnancy. I will begin with the basic idea of conception and discuss the role of the mother and her rights and the agency of others in bringing about the conception. I will then discuss the role of women by examining the nature of the womb, the mother's role, and her powers during gestation. Doing so helps in understanding Indian premodern views on sacredness of life and the mother and child paradigm in India, and how these views may persist in modern attitudes in India.

PREGNANCY AND THE BEGINNING OF LIFE

Pregnancy and conception are clearly understood and enumerated in classical texts of India, including the *Brihadaranyaka Upanishad*, *Ayurveda* texts, as well as the *Puranas*.[12] Since my main purpose is not to examine the medical conceptions of motherhood and pregnancy, but a sociocultural understanding, I will limit my examination to the mythologies of childbirth to understand the concepts of pregnancy and childbirth and its implications for current understandings of women's health and fertility.

> As soon as (the soul) is released from hell, or from heaven, it arrives (in the womb). Overpowered by that (soul), the two-fold seed becomes solid. It becomes a speck of life, and then a bubble, and then flesh.[13]

Similarly, in the *Brahmapurana*[14] the soul goes to the semen and then develops into an embryo by joining the fertile ovum.[15] It means that the semen carries the soul, which begins to develop once the semen joins the ovum. This means that life is present in semen, that is, semen could fertilize and grow to life, under favorable circumstances even though a womb may not always be available. Even though the process of impregnation and the development of the fetus are well known, as noted in the descriptions above, it has remained the one subject of contention on the question of beginning of life, as a number of classical narratives of birth happen in the absence of womb. Women's role and the role of the "ovum" have received less attention almost to the point of obscurity, while lengthy descriptions in the process and the cause of birth are assigned primarily to the sperm. Thus, a perspective, which can be called "womb jealousy," characterizes a number of birth stories in the *Puranas*. Numerous stories depict various processes of birth, substituting women with that of water, reed, fire, and so on. The cause of birth is also narrated differently in many stories, in which women play a negligible role in choosing their partner for cohabitation or have no knowledge of conception until the delivery of her child has taken place. Similarly, numerous stories relate the fetal processes where the fetus is transferred from one woman to another or protected in isolation until birth, without her knowledge or involvement in the process. As narrated in numerous stories, women's fertility can also be taken advantage of without her involvement. It is important to analyze these stories to understand the position of a woman in connection with fertility, childbirth, and her relationship with the child. Earlier studies have assumed that the man has authority over the child as the woman is seen as the earth with a passive role in conception and childbirth.[16] However, an examination of stories of childbirth begs for a reconsideration of this assumption with a view to establishing women in better status in regard to childbirth. I will examine two stories briefly here.

THE MOTHER AS AN UNINVOLVED/UNKNOWN PARTICIPANT IN THE PROCESS OF CHILDBIRTH

The creation (or replication) of life inside a woman is intriguing and has been dealt with in numerous stories. I discuss below varied conception processes where the normal process of formation of an embryo through intercourse, and in the womb, is avoided and the conception is said to have happened in strange, unimaginable processes leading to the birth of children.

Usha acquired the form of a mare, and her husband, Vivasvat (the sun), also acquired the form of a horse and reached her. He touched her with his mouth and she emitted the semen from her mouth. From it were born the Asvins in the Ganga River.[17] Here although the conception is depicted as that of the male touching the female, thus resulting in an embryo in the mouth of the female (in the mare), the actual agent of conception and birth is an external womb—in this case, the Ganga River. Ganga, or water, is depicted as the surrogate womb in many stories. In another version of this story, the Asvins are said to have been born from the semen sneezed from the nose of the mare.[18] Similarly, the birth of Daksha happens in a very strange manner.[19] Mārisā, the wife of the Pracetasas (the ten sons of Samudri), followed them when they decided to renounce everything and live in the forests. There they copulated and the Pracetasas continued their journey with Mārisā following them. The sperm came out of her body in the form of sweat and was deposited on the leaves as she was walking past the trees in the forest. The leaves put together drops of her sweat, which gave birth to Daksha. Here a womb or a womb-like structure is completely absent, with leaves facilitating the formation of the child from scattered semen-sweat, akin to the idea of scattered genes, collected to reach a final form. Another story presents a different version and says that Daksha was born from the right thumb of Brahma, while Daksha's wife-to-be was born from the left thumb of Brahma.[20] Again the absence of a womb or an ovum is notable.

These stories depict women as peripheral to childbirth and the womb as a completely unnecessary organ for the birth of a child. In order to understand the concept of womb or the description of other media as womb, a number of well-known birth stories can be mentioned briefly here: the stories of the birth of Agastya (pot born); Suka (fire born); Draupadi, also known as Yagnaseni (born from sacred fire); Sita (earth born); and Satyavathi (fish born). Another unnatural conception and birth is also seen in the stories of Bhagiratha (born from two women) and Ayyappa (born from two men). Granted that stories of unusual personages often include unique circumstances for their births, the cumulative effect of so many stories of special births indicates a process to mask or belittle or even negate the role of women in childbirth.

Curiously, the absence of the mother's womb in the above stories foreshadows the role played by test-tube babies and surrogate pregnancy currently commonplace in India. These stories simplify the unnatural aspects of conception and childbirth and diminish the taboo commonly attributed to anything new or unknown.

WOMEN AS ACTIVE PARTICIPANTS IN CHILDBIRTH

In order to understand the depiction of women as active agents in conception and its consequences, I will examine the stories of levirate in the epic *Mahabharata* (the birth of Dhritarashtra, Pandu, etc.; of Vyasa; of Bhishma; of Skanda [Ganga as the mother]; of Pandavas; of Krishna and Balarama; the failed conception in the story of Martanda and the birth of Kauravas). Although a male sperm can result in a pregnancy even in the absence of a womb or an ovum, the women could not do away with male sexual contribution should they desire offspring. Thus, these stories place the special circumstances under which women acquire pregnancy by the contribution of a male other than their husband. The husband/father, on the other hand, could produce children from anywhere, just by dropping his sperm and does not really need a womb/woman.

Kunti and Madri obtained the Pandavas (the five sons of Pandu, namely, Yudhishthira Dharmaraja, Bhima, Arjuna, Nakula, and Sahadeva) through their own active involvements with permission from their husband, Pandu. This is very similar to sperm donation, but with a difference. The donors were known, but not involved with the children in any way.[21] In the stories of the birth of other heroes such as Rama, the conception happened after the *prasada/yagnaphala* was consumed by king Dasaratha's wives. Among these women, Gandhari, upset that Kunti had already given birth to a son, tries to abort her undeveloped fetus by hitting herself in the stomach. The resulting embryo was only a ball of flesh that looked like an iron ball. Vyasa then advised her to cut it up into a hundred pieces and nurture them by keeping them in a hundred pots and pouring over them clarified butter. These pieces of flesh then developed into a hundred sons, the *Kauravas*.[22] This is almost like a test-tube baby development, obtained from something like stem cells derived from an aborted embryo. The story of the birth of the

Pandavas and the Kauravas depicts the mothers as active participants in obtaining their children, and they are also seen as very involved mothers in their growth. Stories like these show a culturally based awareness of various types of birth procedures, where mothers are active decision makers while the husband and others may be passive. This type of cultural awareness is reflected in the acceptance and easy availability of contraceptives including the morning-after pill and abortion services as part of a broader medical practice rather than secluded abortion centers, as seen in some countries of the world. The use of contraceptives by women is culturally acceptable, even though social status and economic problems may prove to be limiting issues for their adoption by women. However, there is still a need for women to take charge in the issues of childbirth and child rearing in addition to the use of contraception and limiting family size.

I now take up the examination of fetal narratives in Jain texts and compare the findings with regard to childbirth and women. The Jain texts deal with similar concepts, but the descriptions and stories differ in order to support the Jain philosophical understanding of birth and child. In the second section, I examine a number of stories of the conception, womb, gestation, and fetuses (dreams of birth, birth of Kamsa and of Krishna, Balarama, and Jarasandha). The embryo of Mahavira is transferred to Sumitra, who understood the significance of pregnancy through a number of symbolic dreams. Kamsa was found by his parents in a box of bronze found floating in a river, hence he was named Kamsa (a word derived from *kamsya,* a Sanskrit word for bronze),[23] and the births of Balarama and Krishna were preceded by the transfer and death of *shadgarbhas* (six fetuses), a feat accomplished by Nigamesha, a god related to fertility and childbirth in Jainism.[24]

CLASSICAL CASE OF MADHAVI: SURROGACY AND FERTILITY

In this story, Vishwamitra requires Galava to pay 600 horses as his *gurudaksina,* which he needed for a sacrifice.[25] Galava did not own, and could not afford to pay for, those many horses. Instead, he gave his daughter, Madhavi, to Vishwamitra to use to procure the horses. Vishwamitra then visits a number of kings and requests them to provide him with the horses, for which he could offer Madhavi to produce a son for that particular king. After a number of sons were produced to a number of kings, Vishwamitra acquired his required number of horses and returned Madhavi to Galava, her father. This story depicts Madhavi as the necessary participant and a surrogate mother, but passive in role. Vishwamitra is the active participant seeking donors, in return for the womb/surrogate he offered them in the form of Madhavi. Similar passive roles still prevail in the present artificial insemination and surrogacy practices in India, which will be discussed in the following section.

Fertility, Childbirth, and Motherhood: Current Practices

Gender awareness and efforts to legalize the status and rights of women began gradually during the colonial period, gaining momentum only after the independence of India in 1947, with the enactment of the Constitution of India. Article 15 of the Indian Constitution grants equal rights to women and men, in all walks of life. The first report on the development of women released by the Government of India, in 1974,[26] on the occasion of the United Nation's Year of the Woman, showed a dismal picture of women's status in India.[27] However, the status of women as dependents in the Hindu patriarchal system continued to dominate the lifestyle of people. A woman who is not able to take care of her body, health, and basic needs would not be able to enjoy her civil rights in society. Even though several health and population policies exist, many of these policies that might directly affect women were not planned with a women-centered perspective.[28] Hence, numerous government policies do not yield the desired results with regard to female health.[29] I will discuss below the population control policies enacted by the Government of India, which were poorly designed ignoring the women and hence failed in yielding the desired results.

New Issues in the Global Century

1. Fertility, contraception, abortion, and prenatal and delivery care
   The Medical Termination of Pregnancy (MTP) Act passed by the Parliament of India in 1971 clearly states that when a pregnancy can be terminated, the limit is placed at 20 weeks of gestation, beyond which no pregnancy can be terminated.[30]
2. Egg donations and stem cell research is carried on by numerous private clinics with utter secrecy. Although the Medical Council of India lays down guidelines, there are no clear rules on intercountry transfer or sale of eggs, which might be of concern, as stem cell research is becoming a multibillion-dollar industry and leads to underground trading and marketing.

Reproductive Rights of Women

Reproduction and fertility rights entail another major issue of aggression against women.[31] Lack of feminine health care and lack of availability of free contraceptive aids is common. Female selective abortion, while not common, is still practiced, which is a two-pronged violation of human rights with regard to women, and the issues of surrogacy and adoption have further questionable consequences due to the lack of appropriate legal codes.[32] This leads to numerous pregnancies not known or registered in the official statistics,[33] and a woman's body in the case of pregnancy becomes a marketable commodity. Although commercial surrogacy has been legal in India since 2002, India faces numerous bioethical concerns and legal issues due to the lack of clarity in the law.[34] According to this law, neither the mother nor the child has any rights. A recent law, Assisted Reproductive Technology Bill and Rules, enacted in 2010 provides nominal rights, but leaves much to be desired.[35] Most often women are lured into this process for monetary gains (up to $7,000–$10,000, which results in 3.5 to 5 *lakh* rupees, a hefty sum when compared with the daily wage of $5–$10). Indian law does not adequately address the health issues or concerns of surrogate mothers, which are largely regulated by the fertility industry, under nonbinding guidelines set by the Indian Council of Medical Research.[36] Several physical as well as emotional issues faced by surrogate mothers are completely ignored by the government policy and law on commercial surrogacy. It is especially important to address these health aspects for surrogate mothers since the maternal mortality rate is also high in India. A mother is left with numerous physical and psychological issues after the childbirth, since the child is immediately separated from its mother and given to the commissioning parents. Postpartum care of surrogate mothers is completely neglected.

Commercial surrogacy also entails a lack of rights for the child, and the citizenship of the child remains in limbo, until the commissioning parents register the child.[37] This is brought to light in the case of a child, Manji, born in India commissioned by a Japanese couple.[38] However, by the time the child was born, the Japanese couple divorced and refused to accept the child, thus leaving the child in limbo. The issue was resolved only when her grandmother adopted Manji and took her to Japan. However, such issues might not always end with a positive result. This brings the concern of the rights of the child that need to be addressed by another bill.[39] To ensure a safe home and bonding with parents, the commissioning parents (as expectant parents) should be mandated to spend time with the surrogate mother from the time of commissioning a baby, since it is not a simple commercial transaction, but involves familial bonds and emotional attachment. But prevailing cultural norms as seen in the story of Madhavi, and others noted in the first section, compounded with the lack of gender sensitivity negate such an engaging role for either the surrogate or the commissioning mother involved in the surrogacy process. ART legislations do not provide the necessary measures of safety and security for health risks of surrogate women. If any unforeseen circumstances were to occur during her pregnancy or if the surrogate mother were to lose her health due to her pregnancy or miscarriage, there is no help for her. She may be left to suffer the consequences alone for the rest of her life. A surrogate woman is just a tool, and care is provided only for the duration of the pregnancy, but not for her as a person or a mother, and postpartum care is absent. Women are exploited in the current system.

Female health and hygiene needs call for a specially designed educational and awareness campaign in addition to the availability of health care centers. Studies have shown a close connection between the success of policies designed with gender-sensitive strategies and planning.[40] The Government of India successfully carried out rural electrification and communication projects (with cell phones widely used even in remote regions), yet rural sanitation projects still lag behind. It is not the lack of resources but the lack of willingness, commitment, and gender sensitivity that creates this dismal picture. The then rural development minister of India, Jairam Ramesh, even remarked to journalists, during the launch of the Millennium Development Goals, that "women in the country demand cell phones over toilets,"[41] which is a demonstration of the misplaced and misogynist policies prevalent at the administrative level of the ruling party at that time.

CONCLUSION: PRESENT ISSUES AND FUTURE PROSPECTS

A comprehensive women's act is necessary, similar to the SC/ST Act (Scheduled Castes and Tribes Act). It would outline and provide rights and facilities required to ensure the progress of women and also would address the following: (1) education; (2) job and pay equality; (3) maternal health; childcare, including fertility rights; and protection for life and health; (4) security and legal and political rights; and (5) domestic and property rights.

Women may venture into a number of fields, or may prepare to fly into space or pilot a submarine, but the ground realities for most of the women in India are debilitating. The legal and administrative mechanisms have not kept pace with the development of women and do not provide a decent standard of living. A bus or a train, which women may board, lack the basic amenities such as security, a bathroom, and clean drinking water. Minimal sanitation, health care facilities, and legal rights of equality still leave a lot to be desired for women's development. Women are also exploited in the current ART and surrogacy practices. Until all these systems are addressed and suitable laws are created, women's development will remain incomplete. Development is not just about attaining measurable achievements in selective fields, but should entail good quality of life and tangible benefits for all the people in a society. A number of new issues arise in the new millennium for women in addition to the health and sanitation issues that have plagued the Indian women for millennia. Surrogate mothers and children are left in a limbo and their rights to life are severely compromised under the existing law.

Legislative mechanisms need to be enacted to protect the mother and the child in such types of contractual birthing practices. Another area that needs to be regulated is ART, which encourages egg donations for monetary gains, which might be used in illegal stem cell research, without informing or seeking the consent of the donor, who may not understand the consequences of such donation. For donors of eggs, or participants in surrogate motherhood, guidance needs to be developed about three programs: social, economic, and ethical issues. Issues discussed in this chapter, including health and fertility, need to be regulated, and legal procedures need to be established immediately. Clearly, these matters merit the attention of fair-minded citizens of India. And certainly there is room for improvement, and the need for expertise and support of men and women from around in the world. Hopefully, the situation of women will improve in the 21st century.

ACKNOWLEDGMENTS

First, I thank Dr. Zayn Kassam for inviting me to contribute this chapter on issues concerning women in modern India. I also thank my friend R.L. Mohl, interpretive specialist, Hopewell Museum and Historical Site, Hopewell, Ohio, for his reading and valuable advice on an earlier version of this chapter.

NOTES

1. See Mahr et al. 2013, 12. Although it was not the first time a woman was raped in India, Nirbhaya's rape and murder drew wide media and public attention forcing the government to reconsider the security of women in the public, passing a bill named after Nirbhaya in order curb the recurrence of such incidents. See also Bahadur 2014, 35–39.

2. See Banerjee 2006, 85–101; Vanaja 2012, 1–3.

3. See Berry 2011, 136–152.

4. Klaveren et al. 2010.

5. www.unwomen.org; http://www.un.org/millenniumgoals/bkgd.shtml, accessed August 31, 2014.

6. See Kumar 1993.

7. See Arya 2006, 293–328; Berry 2011, 136–152.

8. See Halder and Jaishankar 2008, 663–687.

9. See Agarwal 2003, 184–224; Patel 2006, 1255–1268.

10. Hume 1921, 6.4.4.

11. Preference for sons, instead of daughters, intensified in light of the modern family norms where families raise only one or two children. Female selective abortion is one of the serious concerns noted by scholars and policy

makers. A recent study also notes that education and empowerment of women have shown limited effect on the birth and survival of a girl child. See also Mukherjee 2013, 1–28.

12. See Das 2003; Selby 2005, 254–275; Kapani 1989, 181–196; Bhattacharya 2006.

13. See Pargiter 1923, 11.1–21.

14. See Shastri and Bhatt 1985, 234.9–42.

15. Ibid., 217.26–27.

16. See Doniger 2002, 15–32.

17. Shastri and Bhatt 1985, 89.34–36.

18. Ibid., 6.44–45ab.

19. Ibid., 178.99–104.

20. Ibid., 2.47; 2.51–53.

21. See Suktankar 1933, 133–66.

22. Ibid.

23. Vaidya 1969–71, Ch. 25.

24. See Jain 1962, Ch. 30.

25. Ibid. *Mahabharata Udyogaparva* 119–122.

26. Government of India, Department of Social Welfare, Ministry of Education and Social Welfare 1974.

27. Indian Council of Social Sciences Research 1975.

28. See Gill and Stewart 2011, 12–18.

29. See Ghosh and Bharati 2005, 194–211.

30. The UK Abortion Law 1967, on which the Indian law is based http://www.legislation.gov.uk/ukpga/1967/87/contents, accessed August 28, 2014, also allows abortion only until 20 weeks of gestation, although in UK it was raised to 24 weeks in 1990. Other nations permit abortions between 12 and 24 weeks of pregnancy. Abortion is also allowed after 24 weeks of gestation in UK if the continuing pregnancy is deemed to cause a health risk to the mother or shows evidence of grave fetal abnormalities.

31. See Kaur 2012, 21–30.

32. See Ross-Sheriff 2012, 125–128.

33. See Rimm 2009, 1429–1462.

34. See Chang 2009, 11–12. Chang notes that India has become a global destination for commercial surrogacy as the cost of surrogacy is low in India, almost one-seventh the cost of such a procedure in the United States, although commercial surrogacy in India is still embroiled in numerous bioethical, legal, and women's rights issues, while the state is still attempting to regulate the industry to better protect the mother and her child in this new commercial enterprise.

35. See Malhotra and Malhotra 2012, 31–41.

36. See Mishra 2009, 9–14.

37. See Smerdon 2012, 341–358; Kanojia 2008, 92–93.

38. See Parks 2010, 333–340.

39. See Unnithan 2013, 287–313. A number of acts were passed between 2001 and 2013 regulating a variety of aspects of commercial surrogacy; however, certain questions on the surrogate woman's consent and agency still remain ambiguous.

40. See Gill and Stewart 2011, 12–18.

41. http://articles.economictimes.indiatimes.com/2012–02–17/news/3107 1471_1_mobile-phones-toilets-jairam-ramesh, accessed August 31, 2014.

PART II

Socioeconomics, Politics, Authority

CHAPTER 5

From Secession to Social Activism: Muslim Women's Movements in the Philippines

Vivienne SM Angeles

INTRODUCTION

Women's studies and advocacy are vibrant fields in the Philippine academic and nonacademic landscapes, and numerous studies have been conducted and published in the areas of gender equity, empowerment, economic activities, women's roles in development,[1] transnationalism, and Filipinas as overseas workers.[2] The situation, however, on the specific subject of Filipino Muslim women is different. There are studies on the changing roles of Muslim women,[3] but there are other aspects of Muslim women's lives that deserve serious attention. Brecht discusses the leadership roles of Maranao women in a localized setting marked by a no war–no peace situation,[4] while Hilsdon notes that perceptions of Muslim women as simply assisting men impede the acknowledgment of women's participation in the peace-making process.[5] Alojamiento (2004) recognizes this invisibility of Muslim women and attributes the absence of feminist discourse in Mindanao to the dominance of male religious authorities in discussions on revolutionary organizations and mass politics.[6] Other studies on gender and Philippine Muslim women are done by funding agencies, designed to assess the impact of the war on women and children and to determine how aid programs can improve conditions and prospects for women in conflict areas.[7] Women were also involved in Muslim secessionist movements, but aside from studies by Siapno (1994) and Angeles (1995), works[8] on the subject have ignored women's participation. In spite of this lack of attention, Philippine Muslim women's engagements in the public square have continued, in various forms and with diverse goals.

This chapter discusses the forms of Muslim women's activism in the Philippines from the early 1970s to the present. I argue that the evolving pattern of women's activism is multivalent and has expanded to include Muslim women of varied backgrounds and interests. In covering this 45-year period, I look at women's activism in terms of their participation in the secessionist movement and, in the later years, in their involvement in transnational discourses and conventions like the CEDAW (Convention on the Elimination of all Forms of Discrimination against Women), DEVAW (Declaration on the Elimination of Violence against Women), and domestic legislations that have to do with women's rights.

I focus on the activism of born-Muslim women who also refer to themselves collectively as Bangsamoro (Moro nation) women, who have either experienced or whose parents have lived through the conflict in southern Philippines. I begin in 1970, the height of the war between the military and the Moro National Liberation Front (MNLF). The MNLF was pushing for secession and the establishment of an Islamic state in southern Philippines. I end in the present, after a period that witnessed Islamic resurgence in the 1970s; the United Nations Decade for Women's Equality, Development and Peace; the end of martial law in 1986; the signing of a peace agreement with the MNLF in 1996; increasing global attention to women's rights; and in early 2016, the peace negotiations between the Philippine government and another secessionist group, the Moro Islamic Liberation Front (MILF). These events, together with increased access to education and technology that facilitates globalization, have influenced and shaped the nature of Filipino Muslim women's engagement in the public space.

This study comes from continuing interviews, communications with Muslim women, email and phone conversations, news reports and articles that deal with Philippine Muslim women's activities, and other relevant materials. I look at the contexts and causes of Muslim women's activism and focus on their engagement outside the home, where they exercise their agency in activities that impact their lives as Muslims and as women.

PHILIPPINE MUSLIMS

Muslims constitute five percent of the estimated 100 million population[9] of the Philippines. The country is predominantly Christian, with

80.9 percent professing Roman Catholicism and the rest belonging to variations of Christianity and other religions.[10] Historically, Philippine Muslims were concentrated in the southern parts of the country (southern Palawan and Mindanao), and their religious identity has been tied with ethnicity.[11] They are mainly Sunnis, but since the 1970s, other expressions of Islam have been manifested in the Philippines so that now there are the Shi'a, Jami'at Tabligh, Ahmadiyya, plus converts who call themselves reverts,[12] or *Balik Islam*,[13] and may be affiliated with one of the Muslim sects. Another distinction has recently emerged among Philippine Muslims: Moro and *Balik Islam*. The Moros trace their lineage to precolonial families in Mindanao and Sulu who are also identified with the 13 ethnic groups.[14] The Spanish colonizers called the Muslims "Moros" (Moors) in a derogatory way, but in the course of the Muslim rebellion in the 1970s, members of the MNLF began to transcode (Hall, 1997) the word to connote the courage, bravery, and heroism of the Moros, whose rich political and cultural heritage was not diluted by colonialism. Ethnic Muslims have now been using the term *Moro* for individuals and *Bangsamoro* for the collective.[15] While being Muslims, too, the *Balik Islams* do not share the historical experiences of the Moros nor participate in the secessionist movements.

Sixty percent of the estimated 5 million Muslims in the Philippines are women. The ethnic Muslim women are now present in other parts of the country due to internal migration motivated by educational opportunities in the capital region, economic needs, and internal displacement caused by the war in the 1970s. Muslim women are now a common sight in universities in Manila, are engaged in different careers including law and medicine, and several of them have been elected to national government positions. Their participation in varied forms of activism has expanded, from involvement in the secessionist movement, to heading nongovernment organizations (NGOs), to campaigning for women's rights and running for political office.

Defining the Terms: Muslim Women's Roles, Identity, and Agency

Colonial and postcolonial literature and the Philippine media portray Moro women as participants in arranged marriages, dutiful daughters, docile wives, mothers, and caregivers. The Moro men, in contrast, are presented as brave and courageous, heads of households, economic providers, decision makers, and guardians of the socioeconomic and political structure. In addition, interpretations of the Qur'ān in the local setting present women as being under the care of male members of the family. There were women who wielded power and influence, but they were exceptional Moro women, members of the aristocracy, like Tarhata Kiram and Dayang Dayang Hadji

Piandao, nieces of the Sultan of Sulu, Jamalul Kiram, who reigned from 1894 to 1936. Traditional presentations of Muslim women, however, have undergone changes as more women became educated and joined the workforce either in their localities or in larger cities like Manila.

Islamic resurgence, which in a way was facilitated by government response to the secessionist movement,[16] has also affected Muslim women's sense of identity, which is increasingly expressed visually, through the use of the head cover and in conformity with their understanding of the prescriptions on modesty in the Qur'ān (24:31). As indicated previously, Philippine Muslims, who also represent different ethnic groups, possess varied characteristics that include modes of dressing peculiar to their tribes. Before the 1970s, women rarely wore the head cover in their everyday lives, wearing them only to the mosque or if they went on a pilgrimage to Mecca to indicate their completion of the fifth pillar of Islam. From the 1970s on, however, the use of the head cover has become more popular, with both the MNLF and the MILF promoting its use. For women in these movements, wearing the head cover, whether a turban or a hijab, has become a symbol of identity and also functions as a political statement especially at a time when Muslims were asserting their rights in the course of the war in the 1970s. There are also women who have taken to the Arab *abaya* and the *niqāb*, as influenced by the increasing contacts with Saudi Arabia and the training of Filipino religious teachers there. The traditional ethnic clothing has given way to what is now defined as Islamic clothing.

My interviews with Muslim women indicate that the use of the head cover is usually a woman's choice, an exercise of their agency as Muslim women. Agency here refers to Mahmoud's definition of the term as "the capacity to realize one's own interests against the weight of custom, traditions, transcendental will or other obstacles."[17] In addition to adopting what has been defined as Islamic clothing, Philippine Muslim women have also used this agency to break away from the traditional notions of women's subordination and in the quest for and promotion of their rights as Muslim women in the public square.

THE 1970S: MUSLIM WOMEN IN THE SECESSIONIST MOVEMENT, UNITED NATIONS' FOCUS ON WOMEN, AND ISLAMIC REVIVAL

The MNLF was established in 1969 and, in a short period of time, emerged as the largest and most organized Muslim secessionist movement in the country, claiming an army of 15,000 and countless other sympathizers in the early 1970s. Their goal was to establish an independent state in southern Philippines after centuries of continued marginalization by the Spanish, American, and Philippine governments. The MNLF described itself as a popular revolutionary movement guided by the Qur'ān and ideas of nationalism.[18] President Ferdinand Marcos claimed that one of the reasons he declared Martial Law in September 1972 was the existence of this movement. Although the leadership of the MNLF consists of male Moros, the membership includes women who joined for various reasons, among them land-grabbing by Christians and those favored by the government, military abuses, massacres of Muslims,[19] and government oppression and neglect. One of the early women MNLF members, a graduate of the University of the Philippines, attended the training camp in Sabah and was the only female in the group who trained in jungle survival and the use of weapons. Many women in the movement were university students and employees, with several having the support and encouragement of their families who believed in taking action against government neglect of and discrimination against Muslims. Other families asserted that it was safer to be in the mountains than be subject to military abuses. Students organized in colleges and universities and in the countryside, where they encountered difficulties in getting other women to join the movement, because of traditional perceptions of gender roles where women were viewed as protected and families were concerned about the risks their daughters would be taking. Generally, women were not expected to be revolutionaries.[20] Eventually many more women became involved with the MNLF either by joining the latter in the mountains or as sympathizers/supporters while they continued their usual daily lives.

The MNLF women came from different socioeconomic backgrounds—some from the old aristocracy, others from political families, and still others from the rural masses. I interviewed these women for the first time in 1995 and continue to communicate with some of them up to the present. The majority of these women worked outside the home, while others were students or homemakers. Their range of activities covered intelligence, propaganda, smuggling small arms and ammunitions, delivering medicine and supplies to the MNLF forces, and for some, involvement in actual combat.[21] Women in combat were more the exception than the rule, but there were a few women killed in the battlefields, or "martyred," in the language of the MNLF. The main task of the women in the battlefield, however, was to provide moral and medical support to the men. Stay-at-home mothers contributed to the war effort by sewing uniforms and patches for the fighters. There was a select group of women trained to produce homemade bombs and bullets. The war became personal for many women whose husbands, brothers, and male relatives were among the estimated 70,000 who perished in the early 1970s. A Muslim woman who is presently involved in an NGO for Muslim women in Cotabato city commented that she is now working for Muslim women; she did not participate in the MNLF but considers herself a victim because her brother was killed in the course of the conflict.[22]

In 1972, the MNLF formally created the Women's Committee, whose main function was to support the MNLF and to perform whatever duties they would be called upon. The leadership of this committee came from the women who had been actively involved in the MNLF since its inception—among them Eleonora Tan and Bainon Caron. Their primary concern in the early years, aside from supporting the MNLF, was recruitment and consciousness-raising among the women in Mindanao.[23]

As the conflict wore on, causing deaths, destruction, and displacement of peoples, the international Muslim community pressured the Philippine government to find solutions and resolve the conflict, resulting in the Tripoli Agreement of 1976 and, two decades later, the Final Peace Agreement with the Philippine government under Fidel Ramos in 1996.

When the MNLF and the Philippine government started negotiating for a peaceful resolution of the conflict, women were not present in the negotiation panels, but the Women's Committee of the MNLF fulfilled critical tasks behind the scenes, providing clerical support, research, and propaganda. However, the public face of the movement was always the male leadership, with the women as the invisibles whose critical tasks were perceived more as "assisting men."[24] Interestingly, the MNLF women did not clamor for a greater role in the movement, and as one of the women members noted, their focus was on the struggle and the goal of the movement—the establishment of a separate state.

It was also in the 1970s that the United Nations declared 1976–1985 the Decade for Women: Equality, Development and Peace. In 1979, the United Nations General Assembly passed the Convention on the Elimination of all Forms of Discrimination against Women (CEDAW). The Philippines, which has had several women serving in the UN Commission on the Status of Women,[25] became one of the countries that actively promote CEDAW. Muslim women's organizations like the PHILMUSLIMA and MUSLIMAH (established in 1975) were among those involved in the promotion of CEDAW at the time. This involvement, however, was largely limited to Muslim women in the Manila area as those in southern Philippines were still grappling with the displacement and effects of war.

THE 1980s: MARTIAL LAW ENDS, THE WAR SLOWS DOWN

By the 1980s, the war had slowed down but there were intermittent conflicts, especially since there were other competing Muslim groups that had their own separatist goals. Many MNLF women started working in both private and government sectors and, at the same time, continued to support the MNLF men in the frontlines in various capacities—providing supplies, acting as "urban operatives" passing crucial information, and giving moral support to the continuing, albeit reduced armed conflict.

In February 1986, a People's Power Revolution ended the rule of Ferdinand Marcos and ushered in Corazon Aquino as the new president of the Philippines. Among the crowds that congregated in the historic peaceful "revolution" were Muslim men and women who, together with the other Filipinos, demonstrated against the Marcos government. Corazon Aquino, the first woman president, was the wife of Benigno Aquino, an opposition leader who was assassinated when he returned to the Philippines. It was during Corazon Aquino's term that negotiations with the MNLF resumed, and a new Philippine constitution was promulgated in 1987, which provides for an autonomous region in Mindanao.[26] This provision was the basis for the creation of the Autonomous Region of Muslim Mindanao (ARMM).[27]

THE 1990s: FROM THE BATTLEFIELDS TO NGOs AND BEYOND

In 1996, the Philippine government under President Fidel Ramos signed the Final Peace Agreement with the MNLF. As the MNLF leadership was signing the documents in Malacanang, the presidential palace, many of the MNLF members were downstairs, and as Bai Embai Baraguir, one of the MNLF women in the group noted, they were crying and wondering whether all their efforts in the struggle for the rights of their people were for naught.

Although the war was supposed to have ended, there was still some fighting going on with other Muslim secessionist groups, but the MNLF women returned to their homes and continued on with their lives although still meeting, planning, and organizing seminars and other activities through the Bangsamoro Professional and Employees Association. Many Bangsamoro women were among the employees of the ARMM administration and served in the office of the Regional Commission on Bangsamoro Women.

After the signing of the peace agreement in 1996, the Bangsamoro women started to be involved in NGOs designed to benefit women and children affected by the war. Government and international aid agencies started to pour money for the economic development of Mindanao, which included programs that would generate employment and promote vocational and skills training for women, as part of the postwar reconstruction programs. Since women were the most disproportionately affected by the conflict, either as refugees or left to fend for themselves since the men were either involved in the war or had to stay put because of security concerns, women had to perform dual roles as care givers and family providers.[28] Muslim women took it upon themselves to organize NGOs that would support the women and teach livelihood skills. Such organizations received funding from the United Nations, the World Bank, United Nations, Asia Foundation, as well as the United States, Canada, Japan, and European countries.

Among the early Muslim women's NGOs created as a result of the peace negotiations with the Philippine government under President Ramos was the Bangsamoro Women's Foundation for Peace and Development (BWFPD), chaired by Eleonora Roida Tan, one of the early women members of the MNLF. The BWFPD's projects are geared toward empowerment of women in the conflict areas, providing training and assistance on livelihood projects, financial management, as well as seed capital for livelihood projects. Others, like Tarhata Maglangit, Fatmawati Salapuddin, and Hadja Bainon Caron, all active MNLF women, also started NGOs. They became involved in government-hosted seminars and also had the opportunity to attend international meetings, workshops, and training under various government programs, some sponsored by the U.S. State Department, on conflict resolution projects. In their localities, their NGOs implemented programs geared toward improving the lives of women and empowering them especially since many of them had become war widows.

Aside from MNLF women, there were also others who created successful NGOs like the Magbassa Kita Foundation, organized by former Senator Santanina Rasul. The foundation initially focused on adult literacy programs but has expanded to include skills training programs, microfinancing, and peace advocacy. The Magbassa Kita Foundation, like the Bangsa Moro Women's Foundation for Peace and Development, has been a recipient of the United States Agency for International Development grants as part of the latter's efforts to empower Muslim women and encourage women's leadership. Zenaida Tan-Lim created the Sarang Bangun Foundation and established a school for children, skills-training workshops, and literacy programs for war widows in memory of her sister Desdemona, whose *nom de guerre* was Sarang Bangun and who was the wife of Nur Misuari, the chair of the MNLF.

Muslim women's advocacy also includes the promotion of democracy. Amina Rasul Bernardo, a cabinet member during the time of President Ramos and the daughter of Santanina Rasul, together with Nasser Marahomsalic, a former human rights commissioner, and Abraham Iribani, former spokesperson of the MNLF, organized the Philippine Center for Islam and Democracy (PCID) in 2002. The PCID is an NGO dedicated to the study of Islamic and democratic political thought and is also involved in promoting peace, democracy, and development in Muslim communities through seminars and workshops. Amina Rasul Bernardo received the Muslim democrat award from the Center for the Study of Islam and Democracy in Washington, DC, in 2007. She is also the founding member of Women in International Security—Philippines and Muslim Women Peace Advocates—Sulu.

The 1990s saw the emergence of a new generation of Muslim women pursuing activities markedly different from those pursued by the generation before them. In 1997, Yasmin Busran-Lao established the *Al Mujadilah* Development Foundation (AMDF), an organization for social development committed to promoting women's rights, good governance, and peace building toward gender-fair, humane, and sustainable communities. In the pursuit and attainment of this mission, AMDF members see themselves serving as Allah's Vicegerents (*khalifah*), who are guided by the principle of *tawḥīd*,[29] which, to them, reflects the unity of creation. This is a new development among Muslim women's groups that explicitly invokes the teachings of Islam as they pursue the organization's goals. Busran-Lao talks of issues of gender justice within the parameters of Islam, which they are still in the process of defining. While cognizant of the injustices toward Muslims and calls for ending the conflict between the Christian-dominated government and Muslims that has persisted through centuries, Busran-Lao's work is more focused on issues of gender equity and justice. One of the programs of the AMDF is the popularization of the Code of Muslim Personal Laws (CMPL). Busran-Lao organized the AMDF shortly after attending the Beijing Women's conference in 1995 and, together with Raissa Jadjurie, established *Nisa ul Haqq fi Bangsamoro* (Women for Truth and Justice in Bangsamoro). This organization advocates for women's rights in the context of religion and culture. Raissa Jadjuric is a lawyer, who, in addition to her responsibilities in *Nisa ul Haqq fi Bangsamoro*, is also involved with the Center for Alternative Legal Care. They organize workshops promoting CEDAW and understanding the CMPL although they believe that certain parts of the CMPL need to be reexamined and revised, like the minimum age for marriage.[30] Their extensive research on the effects of early forced marriages support their position in rising the marriage age in the Code. They organize training sessions on gender and Islam for Muslim women and contend that the interpretation of local religious scholars with limited understanding of Islam perpetuates discrimination. Busran-Lao and Jadjurie come from prominent Muslim families and were educated in Manila. They have traveled abroad and attended workshops and seminars on women and gender, sponsored by the United Nations and other organizations, and are very much in the forefront of the discussions on gender and Islam among Muslims in the Philippines.

A radical departure from the previous peace negotiations between the MNLF and the Philippine government is the inclusion of women on both sides of the negotiating panels with the MILF. The chief negotiator for the Philippine government was Miriam Coronel-Ferrer and also included Muslim women like Yasmin Busran-Lao, who at the time of her appointment was also a presidential assistant for Muslim affairs. The legal team of the Philippine panel included two young Muslim women lawyers, Johaira Wahab and

Tarhata Basman. The MILF side included Raissa Jadjurie and Cabaybay Abu Bakar in its MILF Board of Consultants. On both sides of the negotiations, women were very visible but admitted being subjected to gender-sensitive remarks, like those from the chair of the MILF panel, Mohagher Iqbal, who asserted that men and women cannot have absolute equality because "they are different, physically, biologically and even emotionally."[31] In the end, the women were able to push for provisions in the Framework of Agreement for the Bangsamoro (FAB) on "the right of women to meaningful political participation, and protection from all forms of violence"[32] and the "right to equal opportunity and non-discrimination in social and economic activity and the public service, regardless of class, creed, disability, gender and ethnicity."[33] The FAB provided for the appointment of members of the Bangsamoro Transition Commission that drafted the Bangsamoro Basic Law. Muslim women were included in the commission: Fatmawati Salapuddin and Johaira Wahab. Salapuddin had been involved with the programs of the BWFPD, while Wahab led the legal panel of the government in the negotiations with the MILF. The Muslim women were active participants in the peace process unlike in previous times when only men represented both government and MNLF sides.

Busran-Lao was eventually appointed to head the National Commission on Muslim Filipinos, a government agency with multiple functions[34] relating to Philippine Muslims, including administration of the pilgrimage. In the earlier years, she ran for senator, and while she acknowledged that her chance of getting elected was very slim, she agreed to be in the Liberal Party senatorial slate because the national campaign would allow her to discuss the situation in Mindanao and inform people that peace would be beneficial for all.[35] Busran-Lao also supported the passage of the reproductive health bill[36] as a measure to educate women on their reproductive rights.[37]

In the May 1916 elections, two Muslim women, Nariman Alonto and Princess Jacel Kiram, ran unsuccessfully for the senate. Both saw the political campaign as a platform for calling attention to the problems in Mindanao and, in the case of Kiram, pursuing the Philippine claim to Sabah, which is part of Malaysia.[38] So far, there has been only one Muslim woman senator, Santanina Rasul, but there have been others who have served in the House of Representatives from the 1990s to the present.[39]

There are several organizations of young Muslims in Mindanao and in the Manila area that are engaged in peace making. One of them, the Young Muslim Professional Network, headed by Samira Gutoc, organizes seminars and workshops and also promotes a "halal lifestyle," which, they believe, will help promote lasting peace in Mindanao.[40] Gutoc is a freelance journalist who spent part of her life in Saudi Arabia, where her father was in the diplomatic corps. She concedes that today's Muslim youth inherit the activism of those who had responded to the Jabidah massacre of 1968,[41] but she recognizes the need to work within the mainstream for the promotion of peace and development.[42] Aware of the multiple problems in Mindanao as well as the sacrifices of those involved in the secessionist movement, she believes that "freedom of the Moros from hunger, want and all the walls that divide us from the North" assume priority and that they "seek to create a history of our own that is shared to contribute to the national psyche." She adds that they "seek to build our communities so ours would be a shared country."[43] Secession is not an issue for this group, but working within the context of Philippine society and overcoming the differences that divide Muslims and non-Muslims are essential in promoting peace.

Teaching Islam used to be the privilege of men in the Philippines. However, there are increasing numbers of women, like Khadija Mutilan, who underwent religious training at Al Azhar University. They are engaged in studying, teaching, and interpreting the Qur'ān, hadith, and other aspects of Islam to fellow women and students in the *madaris* (schools for religious instruction) but have also experienced the difficulty of being a woman in a male-dominated field. Mutilan helped institutionalize women's participation in the *ulama* organization of Lanao and organized the *Nisa Ul-Islam*, a group of women graduates of Islamic theology. The group has been promoting Islamic awareness and holding seminars on Islam in public places, exposing other citizens of Mindanao to Islamic learning.[44] The PCID, under the leadership of Amina Rasul Bernardo, has been engaged in organizing female religious teachers into the *Nur al Salaam* (Light of Peace), and their advocacies include peace and health issues, access to economic resources, and promoting interreligious dialogue, among other things.[45]

Muslim women are also asserting their right to express their Islamic identity through the wearing of the head cover. There have been several situations in Mindanao where the wearing of the head cover was an issue, like the case in 1993 when Notre Dame University in Cotabato prohibited the use of hijab by medical and nursing students when working in the hospital. This was based on a memorandum of the Department of Health, which prescribed a standard uniform for all government health personnel under the Department of Health. Muslims of Cotabato organized the Islamic Resistance against Hijab Prohibition and staged demonstrations against the university. The Department of Health amended the previous memorandum and allowed the use of the head cover. In 1991, Pilar College, a Catholic institution run by the Religious of the Virgin in Zamboanga but open to non-Catholics, informed the students that since it was an all-girls school, wearing the head cover was not necessary. There was a meeting between the school administrators and Muslim students, and the nuns explained that while it is customary in Saudi Arabia, it is not really required by the religion.

There were girls who continued to wear the head cover but eventually they stopped. In July 2012, Pilar College banned the use of hijab, thus becoming the first school in the Philippines to do so. By then, the college had become coeducational with a much bigger enrollment. The school claimed that the policy banning the hijab "is part of academic freedom in connection with which the school has the right to choose whom to teach."[46] In this age of social media, the response to the Pilar College directive was immediate, with the Hijab-Niqab Advocacy Network using Facebook and text messages to generate resistance to the college policy. A parent created the Right to Hijab Movement page on Facebook, and the National Commission on Muslim Filipinos called for a dialogue with the school administrators. On September 20, the school rescinded the ban.

CONCLUSION

Muslim women's engagement in the public square in the last 45 years has seen their expanded roles not only in their localities in southern Philippines but also in the capital region. Looking at the years prior to the 1970s, Muslim women's involvement in the public square was largely a function of their having been from the traditional prominent families or the aristocracy where their positions of prominence gave them visibility and privileges unavailable to ordinary Muslim women whose lives were more anchored on the traditional roles of wife, mother, and caregivers. Since the creation of the MNLF, the first large-scale secessionist movement in 1969, Muslim women became involved in activities that have far-reaching implications in their lives as Muslims, Moros, Filipinos, and women. Although not all Muslim women were involved in the MNLF, there was a significant group of women from different Muslim tribes who made important contributions to the cause of the movement. The overriding goal of the MNLF in the early 1970s was creation of an independent state, and women's participation in it was motivated by many factors that include belief in the cause of charting their own destiny as Muslims after centuries of marginalization by the colonial powers and the Christian-dominated government. As the years wore on and the peace agreements failed to deliver the promise, the women returned to normal lives without giving up their loyalties to the MNLF. For the women of the MNLF, their lack of leadership roles within the movement particularly in the early years was not seen negatively, but they claim that their experience in various activities, like organizing, recruiting members, consciousness-raising, fulfilling support roles, and even working as "urban operatives," helped in their work in the postconflict situation as they created NGOs directed primarily at helping women and children. An MNLF woman member considers postconflict work as part of their struggle, saying, "This is part of our jihad." In a way, the MNLF functioned as an agent of change for the women, a great majority of whom were not involved in any form of activism before joining the MNLF.

In the 1970s and beyond, better educational opportunities, like the scholarships provided by the then Commission on National Integration,[47] helped in increasing the number of Muslim women in higher education and continuing on to varied professional fields. There were MNLF women who were beneficiaries of this scholarship and whose political activism started in the aftermath of the Jabidah massacre in 1968 while they were college students in Manila.

In the last 45 years, Muslim women's movements in the Philippines have expanded and have become multipronged—while those in the rural areas prioritize livelihood skills training, literacy programs, health care, and finding resources for small-scale economic activities for women, in the capital region, the promotion of international conventions on women's rights as promoted by the United Nations and the popularization of the CMPL have been given more attention. The Philippines passed the Republic Act 9710, known as the Magna Carta for Women, in 2008, which established the Philippine government's commitment to CEDAW, and *Al Mujadilah* has been involved in its promotion as well as working for changes in the CMPL since some of its provisions counter those of the Magna Carta for Women. Although this is also a concern of the Muslim women in the south, their priority is more on programs that directly address the needs of women in a postconflict situation.

The MILF, which was sidelined in the course of the government-MNLF negotiations that yielded the Final Peace Agreement of 1996, became the main player in the peace negotiations that resulted in the draft Bangsamoro Basic Law (BBL) in 2014. The draft BBL aimed to create a new Muslim autonomous region in Mindanao[48] but was not enacted into law by the Philippine Congress. Nevertheless, the inclusion of women in the peace negotiations was a remarkable departure from previous times where only Muslim men participated. Muslim women hail this development as a positive step towards gender equity. Interestingly, the promotional posters, news releases, and the campaign for approval of the Bangsamoro Basic Law, all showed images of women and children, thus sending the message that women and children stand to benefit from the passage of the law.

The younger generation of Muslim women is concerned with issues of justice, gender equity, and understanding the Qur'ān as they navigate gender issues. They also demonstrate the right to express their religious identity visually as indicated by the successful campaign against Pilar College's ban on the hijab. It is noticeable that the leadership of the various groups still comes from traditional and politically prominent families but differs in many ways from their forebears. They are highly educated, well traveled, comfortable with the head cover, have benefited from government programs promoting Islam for which their parents had fought, and have been involved in the global discourse on women and gender through international conferences that they attend, which is also facilitated by various grants that Mindanao received as part of the postconflict reconstruction programs. The membership of the movements, however, comes from various socioeconomic situations but demonstrates the same eagerness to exercise their rights as Muslim women. The forms of women's movements have expanded in response to issues and the contexts of their situations, whether in the rural areas or in the capital regions. The demands for change by groups like *Al Mujadilah* and *Al Nisa* would have been radical for their parents but will certainly help in achieving the goal of gender justice for Muslim women. Although the priorities of the movements are different, their courses of action are all geared toward empowerment of women. Contemporary Muslim women's activism in the Philippines that reflects the emerging attention to Islam as the basis for empowerment is evident in a speech by Zahria Muti-Mapandi[49] at the launching of Oxfam's report on gender and inequality in Bangkok in 2015, where she spoke of the situation of Moro women:

> My heart rebels against these realities as I know deep in my soul that these are wrong. For a Muslim taught by my faith to enjoin what is good and forbid what is bad, I am not allowed to sit back and let these things happen. We have to do something about this.[50]

NOTES

1. See Roces 2010, 34–52; Sobritchea 2004; Mangahas and Llaguno 2006, among others.

2. See Choy 2003; Parrenas 2001; Bonifacio 2014.

3. Sarip 1985–1986, 7; Usodan-Sumagayan 1988; Lacar 1992.

4. See Brecht-Drouart 2015, 89–112.

5. Hilsdon 2009, 349–365.

6. Alojamiento 2004, 161–174.

7. Dwyer and Cagoco-Guiam 2012.

8. Abuza 2003; Tan 2003; McKenna 1998; Vitug and Gloria 2002, among others.

9. Philippine National Statistics office projection as of July 2015 is 102,965,300. http://psa.gov.ph, accessed August 1, 2015.

10. 2000 Census cited in http://www.religionfacts.com/religion_statistics /religion_statistics_by_country.htm, The distribution is as follows: Roman Catholic 80.9%, Muslim 5%, Evangelical 2.8%, Iglesia ni Kristo 2.3%, Aglipayan (Philippine Independent Church) 2%, other Christian 4.5%, other religions 1.8%, unspecified 0.6%, none 0.1% (2000 census).

11. The traditionally Muslim ethnic tribes are Maranao, Maguindanao, Tausug, Molbog, Jama Mapun, Kalibogan, Sangil, Yakan, Palawani, Kalagan, Iranun, Samal, and Badjao.

12. The use of the term "revert" has to do with the fact that Islam was already a dominant religion in the Philippines before the coming of the Spanish colonizers and the idea among Muslims that Islam was the first religion of humans. The person converting to Islam, therefore, is going back to the original religion.

13. *Balik* means "return," hence *Balik* Islam means "return to Islam."

14. See note 11.

15. Angeles 2010, 48.

16. See Angeles 2001, 184–200.

17. Mahmoud 1985, 8.

18. Misuari 1992, 1–41.

19. In the Manili massacre of 1971, men, women, and children were killed in a mosque. Although the primary suspect was a Christian group, Muslims believed that the Philippine Constabulary was involved.

20. Angeles 1996, 130–147, 137.

21. Ibid.

22. Simpal 2011.

23. Angeles 1996.

24. Hilsdon 2009, 349–365, 361.

25. http://www.un.org/womenwatch/daw/CSW60YRS/CSWChairpersons.pdf, accessed June 14, 2016.

26. Art. 10, Sec. 15.

27. The Autonomous Region for Muslim Mindanao was created by Republic Act 6734.

28. Dwyer and Cagoco-Guiam 2012.

29. Divine unicity.

30. Ch. II, Art. 6, of the Code of Muslim Personal Laws defines the marriageable age for males as 15 and for females the age of puberty and upward. It assumes that a female reaches the age of puberty at 15. However, marriage may be allowed for a female under 15 years but not below 12 if a proper *wali* (guardian) petitions the Sharia District court.

31. Coronel-Ferrer 2014, 3–7.

32. Philippine Government (GPH) and Moro Islamic Liberation Front (MILF) 2012.

33. Ibid., Art. VI, i.

34. For functions of the National Commission on Muslim Filipinos, see http://www.ncmf.gov.ph/about-ncmf.html

35. Rallonza 2014, 8–9.

36. Republic Act 10354 (Responsible Parenthood and Reproductive Health Act of 2012).

37. Barlaan and Cardiente 2016.

38. Francisco 2016.

39. Among them were Bai Sandra Sema (First district, Cotabato), Faysa Dumarpa (First district, Lanao del Sur), Nur Ana Sahidulla (Second district, Sulu), and Sitti Djalia Turabin-Hataman (Party-list representative).

40. Banes 2011.

41. Massacre of Muslims being trained by the military in the island of Corregidor. The purported reason for the training was the possible invasion of Sabah. The incident served as a catalyst for the formation of the Moro National Liberation Front.

42. Gutoc 2009.

43. Ibid.

44. Rasul 2008.

45. Berkeley Center 2015.

46. Barawid 2012, 1.

47. McKenna 1998, 140.

48. Congress Adjourns, Fails to Pass BBL 2016.

49. Zahria Muti-Mapandi is Executive Director of *Al Mujadilah* Foundation. See Catada 2015.

50. Ibid.

CHAPTER 6

Speaking Shadows to Light: Vernacular Narrative as a Vehicle for Rajasthani Female *Sādhus* Voicing Vulnerability and Violence

Antoinette E. DeNapoli

THE CONTEXTS OF RENUNCIATION AS AN IDEAL
AND AS LIVED: GANGA GIRI'S STORY

This chapter proceeds to tell the story of the most powerful *sādhu*, the late Ganga Giri Mahārāj, whom I met during my 10 years of research in the north Indian state of Rajasthan, describing the powerful rhetorical practices I witnessed through which she carved out a critical insight on Indian culture while instructing her disciples in moral lessons that speak particularly to the plight of women in a patriarchal religious symbolic. I identify three distinct moral narratives, showing how each works as a "shadow story" that casts critical light on the moral character of India and particularly the blindness of patriarchal renunciant institutions to the value and work of a female *sādhu*. Ganga Giri's tales accentuate a crucial issue: female *sādhus* practice a unique kind of detachment that does not follow a masculinist model, but, because they are not recognized in the most holy of sacraments—the provision of water, food, and burial—they require the devotion of disciples to secure what male *sādhus* are typically guaranteed. If understood in this light, Ganga Giri's repeated words "I am alone" shift from appearing like the complaint of a woman who has renounced all goods to indicate instead the value that she is claiming: her shadow stories bring to light her human dignity as a *sādhu* in the male-dominated religious world of renunciation that would rather remain unseen. Through the storytelling path, Ganga Giri crafted herself as the roaring lioness, empowered to change her world and the conditions weakening her quality of life.

Sādhus like Ganga Giri are characterized as world renouncers (*sannyāsin*).[1] Their uncommon way of life is known as renunciation (*sannyās*).[2] As renouncers, *sādhus* ideally leave behind everything, like marriage and family, work, class and caste status, and the social-religious obligations that once defined their everyday lives and worlds, in order to dedicate themselves to the worship of the divine. As the ideal suggests, renunciation represents a radical life path; an alternative to the norm of householding and its worldly concerns. The practices, ideologies, and institutions commonly associated with the standard (and text-based) idea of *sannyās* express its classic values of detachment (*vairāgy*), solitude and isolation (*ekānt*), a life of voluntary poverty (*bhikhāri honā*), and separation from the world (*sansār*). Breaking free of their illusions, *sādhus* are viewed as human penumbra on the mercurial margins of existence who cast doubt on received ways of thinking and acting in the world. Their shadows reveal another truth.

Ganga Giri passed away or, in *sādhu* terms, "took *samādhi*" on July 26, 2008, five days after the Hindu holiday of *Guru Pūrṇimā*. She was 98 years old. She received initiation into renunciation from the orthodox Shankaracarya Dashanami Order of *sādhus*. It constitutes one of the two Shaiva-based,[3] pan-Indian *sādhu* organizations—the other is the less-orthodox Gorakhnath Kanpatha Yogis—and has 10 administrative branches (*daśa* literally means "ten").[4] As her spiritual name indicates, Ganga Giri took initiation from within the Giri branch of the Dashanamis, which is one of only five branches that initiate women as *sādhus*.[5]

THE SHADOWS OF *SANNYĀS*: STORYTELLING AS TESTIMONY TO EVERYDAY STRUGGLES

Writing about the lives of New Zealand veterans of World War II, and of mixed-descent Australians traumatized by the "erstwhile assimilationist policies" enforced by federal and state laws during the post–World War II period, anthropologist Michael Jackson says that "storytelling is crucial to the process of reempowerment."[6] It transforms lives because "the act of sharing stories helps us create a world that is more than the sum of its individual parts."[7]

The tales that Ganga Giri tells are transformative. They allow her to voice what *sādhus* are typically expected to relegate to the penumbra of everyday life and to complicate the more official notions about what *sannyās* means and how it should be lived in "an age in which many individuals feel that they are drawn into, diminished, and damaged by global force fields that they cannot completely control or comprehend."[8] In pushing the shadows of *sannyās* to the center of public renunciant discourse and practice, Ganga Giri enacted, as Jackson describes of the war veterans and the part-Aboriginal Australians whom he knew, "truth to power"[9]—the existential "possession of being" that a person experiences when she feels that the society recognizes her human value and rewards her contributions to what is perceived as the larger existential good.[10] However, more than "the human need for recognition" remains at issue. There is also the need to imagine the moral possibility that "one's voice carries and one's actions have repercussions in the state, nation, or community with which one identifies."[11]

In this chapter I argue that Ganga Giri performed shadow tales as a constructive means to change undesirable circumstances as concerns her (lack of) access to life resources, to challenge broader structural powers of inequality that violate *sādhus'* humanity in part because they are not wage-earners in India's postindustrial cash-based economy, and to protest against what she viewed as the paralyzing human apathy toward four categories of vulnerable populations. These are the aged, the poor, women, and *sādhus*. All of these lenses applied to Ganga Giri and oriented her experiences. Storytelling empowered Ganga Giri to create "balanced reciprocity" in her life, to right what she perceived as the wrongs of her society. Telling shadow tales also made it possible for Ganga Giri to negotiate the gap between the ideal and the real and construct a meaningful life that bridged the concerns of these worlds. In the years that I spent with her, I recognized that Ganga Giri grappled daily with the tensions inherent in her way of life.[12] After all, she was a woman pursuing a path traditionally associated with men. She demanded to live independently of the social-biological networks with which she had identified as a householder, but made it clear that without those cultivated connections she would die. She lauded the peace of mind that taking *sannyās* gave her but described the daily "troubles" (*pareśāni*) that plagued her. She trusted that God met all her needs but spoke anxiously of "having no one" to depend on.

In her expressive practices Ganga Giri reworked in both subtle and obvious ways her vision of an ideal *sannyās* to include her individual experiences as an old, poor, and uneducated Brahmin woman as much as she constructed her *sannyās*-as-lived to actualize that ideal. She realized that the dominant model of what "counts" as *sannyās* carried enormous cultural currency. It constitutes the "charter myth" of Brahmanical renunciation.[13] And yet, the everyday (and unavoidable) realities of gender, ageing, sickness, and, eventually, incapacitation prevented her from absolutizing the ideal as anything but that. The negotiations she made through storytelling demonstrate, then, her creative attempts to comprehend the changes happening in/to her body and in/to the larger body politic. I present here Ganga Giri's practices as a critical case study, as she was one of the few *sādhus* who sought to model the ideal. On this account, her life exemplifies in high relief the contradictions faced by many of the female *sādhus* I knew. I am also convinced, however, that her situation and her responses to it are not at all exclusive to her. Ganga Giri's story illuminates the shadow lives of female *sādhus* in particular and what is at stake for *sādhus* in general, that is, for those individuals who live in a rapidly changing and globalizing India where storytelling becomes a strategy against the "nullification of being."[14]

Ganga Giri told a collection of personal stories in her repertoire of vernacular narratives. The stories I document below are also illustrative of the tales that seemed predominantly to occupy Ganga Giri's focus and that dominated her *satsang* performances, between the years 2004 and 2006. I arrived in Rajasthan at the end of the year 2004 and conducted a full 16 months of ethnographic research with Hindu *sādhus*, men and women, until I left India in the late spring of 2006.[15] At the beginning of my fieldwork, a constellation of factors impinged on Ganga Giri's well-being and colluded in lessening her quality of life. Specifically, eight months before my arrival she fell in a local bazaar and broke her right hip bone. She had to be hospitalized for six weeks. When I returned in 2004, she could barely walk, and when she ventured beyond her hut, she had to use a wooden cane and traveled only when someone accompanied her. Besides the increasing physical difficulty she experienced in getting around, Ganga Giri's eyesight and hearing had drastically diminished. But on top of all this, when the water tap she used broke, the Mahakaleshwar Temple Board of Trustees refused to repair it. Not surprisingly, during this period I noticed a substantial shift in Ganga Giri's self-representation. No longer the "wild" (*junglî*), fiercely independent, and indefatigable 91-year-old, she portrayed herself to be just four years earlier (2001), she now saw herself as "cool" (*thaṇḍā*) and vulnerable, as "all alone" and with "no strength in this body" (2005). Feeling abandoned and forgotten by those with whom she shared her love, time, and energy (such as, other renouncers, householders, and disciples), Ganga Giri commented, "People don't take care of *sādhus*. They think, 'to hell with *sādhus*!'" It is against this backdrop that Ganga Giri's stories and the shadows they speak of can come to light.

"WHEN THERE WAS STRENGTH IN MY BODY, NOBODY WOULD HAVE TOUCHED ME!": GANGA GIRI'S PERSONAL NARRATIVES

In performing personal experience narratives, Ganga Giri made apparent the everyday difficulties she brooked across the lifecycle as a female *sādhu* living in a patriarchal culture—challenges that push to the center of renunciant discourse issues directly related to gender, ageing, and poverty. By sharing life stories, Ganga Giri performed resistance to the injustices and hegemony that she has experienced. She told the following story to seven householders, including my assistant Manvendra Singh and me.

> *Sādhus* do not have to pay for tickets [to travel in trains]. We are the *sādhus* of India. We have the right [*adhikār*] to sit on the skin of a lion. We don't have to pay [for tickets]. I use to wander when there was strength [*tākat*] in my body without a ticket. I travelled in trains. Two or three ticket takers used to come. There was glory [*vaibhav*] in my body. Nobody would have touched me! If they would have touched me, I would have made them leave their jobs. They're bastards [*sāle*]. I would have made those bastards fired off [from their jobs]. I have travelled so much, at least fifty thousand rupees [approx. one thousand dollars USD] worth without tickets. Even today if I sit in the train, I don't have to give the ticket. [Sohan Lal speaks:] You can go anywhere and they don't take tickets? [Ganga Giri answers:] I don't give tickets when I travel by rail. But I have to pay for the bus. I don't pay for the trains, because it is the vehicle of India [*bharat kī gārī*]. [Sohan Lal says:] In India, if you're past sixty-five years, you don't have to pay. [Ganga Giri retorts:] We are the *sādhus* of India. Why should we pay? It's not the ticket takers' train? The ticket taker is a servant [of India]. I will not pay a single penny . . . I traveled a lot and returned. Now everything pains. Now I can't go anywhere. I can't go from here to there [showing with her hands the distance between her hut and the tree right outside the hut]. Now the body [*saīr*] is of no use. It doesn't work anymore. It has become weak.

In the tale below Ganga Giri spoke directly about her somatic experiences of ageing. While sitting on the platform where her *dhūnī* was established, she told this tale to my Brahmin host sister, Kalpana Sanadhya, and me. The story came about in connection with Kalpana's observation that Mahakaleshwar Colony has changed substantially in the last 20 years.

> When I came here, everything was jungle. I lived alone in the jungle. I am still living alone in the jungle. In the end [*akhir men*], I am a woman [*aurat kī jāt hūn*] and I am [living] alone in the forest. I don't have anybody. The one who has no one, God is for her. For her, God is everything. Anyone can come on his own at my place. It has been so many years [since I've lived here]. Before, there was nothing here. At that time when I started to live here there wasn't a single bungalow around. Now people have built these big bungalows. How many years has it been? It's been so many that

I have lost count. Now, I don't go outside because I've become weak; I've become old. As long as there was power [tākat] in the body, I would take a stick and go outside whenever I wanted. It didn't matter what time was striking the clock. I wasn't afraid [dar]. If someone would have come, I would have torn him into pieces. I used to be so strong. But now I don't go outside because there isn't any power in this body. If someone pushes me, I will fall down. I will die. Now where is the strength [that used to be in this body]? I ask God, "Don't make my eyes weak." My eyes have become weak and I can't see. If I can't see you, I feel separate from you. If I get you through my eyes, I feel we are the same. "Don't make me blind, God. I don't have anyone to do things for me. Don't make my eyes weak, Lord." If I become blind, who will grab and move me? I don't have a single person. God has mercy on me. God has all the news.

Our third story casts light on Ganga Giri's cultural experiences of ageing and their effects on her renunciation. Besides Manvendra Singh and me, the audience members also included Manvendra's mother and youngest sister, who was on holiday from law school. They joined us on this day because of Ganga Giri's insistence to Manvendra earlier that week that he bring his family to meet her and earn the merit (puṇya) of seeing (darsan) a sādhu. The story she told emerged somewhat circuitously. Ganga Giri was about to lead a group recitation (pāṭh) of the vernacular-language text, the Rāmcaritmānas.[16] As she began the recitation, Manvendra's mother remarked how surprised she was that Ganga Giri could read the text without "specs" (glasses). Here is the story Ganga Giri narrated in response to Manvendra's mother's comment:

Before making this hut, I always used to wear specs. There is a village near my village called Tera. All of a sudden this desire came into my mind. It's a Brahmin village. The desire came that I should do the caturmās over there, in the temple over there. [Manvendra's mother asks:] What do you mean by caturmās? [Ganga Giri replies:] It's only that you have to stay at one place [during the rainy season]. Don't go in the village; don't cross the river. So, I went there [to Tera] to do the pūjā. The villagers said that earlier Patels [a farming community] used to live there. Brahmins did not live there. I left that village twenty-five years before settling here [at Mahakaleshwar Colony]. They [the villagers] all told me that "No one who is an outsider has lived for more than seven days in the temple. No one has lived for more than seven days in that temple. Neither a Brahmin nor a sādhu has ever gone [in the temple] and come out alive. Even guṇḍas [thieves] never come here [in the village and in the temple]. And if the guṇḍas come in the village, they enter from a different way. They don't come through [the way of] Mahadev's [Shiva's] temple. The guṇḍas don't come here. But witches [*cudail*] come here. Also many ghosts come here. The temple becomes a crowd of ghosts in the night.

The *caturmās* is four months, but after hearing this, I decided to do the *caturmās* for six months. I used to say "Om Namah Shivaya. Om Namah Shivaya. Om Namah Shivaya." I put my seat [*āsan*] on the temple platform [*cabhutra*] and my feet used to hang like this [gives a demonstration]. There was a temple to Hanumanji right in front of me [where she sat]. I sat there for eight days. I didn't eat anything. I didn't eat any bread. I didn't drink tea or milk for eight days. But there was strength [*bal*] in the body at that time. Many people started coming. Many people used to come and take my *darśan*. Many men and many women came. But nobody talked to me, nor did I look at them. Then I started cursing them. Man or woman. Whoever used to come, I cursed them. Whatever came into my mind, I used to speak. [Manvendra's mother asks:] Who gave curses? You gave the curses? [Ganga Giri says:] I gave curses, many curses. Man, woman, whoever used to come. I was wild [*junglī*]. . . I remained in the dark [in the temple at night] for eight days. There are lights now [in the temple]. The Harican [kerosene lamp] was introduced. The girls used to come and bring water, and I cursed them, too.

I used to have specs at that time. I used to take a bath, I used to do the *pūjā*, and I used to do the *pāṭh*, and I used to put on specs. I couldn't read the letters [*akshar*] before making this hut [without specs]. Then one day I was reading a book. I used to keep my specs in a box. But when I opened the box the specs were gone. The box was empty! There were no specs in the box! There were no specs! I cannot read without specs! So, how to do the *pāṭh*? I cursed Mahadevji. I gave him many curses. I kept the empty box with me. I said to myself that I am not going to buy new specs. So, I didn't do the *pāṭh*. Because I couldn't see. And I didn't buy new specs. The thieves came and took the specs, and I cursed Mahadev a lot. I said "Where have you been? What kind of a god are you?" After fifteen days, I started seeing and I can still see . . . I have lived alone with the sound of snakes. I have wandered alone and returned. I used to be sharp [*tej*]. But now I have become cool [*thanḍā*]. I have become patient. This body has no power anymore.

Common motifs surface in each of the three stories, which we might label as the "train story," "the jungle story," and "the specs story," respectively. The dominant theme that recurs in every single story has to do with the potent contrast Ganga Giri constructed between her idea of herself in the past and the present. Ganga Giri went to great lengths to make her interlocutors aware that appearances are not what they seem to be, that she, too, was once youthful, strong, and capable. In her stories the past represents an extended period of time, beginning with her becoming a *sādhu* at the age of

45, until about the age of 95, when she had her traumatic hip injury. The former also constitutes a time when Ganga Giri had, as she said, "strength in the body." She was mentally sharp and physically strong. She viewed herself as "glorious." The image that Ganga Giri retained of herself in the past seems a far cry from how she imagined herself in the present. She characterized herself as "old," "weak," and with a "body that no longer works." As she emphasized in every storytelling context, "This body has no power anymore." Her stories underscore idioms centering around "losses and waning powers"[17] and the fear of being forgotten (and dying alone) in her old age. Ganga Giri's self-representations recall the characterizations that old Bengali women (and some Bengali men) used to talk about themselves in their stories. The groundbreaking gerontological data documented in the works of anthropologists Sarah Lamb[18] and Katy Gardner,[19] both of whom researched the impact of ageing, gender, class, and poverty on Bengalis in South Asia and in the West,[20] has shown that ageing is imagined and experienced in both physical and social-cultural ways. Lamb explains:

> The Bengalis I knew definitely used the body to define gender differences, but not in terms of a fixed, binary male/female distinction; instead, they often explained the biologies of the sexes in terms of differences in the relative amounts of qualities, such as "heat" and "openness," that all bodies and persons possess. All bodies (male and female, young and old) possess relative amounts of heat (or coolness), fluidity (or dryness), and openness (or boundedness). . . . But these qualities fluctuated significantly over the life course, with important somatic as well as social, political, and spiritual implications.[21]

The physical and social dimensions of ageing as a female *sādhu* are drawn out in Ganga Giri's narratives. The stories similarly clarify that her experiences of ageing, physical and social, shifted dramatically over the 50 years that she has lived as a renunciant. Physically, ageing has meant (and brought) increasing incapacitation, frailty, and vulnerability for Ganga Giri. She cannot see like she used to. "My eyes have become weak and I can't see." But just as significant, she cannot move like she used to. "Now everything pains. Now I can't go anywhere. I can't go from here to there. Now the body [*śarīr*] is of no use. It doesn't work anymore. It has become weak." The loss of her independence has been concomitant with the loss of her mobility and her eyesight. Because her capacity to move on her own decreased substantially between 2002 and 2005 (she walked only with difficulty and with a cane), Ganga Giri became dependent on others for help. Not surprisingly, perhaps, Ganga Giri seemed ambivalent about her dependency.[22] On the one hand, her physical dependency meant that Ganga Giri could give devotees the chance to care for her and earn much spiritual merit. On the other hand, being dependent meant giving up the ideal of the independent *sādhu* who survives on her own. A "theological fiction,"[23] indeed.

The cultural aspects of ageing are equally apparent in Ganga Giri's life stories. She emphasized two crucial words that distinguish between her vision of herself in the past and in the present—they are *tej* and *thaṇḍā*. I have translated *tej* as sharpness,[24] but it could also be glossed as "hot." *Tej* further describes the (mental/physical) brilliance or luster produced by intense spiritual (or renunciant) practice. The Sanskrit noun form *tejasvin*[25] characterizes a renouncer, who engages in the intense practice of penance (*tapas*) and, as a result generates heat (*tapas*) and brilliance (*tejas*) which, in turn, purify the body and mind of negative (*karma*-based) impurities. In Ganga Giri's jungle story, *tej* lends itself, therefore, to double signification: as the heat/power/sharpness that results from *sannyās* as well as from youthfulness. Relatedly, heat has sexual and religious underpinnings. It can manifest physically/emotionally as sexual desire or spiritually as the devotional/psychic power that controls and subdues sexual desire. Ganga Giri talked about heat in both senses of the term. In 2003 she told me in the company of Sohan Lal's eldest son that the practices of meditation, yoga, and singing that she had learned from her guru and other *sādhus* helped to control the *mastî* (desire), which she continued to experience until she reached menopause in her late fifties.

In contrast to heat, Ganga Giri associated old age with "coolness" and "patience." No longer the quick-tempered and confrontational *sādhu* she once was, Ganga Giri saw that she had instead become soft, mild-tempered, and easy-going because of her old age. Even the contrasting idioms of mobility and immobility, independence and dependence, that Ganga Giri tied to her idea of physical ageing have broader social implications. Ganga Giri's interpretations of mobility/independence, which she linked to youth, signify an implicit cultural association of youthfulness with openness or unbounded potentiality. Insofar as she was young and strong, Ganga Giri viewed the world as an expansive place that she could fearlessly explore. Her association of immobility/dependence with ageing, however, connotes an underlying cultural understanding of old age as a bounded and constricting experience. "This body grows weaker day-by-day," she said, "I may not be here tomorrow." To the extent that she could no longer move around on her own and see (with or without specs) the world that presented itself to her senses, Ganga Giri imagined herself as being isolated from, and forgotten by, that world. What was once bright and welcoming had now become dark and dangerous. Day by day Ganga Giri felt that the world was shutting her out.

Gender is a muted theme in the train and specs story, and yet, it stands out as a defining narrative element in the jungle tale. "In the end, I am a woman and I am [living] alone in the forest," Ganga Giri emphasized to Kalpana and me. As with old age and illness, gender, too, has shaped and structured Ganga Giri's everyday experiences of renunciation. While what it means to be a woman (and a female *sādhu*) has changed substantially over the course of Ganga Giri's *sādhu* life, gender never goes away. It is no coincidence that Ganga Giri threaded her tale around gender in a context that consisted entirely of women. It is, after all, a social aspect of human experience that Ganga Giri, Kalpana, and I shared. Ganga Giri herself divided humans into two "castes" (*jāt*), that of "woman" and "man."

Thus, from her perspective, the three of us, as she described in her story, belonged to the "*jāt* of woman." Maybe, too, seeing Kalpana and me, two women traveling in the world with "strength in [our] bodies" and "sharpness in [our] minds," reminded Ganga Giri of the robust and independent woman she envisioned herself to be at our age. In making this statement Ganga Giri suggested that being a woman compounded her vulnerability as an old/ infirm *sādhu* who lived alone and "ha[d] no one." Becoming old and weak, of course, crosscuts the gender of the *sādhus* I worked with. But being female puts *sādhus* like Ganga Giri at risk for male sexual violence. This fear is implied in her story. Even though the male *sādhus*, most of whom were over the age of 65, discussed openly the problems that come with old age, such as those associated with loss of hearing, eyesight, and mobility (several of the *sādhus* suffered from chronic emphysema, tuberculosis, and congestive heart failure), none of them ever said that being a man was something that they had to worry about as *sādhus* or as persons. Gender, however, mattered in a crucial way for the female *sādhus*. In fact, it mattered to the old and to the young female *sādhus* in my field study.[26] Along with gender, though, choosing to live by oneself doubles a *sādhu's* risk for sexual attack; add old age to the mix and the risk triples.

Ganga Giri relied on the extended network of devotees that she had carefully cultivated and sustained over the last five decades of her life in a manner that preserved her *sādhu* integrity. Having a stream of devotees come to her ashram every day for the purpose of helping her constituted an expression of selfless service (*sevā*) to the guru. It also demonstrated balanced reciprocity in the devotees' relationship with Ganga Giri.[27]

The system of exchanges underlying the guru-disciple relationship extends more globally to transactions made between *sādhus* and, as Ganga Giri indexes in her train story, the people of India. The train image works well as a metaphor for the implied role of *sādhus* as transmitters of spiritual teachings that advance and reinforce the moral upliftment of the society. *Sādhus* travel the countryside offering their words and wisdom to the masses, regardless of religious affiliation and, in theory, create a more peaceful and less fearful world. But what does society give back to them? The logic of reciprocity, then, is at play in Ganga Giri's train story and illustrates another shared theme in her life narratives. "We are the *sādhus* of India!" She makes this statement twice in the train tale. That is, in Ganga Giri's view, why should *sādhus* pay to travel in trains (and buses) when they promote (and protect) the existential good of the nation? India, therefore, Ganga Giri's story suggests, should repay its moral debt to its *sādhus* by not "taking tickets" from their hands. To do so violates balanced reciprocity. India, according to Ganga Giri, owes *sādhus* a lot. Hence, by not taking money from them, India shows that it values *sādhus* and the ongoing spiritual work that they do for the state and, by extension, the world.

But there is more. *Sādhus*, Ganga Giri implied, should not have to pay to travel on trains on account of the fact that they are not wage-earners. *Sādhus* do not make money simply by casting the world aside. When *sādhus* renounce the world, they make a life-long commitment to voluntary poverty. Unless they live in an institutionalized setting (e.g., a monastery or nunnery) that provides them with food, supplies, and shelter, *sādhus* have to beg for alms in order to survive in the world or, as Ganga Giri's life shows, rely on the compassion/generosity of their devotees for these essential life resources. Either way, the exchanges given and received in those transactions create and establish symbolically the ideal of reciprocity that Ganga Giri not only performed as significant by means of story, but also herself depended on to be able to live independently as an elderly and infirm (female) *sādhu* outside the mainstream. Her critique that she had to pay to travel on buses expressed a coded protest against what she perceived as the failure of reciprocity between the Indian state and *sādhus* and, more generally, between *sādhus* and householders.

Furthermore, Ganga Giri's comment in the jungle story that she is surrounded by the biggest and most expensive bungalows in Udaipur and yet sees herself as "all alone in the forest" criticized the social apathy that she, like other *sādhus* I met, readily associated with the urban/educated Indian middle class and upper middle class. Performing personal narratives gave Ganga Giri an opportunity to reflect on (and debate) what she saw as larger societal problems. Her practices indicated that apathy toward *sādhus* and their maltreatment represent interrelated issues. The former contributes to the latter. It is relevant that, in my experience, the people who visited Ganga Giri on a daily basis were primarily poor and uneducated people from across the caste spectrum and from outlying villages or towns. This constituency of people wanted to hear her tales and continued to value her role in a rapidly changing society that has become increasingly motivated by consumer-based capitalist concerns and values. Storytelling, as anthropologists have said, constitutes a political act. It is political in two senses: first, in terms of the kinds of tales that performers tell and, second, in terms of the people who are willing to listen to those tales. The performance contexts of Ganga Giri's storytelling themselves reveal the global transformations occurring in the larger body politic.

CONCLUSIONS: CREATING CHANGE THROUGH STORYTELLING

The stories that Ganga Giri told over the course of the 16 months that I conducted fieldwork in Rajasthan, and the shadows those tales revealed, evoked concerted action from members of her extended network of devotees. Everyone, women and men, retired and employed, high caste and low caste, Indian and foreign, pitched in their time, effort, labor, and resources as means to elevate Ganga Giri's sense of well-being and alter those conditions, like the water tap busting, that went beyond her control. By the time I left the country for the United States in the spring of 2006, Ganga Giri had access to fresh drinking water. To see the look of anticipation on her face every time she opened the tap to drink or wash soiled dishes filled devotees with a keen sense of accomplishment. It seemed that whenever I met with Ganga Giri, something had transformed, and for the better. Someone had brought gas for the stove, someone had donated ghee, someone had purchased cotton wicks for the lamps, or someone had shared news in connection with Mahakaleshwar's decision about the tap. Her stories created change.

As I witnessed these changes, I began to see more clearly, something of the contradictions, complexities, and ambiguities that female *sādhus* like Ganga Giri have to negotiate everyday as they struggle to make their voices carry and their actions have repercussions in a world where they are often unrecognized and marginalized. The *samādhi* shrine that Ganga Giri's daughter had constructed for her after she passed away, which sat on the north side of the property, served as testimony to Ganga Giri's life struggles and her individual quest for truth to power. The saffron-colored flag that marked the shrine and crinkled with the wind's touch functioned as a reminder that the ideal and *sādhus*' everyday experiences of *sannyās* often clashed; that, in Ganga Giri's case, the realities of gender, old age, and infirmity exposed the notion of needing nothing and no one to survive in the world for the fiction it really is.

And yet, Ganga Giri crafted her world in a manner that sought to bridge the ideal and the real with integrity and dignity, and she managed to construct that intersection at the crossroads of storytelling and everyday life. Telling the kinds of tales analyzed in this chapter allowed Ganga Giri to reflect on the ambiguities and contradictions inherent in *sannyās*-as-lived. She saw the potential that storytelling held as a means for bringing balance back into one's world, for critiquing a society's (and a temple's) poor treatment of disadvantaged groups, and for challenging people to move beyond stymy-ing false views and see the interconnectedness of creation. Her stories acted as a vital resource in creating community amongst her constituency and in celebrating the power that comes with the human intention to make a dif-ference in the world. Ganga Giri's capacity to act within, and in light of, the circumstances that shaped as well as constricted her life choices arose, in part, by means of the stories she told every day, to people who were willing to listen to them and apply their teachings. Ganga Giri's stories, of course, did not resolve all the tensions and problems in her life. But they did not have to. Their power lay in what their tellings created and established as human pos-sibilities.[28] Ganga Giri's stories helped her and her audience to make sense of their worlds and construct lives that had both value and meaning. And, as people gathered to remember Ganga Giri and the stories she once told, it is clear that Ganga Giri's voice continues to be heard and create change.

Acknowledgments

I thank Zayn Kassam, Kathleen Erndl, Mary Keller, and Bonnie Zare for reading and commenting on drafts of this chapter. Their insights and suggestions provided invaluable feedback and made the chapter stronger. The research on which this chapter is based was conducted with the assis-tance of an American Institute of Indian Studies Junior Fellows Dissertation Research Grant (2004–2006) and with the help of a Basic Research Grant and International Travel Grant from the University of Wyoming (2011)

Notes

1. *Sannyāsî* represents the gendered masculine form; *sannyāsinî* is the gendered feminine form.

2. The italicized words (e.g., *sannyās, mokš, vairāgya*) represent the ver-nacular Hindi-language pronunciation of these terms as I heard them in the rhetorical practices of the *sādhus* with whom I worked.

3. Shaiva-based forms of *sannyās* describe orders that patronize the deity Shiva. In Hindu mythologies in which Shiva figures as the supreme deity, he is represented as creating, maintaining, and destroying the world. He is also known as the renouncer *par excellence*. He is considered to be the patron-deity of Shaiva *sādhus*.

4. *Sannyās*-as-lived in contemporary India has two major "forms," namely, the Shaiva and Vaishnava expressions. Whereas the Shaiva forms of *sannyās* patronize Shiva, the Vaishnava manifestations patronize Vishnu.

5. The other branches that offer initiation into renunciation for women are the Bharati, Saraswati, Puri, and Dandi Swami.

6. Jackson 2013, 170.

7. Ibid.

8. Ibid., 182.

9. In his use of the idiom "truth to power," Jackson draws on the language described by Tim O'Brien. See Jackson 2013, fn 38, 308.

10. Ibid., 172.

11. Ibid., 170.

12. For an excellent discussion of the tensions that emerged in female renouncers' lives, see Khandelwal 2004.

13. Brahmanical renunciation refers to the concept and model of *sannyās* as constructed in Brahmanical texts, such as the *Samnyāsa Upanišads* and the *Upanišads*. See Olivelle 1992, 1996.

14. Jackson 2013, 181.

15. I also spent the summer of 2001 and another 15 months between 2002 and 2003 conducting preliminary research with *sādhus* in Rajasthan.

16. The *Rāmcaritmānas* characterizes a vernacular-language (Hindi) narrative text of the *Rāmāyan* story. It is attributed to the 15th-century poet-saint Tulsidas.

17. Lamb 2000, 1.

18. Ibid.

19. See Gardner 2002.

20. Sarah Lamb worked with Bengalis, Hindu, and Muslim, in India and in the United States, while Gardner worked with Bengalis across religious affiliations in east India, Bangladesh, and London.

21. Lamb 2000, 14.

22. Gardner (2002) similarly concurs that the Bengali elders in Britain with whom she worked talked about their dependency on others with ambivalence.

23. Olivelle 2007.

24. One definition of this term that the McGregor Hindi-English (1992) language dictionary provides, and which I particularly like, is "awesomeness." McGregor 1993, 460.

25. *Tejasvî* (masculine) represents the masculine form, and *tejasvinî* represents the gendered feminine form.

26. For a discussion of how the younger female *sādhus* I worked with talked about the relationship between gender and *sannyās*, see DeNapoli 2014, chapter seven.

27. Cited in Jackson 2013, 171. The notion of "balanced reciprocity," as Jackson discusses, is derived from anthropologist Marcel Mauss. He defined this concept in terms of three elements: giving, receiving, and repaying.

28. The work of Joyce B. Flueckiger discusses the ways that performance of stories creates and establishes possibilities with which humans imagine their worlds. See Flueckiger 1996, 2006.

CHAPTER 7

The Martyr Bomber Becomes a Goddess: Women, Theosis, and Sacrificial Violence in Sri Lanka[1]

William Harman

Normally, the term "suicide bomber" is used to designate someone who inevitably and willingly dies in a destructive explosion he or she causes, an explosion intended to injure or kill others. In common conversation the word "suicide" tends to be pejorative and judgmental, and is associated with aberrant, destructive intentions.. It implies that the person or persons perpetrating the act are intent *primarily* on a deviant form of self-destruction, with emphasis on self-destruction first, and only secondarily on accomplishing something else. But there is another perspective: these bombers almost always see themselves less as people who are pledged to commit suicide and more as people who, in performing an act crucial to advancing their cause, are likely to be sacrificing their lives in the process of accomplishing that cause. Because I believe that people have the right to represent themselves with a term that reflects their intentions and their self-understanding—rather than others' judgments of them—I have decided to use the term "martyr bomber." The term I propose accords people who die in this way a certain respect. Many of us may feel they do not deserve such respect. I am not claiming that we should honor martyr bombers for what they do. Indeed, what they do I find quite abhorrent. But to understand them, we must respect their motivation to give their lives for a cause in which they deeply believe. Unless we do that, we shall never understand why they do what they do, and without some understanding of motivations, we will not be likely to deal constructively with this phenomenon.[2]

I will be discussing female martyr bombers in the civil war of Sri Lanka. I choose to focus on this issue for several reasons. First, as my venerable teacher, the late Mircea Eliade, was fond of saying, "The scale makes the phenomenon." The very scale of female bombers during the Sri Lankan civil war was remarkable. Worldwide, in other struggles where female martyr bombing has occurred, about 8 percent involved females. In Sri Lanka, that percentage was considerably higher, reaching over 30 percent according to Sri Lankan government sources.

A second reason is that much of my scholarship has focused on village goddesses in Tamil-speaking India, and I have been struck by how the sacred life stories of these goddesses suggest elements found in the stories of female martyr bombers. About this I will say more shortly. Finally, many religious traditions—including Christianity, Islam, and Buddhism—teach that it is admirable and praiseworthy if a person is willing to sacrifice his or her life for a cause dedicated to justice and higher ideals that point beyond creature comforts and simple survival. War memorials the world over suggest as much. Yet, at the same time it strains my sense of what is right, proper, and just, to know that martyr bombers are willing to take not only their own lives, but also those of innocent civilians who are considered "collateral damage." The martyr bomber condenses in the very body she destroys, values I both admire and values I deplore. The tension between values that, on the one hand, affirm acting out of a profound willingness to sacrifice for one's people and, on the other hand, encourage randomly destroying the lives of innocent people fuels my need to understand this phenomenon. Spreading fear, terror, confusion, and even despair in the ranks of the enemy supposedly justifies these extreme means.

I want to make it clear that my analysis at this point has occurred in a context in which I have sought primarily to *understand* rather than to judge the events surrounding the activities of these women. I do not endorse murder. But I do not begin with the assumption that these women are crazy or evil. Such a perspective, while tempting, is motivated by what I would call a lazy hermeneutic. These women are human beings acting out of a sense of commitment to principles for which they are willing to give their lives. Whether we agree with those principles or not, it will be impossible to understand these events by simply dismissing the women and their motives as insane.

And what good will understanding these women do? Hopefully, it will allow us to bring an end in future conflicts to the tragic loss of life involved in such bombings: the losses among innocent victims and among the people who do the bombing, who themselves are also victims of this conflict. Circumstances are clearly tragic when women—as well as men—reach the point of feeling they must sacrifice their lives in order to accomplish such a diffuse purpose as sowing random terror and fear in a particular population.

Well before female martyr bombing became a morally and religiously sanctioned strategy to respond to perceived oppression in Palestine, Israel, Iraq, and Chechnya, it had become a routine tool in the civil war waged between the Sri Lankan government and the *Viṭutalai Pulikaḷ Tamiḻ Illam*, that is, the Liberation Tigers of the Tamil Homeland, abbreviated as LTTE. Much has been written about what Stanley Tambiah has termed this "ethnic fratricide,"[3] but two of the most dramatic developments since 1983 in the Sri Lankan civil war were the routinization of martyr bombing and the participation in martyr missions by Tamil women. It is with this issue that I am especially concerned in this chapter.

Sri Lanka is a lush tropical island-nation, with pristine beaches and beautiful interior highlands. It lies just 26 miles off the southern coast of India. It is home to about 20 million inhabitants, though that number has been eroding with the flight of so many Tamil refugees to Germany, India, Canada, Denmark, France, and several other countries.[4] Seventy-four percent of the Sri Lankan population are Sinhala-speaking Buddhists; about 22 percent are Tamil-speaking Hindus, Christians, and Muslims. After 25 years of serious failures alternating with great successes, the Tamil Tiger insurgency, led by the charismatic and ruthless Prabhakaran, was in 2009 finally and definitively defeated. From 1983 until 2009 Sri Lanka experienced a devastating civil war. Almost 100,000 people died; well over 30,000 are counted among the "disappeared." This conflagration arose from the determined rebellion of the Tamil-speaking Tigers against the Sinhala-speaking Buddhist majority national government. At issue was the survival of the Tamil language (its use had been seriously proscribed in day-to-day dealings), the associated Tamil culture, and a governmental attempt forcibly to remove Tamils from their homes and to integrate them into Sinhala culture.

Tracing the sources of this conflict is not simple: differences between the two groups include linguistic, religious, and allegedly racial divides. However, genetic research reveals few distinctions between Tamil and Sinhala speakers. Both groups have inhabited the island of Sri Lanka and have intermarried for nearly 2,000 years. Additional Tamils, several hundreds of thousands of them, were brought to Sri Lanka from India as coffee and later as tea plantation workers when the British established a colonial empire there in the early 1800s. For reasons still not completely discernible, the British established their educational systems primarily among the regions populated by Tamils in the North and the East. When independence came to Sri Lanka in 1948, the reserve of educational, administrative, and managerial talent among the Tamils gave them a disproportionate advantage over the Sinhalese for obtaining government positions. This situation caused enormous tension and led eventually to a form of reverse affirmative action, a law that banned the use of Tamil and therefore barred Tamils from holding many important government positions in the country. Tensions between Tamils and Sinhalese, tensions that the British learned early to exploit with a "divide-and-conquer" strategy, slowly, almost relentlessly, became exacerbated.

By 1977 the sense of oppression among Tamils was so acute that they began to call for a separate Tamil state: "Tamil Eelam." At least two separate Tamil auxiliary armies began to form, but by 1983 they had coalesced into a single, tightly knit group that made itself known throughout Sri Lanka by staging a deadly attack on a government army base in the North. That installation was intended as both a symbolic and a de facto control over possible Tamil rebellion, and its fall signaled the grim seriousness and the deadly commitment for which the Tamil Tigers have come to be known. Not until 1987 did routine martyr bombing become a weapon in the arsenal of the LTTE when a truckload of explosives driven by two Tamil males destroyed a second Sri Lankan army camp. Among the hundreds of subsequent martyr bombings, two prime ministers of Sri Lanka, one prime minister of India, four Sri Lankan army generals, and three moderate Tamil politicians[5] were victimized, as were hundreds of bystanders.

Between 1987 and 2002, 76 different martyr bombings were perpetrated by the Tamil Tigers. But from the earlier days of the resistance, the willingness to die for the cause of Tamil Eelam (the Tamil Homeland) was considered basic to the Tamil cause: training for fighters in the Tamil army included instructions to avoid capture at all costs by wearing a cyanide pill necklace, called a *kuppi,* which was to be swallowed when capture became inevitable.

The year 1987 marked the period when women became formally active agents in the organized insurgency: this was the period when the Tigers developed a fleet of hit-and-run attack boats that were light and fast and manned (so to speak) by cadres of women whose lighter body weight gave the boats greater maneuverability. Several of these boats launched deliberate group-martyr missions. But it was not until May 1991 that the first prominent female martyr bomber grabbed international attention. On May 21, 1991, a young, purportedly modest Tamil Hindu woman named Tēnmoli ("sweet speaking") Rajaratnam arrived early in the evening in Sriperumputur, India.[6] She was hoping to catch a close glimpse of Rajiv Gandhi, the prime minister of India, as he campaigned for a second term. Clad in a green and saffron *salwar kameez,* her hair covered in fragrant jasmine and kanakāmparam flowers, Tenmoli approached Gandhi respectfully as he received people all evening long prior to a Congress Party celebration. She patiently waited as he blessed the four or five women ahead of her in the crowd. When she was next, she advanced and garlanded him with a lovely sandalwood chaplet. She smiled warmly and bent down reverently to touch his feet. She then ignited her explosive-laden bomber belt, obliterating herself and Gandhi, and killing 14 others. Earlier that year, Gandhi had sent Indian troops to Sri Lanka to help suppress the Tamil civil war. His death meant that his campaign promise to do so again would never be fulfilled.

Stories—mostly unverifiable—about the daring Rajaratnam (who also went by the name "Dhanu") immediately began to circulate: she, like several others of the female martyr bombers, had been raped in Sri Lanka by Indian army troops. It was said that one tool of "pacification" used by Sri Lankan and Indian government forces to disrupt the morale of Tamil Tiger insurgents has been systematic rapes of Tamil women. Once a woman is raped, in the traditional South Asian context, her future is sealed: no self-respecting man will wed her, and a family will never be a possibility. If she is married, her husband must renounce her. And so, the result has been that several women who have endured this abuse have "married," if you will, the cause of Tamil liberation. Anecdotal information points to the conclusion that rapes have been instrumental in creating a cadre of female martyr bombers. In the case of Rajaratnam, after years of training, she eventually vowed to become a martyr bomber. So vividly did she capture public imagination that a famous Tamil film was produced based roughly on the few facts known about her. This film, called *The Terrorist*, celebrated the valor and courage of female martyr bombings and received a wide international showing.[7]

The fact that this film represented in India so sympathetically the exploits of someone who had murdered the Indian prime minister, and 14 other innocent Indians, suggests a certain predisposition to exalt martyr bombing or, rather, to exalt a female who perpetrates a martyr bombing. Indeed, there are some basic elements in both Indian and Sri Lankan culture that suggest how such a woman might be more likely to become a martyr bomber. Traditionally, women are regarded as less threatening and less dangerous than men, and so are able to gain access to sensitive or protected targets with greater ease. And in a culture where bodily searches of women by men are considered tantamount to molestation, concealing explosives becomes much easier for women.

The Tamil-speaking southern portion of India had long offered illicit support to the cause of the Tamil Tigers, but Rajiv Gandhi saw an opportunity to insinuate Indian power into Sri Lankan affairs by sending a peacekeeping force supposedly to mediate between the Tamil and Sinhala factions. When the Tamil insurgents refused to surrender their arms to Indian "peacekeepers," serious conflict between Indian and Sri Lankan Tamil forces erupted.

Reports of widespread abuses by Indian forces soon surfaced in the Tamil community: pillaging, rape, and summary executions of recalcitrant Tamils seemed the norm. Thus, the Tigers did not want Rajiv to be reelected, lest he send the Indian forces once more.

My hypothesis builds on these details. Specifically, there are certain basic cultural norms found in Tamil society that promote the notion that a woman's body is the repository of special powers when it comes to constructing and influencing a society in which justice and prosperity may prevail. A female has the capacity to be the ultimate personification of virtue, justice, fidelity, and health. "Keep women virtuous and the whole of society will follow suit" seems to be the basic attitude. When women are virtuous, their bodies become the repository of a powerfully magical force that has destructive capacities when faced with any evil that threatens them or society in general. This force, cultivated exclusively in virtuous women, is called *"aṇaṅku."* The more virtuous a woman, the more powerful is that *aṇaṅku* and the greater danger it becomes to compromise that virtue. For this reason, dedicated, chaste women who for the sake of righteousness suffer unjustifiably are imbued with a power to reverse injustice and oppression, especially after their deaths, when they become deified as goddesses.[8]

In becoming a martyr bomber, a woman becomes much more than simply a martyr. She becomes a goddess, reborn after her death to a new and higher calling, with fearful powers to avenge evil, oppression, injustice, and corruption. The religious culture of South Asia, whether Hindu, Buddhist, Christian, Muslim, Jain, or Sikh, places extraordinary emphasis on conduct regulated by vows.[9] Most often, those vows are promises made in public to a sacred figure. Women who become martyr bombers almost always do so by making a vow to do so, either to a deity or to the movement, personified by the deity/leader Prabhakaran.[10] They are accorded respect and honor—similar in many ways to that accorded to animals set aside for religious sacrifice. In this liminal state they lead a disciplined, celibate life dedicated to a single purpose. Preparations for the event are understood as part of a physical, spiritual, and psychological discipline.

I deal here with what has to be a decidedly blood-and-guts phenomenon in which human beings blow themselves and others to bits in a deliberate and calculated way. Given the elemental nature of the topic, I move now to specifics inasmuch as I am able to do so. The particulars I have to offer come primarily from the Tamil culture of southern India, though there is widely verifiable evidence that we will find the same particulars on the ground in Sri Lanka. Throughout Tamil culture, and especially in Sri Lanka and Tamil Nadu, we find widely worshipped goddesses whose powers and images Tamil people invoke and respect. Narrative accounts about these goddesses can, on occasion, become models for Tamil women's understanding of themselves and of how they should function in society. The stories of these goddesses provide, if you will, a logic and a framework for apprehending how Tamil women might take charge of things under duress. Acting as the deity acts (in Latin, *imitatio dei*, or "imitating the deity" in religious studies terminology) is as much an operative devotional injunction among Tamil devotees as is the acronym "WWJD" (What Would Jesus Do?) among pious Christians who take Jesus as their model.

The first goddess is Māriyamman. Her shrines can be found throughout the northern and eastern areas of Sri Lanka, in much of Tamil Nadu (India), and even in such places as Paris, Hamburg, and rural Michigan, where migrating Tamils from Sri Lanka and India have constructed temples. The stories about Māriyamman vary widely, but nearly all of them have a central theme. They speak of how a once-human, but now divinized female was somehow deceived, mistreated, irresponsibly cared for, and downright abused. In nearly every case, the abuse was perpetrated by males who should have protected or cared for her: her husband murders her, a priest rapes her, and a brother marries her off to someone he knows to be inferior. As a result of that abuse, and her stoic willingness to endure it, the woman derives from her sense of righteous purpose and dignity a superhuman strength and ferocity. Māriyamman deserves in no way such treatment. Her purity, or *karpu*, empowers her to return from the dead as a powerful spirit seeking vengeance and justice on those who have wronged her and women like her. In many cases, she literally explodes in anger, destroys the always-male figures responsible for her mistreatment, and dies herself in the conflagration. She then becomes a goddess who must be worshipped fervently. She insists that her followers be willing to sacrifice considerable energy and blood in their worship of her. Firewalking, excruciating pilgrimages that involve rolling one's body on the ground for miles, and submission to the insertion of sharp metallic lances into one's flesh are just a few of the many demands she makes.

I will not belabor the ways in which Māriyamman could easily be seen as a role model for the female martyr bomber: a virtuous person submits to a violent blazing death that is necessitated by injustice. Resurrected in the form of a goddess, she now demands a devotion from her followers that reflects and embodies their willingness to sacrifice, as well.

A second goddess whose narrative history serves as a model for Tamil women is named Pattini.[11] Her shrines can be found in much of Sri Lanka; she is actively worshipped by both Hindus and Buddhists on the island. Though her roots are in India, she is far more popular and her shrines are far more widespread in Sri Lanka. She has become, in fact, one of the more visible goddesses of Sri Lanka. Her story comes from a Buddhist document dating to the fifth century called the *Cilappatikāram*.[12] In that document she is introduced to readers as a woman named Kaṇṇaki, married to a man named Kōvalaṉ. Kōvalaṉ, however, fell in love with a courtesan named Mātavi and frittered away all his money on her. Despondent, Kōvalaṉ returned to his chaste wife Kaṇṇaki, who forgave him and took him in without question, displaying the quality of chastity that would eventually provide her with such remarkable postmortem powers. She gave him one of her family treasures, a precious golden anklet, which he was instructed to take to the city of Madurai and sell there so that he could refinance his trading business. But in trying to sell the anklet, Kōvalaṉ was framed by a goldsmith who claimed Kōvalaṉ stole the anklet from the local Pāṇṭiyaṉ dynasty queen. Hauled before the king on this mistaken charge, Kōvalaṉ was immediately beheaded at the king's order. When Kaṇṇaki found out about this unjust murder, she flew into a righteous rage. She appeared before the king, and produced the paired duplicate of the anklet Kōvalaṉ was said to have stolen, thus proving definitively that the anklet Kōvalaṉ tried to sell was not stolen. She then cursed the king and his entire court to a fearsome death. Her righteous indignation took on new power when she ripped off her left breast, threw it in front of the palace, thereby (and somehow) causing a massive conflagration that consumed her, the king and his court, and eventually the entire city. As the city burned to the ground, Kaṇṇaki was assumed into heaven, becoming the goddess Pattiṉi. Today, as a goddess, Pattiṉi is understood to be a powerful instrument for justice. Her worshippers pray to her for healing, retribution, and assistance at times of difficulty. One of the most common ways to approach her, to enter her world in worship, is to flirt with injury and death by walking on fire. While her temples dot the landscape in Sri Lanka, there are fewer in India, but there is a major carved stone statue of Kaṇṇaki/Pattiṉi about 20 feet high on the marina of the beach in Chennai (earlier Madras). The statue of Kaṇṇaki holds up that jeweled anklet as she denounces the Pāṇṭiyaṉ king in an inscription on the base of the statue that comes directly from the epic ballad.

The images and narratives associated with the two major female deities worshipped by Tamils in Sri Lanka share some basic characteristics: pure, chaste women have suffered enormous injustices at the hands of uncaring, callous males. They finally erupt in righteous anger, destroying themselves and their persecutors. Then, they live on as goddesses to whom people pray for protection and assistance, and especially for the rectification of injustice.

Female Tamil martyr bombers seem to have reenacted in strikingly parallel fashion the careers of these two goddesses. The mythic traditions of these two goddesses are traceable to the fifth century for Kaṇṇaki and at least the 15th century for Māriyamman. I can only be impressed by the fact that some of the most visible tactics for guerilla campaigns in South Asia likely find their roots in religious traditions describing how women might experience apotheosis. The extent to which women and those who assist them deliberately and self-consciously invoke the memories and names of Māriyamman and Kaṇṇaki remains to be seen. Discussions with female martyr bombers who have taken a secret oath to give up their lives are very difficult to arrange. But I maintain that these religious traditions provide for them models, implicit support, acceptance, and encouragement, if not inspiration. Māriyamman and Kaṇṇaki are the forbearers of the tradition of martyr bombing in South Asia and provide a cultural context in which martyr bombing is understood, accepted, and lauded by those dedicated to the cause of the Tamil Tigers.

WOMEN'S BODIES AND MARTYR BOMBERS

In the media coverage of the civil war in Sri Lanka, Tahira Gonsalves has noted a particular concern with the appearances of the bodies of women who have enlisted as combatants in the struggle.[13] Normally, she claims, "women are expected to conform to gendered stereotypes which cast them in roles of the demure and passive nurturer, linked to the land, nation, and culture. However, in the context of war, these stereotypes are often thrown open and women are forced to or volunteer to play 'men's roles.'"

Female Tamil combatants in the Sri Lankan civil war have frequently attracted the fascinated attention of media and government because they are perceived to have given up their essential "femaleness," represented by the female body adorned in a flowing sari, wearing bangles, necklaces, toe rings, makeup, and fragrant flowers in their long hair. As trained combatants, female Tamil Tiger army recruits have become much more "male," wearing combat boots, battle fatigues, no makeup, their hair either tightly braided or cut short beneath their standard issue military caps. Their training is rigorous, with few concessions made to the traditional notion that women are unable to endure physically demanding exercises. They are taught to kill rather than to preoccupy themselves with what is considered quintessentially female, giving birth. The values of fertility and beauty, normally prized among women, are eclipsed by the ideals of ferocity and intimidating violence.

The leader of the Tamil Tiger cadres, Prabhakaran, insisted on a relinquishing of gender identities among the soldiers who serve under him. In his speech given on International Women's Day (1992), for example, he spoke of "the need to eliminate male chauvinistic oppression, violence, the dowry system, and casteism."[14] He exhorted them to live lives of strict celibacy and to regard each other as brothers and sisters. But it is the women for whom the gender transformation is greatest. In terms of customary roles and dress, they must relinquish their feminine identities. In general, in the Tamil culture—as in much of South Asia—the body of a woman is considered to be "fungible," which is to say that women's bodies are understood to be able to incorporate and sustain basic changes in their gendered and ancestral identities. Inden and Nicholas have written about how a woman, at the event of marriage, becomes the "half-body" of her husband.[15] She takes on the physical properties of her husband's clan, eats the food common to her husband's extended family, worships the new deities of her husband's house, and in so doing assumes a physical transformation initiated by the ceremony of marriage and sustained by a new lifestyle. In Tamil culture, women are seen as the mediators between lineages, for they can move from one to the other in a way that men cannot. Traditionally when they marry, they transfer their residences to the homes of their husbands. When they bear children, those children become members of the family lineage into which she has married.

This "fungibility in bodily substance" (if I may call it that) suggests how these Tamil women who take on male roles and appearances as foot soldiers can then assume another major change when they are selected to become elite martyr bombers. Nearly all women who become martyr bombers first train as combat recruits, as foot soldiers in the Tamil Tiger army. Having undergone this radical change in identity and in appearance, they are then called upon to change once more. The quintessential female martyr bomber must once again effect a transformation. She must become the epitome of the South Asian female. She forsakes any hint of the militant male and becomes effective as a martyr bomber only to the extent that she becomes once again, in appearance at least, the feminine, retiring, unthreatening, sari-clad female. Indeed, the Tamil Tiger strategy in designing the explosive belt to be worn on the torso has sometimes sought to make women appear to be pregnant. One of the more recent martyr bombings occurred in April 2006 at the Sri Lankan Army Headquarters Hospital when a Tamil woman who had visited earlier for neonatal care strapped onto her body a belt of lethal explosives and detonated them inside the hospital compound. Eight were killed and 26 were seriously wounded, including Sri Lanka's top-ranking military officer General Fonseka. Interestingly, the Tamil Tiger propaganda wing insists vehemently that the martyr bomber was pregnant at the time. The Sri Lankan government denies this. Little independent evidence supports either position, but the heated public information debate is revealing. If a pregnant woman commits an act of martyr bombing, the act takes on an air of forceful intimidation. A woman willingly gives up her life and the future life of her unborn child in dedication to the Tamil Tiger cause. This kind of resolve and self-sacrifice on the part of a woman, a woman who, by all appearances, is doing what real women do, that is, nurture and give birth, calls attention to the seeming determination and dedication of those enlisted in the cause of the Tamil Tigers. It suggests that all the normal rules of military engagement are suspended and that no strategy and no sacrifice in this war is unthinkable. Here, strangely enough, the melody sung by the late Janice Joplin seems to echo: "Freedom's just another word for nothing left to lose."[16] When a woman, possibly a pregnant woman, can perform a martyr mission, she and her trainers have been released, are free, from all normal constraints, and what some would call basic humanity, and they have done so in unthinkable ways. The very act invites fear, awe, dread, and disgust. It is much easier to face women dressed and acting like men on the field of combat.

The final transformation a female Tamil martyr bomber's body undergoes is from human being to goddess. Reports I have read indicate that of the shrines constructed in honor of martyr bombers, those built in memory of women-become-goddesses are more often frequented by worshippers and are more enthusiastically worshipped than are shrines of male martyr bombers. For females the transition from human to goddess is more natural, much easier to accept and to affirm. I believe this has much to do with the perceived fungibility of the female body. In Tamil villages, both in India and in Sri Lanka, most village shrines traceable to human apotheosis are associated with female deities. When a heroic woman dies, let us say in childbirth, she may be enshrined in the village into which she has married. But it is also possible that an ancillary shrine will be constructed in her natal village and, in some cases, in villages into which she might have married. Shrines for male heroes[17] are more unusual, but hardly ever do these shrines migrate outside the village and lineage into which the men are born. A male's transition into a deity is usually slower and always much more spatially limited. A male body is always less fungible.

As we look at how Tamil women became martyr bombers in the Tamil Tiger rebellion, we see a reprise of several notions about the female body in South Asia. (1) Women's bodies are capable of becoming the ultimate cultural repository of justice, virtue, and purity in society. When women are virtuous, they accumulate extraordinary powers to protect themselves and the society in which they live. (2) When virtuous women perceive that they are violated or betrayed (and this includes the violations by their husbands, sons, daughters, and larger social circles), they have the capacity to erupt in violent, fiery destruction wreaking havoc on the usually male forces threatening them. (3) Women's bodies are especially sensitive to transformations involving gender, lineage, and spiritual status. This transformative "fungibility" enables them to adapt to the requirements of guerilla warfare, to do men's work when needed, and to become goddesses when their inspiration and protection can become a resource for those who continue the struggles required of those still living.

Notes

1. With most proper names, I have chosen to use the more conventional transliterations of Tamil terms, such as those found in English newspapers, on maps, and in common publications. For less familiar Tamil terms, I have entered them using the Tamil Lexicon transliteration system.

2. This reconsideration of terminology is the result of conversations with a colleague, Dr. Ralph Hood, who pointed me to an article that first suggested using the term "martyr bomber." See Guss et al. 2007, 415–445.

3. Tambiah 1986.

4. Informal estimates suggest that fully 35 percent of the Tamil population in Sri Lanka have left the country in the past 20 years. In the Wellawatta District of Colombo, a Tamil temple to the Hindu deity Ganesh sprang up during the early years of the conflict. It was notable partly for the fact that the image of the deity was installed on the back verandah of the home of three women, who served as the primary priestesses for the deity. It was most unusual that women would be serving in this role. Each evening the temple attracted several hundred worshippers who thronged the road that bordered the Indian Ocean waterfront. The temple was known as the "Visa Ganesh" temple, and it housed a form of Ganesh reputed to grant the wishes of Tamils seeking an exit visa from Sri Lanka. Such visas were difficult to get. I lived near this temple and was impressed with the size and fervor of the crowds.

5. Moderate Tamil politicians who did not support the violent goals of the LTTE were considered to be collaborators with the Sri Lankan government and were often murdered.

6. See, for example, Michael Roberts's article (2009, 25–41).

7. See the 1998 film, directed and written by Santosh Sivan, who admits that the murder of Gandhi was his model for the plot.

8. Though he has been challenged on some of his interpretations, notably by Rajam (1986, 257–272), George Hart's seminal article remains the standard work. See his (1973, 233–251).

9. See, for example, Raj and Harman 2006.

10. Note that Prabhakaran was revered by many as a deity, as the Sun God. Many refused to believe the report of his death, considering him immortal. See, for example, *The Sydney Morning Herald*, "Sri Lanka's 'Sun God' Tamil Chief Killed," at http://www.smh.com.au/world/sri-lankas-sun-god-tamil-chief-killed-20090518-bcor.html.

11. For more on Pattini, see Obeyesekere, 1984.

12. Ilankovadigalin 1973.

13. See her article, "Media Manipulations and Agency: Women in the LTTE (Liberation Tigers of Tamil Eelam of Sri Lanka)," *Ahfad Journal*, December 1, 2005, accessed online 8/22/2015. See also a more general coverage of this issue in Bloom (2007, 94–102, 97), who says, "A growing number of insurgent organizations are also taking advantage of the fact that suicide bombing,

especially when perpetrated by women and young girls, garners a lot of media attention, both in the West and in the Middle East. Attacks by women receive eight times the media coverage as attacks by men, again largely because of the expectation that women are not violent."

14. Schalk 1994, 166.
15. Inden and Nicholas 1977.
16. "Me and Bobby McGee," written by K. Kristofferson and F. Foster, 1977.
17. See Blackburn et al. 1989.

CHAPTER 8

Women of the Clouds: The Cordillera Religion and the Shaping of the Economic, Political, and Social Empowerment of Women[1]

Jae Woo Jang

INTRODUCTION

This is how they avert war and conflict. There is a priestess, in a red-and-black checkered garb, surrounded by the elders and the village chieftain in a headdress topped by crimson rooster feathers, who sits legs crossed, laying down a wooden vessel on which she places the offering of pigs and chicken, tied and readied for their throats to be slit for a blood offering. Then, their songs begin—a prayer to Kabunian—an exhortation to mediate in a conflict between the intruders of the forest and its owner Amaya, heir to the *Muyong,* a forest watershed on the edges of the mountain peaks that irrigate the terraces below.

In the olden days, an intruder to Amaya's property, the Muyong, would probably be put to death. The Muyong is the center of their world: the source of water to irrigate the rice fields and drinking water for the villages below; a home for their dead ancestors; a repository of hundreds of species of plants and trees, many of which are used as medicinal herbs; and timber for housing and firewood. Amaya has sought the advice of the Council of Elders who offered to officiate the ritual. Now, they must watch closely the chicken bile as the Baki priestess holds the chicken's head in between her thumb and forefinger, gently cutting the hen's throat with a sharp blade, and as soon as the blood surfaces, she lets it drop to the hollow wooden vessel shaped like a bowl. The priestess must now inspect the bile. If the bile is bad, they must conduct another ritual; if it is good, the intruders from a neighboring village must bring in pigs and chicken as offering. If they refuse, Amaya and the elders must prepare the male warriors for a retaliation, and this is the conflict Amaya tries to stay away from, but as a woman of status and wealth, she must do her duty as required: to take care of her forest that has now become a communal property on which their lives and livelihoods depend.

The women and men now gather closer as the priestess dissects the chicken, pulling out the bile and softly running her fingers around it. "It is a good healthy bile," she says, and the crowd erupt in cheers of relief. The dancing and chanting continues and ends with a feast and the sharing of the Tapuy, wine made from rice.

This is only a glimpse of the life of a woman in the Cordilleras, a mountain range in northern Luzon in the Philippines, whose egalitarian society, brought about by her religious traditions that govern the life of every person, has bestowed her significant roles and a status revered in her community—status that encompasses every aspect of her existence, rendering her socially, politically, and economically empowered.

OVERVIEW OF THE RELIGION AND THE CORDILLERA

The Cordillera Administrative Region is geographically located at the landlocked north-central area of Luzon, one of the three major islands of the Philippines. The Cordillera is comprised of six provinces: Benguet, Abra, Kalinga, Apayao, and the Mountain Province, whose capital is Bontoc and Ifugao, where the world-renowned Banaue Rice Terraces are found. The region thereby harbors eight major ethnolinguistic groups: the Ifugao, Ilocano, Ibaloy, Kankanaey, Kalanguya, Kalinga, Itneg, and Isneg. Linguistic variations within these groups occur as manifested in the existence of dialects within a linguistic group.[2] The Ifugao language and ethnic group, for instance, comprises four distinct dialects, which include the languages Amganad, Batad, Mayoyao, and Tuwali.[3] These linguistic differences are minimal, and although the groups and subgroups differ at times on religious terminology, religious beliefs vary little, with a few distinctions on the officiating of rituals. It is also important to note that the sublinguistic division is sometimes used to refer to a particular ethnic group or subgroup. For instance, the Ifugaos are an ethnic group who speak the Ifugao language.

The demarcation among each ethnic group is determined through regional and linguistic differences.

Religion in the Cordillera is tied to its topography, whose features include rugged mountainous regions, forests, gorges and ravines, river, pasturelands, and cascading farmlands that reach nearly 4,522,030 acres of land. Its terrain contrasts with steep slopes by the North and plain lands by the South.[4] Eighty-five percent of these areas are forestlands that could potentially be utilized for human settlement, but people tend to inhabit areas that surround river basins or open valleys in order to upkeep the most prominent functions of the lands—rice cultivation and watershed maintenance, activities delineated by their religious belief. Therefore, people established permanent settlement near water sources to ensure their water supply for efficient rice cultivation. However, the total watershed area in the Cordillera that accounts for the major river valleys, such as the Cagayan and the Agno River valleys, is 18 times larger than the land occupied for farming. If I were to make sense of these numerical values, the Cordillera is literally a giant water cradle for the entire Luzon, supplying fresh water for the country's capital.[5]

The first major inhabitants of the Cordillera emerged roughly 4,500 years ago, and the rice terraces were first constructed for a strategy to improve sustainability of the environment and improve agricultural production through the progression of time, modifying their lifestyle to suit to the conditions and situation that spring from the demands and requirements of their religious beliefs.[6] The result of this adaptation is the rice terraces for which the Cordillera is most famous, emerging as one of the country's engineering feats, dubbed the eighth wonder of the world. How much do these forests and land mean to the people of the Cordillera?

Religious life in the Cordillera is governed by a combination of polytheism, mythology, and animism whose basic tenets encourage believers to interact with the spiritual and the natural world. It is significant to remember that the natural world parallels the spirit world; hence, nature is the abode of the spirits, and gods manifest themselves in objects, carved statues, the environment, rivers, or forests. Appeasement of the gods for good fortune is carried out through communal rituals and ceremonies.[7] The belief that every action or intention is governed and supervised by the spirits allows people to follow a zealous religiosity. The gods are always watching over the people, and it is this assurance that motivates individuals to live and act according to their religious ideals and the values. If the gods are pleased, the Cordillera people believe that the world will be rewarded with prosperity; on the other hand, if the gods are displeased, society shall be beleaguered with a series of misfortunes. The traditional religion in the Cordillera is carefully followed and its values, tenets, and doctrine exemplified through oral literature such as chants, orations, songs, and epics, which constitute religious doctrine in the region. These provide an individual existence with the "Thou Shalts," allowing the underlying cultural values to sink into their subconsciousness. As children are taught to memorize the epics, tales, myths, and legends that exist in everyday life, especially those with religious attributes, the information is ingrained in the children's minds effectively.

THE GODS OF THE CORDILLERA

The Cordillera belief in a god that governs the lives of the people is based upon three supreme beings. The first is the supreme god called *Lumawig*, the skyworld god, often referred to as the "rice god," who had designed the beauty and the serenity of the world and the Cordillera rice terraces in particular, depicted as an anthropomorphic figure. In Ifugao and in most areas of the region, this takes the form of a wooden sculpture of a human form, standing or crouching or at times holding a bowl. This is referred to as the Bulul in Ifugao. Secondly, the Bulul also represents other gods or goddesses—the invisible powers that establish the law and order of nature including those on earth and in the underworld. These types of deities that can manifest themselves in the Bulul number more than 1,500. They are present in trees, rivers, mountains, and other natural phenomena. Lastly, Bulul can likewise represent spirits of the ancestor or "anitos" who live in the underworld as the indigenous population in the Cordillera believe that the spirits of their ancestors remained on earth as a vestige to protect and govern the lives of the family.[8] Therefore, the ancestral domain became a significant factor in one's identity, and the Ifugao considered the continuation of the family line as prosperity. As the Bulul is tied to all these numerous beliefs, the Ifugao culture values and honors gods as they believe that their lives are intertwined with and influenced by many forms of these gods.

It is important to note, however, that the term "Bulul" connotes a specific reference to the gods in Ifugao and similar variations on the names and functions of these gods exist within the different regions and among sublinguistic groups throughout the Cordillera. But their core belief is structured similarly into the belief in the tripartite figures of the supreme god, deities, and ancestral spirits. Therefore, below, the word "god" will refer to the gods of the Cordillera and not only to the Bulul, while the diction "religion" likewise shall refer to the religion of the Cordillera. Gods in the Cordillera, as similar to the Bulul, are represented in a carved wooden figure that represents the aforementioned three spiritual entities.[9]

As children are exposed to and first taught the deluge of oratories that address the concept of nature, value, cooperation, and agricultural success, people in the Cordillera region subconsciously behave in accord with these values. If you were to ask an elder whether his or her belief and religion provide its followers with a set of prescribed actions, ideology, or commands that govern their lives, many would simply answer "not really." However, through empirical observations of the wise aged women and their interactions with society, the indigenous Cordillera culture is identified as contributing largely to shaping its societal perception and treatment toward women as ordinate and as equally important to the well-being of the society as are men.

This society, however, is susceptible to deterioration. Its history is tarred with a series of conflicts and uneasiness against the imperialist rule of the Spaniards as early as 1572 until the very late period of the 1900s, the American and Christian influence that trickled in until 1915, and the independent Philippine government since its independence in 1946.[10] Even after overcoming the foreign attempts to assume power over the Cordillera or to force the indigenous people into the process of assimilation, Cordillera still exhibits vestiges of its traditional culture and belief. However, its annals of history, the series of struggles to deny its "subjugation" under the mainstream, Christianized and foreign culture, had lunged a gasp, a chasm of space, in the heart of its tradition, leaving room for assimilation and the deterioration of the authenticity and the sincerity of a culture that based its core values upon the tripartite of communal responsibility, familial attachment, and respect toward nature. The application of these core values that are attributed to their religious framework has spawned a society that empowers women through economic, social, and political means—an egalitarian community in which a person is measured not by the amount of his or her possession of materials and property but by his or her character and spiritual fulfillment.

WOMEN AND RELIGION IN SOCIAL LIFE

The women of the Cordillera region play a significant role in society. As her laws and traditions, a consequence of her religious beliefs, provide her with the status equal to that of a man, the Cordillera woman occupies an important rung in the social ladder.

The life of the people in the Cordillera region is guided by beliefs in taboos known as the *paniyu* in Ifugao. Laws, customs, and interactions among individuals and families are regulated by these taboos as violations of these may lead to insanity, diseases, and misfortunes. Taboo or *paniyu* in the Ifugao language, therefore, proliferates the notions of good and evil actions and in many ways regulates relationships among individuals. Taboo, in fact, is a significant aspect of the region's traditional laws whose promulgations necessarily aim for the protection of women. For instance, in Ifugao, it is taboo to use offensive language with reference to sex in front of a female or the opposite sex. Cruelty against a spouse and infidelity are taboo and are serious offenses that could result in divorce and the payment of a fine to the aggrieved party. Violating taboos under traditional law require remedy in the form of a fine and in some instances severe punishments.[11]

Hence, a woman is bestowed with important functions that begin in her family and household. While both genders are treated equally, boys and girls of the Cordillera regions have similar functions: they tend to the house chores when their parents are in the fields, take care of their younger siblings, and are tasked to manage the household. The enculturation of the female commences as soon as a girl reaches puberty. During this time, girls live in the dormitory (boys live in a separate dormitory) with single, widowed, or divorced adult women who train the girls in the cultural and religious traditions the community uphold. The women teach the girls chants and songs used in rituals, and girls are expected to memorize them. One of the most important oral traditions among the Ifugaos is the chanting of the Hudhud. The Hudhud epics narrate the legends and beginnings of the Ifugao people, the bravery and the adventures of their heroes and their heroines who are remembered for their beauty and virtue. It is through the Hudhud that cultural values are exemplified by the ways of their ancestors and their gods who intervene with the daily affairs of the village folks.[12] The chanting of these tales in the Hudhud highlight the values that their ancestors hold dear such as the reverence afforded to women. In the Hudhud, the hero's mother, although a secondary character in the story, is consulted first with regard to decisions on major festivals and feasts especially in the arrangement of the marriage rituals and feasts for her children.

The Cordillera oral literature, which includes poems, epics, chants, and orations, has helped in laying the foundation of a culture that highlights gender equality and ensures women's prospects and dignity. These oral traditions are significant in that they have paved the way for the establishment of customs and taboos that regulate social interactions between neighbors, between men and women, and among members of the society. Hence, the consequences of these customs and taboos translate to favorable treatment of girls, of a child, or of any member of the society. For instance, it is a taboo to disrespect women or inflict harm on them or any member of the community. As women's duties and functions are viewed as complementary to those of men, the ideals of equality are quite disparate to those of the Western feminist movement. Women are expected to work in the fields during rice planting season while men take care of the children. Men take their turn tilling or plowing the fields, and fixing the stonewalls of the rice terraces before harvest, while women tend to the children. During harvest, both men and women can take part, and when the children needed tending, only the men do the work. These distinct roles are not perceived as unfair or discriminatory.

In contrast to most of the cultures across Asia in which traditional marriages were usually arranged, the choice of marriage partners within the region of the Cordillera rests upon the individual. Society refuses to fetter women to their choice of partners, and although parents could influence these choices, it is never imperative for both men and women to yield to their parents' wishes. At times, trial marriage is practiced to determine compatibility because incompatibility could count as grounds for divorce. Cheating on a spouse could result in divorce and the payment of a severe fine to the aggrieved party with no consideration to gender. Traditionally, children whose parents agree to divorce live with the mother and are entitled to their father's property.

The social status of a woman is tied to her wealth and her occupation as social stratification exists in the Cordillera to some degree. However, because every endeavor is tied to rice production and good harvest to produce rice wine, *tapuy*, used in rituals and ceremonies for the appeasement of their gods, the existence of the social divide easily dissolves as individuals of both sexes take part in the management of the rice fields and in ensuring a bountiful harvest. In the eyes of their gods, they are all producers. On the other hand, wealthy landowners allocate much of their property for communal use as a source of timber or firewood, produce, and water.

In addition, as rituals and ceremonies govern the lives of the people in the Cordillera, women take on the significant function of orators and chanteuses during festivals. Although in some parts of the region women do not hold the authority to become priestesses, there are numerous instances in which women are allowed to officiate and lead rituals. This is especially true in the province of Ifugao, in which *mama-o*, or priestesses, with the functions and status equal to those of priests, narrate traditional myths in a ritual to cure sickness.[13] The same is true in the province of Kalinga, in which the priestess called the *mandadawak* acts as the spirit medium to communicate to the spirits of the Sangasang, the village shrine in which members of the community believe the spirits reside. The *mandadawak* calls on the spirits of the Sangasang for the blessings of favorable fortune and good health. If members of the community fail to observe taboos and conduct rituals that involve the blood sacrifice of chicken or pigs, the people of the Kalinga believe that they will suffer from afflictions and diseases that cause trembling, gaping mouth, and screaming and shivering spells brought about by the spirits of Tayadan (shiver), Pakkuyan (scream), and Takang (Gaping Mouth).[14] The *mandadawak*, priestesses of the Cordillera's Kalinga, accompany war parties of head hunters whose attacks against the village enemy commence with her shrill high-pitched cry as she lunges her sacred war spear toward the village of the enemy. Head-hunting parties, in fact, rarely occur in the region, and headhunting is done only as a form of retaliation against enemies who refuse to redress wrongs or when rituals and ceremonies have failed to fend off bad omens.[15] As a result, the Cordillera region during the past few centuries has become synonymous with headhunting despite its rare occurrence. Nonetheless, the contributions of women in every aspect of social life even during wars and conflict remain substantial and significant.

WOMEN IN RELIGION AND POLITICS

The overlapping of religion, society, economics, and politics in the Cordillera life confounds in some ways the extent of women's empowerment in politics. This power results from the belief in taboos, a consequence of religion, which in turn justify customary laws and political roles. Added to that dilemma is the absence of a central government that could regulate and influence political life, but this is easily compensated for by the well-established and effective laws that govern their lives. The region's governance system, therefore, does not exert internal authority but rather an external one that does not impinge much on individual freedom. Barton observed this when he posited that the Ifugao of the Cordillera enjoyed much freedom and yet remained consummate diplomats. Others see the political structure as akin to anarchy although this perception is an oxymoron as the people of the region live at peace with each other.[16]

The closest to a political system that governs the lives of the villages in the Cordillera is the *Dap-ay* (in Ifugao language as well as in most parts of the region) or *Ato*, which is a place for meetings and gatherings as well as a setting for rituals and ceremonies. The stone-paved structure also acts as a training center for boys, and in which the male elders gather to decide on pressing issues that confront the community. *Dap-ay* can also connote a council of elders who settle issues that beset village life. The council of elders, however, is exclusively comprised of prominent men in the village whose experience, age, wisdom, and wealth have bestowed this office upon them. The influence of women remains on the sidelines in specific regions of the Cordillera such as Sagada, as women have limited direct participation in political decisions. However, women do exert influence over their husband's decisions as the cultural norm of familial solidarity always enables a husband to consult with his wife through informal discussion about important decisions regarding their family and community.

In the Ifugao province, however, the status of a man in the community is tied to his wife's. The Ifugao chieftain occupies a significant leadership role in the village as he functions as a peacekeeper, is tasked to mediate in conflicts, and to lead ceremonies, rituals, and festivals. These responsibilities are passed on to the wife when a chieftain passes away.

The role of a priestess/*mumbaki* also holds significance in Cordillera politics as issues that are political in nature require religious solutions. During conflicts with other villagers and tribes, a community gathers for a ritual and slays a chicken and pigs for a blood offering, followed by chants, dances, and orations, after which the priest or priestess inspects the chicken's bile used as an offering to determine if it signifies a good or bad omen. A healthy bile means a good omen and an unhealthy one could mean war. The priestess therefore holds the power to declare war against a neighboring tribe as she deems necessary or to avert it. Barton, however, observed during his nearly a decade of stay in the area conducting ethnographic research on the Cordilleras that a war had never occurred as the bile "was always good."

The best gauge for women's empowerment in politics in the Cordillera, however, manifests in the women's right to inherit, purchase, and manage the Muyong, a forest watershed and a sociopolitical structure that regulates village life. In the Cordillera, the Muyong or Batangan is the center of the world and this means that the owner of this wields much power, although, of course, community members hesitate to exercise much of it as it defeats the purpose of equality.

The Muyong is a watershed forest recognized worldwide as an ideal forest management strategy, an assisted natural regeneration system for the flora and fauna that thrive in it, and a watershed rehabilitation system.[17] Harboring hundreds of traditional species of plants and animals, it spans to about five hectares; the watershed functions for communal use as a source of firewood, timber, fruit products, herbal medicine, and housing materials.[18] Any villager can take resources from the Muyong, with the sole caveat to help with its management and care. Hence, the tending of the forest remains a collaborative and a cooperative effort. Although more consideration is given to the poor whom the owner allows to take housing materials from the woodlot, every villager takes seriously his or her responsibility for the management of the Muyong.

Normally perched on the peak of the rice terrace and on the verges of hills, the Muyong provides water for the rice paddies that make up the terrace and spring water for household consumption. As the Cordillera culture, politics, and society are tied to their land, rice cultivation, farming, the tending of forests, and the management of the environment, the Muyong ranks as the most valuable property. This forest watershed functions as a major constituent of spiritual life as it is where thanksgiving rituals are conducted in order to delineate the significance of the forest as a provider of air and water. The center of tribal life and culture and a burial site for the villagers' ancestors, the Muyong, viewed as the abode of the spirits present in nature and ancestral spirits, provides a safe haven for those who reside within its clusters. It is within this forest that the people of the Cordilleras perform their rituals and conduct their feasts to appease their gods and beseech good fortune and good health.[19]

That a woman can own a Muyong, inherit, purchase, and manage it, bestows her with not only a status equal to that of a man but also with political clout in which her decisions with regard to her property carry political, religious, and economic consequences.

WOMEN AND THE CORDILLERA ECONOMY

Quantifying the wealth and economic capability of any individual within the Cordillera can be taxing as one's property intertwines with or is jointly owned by their spouse, parents, or extended family members. The traditional culture of the Cordillera region in fact measures one's affluence through her contentment with her life and, therefore, within such a nonmaterialistic culture, economic empowerment does not refer to a woman's ability to purchase material goods but her ability to maintain and secure her property for subsistence farming. Religion takes on a crucial role in defining the customary laws of the Cordillera that allow women to take hold of her own inheritance or to benefit from her occupation, marriage, or divorce. Women's economic empowerment, therefore, is the by-product of the prevailing religious and traditional belief.

The belief that the spirits of their ancestors live among the sodden earth of their family farmland prevails in the society. This thereby compels individuals to heed much effort and power to maintain the land.

Therefore, the notion of ancestral domain and family unity is greatly emphasized in the Cordillera, which induces many families to cultivate crops in their lands not only to meet economic needs but also to appease the spirits of their ancestors with a successful rice harvest. Abundant crop produce signifies the land's fertility; therefore, producing a substantial quantity of rice is the responsibility of the owner, a duty that she must fulfill as a member of her own family. As nearly 20 percent of the Cordillera region is registered under ancestral domain, the indigenous people are still very devoted to their religion as to satisfying their ancestors and maintaining the land to its optimum condition.[20] Therefore, the religious value of this ancestral attachment is likewise eminent in Cordillera customary law, which varies slightly among the different ethnolinguistic subgroups in the Cordillera region. Although the law differs depending on region, Ifugao customary law, as transcribed by Roy Franklin Burton, presents an insight to women's empowerment that endows them with freedom to hold and protect their property, especially the land inherited from parents. These definitions of rules on property apply all throughout Cordillera.

Families ensure the maintenance of their land through inheritance. Children are given their parcel of the land as soon as they are married or separated from the household. The process often follows the concept of primogeniture, with the eldest child regardless of gender partaking of the biggest portion as he or she is deemed to hold the most burden in ensuring the maintenance of the land and to care for his or her other family members and neighbors. However, this applies differently from one family to another.

The Sagada Ganduyan museum owner Christina, for example, who is only the third-in-line among her siblings, was bestowed the largest parcel of the family land upon her marriage, with a land area of 80 hectares from her chieftain grandfather. Against all odds, her grandfather had given Christina above her two older brothers the privilege of receiving her land. As she clarifies, although the law of primogeniture is the cultural norm, parents often consider which child would be best apt in taking good care of the land—this does not necessarily compel the parents to bequeath their lands to their firstborn. As compared to a patriarchal society in which the eldest son is rightfully bestowed with the largest parcel of the property, people of the Cordillera region do not exclude women from receiving property from their parents. As a consequence, not only do women earn income and produce crops and commodities but a woman also gains honor from satisfying her ancestor's expectations by cultivating rice on the land on which her forefathers likewise used to nurture their crops.

A landless woman could earn monetary support for herself and her family if she works diligently as a tenant farmer. In the Cordillera, tenant farmers are not repressed with debt or the laws that enforce the payment of rent. Tenant farmers are paid a share of the produce divided strictly equally with the other tenants and farm workers as well as with the landowner. Landowners also provide their tenants free housing on a piece of land apportioned to them.

Even during cases in which the couple decides to divorce, the customary law carefully demarcates the division in the conjugal property to return to its respective owners.[21] If, in the worst case scenario, the woman did not own any property upon her marriage, she may take the role of a tenant farmer. Women are not disadvantaged in seeking a job as a tenant, as harvesting is performed primarily by men while plowing is often conducted by women. In a sense, gender roles also equate to specialized roles in farming; therefore, men are not, customarily, an easy replacement for women.

However, in the case where a couple has a child, the two partners must consider who should manage their property in order to pass it on to their child. Therefore, couples may separate, but when a child is already born, they are both committed to giving their lands to their child. The religious value of land passed on as inheritance to their subsequent generation shapes the customary law allowing mothers, who are the child bearers, to maintain their own property and even the property of their ex-spouses.

CHALLENGES AND STRUGGLES

The indigenous ways of life in the Cordillera lie lacerated with numerous scars and struggles that indirectly or directly attempt to compel the Cordillera region to assimilate into the mainstream and foreign culture.

The Spanish had dispatched military units to find a potential source of gold in the Cordillera since 1572 but succeeded only in establishing a colonial government in the Lepanto Province by 1787—almost 200 years after the Spanish's military expedition. Although lowlanders in Pangasinan and Ilocos were subdued by the Spanish authority, the Spanish failed to dominate the Cordillera highlanders of the Ifugao, Kalinga, Bontoc, and other elevated regions as the terrain was harsh and adverse to those who attempted to enter the area. Although the Spanish could not subjugate the Cordillera region into its command, the Spanish administration still reigned over and Hispanized a substantial area along the lowlands as with the majority of Luzon.

During this 300-year period from the late 16th century to the late 19th century, the Spanish and the Cordillera both responded with a series of retaliations. What ensued was a bitter relationship. The governor general in Manila had garnered an anti-Cordillera view as he described the Cordillera people as primitives who murdered people for vindication, theft, intimidation, or extortion and mutilated their bodies.[22] The Cordillera people were perceived as savages and lawbreakers whom the Spanish resolved to "salvage" by introducing Christianity throughout the region. Amidst all of these progressions, we must note that the religion of the Cordillera had upheld the values and the customs that empowers women and shapes a society that benefits all its people. But as the Spanish entered these villages and witnessed the traditional dances, rites, performance chants, and oratories that seemed so foreign, unchristian, and exotic to the Spaniards at the time, the Spanish sought to induce the Cordillera region into Christianity and "civility."

The Spanish enforced the process of *reduccion,* which converted the society into Christianity and replaced the indigenous customary laws and values with foreign religious instruction and guidance that the people were obliged to follow as clarified by an organized and legitimate set of authorities. Those who opposed such enforcement were mostly the highlanders such as the Kalinga and Ifugao as they remained devoted to the traditional culture. As these highlanders continued to resist direct contact between the Conquistadores in 1826, the Spanish responded by forming the *Comandancia del Pais de Igorrotes,* a special military administration in order to monitor and sequester the insurgent and the "barbaric" tribes.[23] Still, in an overall sense, *reduccion* or any other Spanish administration had not inflicted a comprehensive change within Cordillera, but it was the first stage to leave the Cordillera exposed to the belief of Christianity and foreign culture that challenged the indigenous way of life.

Following the Spanish colonization was the American occupation in 1898. Unlike the Spaniards, the Americans took a different approach to assimilating the indigenous Cordillera into the foreign culture. The U.S. government in 1903 categorized the Cordillera into two: those who were Christianized and obedient to the American government as civilized and those who were unchristian and noncompliant to American colonization as uncivilized and primitive. Many classifications of cultural zones were indicated through ethnographic research as to divide the regions into ethnolinguistic subgroups. Some of the prominent ethnographers who have studied the indigenous cultures of the Cordillera were Roy Franklin Barton and Albert Jenks. These ethnographic studies, which to some extent I have referred to in my essays, provided the U.S. government with a better understanding of the Cordillera as compared to the Spanish administration, thereby allowing the Americans to implement a better systematic approach in dealing with the indigenous tribes.[24]

By 1902, Reverend John Stauton had entered the Cordillera, paving the way for both the Protestant and the Catholic Church to establish ground in the indigenous communities. In the preceding paragraphs, I have elucidated the dangers of introducing the Spanish culture into the Cordillera society, where people uphold a traditional belief that contradicts with the foreign culture. The indigenous culture will deteriorate and the society will confront a conundrum as to which culture it should adopt. In 1907, the first Catholic foundation, *The Congregation of the Immaculate Heart of Mary,* had emerged in the lowlands of Bontoc, while the Episcopal Church had also established religious institutions in highland mountain provinces, such as in Sagada, a tourist town in Mountain Province. These initial formations of the Catholic and Protestant Church soon expanded over to the provinces of Kalinga, Ifugao, and nearly the entire Cordillera, including those in Mountain Province and among the highlanders that had resisted the Spanish occupation. The power over the Cordillera region was placed into the hands of the Americans as they enacted the Public Land Acts of 1902 and 1905 that deprived the Cordillera people of their ancestral land. The confiscation of the population's family land is a huge, almost irreparable, offense toward the Cordillera religion.[25] The Cordillera had sought to sign petitions and demonstrate resistance toward the American not through force but through diplomacy.[26]

The Cordillera in the 21st century exhibits a much amplified Catholic and Protestant influence with churches protruding by the center of most major villages. The three regions that I have visited for my ethnographic fieldwork—Ifugao, Sagada, and Bontoc—all contained churches as open spaces used for *Dap-ay* meetings or communal gatherings that were preserved as the reminiscence of the past. The Catholic nun who was managing the library of the Bontoc museum explained the traditional culture of Bontoc using the past tense, language that unconsciously implicates that the indigenous Cordillera culture no longer exists as the mainstream culture within the region. I have witnessed such similar implications with the tour guides in Sagada and the inn manager of St. Joseph's, both of whom referred to the Western culture as civilized and the indigenous culture as almost barbaric. My reference here does not intend to rebuke or criticize anyone but only points out the change in perception and the loss in traditional religious prominence that has so deeply affected the Philippines even after 60 years of independence. The teachings of indigenous culture and traditions, which mostly are justified through its religion, are perceived as impractical, diminishing the emphasis on family solidarity, respect for elders, social prestige over economic wealth, and most importantly, the prominence given to women.[27] The norm of the modern culture, which regresses women into the state of domesticity and provides women with less variety in career opportunities, will partially replace the indigenous norms. Women's status and their influence over the society will be much affected by such cultural change.

The indigenous religion and its culture were further threatened, even after Philippine independence in 1946 and the establishment of the Cordillera autonomous region in 1987, by the process of modernization, enticing younger generations to follow the concept of materialism and individualism over their devotion to the traditional way of life. The introduction of modernized agricultural practices devalued the necessity to perform rituals to appease the gods that were directly or indirectly responsible for the success of rice farming. This as a consequence delegitimizes the credibility of tales, myths, and religious legends for the younger generation. The former Ifugao Chieftain Noel laments that rice rites and oratory performances occur very rarely. Women no longer participate as regular orators and their influence over social teachings is now very limited to only their children. Especially, the use of modern technology and techniques has allowed farmers to become less reliant on the Muyong and its natural irrigation system. The consecration of the rice god or the gods of nature, therefore, is no longer considered the primary factor of their agricultural success. As the modern culture gave Cordillera exposure to different modes of agricultural practices, the religious and cultural attributions toward rice cultivation have been devalued with the adoption of new technology.

The owner of Ganduyan museum in Sagada likewise depicts the cultural changes that she has had to watch so excruciatingly over the past few decades. With the increasing contact with foreign tourists, the Cordillera region, especially the younger generation, began to lean toward the concept of materialism. Such changes led communities to adopt a more individualistic society that replaced the sociopolitical structure of Muyong, with its emphasis on the notion of communal responsibility and cooperation. Therefore, the religiously implicated familial attachment, to some extent, dissolved letting specific individuals hold their property as opposed to the traditional norm of referring to lands as family property. Disputes between families are often settled through third party intervention through the *barangay* (village) administration, all of which show evidence of the decay in the concept of communal living and the promotion of individualism and self-interest. The museum owner mentions that her grandchildren and her children all are willing to purchase an automobile; she is discontented with the society's growing appetite for materialism and complains that the Sagada community will soon be overwhelmed by traffic congestions along its community's narrow alleys. The evidence of growing individualism in the Cordillera could also be attributed to property disputes within families. Virtual conflict arises between the traditionalist and modernist worldviews. The word "virtual" in this context indicates that there is no directed hostility between both sides but rather an ideological tension that is slowly consuming the society. Such conflict is manifest, for example, in a person's questioning the legitimacy of his cousin's communal ownership over family land. Christina has likewise experienced this tension within the family when one of her cousins resolved, without permission, to develop a portion of their 80-hectare family Batangan land, which would be equivalent to the Muyong in Ifugao.

The traditionalist Christina, upon narrating her answers to my questions, began to tear up involuntarily perhaps by nostalgia or her yearning for what was beautiful in the past. Her tremulous hands wiped the side of her sagging eyes as she sought counsel for her family problems and her decision to confront her cousin's exploitation of her family's land. I asserted to Christina that the land had been bequeathed specifically to her from her deceased grandfather—so to some degree, she should hold the political power to make the final decision for the land.

While I did give her some bleak reassurance as to the continuity of her family land, she of course contemplates the changes that have come about through the progression in time and it is above all her hope to return to a traditional community in which "everyone, during those days, was all content with his or her life." Amidst of all this desolation, she concludes our conversation with her hopes of preserving the artifacts, tools, and the traditional huts in which she would like to live in the future.

CONCLUSION

It would be unfair to describe the Cordillera as a region completely deprived of its traditions and culture. Many in Cordillera society, in spite of the overarching Christian influence, still unconsciously live their daily lives in accord with their traditional religious values of familial solidarity, respect toward women and the elderly, mindfulness of the ancestral domain, and prominence given to women—all of which merge together so as to shape a culture and a customary law that empower women in all areas of life. The key attribution to this empowerment is the recognition of women as independent and prominent contributors to society; a person's gender is never the factor in determining social, political, and economic status. Religion relegates individuals into their family, and regardless of their gender, the Cordillera inhabitant strives to preserve the past, the memento of the fathers and mothers that are spiritually bound to the gods of the sky, nature, and environment.

These gods, during a girl's visit to her hometown, after a long absence, are engraved in her mind. She sits there in an arched semi-circle with adults perching down on a stone at the brim of the hills while the children cuddle together as penguins huddling for warmth during a long and cold night. She fills herself with cups of steamed rice, roasted chicken, and chopsuey after watching the women dance with the gong. Then, a group of elderly women wearing those traditional garments come up and sing the tales of the Aliguyon and the other legendary heroes with which she had grown up.

But even if this traditional culture exists with some mixtures of other foreign culture, religion lies underneath as the basis of the Cordillera psyche. It is the duty of the children, both girls and boys, to invest all their time and energy to allow for the prosperous harvest on their family land. It is one's honor to take on this responsibility and it marks the continuity of the family's success.

Thus, as women are given the opportunities to own land themselves, this empowerment brings out a rippling effect over her ability to exert control over the politics, economics, and the society. It is the perception that brings women up onto a pedestal, placing equal emphasis on the importance of women and men in shaping societal, familial, and individual harmony.

I ask myself could a society get any much closer to utopia than the society found in Cordillera? Perhaps this is a misleading question as all societies have their distinctions of beauty inherently immeasurable within the spectrum of "better" or "worse." Yet, the traditional Cordillera religion juxtaposes, almost impeccably with the rugged mountains and the sinuous virgin rivers, women and men living in a balance, as each perceives the other with respect and dignity, interweaving individuals to families and families to community, compelling all individuals to take responsibility as members of the larger group. It is this responsibility that also ushers empowerment, equality, and peace upon women in the Cordillera.

NOTES

1. I would like to acknowledge and thank my research assistant Jun Woo Jang for his tremendous efforts in organizing my ethnographic notes when writing this chapter.

2. National Statistical Coordination Board 2010.

3. Pyer-Pereira 2015.

4. Conklin 1980, 1–12.

5. National Statistical Coordination Board 2010.

6. Reid 2009, 3–26. http://www2.hawaii.edu/~reid/Combined%20Files/A77.%202009.%20Who%20are%20the%20indigenous.pdf, accessed July 13, 2015.

7. Shedden 2010, 24–28.

8. Bulul Artifact. Bontoc Museum. Bontoc, Mountain Province, Cordillera Autonomous Region.

9. Cordillera Schools Group Inc., 2003, 116–134.

10. Stephen 2010, 17–34. http://www.anthropology.hawaii.edu/people/alumni/phds2010-present.html, accessed July 12, 2015.

11. Barton 1919, 1–33. http://www.freefictionbooks.org/books/i/47715-ifugao-law-by-r-f-burton, accessed March 8, 2013.

12. Jang 2012, 169.

13. Sianghio 2013.

14. Krutak 2013.

15. Krutak 2013.

16. Barton 1919, 1–33.

17. Jang and Salcedo 2013, 5–7.

18. Dacawi 1982; Jang and Salcedo 2013, 5–7.

19. Jang and Salcedo 2013, 5–7.

20. "NSCB Fact Sheet," National Statistical Coordination Board 2010. http://www.nscb.gov.ph/rucar/pdf/fs/FS_ancestraldomain_Oct10.pdf, accessed March 8, 2013.

21. Barton 1919, 1–33.

22. Ibid.

23. Florendo 2011.

24. Ibid.

25. Ibid.

26. Ibid.

27. See Dulawan 2005, 115–125.

PART III

Body, Mind, and Spirit

CHAPTER 9

Gender, Popular Religion, and the Politics of Memory in Taiwan's Urban Renewal: The Case of the Twenty-Five Ladies' Tomb[1]

Anru Lee and Wen-hui Anna Tang

The Twenty-Five Ladies' Tomb was the collective burial of the female workers drowned in 1973 in a ferry accident on their way to work at an export-processing zone in Kaohsiung, southern Taiwan. The fact that of the 70-plus passengers on board all 25 who died were unmarried young women, and the taboo in Taiwanese culture that shuns unmarried female ghosts, made the tomb a fearsome place. Young men encountering beautiful young women who turn out to be ghosts is a common theme in Chinese literature and folklore (classic and contemporary) and movies. Oftentimes these women are said to be waiting to find a husband, especially if they died unmarried. Although coming across a phantom is rarely a welcome event to the Taiwanese—and many people would actively try to avoid such an experience—there is apparently something enlivening about meeting a beautiful female ghost. A survey conducted at a university near the Twenty-Five Ladies' Tomb shows that the tomb was a popular topic of banter among students.[2] Male students would jokingly remind one another that they should have a female friend occupying the back seat before they ride their motorcycles through the tomb site; otherwise they might have an unexpected "love encounter" with one of the ladies.

Yet, it is precisely these mostly negative emotions and responses provoked by the "maiden" status of these deceased young women that propelled feminists in Kaohsiung to voice their disapproval of the way these women were treated, both when they were alive and after they died. For some years these feminists had wanted the Kaohsiung city government to change the name of the tomb. They also wanted the city government to renovate the tomb site. However, their calls were not answered until the Kaohsiung city government began to incorporate tourism into its urban revitalization plans. In order to reinvent the city's economy, the Kaohsiung Mayor's Office finally allocated money to clean up the gravesite and remake it into a tourist-friendly "Memorial Park for Women Laborers."

Against this background, this chapter looks at the recent renovation of the Twenty-Five Ladies' Tomb and examines the politics of memory as they are expressed through the various meanings given to the deceased women. People involved in the renovation included the families of the deceased, the Kaohsiung city government, and Taiwanese feminist groups—most notably the Kaohsiung Association for the Promotion of Women's Rights (hereafter, KAPWR). They all had different considerations and therefore diverse expectations regarding the future and purpose of the tomb. At the center of the controversy was the unmarried status of these women upon their death. Anthropologist Arthur Wolf postulates in his seminal article "Gods, Ghosts, and Ancestors" that three different beings exist in the pantheon of Taiwanese popular religion, and together, they closely reflect the social world: gods, who were previously mandarins representing the emperor and the empire; ancestors, who were senior members of the patrilineal family representing the line and the lineage; and ghosts, who came from a heterogeneous group of strangers and outsiders and are thus dangerous and despised.[3] However, in this supernatural world, the status of these three categories is relative. For example, whether a particular spirit is viewed as a ghost or an ancestor depends on the standpoint of a particular person. One person's ancestor is thus another person's ghost.[4] Also, Taiwanese popular religion has always been "flexible and individualistic in the sense that there is no one authority, church, or theocratic state [that] establishes dogma and determines belief."[5] Therefore, hypothetically, every spirit or any spirit can become a god or attain some godly or god-like standing. Yet, practically, whether a spirit can convince other people about its godly status is closely related to its spiritual power or efficacy, that is, whether the spirit can answer requests or grant favors.[6]

A son by his birth right is a part of his father's patrilineal line, and he is entitled to a place on his father's ancestral altar; he will become an ancestor after his death. A daughter, however, is not given this privilege. Patrilineally, a daughter is a temporary member and, eventually, an outsider of her father's family. Therefore, marriage as a social institution is particularly significant for women, for it serves as both a symbol of and a gateway to their ultimate (though subordinate) position in the Taiwanese kinship system.[7] Normatively, it is through marriage that women are accepted into their husbands' families and permanently integrated into a lineal line, although there are variations of and exceptions to this practice.[8] Correspondingly, if a woman dies a violent death before marriage, she can become a ghost if she is not properly prayed for. Spirit marriage—where a female ghost marries a living man—has been strategy adopted by such a woman's family to ensure that she is cared for in her eternal life.[9] Marriage also provides the opportunity for men and women to perpetuate the family line through childbearing, the failure of which is considered a serious breach of filial piety in Taiwanese culture even today. Economically, marriage also grants, especially to women, some financial support and social security as men continue to be seen and act as primary breadwinners in contemporary Taiwanese households. Together, these concerns—religious/spiritual and economic/material—have made many generations of Taiwanese parents anxious to find their sons and daughters a suitable spouse; it is a priority for them as parents.

The parents of the 25 deceased women thus faced the quandary of how to ensure a final settling place for their unmarried daughters who died an untimely, violent death while acknowledging that these daughters are essentially outsiders, strangers, and thereby ghosts to their natal families. The ghostly connotations derived from these women's unmarried status are also at the root of the feminists' critique. However, for many of these families, the "ghosts" are not merely metaphysically but literally ghosts with whom members of the families interact. They appear, express their sorrow, and demonstrate their grievances. The reestablishment of peace and order essential to residents of both the living world and the afterlife thus hinges upon mutual understanding and close collaboration between them. Yet, as meanings are constantly contested, so is the nature of the deceased's requests. The different interpretations that the (living) sociopolitical forces give to the deceased's needs open up new terrains of contestation for the memory of the past and the rights and obligations at the present. The deceased are hence agencies that inform changes in the social life of the living.

THE FERRY BOAT INCIDENT AND ITS AFTERMATH

Taiwan had been a manufacturing powerhouse in the world. The export-processing zones in Kaohsiung were the first of their kind in the world. They were established to attract foreign direct investment, which has proven crucial to Taiwan's post–World War II economic development. The manufacturing jobs created by the factories inside the export-processing zones and elsewhere in Taiwan not only contributed to the success of Taiwan's export-oriented economy but also helped to bring employment opportunities to many families, especially those families with young daughters.[10] Indeed, the image of thousands of young women riding bicycles—and, later, motorcycles—out of the entrance gate of an export-processing zone is a part of the collective memory of the Taiwanese who lived through the heyday of Taiwan's export-oriented industrialization in the 1970s and 1980s.

Cijin used to be a peninsula attached to Kaohsiung. However, it was separated from Kaohsiung and became a tiny island of a few fishing villages as a result of the expansion of the Kaohsiung Port in 1967. For many years thereafter, people had to rely on privately owned ferries to travel between Kaohsiung and Cijin. Traditionally, many parts of Cijin were poor fishing villages, and the local families were able to raise their family incomes only when their daughters started manufacturing jobs. Every morning, these young factory workers would meet up with other Cijin residents to take the ferry to work. On the morning of September 3, 1973, a small boat with a maximum capacity of 13 passengers was loaded with more than 70 passengers, many of whom were export-processing-zone workers rushing to work. This in and of itself was not unusual; the ferry owner had been doing this for quite some time even though it was illegal. Only on that fatal morning, the boat capsized: 46 passengers were saved and 25 were drowned. All of the 25 drowned passengers were unmarried young women. Many people in Kaohsiung did not perceive this as a coincidence but, rather, a sign of supernatural significance. A widespread story supporting this ghostly interpretation of the fatal event tells of one of these 25 women, one who was first rescued and sent to the hospital for treatment. Just when everybody thought she was about to be saved, she suddenly turned to her mother waiting at her bedside and said hastily: "I am going to be late. My sisters, they are waiting for me. I have to go now." After that, she died and became the last casualty of the ferry incident. To further support the otherworldly interpretation, one married woman was first rescued but then pronounced dead; yet, she miraculously came back to life later on.

Shortly after the ferry incident, the Kaohsiung city government intervened and helped to settle the pension and compensation issue. The city government also helped to find a plot of land big enough to accommodate the graves of all these 25 women after their families decided to have them buried in one location. Parents of the deceased also began to address these women as "sisters" and refer to the collectivity as a "sisterhood." Later, in 1988, because the land of the tomb site was acquired for the expansion of the Kaohsiung Port by the government, the tomb, along with other graves from Chong-chou village, where the families of the deceased lived, was relocated to a new seashore site. This time the Kaohsiung city government also erected a memorial gateway (inscribed with the "Twenty-Five Ladies' Tomb") for the new site. Compared to the original burial ground, which was at a fairly remote corner of Cijin Island to which not many outside visitors would usually go, this new location is right beside a main road of Cijin. It sits facing the Taiwan Strait, enjoying a scenic view of the coastline. The public land across the road from the tomb has been renovated and made into a part of the Cijin Tourist Port Area since the relocation of the tomb.

Families of the Deceased Telling Stories

As far as the Kaohsiung city government was concerned, the ferry incident had come to a relatively satisfactory conclusion when the legal and political responsibilities of the ferry owner, the ferry captain, and other concerned parties were settled; when the bereaved families were financially compensated; and when the collective burial of the 25 deceased was established. For the families grieving for their lost daughters, however, there was still unfinished business. Specifically, where and how to place the spirits of those who died unmarried presented a great challenge to these families.

These families, however, were presented with something other than a spirit marriage to care for their daughters. A few years after the ferry accident, after the collective burial was completed, some members of the grieving families began to report paranormal incidents. Mr. Kuo, the father of one of the deceased women, told us about the nature of these incidents that was later repeated by many other families. He said:

> I heard this from my wife . . . [It all started with] that mother down the block. She went to consult a tang-ki [spiritual medium] in our village [about her daughter]. The tang-ki told her not to worry, because her daughter now learning to become an "enlightened being" on the side of Kuan Yin [the Goddess of Mercy]. The tang-ki also suggested to the mother that she could have a "god statue" made for her daughter and place the god statue at home.

The idea behind the tang-ki's suggestion was that, as the daughter has become a maid of Kuan Yin, she is no longer an unmarried daughter spirit who should not enter the ancestral shrine, but a soon-to-be (if not already a) deity who could be revered by faithful believers including her previous family. Essentially, this suggestion offered the mother a culturally sanctioned solution to provide a permanent and respectable residing place for her daughter who died unmarried.

Shortly thereafter, many families told similar stories, and, before long, the deceased young women, including Mr. Kuo's daughter, received their "god statues." In spite of the fact that many of these god statues were welcomed into their fathers' houses and revered as someone with a pious status, they (except one) were not placed in the family altar along with these women's patrilineal ancestors and other gods worshipped by the families. Instead, they were placed in a separate altar of its own on a different floor of the house. A few other families chose to leave their daughters' god statues at a public Kuan Yin temple in Cijin. In addition, the oldest among these women came back and disclosed herself as "Yi-miao Buddha," a title said to be granted by the Jade Emperor at the Heavenly Court. She also chose her eldest sister to be her spiritual medium, who was stationed at Miao-feng Temple, waiting for her sanctified younger sister to appear and help all the sensual beings coming for help. As a matter of fact, it was through the revelation of Yi-miao Buddha that some of these women were said to be practicing religious virtues. Their god statues were therefore placed at Miao-fen Temple.

The transcendence of these deceased women from being maiden ghosts unable to be incorporated into their patrilineal ancestral shrines to becoming pious beings worshipped by their families provided their families with a culturally reputable solution to care for their daughters in the afterlife. However, as shown above, the variations of where and how these women's god statues are placed also exemplify the ambivalence that many parents of the deceased felt—and continue to feel—about their daughters' said elevated religious position, even though they respectfully had their god statues made. Having a god statue erected for a spirit is a major undertaking. Before the erection of the statue, the regarded spirit should have performed miracles to benefit people. Accordingly, after the statue is bestowed, the relationship between the spirit/deity and the people who made the statue is stabilized and the bonds of mutual obligations between them are established.[11] Private (god) statues may be set up in domestic altars, resonating with the exceptionally flexible nature of Taiwanese popular religion. Whether the gods can attract worshippers beyond the private households, and extend their power and develop themselves into deities of a neighborhood, a village, or even a bigger locality, depends on their ability to perform marvels.

Efficacy was evidently an issue in the minds of the families when their deceased daughters requested to have their god statues made. For example, Mr. Kuo, mentioned above, was not swayed at once by his daughter's request. Later, he was bothered by constant headaches for which his doctor could not find a cause. People told him it was a sign from his daughter, who was asking him to make a god statue for her, but Mr. Kuo still did not think there was anything that supported his daughter's request. Only when he was cured from a cold after drinking a glass of water obtained from the Ladies'

Tomb did he agree that his daughter had shown efficacy that warranted a god statue. He was further convinced when the mother of another deceased woman told him that a couple (husband and wife) had been seen paying respects to the tomb on the 1st and the 15th day of every lunar month, because the 25 ladies saved the husband's life from a shipwreck by directing him to the nearest shore.

That an ailment of unknown causes was first inflicted upon a family member by their deceased young daughter but later also cured by her is cited by many of the families as a proof of the efficacy shown by the deceased woman. Yet, skeptics remained. One Mr. Chuang, who placed his daughter's god statue on an altar separate from the Chuang ancestral altar, commented on the act of some parents as inappropriate—if not to the extent of transgression—of leaving their daughters' god statues at the local Kuan-yin Temple on the assumption that these young women had now become a part of the entourage of the Goddess of Mercy. He did not think that the deceased had proven themselves as holy enough to be worshipped by the general public at a village public temple. Similarly, nearly all the believers seeking help from Yi-miao Buddha came from out of town. When we asked the eldest sister and spiritual medium of Yi-miao Buddha why this was the situation, she said bitterly that local people tended to disregard the deceased women as "ugh, those twenty-five." It appears that the larger local community has not been convinced by the miraculous stories of these women.

FEMINIST FRAMING OF THE DISCOURSE

Just as the unwed status of these deceased young women caused the biggest worry for their parents, it was also the popular cultural and religious assumptions associated with their maiden identity that were at the center of the feminists' critique. On April 2, 2004, right before Ching-ming Day, the traditional tomb-sweeping day in Taiwanese society, the KAPWR called a press conference, in which members rallied for the reconstruction of the tomb and equated the reconstruction with gender equality and with Kaohsiung's status as a progressive city (because of its advocacy for gender equality). Two days later, on Ching-ming Day, then-KAPWR Secretary Wen-hui Tang (a coauthor of this chapter) published an op-ed article entitled "Women Who Cannot Go Home" in *China Times,* a major daily newspaper in Taiwan, in which she commented on the custom that Taiwanese married women could commemorate only their husbands' ancestors but not those of their natal families. The article also highlighted the predicament of Taiwanese women like those young women buried at the Ladies' Tomb who not only did not have an easy life while alive but also did not have anyone to venerate them after their deaths just because they died unmarried.

The timing of submitting this article for publication was carefully chosen. It came right when many people in Taiwan were returning home, reuniting with their families, and getting ready to observe likely the most important duty required of offspring in Taiwanese culture. Therefore, the article came as a keen reminder of a fundamental inequality between men and women in Taiwanese society. The article also resonated with a primary concern of the Taiwanese feminist community at the time. In 2003, the Awakening Foundation, the most prominent women's organization in Taiwan, held a "From Maiden Temples to the Gender Politics of Ancestor Worship" press conference on Ching-ming Day, criticizing the fact that only married women could enter an ancestral hall and acquire a life of eternity, leaving all other kinds of women (e.g., unmarried, divorced, or lesbian) forever uncared for. Ultimately, the press conference concluded that this cultural practice had the oppressive effect of endorsing (heterosexual) marriage as the single most important accomplishment in a woman's life and excluding other alternatives for one's life trajectory. Since this first press conference, the Awakening Foundation has continued to call press conferences on the issue of women and ancestor worship around Ching-ming, the latest one having taken place on April 3, 2009. Another example of feminist efforts along these lines was the publication of *Going Back to My Mother's House on New Year's Day: Culture, Customs, and Gender Equity Education*,[12] a collected volume of essays written by affiliates of the Taiwan Gender Equity Education Association (TGEEA), of which Wen-hui Tang is an active member. The title of this book is meant to be a strong critique of the cultural practice that dictates that a married woman eat "Reunion Dinner" on Chinese New Year's Eve with her parents-in-law, her husband and unmarried children or married sons and their wives, her husband's brothers, their wives and children, and unmarried sisters of her husband. According to the custom, a married woman can visit her natal family only on the second day of New Year, for she will be receiving guests of her husband's family along with her mother-in-law on New Year's Day. It is also said that she will bring bad luck to her natal family if she stays with them on New Year's Eve. Since then, the TGEEA has been working hard to raise the general public's awareness about the gender bias embedded in Taiwanese culture and customs.

As a way to combat the cultural bias against deceased unmarried women, the KAPWR activists emphasized the role of the 25 deceased women as manufacturing workers who helped to build Taiwan's economic miracle. They also highlighted the fact that these women died on their way to work, thereby making their deaths job-related casualties. The feminists maintained that a focus on these women's work roles, as opposed to their unmarried status, would also aid in advancing the public's awareness that Taiwanese women have made great contributions to the economic growth of the country. After its first press conference in 2004, on Ching-ming 2005, the KAPWR held a memorial service at the tomb attended by KAPWR members and their families. Another press conference was held on Ching-ming 2007. Individual KAPWR members, many of whom were college professors, also wrote academic articles, newspaper essays, and commentaries on the topic, and many of these professors incorporated the tomb into their own classroom discussions.[13]

These efforts eventually paid off. The Kaohsiung city government commissioned film director Ke Wan-ching to make a documentary about the lives of the 25 women and the tragic ferry incident that took their lives. Director Ke did more than that. Her film, *The Lost Youth: Women and Industrial Work in Taiwan,* is not just about the 25 women but also portrays the labor history of women, starting from the 1970s when Taiwan's economy began to take off. The film takes the audience through the days when young girls fresh out of elementary school joined the factory workforce and labored for the livelihood of their families and the collective fortune of Taiwanese society, thus giving the life stories of the 25 women some much-needed context. After watching the film at the premier in 2008, then-Kaohsiung mayor Chen Chu, herself a single woman in her late fifties at the time, commented: "The story of Taiwanese female workers is the history of Taiwan. [Our] society should give [all women workers] the long-awaited recognition that they deserve." *The Lost Youth* was later shown on many occasions to the general public and on college campuses as well as at subsequent Kaohsiung film festivals.

The Dead in the Politics of the Living

In spite of the positive responses to the KAPWR's pursuit, the Kaohsiung city government was slow to change the tomb's appearance. Only in early 2006 could one begin to see some signs of action. At a municipal press conference, the Mayor's Office revealed the "Cijin: An Island for Tourism" project, which was a part of the city's larger plan to develop urban tourism. To ensure the overall success of the "Cijin" plan, it was essential to change the public image of the tomb site so that the place did not look or feel like a graveyard. The Twenty-Five Ladies' Tomb would be renovated into a "Memorial Park Dedicated to Workers Dying of Job-Related Accidents."

The announcement of the "Cijin" plan did not win much admiration from KAPWR members. They pointed out that the Kaohsiung city government still addressed these 25 women as "young girls" in its public announcements, in spite of its self-declared effort to change the image of the tomb site. Also, the fact that the new park would be devoted to all laborers, not specifically to female workers, seemed to indicate the city's offhand approach to gender issues. There appeared to be a long process of negotiation before anything further happened. In the end, four mayors later, the city government finally decided in 2008 that the park should be renamed the "Memorial Park for [All] Women Laborers," a decision endorsed by the KAPWR.

During the course, the Cijin District Office, the frontline local government unit in charge of executing the tomb's renovation, also worked hard to communicate with the deceased's families about how to redesign the space. Initially, many of the deceased's families simply could not understand—and therefore were not forgiving of—why the government wanted to dig up their daughters once again. Mr. Lin, the Cijin District Office clerk who served as the liaison to the deceased's families, had to come up with a list of talking points in order to persuade these families what the city government intended to do was beneficial to them, including: (1) As it had been more than 30 years since the ferry incident, and the parents of the deceased were aging or had already passed away, whether the younger generations in the families (e.g., younger siblings and siblings-in-law, nephews, and nieces) would continue to worship and care for their deceased maiden sisters or aunts remained to be seen; (2) The tomb site was susceptible to sabotage—and had been damaged—by gamblers in illegal lotteries or loiterers, and as a result, the tranquility of the deceased was constantly disturbed; the place needed better maintenance; (3) The great contributions of the deceased to the development of Taiwanese economy were conveniently forgotten because of the emphasis on the negative image attached to their maiden status and the supernatural accounts derived from the negative image; (4) The deceased had transcended themselves to be enlightened individuals and elevated their standing in the heavenly order; they were no longer ordinary supernatural beings and thus should be worshipped in a way that reflected their new celestial position; and (5) The tomb would look out of place as soon as the "Memorial Park for Women Laborers" was finished; it was thus in need of a facelift.

To appease the deceased young women and their living family members, Mr. Lin also threw wooden divinatory blocks to ask for the deceased's permissions every step along the way. The families would not agree to make any decisions or changes unless they got a positive answer from their (deceased) daughters. In our interview with him, Mr. Lin actually mentioned that the young women did not always answer positively to the different requests of the city government or their own families. Many a times, it took many tries before the spirits responded, and when they finally responded, they did not always consent to the requests made to them. There were also times when the women simply did not respond. "In the end, I had to consult with religious specialists and learn to phrase my plea in a harder-to-refuse way." Mr. Lin explained, "Once after I pretty much exhausted every possible means I could think of [to plead with one of the spirits,] I told her I was only a minor employee who took orders from some big boss [read: the mayor] and begged her to understand my predicaments. As soon as I said that, she granted us a positive response. [These women] certainly understand the difficulties of being someone's subordinate!" Looking back, Mr. Lin could now speak light-heartedly about the testing moments he had with these supernatural beings. However, from the standpoint of Taiwanese popular religion, not getting a response or a positive answer from a spirit is an indication that the spirit is unwilling to commit itself. It could also mean that the spirit is displeased about the question/request bestowed on it. In other words, the 25 deceased women did not appear to be too keen about the idea of having their resting place disturbed or of remodeling their resting place into a park.

The list that Mr. Lin came up with was significant. His list of talking points had to touch the hearts of these families (Points 1, 2, and 4) while addressing the government's policy in a way that could be understood by these families (Points 3 and 5). This is not to say, however, that there was no difference or disagreement between the city government and the deceased's families. For example, initially, the families of the deceased wanted the tomb to be renovated into something like the Eighteen Lords Temple at the northern tip of Taiwan. The Eighteen Lords Temple was originally "a simple roadside shrine for unidentified bones—the sort that sits unat-tended and almost unnoticed all over the countryside," but has grown into one of Taiwan's major temples and enjoyed unprecedented popularity since the 1980s.[14] From the perspective of these families, the Eighteen Lords Temple resembled the Twenty-Five Ladies' Tomb in the nature of its ghostly spirits who also suffer from the lack of a proper place on an ancestral altar. Its success in attracting a large number of worshippers, believers, or visitors and, accordingly, enjoying exuberant incense burning seemed to present the best kind of prospect for the Twenty-Five Ladies' Tomb for these families. The majority of the families also insisted that the name the "Twenty-Five Ladies' Tomb"—or, at least "Twenty-Five Ladies" or "Twenty-Five"—should be kept. They also wanted the presence of a tomb or an architectural structure of worship where they could place the urns and/or hold memorial services.[15] They also expressed their wish to keep the memorial gate. The parents were concerned that no one else in the family would be making regular offerings to their daughter-gods after they passed away. Essentially, the families of the deceased were envisioning a refurbished tomb/temple/memorial hall with a redecorated memorial gate, surrounded by the new, friendly "Memorial Park for Women Laborers" with flowers and plants. A memorial gate was import-ant; it was to serve as the gateway to the shrine of the 25 enlightened ladies.

However, it had always been the position of the Kaohsiung Mayor's Office that there should be no trace of the tomb left after the renovation. Accordingly, there should not be anything remotely resembling a shrine or temple, and the existing memorial gate had to go. In the end, the government prevailed. The individual graves of these young women were removed, and trees and meadows were planted. At the center of the park is a sculpture of a Buddhist lotus on a pedestal that symbolizes the afterlife status of deceased women. On September 3, 2008, thirty-five years after the fatal ferry incident, the Memorial Park for Women Laborers was inaugurated. Mayor Chen's words, "[Let's] Remember our sisters who labored [and] Wish for a city of happiness," along with a long inscription that explained the purpose of the park, were engraved on the pedestal of the Buddhist lotus sculpture.

The Tomb as a Thrice-Told Story

Although it took a long while and many mayors, the Kaohsiung city government eventually responded to the KAPWR's call and renovated the tomb site and its surrounding environment. The inscription engraved on the lotus sculpture reflects much of the KAPWR's appeal that society should recognize these women as industrial workers who made great contributions to Taiwan's economy and who lost their lives for their jobs. All of these seem to suggest the triumph of the feminist endeavors. However, in retrospect, one wonders why the tomb had to be transformed into a sanitized park in order to make right the gender inequality and social injustice inflicted on these young women. Were there any compelling reasons of why the continuing existence of the tomb—or an unequivocal look of the tomb—would hinder the cause of gender equality or the recognition of these women as hard workers crucial to the post–World War II development of Taiwan?

For the parents who lost their daughters in the ferry accident more than 30 years ago, there was probably never any doubt that their girls were filial daughters and hard workers. During the course of our research, quite a few parents we interviewed had tears in their eyes while telling us how considerate their daughters were that they understood the hardship borne by their parents in order to support a big family. They told us that these girls selflessly shared their parents' burdens, took care of their younger siblings, and always put their own desires secondary to the needs of the family. Some of them also mentioned that their deceased daughters were seen dressing in white coming back to visit and making sure everything was alright with their families. Mr. Chuang, who was mentioned earlier in this chapter, became charged in our interview as he recalled the moment at the funeral of these young women when, according to Taiwanese custom, parents were called upon to whip the coffins of their unfilial children who died before their aging parents: "That was just pure nonsense! How could anybody bear to think these girls were unfilial? They were humble, good daughters." At the funeral, Mr. Chuang tried to stop the parents—and indeed succeeded in many cases—from whipping their daughters' coffins. Yet, Mr. Chuang also had a definite opinion about the spiritual tablet placement of women who died unmarried. "It has been like this since the beginning of history that no parents worship their dead children; [and unmarried] daughters' tablets shouldn't come back home," he insisted.

The parents of the deceased were deeply worried about their daughters, who should have been married and led fulfilled lives of their own, but instead died a violent and untimely death. Yet, they also followed the normative value that dictates against incorporating the spirit of a female descendant into her patrilineal ancestral shrine. This dilemma propelled them to seek help beyond their individual households. A public acknowledgment of their daughters as hard workers (as endorsed by the government and feminists) was certainly welcome, but this was not the point. Ultimately, they were looking for some assurance that the welfare of their daughters' spirits would be continuously and regularly cared for. This became clear to us when Mr. Lin, the aforementioned Cijin District Office liaison, came to us one day with an urgent look. He wanted us (whom he took as having some special ties with the Kaohsiung city government) to reaffirm for the parents the city government's promise to hold a spring memorial ceremony (on Ching-ming Day) and a fall commemoration service (on the day of their daughters' deaths) in front of the Buddhist lotus sculpture every year. The city government made the pledge in order to placate the families before the tomb renovation. While we felt we could not speak for the city government, we promised that we would at least hold a service ourselves with our students the coming spring. However, it was apparent from the expression on Mr. Lin's face that our promise failed to give him and the families the conviction they were seeking. It was the government's firm commitment that they wanted to hear.

Last but not least, the timing of the tomb renovation begs for closer examination. While we credit the KAPWR's persistent efforts to press the government for change, the change came at a time when the development of tourism in Cijin became a part of the Kaohsiung city government's plans to revive the city's economy. Given the strategic location of the Twenty-Five Ladies' Tomb, it became understandable why, from the perspective of the government, removing the phantom image of the place and rebuilding it with a new, sanitized look was necessary. Accordingly, the city government's portrait of the deceased as noble workers dying on their jobs could be a part of the city's attempt to develop urban tourism. After all, what could be a better symbol than the image of 25 young women dying tragically on their way to work to characterize the romance and pathos of Kaohsiung's past as a blue-collar, working-class city? The gender implications of the tomb story are thus subsumed under the government's economically minded urban revitalization effort.

NOTES

1. Portions of this chapter have been adapted from Lee and Tang (2010, 23–49). Used by permission from the *Journal of Current Chinese Affairs*. The article and the journal are available free online at www.CurrentChineseAffairs.org.

2. Tang and Cheng 2010, 33–67.

3. Wolf 1978, 131–182; also see Jordan 1972.

4. Wolf 1978, 146.

5. Harrell 1974, 203–204.

6. Harrell 1974, 204.

7. Martin 1973; Wolf 1972.

8. Hsun 2000, 15–43; Lee 2008, 373–393; Shih 2007, 89–104.

9. Harrell 1986, 97–116.

10. Lee 2004; Anru 2009, 120–129.

11. Lin 2008, 454–477.

12. Chien-ling and Hsiao 2005.

13. Tang 2013, 811–826.

14. Weller 1994, 141.

15. Wang 2006, 11–13.

CHAPTER 10

Shakti's New Voice: Anandmurti Gurumaa and Female Empowerment[1]

Angela Rudert

INTRODUCTION

At some point in the latter half of the 1980s, even though she was at the top of her class, Gurpreet Grover took a hiatus in her academic studies at the Government College for Women in Amritsar, Punjab (India), to attend to matters she would later come to understand and articulate as "more pressing." In just a few years' time and barely into her twenties, Gurpreet would be known as "Swamiji" to many housewives in Amritsar, and then known later (as she is today) by the name Anandmurti Gurumaa, or simply Gurumaa. In 2009 when Gurumaa spoke the words "more pressing" at this same college while participating in an event held in her honor, she was referring to the "more pressing," all-compelling, spiritual quest, which in her early twenties took her away from home, school, city, and family. What might be seen as "running away" in some contexts, in the devotional context, that surrounds the very public guru persona of Gurumaa today; her flight from Amritsar can be seen quite differently, as empowering, and perhaps even as revolutionary.

That Gurumaa, a well-known contemporary spiritual teacher by 2009, with nearly a decade's history of offering discourses (*pravāchan*) on Sony and Aastha satellite television networks, would be invited as an honored guest back to the college she fled says something about the way that people today view the woman she has become.[2] In addition to being a high-profile spiritual teacher, Gurumaa has become somewhat of an activist in matters of girls' education, making frequent and adamant statements about a girl's right to receive an education and putting her organization's money toward that cause through the establishment of a nongovernmental organization (NGO) called Shakti, dubbed in ashram literature as "an initiative to empower the girl child." Shakti's flagship initiative is an education tuition program for girls in primary and secondary schools. The Government College event celebrated Shakti's newest program, one providing scholarships to needy female students at the college. We might view Gurumaa's return and acceptance of the honors bestowed on her as indicative of her gratitude for her own education, and perhaps also to reveal a sense of kinship felt with those who guided her as a young person enabling her to become the woman she is today.

Stories of the lives of spiritual adepts possess a certain power, especially as these stories intertwine with, inform, and inspire the lives of those who admire them and follow their teachings.[3] This chapter explores tradition and innovation in Gurumaa's quest narrative and other ways in which Gurumaa tries to establish a transformation of tradition while remaining deeply rooted in it. Gurumaa's spiritual quest narrative functions paradigmatically for her devotees precisely because it relies on "tradition" inherent to the Indian subcontinent. Another important way that Gurumaa seeks to transform from within tradition is through her invocation and embodiment of the concept of shakti, which theologically understood is the divine power of transformation and change and a power that in Indic tradition has been understood to be feminine. Gurumaa's own feminist theological stance, though it does not stand clearly or solely in any one of the Indian dharmic traditions, nonetheless draws on indigenous spiritual resources rather than those of so-called Western feminism to effect transformation.

Following this introduction, I briefly introduce Gurumaa's activism conducted through her Shakti NGO, the initiative seeking to "empower" and discuss multilayered understandings of power (shakti). I also consider some of Gurumaa's strong words against gender discrimination and women's empowerment, and how she points to herself as exemplar. I follow this with the story of Gurpreet Grover's "running away," and I tell it in the spirit of and from the perspectives of devotee story tellers who told it to me, as a narrative of a valiant spiritual quest. Sometimes, when indicated, I relay narrative I have learned from Gurumaa's own words in both public and private settings. Retaining the devotional flavor helps to reveal the narrative's meaning in the lives of those who admire Gurumaa.

I then briefly point to the ways in which Gurumaa's own evolving narrative has informed and influenced the lives of some of her female devotees who participated in my ethnographic research. These convergences reveal that at least some women see Gurumaa as a model and have even integrated elements of her story into their own lives. Robert Orsi, who coined the term "narrative overlaps," found through an examination of his own family lore alongside the devotional biography of a female Catholic saint from the "home-land" (Italy) that "the two sets of stories regularly intersected so as really to constitute a single genre of popular narrative—a kind of domestic hagiography."[4] Living histories, which we may consider as hagiographies-in-progress, of Gurumaa and of her female disciples, are perhaps more difficult to pin down while lives are so fully being lived than they were in Orsi's study of lives already departed.[5] At yet another level, the stories of female gurus, becoming more prominent and plentiful in our current time than ever before, will also shape and form what future generations may understand to be the *master narrative* of the guru role.

"A Ladies' Guru"

In her now relative position of strength as a public figure and guru in control of some economic and social capital, Gurumaa actively seeks to empower girls and women. I take Gurumaa's "active" efforts, as demonstrated in her words—spoken and sung, then presented in various media forms—as well as her social service endeavors, to be her activism.

Educational aid programs, including the financial aid scholarships at Gurumaa's alma mater, fall under the umbrella of the Shakti NGO. Over a decade ago, Gurumaa's NGO began as a fairly simple tuition donation program for schoolgirls up to 12th standard, allowing needy families to apply for tuition payments made directly to schools.[6] Recipients are predominantly the girl children of widows and single parents, or orphans, thus particularly vulnerable in terms of their access to education.[7] Gurumaa does not characterize herself as a humanitarian or as a social service guru. She once explained to me that social service was not her main "gig," but rather a "side dish," albeit one that had become "very colorful."[8] Shakti programs have since grown to include initiatives beyond tuition donation, such as awareness campaigns.

In one particular case, Gurumaa's actions reflect the common strategy with grassroots feminist activism in India, particularly in her inversion/reinterpretation of a popular regional festival that for generations has celebrated the births of male babies to one that instead celebrates new births of female children. According to Gurumaa, she introduced the practice of making cash gifts to families of girl babies at a *Lohri* celebration in Ludhiana, Punjab, in 2007. Similarly, the Sangtin writers group, grassroots activists in the Sitapur district of Uttar Pradesh, introduced an alternative for the popular festival *Gudiya*. In place of the common tradition of thrashing the *gudiya* (female rag doll), the activists instilled the practice of swinging the *gudiya*. So without "snatching away" a time-honored tradition, they introduced changes from within it.[9]

Beyond her financial efforts to empower girls, this female guru's spoken words indicate that she cares more about social justice than she does censure from religious authority. For this reason, I have heard her characterize herself as a "revolutionary mystic," as "firebrand," and even as "renegade." And, not surprisingly, this is how her disciples see her too. Indeed, it is through her activism toward empowering women and girls that we might best attempt to understand Gurumaa as a "revolutionary." Gurumaa's revolutionary qualities may have less to do with her NGO endeavors—many gurus male and female alike, traditional or New Age engage in similar social service—and more to do with her very direct, verbalized attention to ways Indian society ought to bring about change in the way females are treated from their time in the womb forward as well as the ways parents should be raising their boys to respect women. Marie-Thérèse Charpentier, in her study observing 70 modern female gurus and assessing "female guruhood," acknowledges Gurumaa's revolutionary spirit: "She consciously uses her socially sanctioned position as spiritual master in subversive ways, thus challenging all forms of oppression that support patriarchy."[10]

The multivalent English words "power" and "empowerment" can be understood from varied perspectives. Similarly, the Sanskrit word *shakti* has multiple meanings in contemporary Indian settings, languages and dialects, as well as a history of meanings in Indian scriptural traditions. Theologically, *shakti* is traditionally recognized as the feminine cosmogonic power as well as the creative power existing—however dormant—within all beings. One helpful way to understand *shakti* in the setting of contemporary yogic gurus, like Gurumaa, is to look first at its literal meaning. *Shakti* comes from a verbal root meaning "to be able." As the meaning of *shakti* expands into the yogic context, it can be seen as "that which is an effective power," a "power of transformation, a power of change, a power of creativity."[11] When the power of change comes from within the seeker as a spiritual awakening, or from inside an educated girl who has worked to achieve her education, it can be *empowering*. One of the many clever Shakti NGO tee shirts sold in Gurumaa's ashram reads "Shakti inside," bringing home Gurumaa's message that *shakti* exists "right here" in the embodied human form of the wearer.

On the yogic path of guru devotion (*guru bhakti*), the power of transformation is that *shakti*, which the guru manifests, embodies and emits a power capable of awakening or igniting the *shakti* within another. Modern spiritual teachers have sometimes utilized the metaphoric language of the guru as electrical transformer or power-station (*shakti bhavan*). Such a "powerhouse" has the capacity to transmit power beyond the station. Keeping in mind this yogic perspective of power as *shakti*, and *empowerment* as the awakening of the transforming power already existing within human beings, *shakti* then is both the power itself and the empowering transformation; thus, it is the power and the empowerment.

A more academic way of thinking about empowerment might focus on the multilayered forces of oppression that disempower women. I have found Gurumaa's language to strike surprisingly close to that in Western and Indian feminist literature. I encountered this language in our very first meeting on July 4, 2006, in Hudson Valley, New York. There, I asked Gurumaa how her Shakti initiative empowers girls and asked her to elaborate on what she means by "empowerment." Gurumaa replied that Shakti NGO provides three types of empowerment for recipients of her tuition program.[12] Secular education empowers the girls materially so that they are not dependent on men for subsistence. Meditation instruction empowers them spiritually to realize enlightenment is available to them. And martial arts instruction empowers them physically to defend themselves against unwanted advances from men.[13] With her multilevel scheme of empowerment, Gurumaa attempts to teach young girls already disempowered by intertwining structures of economic, religious, and social hierarchies to claim material, spiritual, and physical powers. Gurumaa's adoption of the Sanskrit *shakti* (f.) to name her NGO constitutes a reclamation of feminine power. Some scholars, and perhaps some of her followers, might see Gurumaa as attempting "to rescue *shakti* from its patriarchal prison."[14]

Gurumaa speaks so frequently about gender, women's discrimination, and women's empowerment that her publishing house compiled excerpts from discourses into video and print media, all under the title *Shakti*.[15] Disciples laud her for "lambasting" traditional religions, and I find strong textual evidence in her writings and discourses to support their claim that Gurumaa is fiery in her critiques, especially in regard to the male dominance of traditional religion. She contends that, historically, male "so-called caretakers of religion and duty" willfully interpreted scriptures to keep women down by continually telling them, "'Because you are a woman, [you] are impure, therefore, you will never gain knowledge. You will not attain salvation.' What madness is this!"[16] Here, Gurumaa speaks directly against Manu and other writers of Hindu *dharma* texts, but she also addresses religious misinterpretations by "caretakers" in other religious traditions that have denied women's aptitude for enlightenment or otherwise stripped them of religious authority. Interestingly, in the Sikh tradition into which she was born, women do have access to salvation apart from men. However, she criticizes Sikhism for not progressing in gender equality beyond that espoused by the original gurus and for the tradition's dearth of female saints and teachers. Gurumaa offers a feminist critique of Abrahamic traditions in these volumes as well.[17] Then, she points to herself to oppose such wrong interpretations, presenting her own "enlightened" female body as demonstration of women's independent access to salvation.[18]

Gurumaa's public speaking is replete with references to the mistreatment of girl children in India, to their lack of equal access to education, to their lack of decision-making power, to their having to carry the burden of family honor (*Izzat*) on their shoulders, and to their incorrectly perceived impurity due to menses. Gurumaa does not shy of directly criticizing an audience made predominantly of listeners from Punjab or Haryana for the skewed child sex ratios in these two prosperous states, which indicate the highest incidences of female feticide in the nation. She goes on to talk about an "imbalanced India" in which the shortage of girls turning marriageable age has led to new social problems for women and the nation. She refers specifically to incidents in which teenage girls are bartered, trafficked, and sometimes forced to serve large families as wife to multiple men. The nation cannot prosper without women, she tells us. When addressing a mostly middle class audience, she not only informs her listeners of these statistical realities, but she does so in a "Yes, I'm talking to you!" tone when she tells them "You *must* educate your daughters before you marry them!"

Making no reference at all to gender, I asked a woman sitting next to me at Gurumaa's public program in Nagpur, Maharashtra, what she liked about Gurumaa, and she replied that Gurumaa speaks to real women's issues, their emotions, and their real lives. I asked, "Is your husband here today also?" (Usually the answer was yes.) She answered emphatically, "No, she's a *ladies'* guru!" I looked around the VIP section where I sat that day and 90 percent of the audience in that section was female. On the rest of the grounds, women also outnumbered men, if only by a slight margin. I thought to myself, women often outnumber men in Indian spiritual gatherings. Gurumaa herself has noted this to me in conversation. So, what about Gurumaa makes her a guru for the ladies?

For at least half of Gurumaa's two-hour program that night, she spoke about the strength of women. In all the places where I heard Gurumaa speak in large, free, public programs, and even in her smaller private settings, in cities large, medium, and small including Nagpur, Gurdaspur, Pathankot, Kolkata, Delhi, and Jaipur, she consistently directed a good portion of her discourse toward raising awareness of women's issues. For instance, when she gave five days of Amrit Varsha talks (usual duration per city), she typically spoke at length about woman-centered topics and her Shakti NGO during one of her program's final days, when the crowd would swell.[19] In various places, Gurumaa drives home these words (paraphrasing): *You should not be so concerned about marrying your daughters. Let daughters choose for themselves to marry or not and concern yourselves with their education, thus enabling them earn for themselves. Life is not about marriage only.*[20] In Nagpur, she continued, "Look, I am not married and I have a life." In all locations where I have listened to Gurumaa, she spends a good portion of her overall time speaking on women's power and women as the embodiment of *shakti*, and she offers practical advice on how to raise stronger, more self-sufficient daughters who have the capacity to earn for themselves and their families. She asks that parents not spoil their boys, insisting they teach them to respect women. She states regularly that a good marriage is a total partnership in which no one is the boss.

Gurumaa's words often challenge the status quo in a way that words spoken from within "traditional" religious perspectives do not. Herself empowered by a modern, Western-styled English-medium secondary and college education, scriptural study of Indic and other religious traditions, and, most importantly for her, experience, Gurumaa levels critique at what she sees as the misrepresentations and misinterpretations of so-called "truth" coming to us as "dogma" from within "tradition." Standing outside of tradition, indeed refusing to be "put into any box," or to be named as belonging to any religious tradition, yet drawing from many, Gurumaa is in a strong position from which to offer critique. No religious authority can yank away her pluralistic and charismatic power. However, she is a revolutionary, one might say, only so far as she is innovative. Thus, it is the degree to which she ably reframes, reshapes, and rearticulates from within tradition (albeit a very broad pan-Indic plurally religious one) that she is able to effect change.[21]

Karen Pechilis has suggested that the public prominence of female gurus occurring today provides a "creative space" for understanding "inherited issues of women's spirituality."[22] Contemporary female gurus take varied stances on womanhood, spirituality, and women's roles, and they offer these stances vis-à-vis their own differing physical forms and appearances.[23] Furthermore, female gurus offer diversity within the already-diversified religious (and multireligious!) role of a guru.[24] Kathleen Erndl reminds us, "Hindu gurus are a non-institutional institution" whose authority often comes from the guru's personal charisma rather than through hierarchical structures.[25] Female gurus independent of authoritative institutional hierarchy, like Gurumaa, who remains independent of both institutional sanction and "ism," occupy a "site of undetermination," a term coined by Kumkum Sangari that Meena Khandelwal finds useful in her examination of Hindu female renouncers.[26] Khandelwal explains that for women, just the act of taking vows of renunciation, in the prominent ascetic order she observes, is a transgressive act. Similarly, just in being a "guru," a woman is already transgressing something. Both Hindu renunciation and guruhood provide already-flexible boundaries ready to be reshaped and restructured by the entry of female spiritual adepts. When we take into account also the fact that traditions of renunciation and guruhood exist outside of what we might call "Hindu," throughout pan-Indic religious forms, then we might begin to see more "sites of undetermination" and "creative spaces."[27]

Looking at the life and work of Gurumaa, a charismatic, outspoken, noninstitutionally aligned female guru alongside stories from the lives of her female followers, not only reveals some "narrative overlaps" but also will allow us to observe guruhood as a contemporary, vibrant example of a "creative space" for women. Furthermore, it offers us a window from which to observe tradition and innovation in a contemporary woman-directed spiritual movement, answering Pechilis's call for a "nuanced approach to tradition and innovation in women's religious leadership."[28]

TAKING FLIGHT

Gurpreet's spiritual journey in the late 1980s dictated that she take a literal journey, a solitary one, all over North India. She traveled for four years visiting famous religious places, sitting with different teachers and seeking answers to her questions and, as disciples attest, achieving enlightenment. When Gurpreet fled from her home in Amritsar, she went beyond the boundaries of home and city and the Sikh tradition into which she was born and from which she attained a wellspring of inspiration. Despite the precedence of such spiritual journeys and the casting aside of one's comfortable life, this journey was well beyond the boundaries of appropriate or proper behavior for a young woman growing up in North India in the 1970s and 1980s. Gurpreet's journey, though it follows a tradition, breaks with it as well. The notion of a solitary spiritual quest and subsequent realization of the self, of God, or of the attainment of enlightenment or Buddhahood could fit into the hagiographies of countless numbers of contemporary gurus as well as those of rishis, sage-kings, *sants*, bhakti poet-singers, and founders in whose names religions would follow, like Siddhartha Gautama, the Buddha. The great predominance of such figures making extensive solitary journeys across South Asia has been male.[29] In other words, such a flight from home is part of the master narrative of the Indian holy man, but not necessarily part of the narrative of a holy woman. When a woman sets out on such a journey, the stakes are often high.

Gurpreet traveled in government buses and in general class seating on trains. She encountered many people along the way who questioned her: "Why are you alone?" "Who is your guru?" Gurumaa explains today that she never felt alone and recounts that she would answer, "God is with me!" (*Paramātma mere sāt hai!*); "My guru is inside!" (*Mere guru andar hai!*).[30]

Certainly Gurpreet's parents, even though they had always been supportive of her all-encompassing spiritual life, would have been given cause for concern when their daughter left home on a spiritual journey with no specific intention to return. Eventually, they heard the word that she was in Rishikesh. The family in Amritsar consulted a clairvoyant, who confirmed for them her location and foretold of her plan for an imminent (solitary) retreat into the "jungle" (or forests) of the Himalayas.[31] As many seekers have done before her, she was about to leave the world for the Himalayan wilderness and would go "the very next day." In 2008, during the first week of my earliest research stint in India, in Gurumaa Ashram, Gurumaa called me for a private meeting. Speaking as a woman who does not see her life merely as her own but rather as an extension of God, she explained to me during this encounter that she had wanted to live in a cave in the Himalayas, but that the solitary life was not her destiny, as yet; rather, she was repeatedly moved in the direction of teaching others, "Students kept coming." My storyteller, a long-time disciple from Amritsar, explained that right after Gurpreet's parents learned of their daughter's plans, a family member searched and found Gurpreet in Rishikesh, bringing her home.[32]

Gurpreet returned to her family home without struggle, the devotional narrative goes, but her family also made certain concessions. There was a renewed understanding on their part that this daughter's spiritual life would take precedence over all else for her. In their modest yet comfortable middle class family home, she was given a room of her own where she could engage in her spiritual practices undisturbed, and it was fully understood that she would not be coerced or expected to marry. She was now a mystic in a state of oneness with God, and therefore, God was all that she needed. There was not room in her life for marriage and family, she has always explained. Besides, to echo her own more current language, who could meet her at her level anyway? In keeping with her very confident air, in public discourses, Gurumaa would later make it clear to those who listened that no man could match her.

Gurpreet's early journey away from home in search of truth serves as a fitting metaphor for breaking with tradition while engaging in the keeping of a good deal of it. Not only did she make her own version of the traditional Indian spiritual journey and, as disciples profess, attain her enlightenment, but she has also adopted the life of renunciation "in her own way," as one devotee puts it. Since Gurumaa teaches listeners coming from primarily Hindu and Sikh religious traditions themselves—traditions in which spiritual knowledge, especially in the form of discourse, more typically comes from males—and she does so in the absence of institutional sanction or lineage, we might surmise that Gurumaa does indeed do things "in her own way."

Gurpreet's return to Amritsar and the end to her solitary journey reflect her early recognition and acceptance of her role as a spiritual guide. According to the story I have pieced together here from its narrative parts offered by a guru and her disciples, instead of leaving the world, as she was tempted to do, Gurpreet turned back and integrated the "treasure" that she had found into her particular life in the world. This was a life surrounded by those who loved and nurtured her to that point, many of whom are still "with her" in various capacities today.[33]

In some ways saints' achievements can seem unattainable, thus making them difficult to think of as models.[34] Often standing out as extraordinary, as a figure who "overlaps with the ordinary social world, yet stands quite apart from it," a living saint may be understood as an exception rather than a model; what applies to the saints is difficult to apply to all.[35] Some devotees do see Gurumaa as such an exception and not a model for their own lives. However, Gurumaa straightforwardly points to herself as an example demonstrating that women can attain the highest spiritual state and that they can do so in this lifetime, in a woman's body. As her story of returning to Amritsar tells her admirers, it is also possible to do so without leaving the world. Her life may tell us that while solitary quests are valuable, indeed crucial in some form on the yogic path, integration of what is discovered in the quest is also possible, even desirable.

For devotees, the stories from Gurumaa's life history become, in a sense, sacred texts. Gurumaa is a 51-year-old contemporary teacher, and therefore, her biography has not yet been written. It is still being shaped. We can see elements, even from this short fragment of Gurumaa's life story, repeated in the lives of some of her female disciples, particularly the courage to go off on one's own and the establishment of one's own space in a home.

Tradition, innovation, and boundary expansion are evident from the beginning of Gurpreet Grover's life, especially in the short story of her flight from and her return to Amritsar. I add to this story Gurumaa's somewhat autobiographical song, *Suno Suno* (translated from the original Hindi), to provide a tangible example of how Gurumaa gives new voice to old ideas, and in doing so reclaims transformative power (*shakti*) and broadens the audience of spiritual knowledge.[36]

The studio mixing of the song *Suno Suno (Listen!)* gives it a global sounding beat. It is a song made attractive to the young with Western rock, Irish folk, Indian folk, and Indian "filmi" melodies. Unaccompanied, Gurumaa sang the lyrics for a studio recording. Her voice was then mixed with recordings of various instruments, the *sārangi*, flute, and penny whistle, and a choir. Despite the loud, rollicking music created by the other instruments, Gurumaa's voice, the "new instrument" (*naya ye sāz*), stands out with clarity, force, and repetition, making the message in her lyrics easily understood.

Gurumaa composed *Suno Suno* for the explicit purpose of inspiring girls to take flight and to soar, to learn to draw their strength from within themselves, to find devotion, and to find the effective power for transformation (*shakti*) already existing within.

Sunno Sunno! Sunno Sunno!	Listen! Listen!
Sunno Sunno! Sunno Sunno!	Listen! Listen!
Sunno Sunno meri awāz	Listen to my voice,
Sunno Sunno naya ye sāz (repeat)	Listen to this new instrument.
mujhe pankh mile hain āj	Today, I have gotten my wings
mujhe leni hai ik parvāz (repeat)	I have to take flight!
Sunno Sunno! Sunno Sunno!	Listen! Listen!
Sunno Sunno! He Sunno Sunno!	Listen! Hey, Listen!
Mujh se chale ye jahān	From me the world turns
Mujh se hai teri ye shān (repeat)	From me comes your glory.
Mujh se mile hai bhakti	From me devotion is received
Main hi hoon teri shakti (repeat)	I myself am your *shakti* (strength, power)
refrain	*refrain*
Kuch chāh jagi hai mann mein	Some desire has awakened in my mind
Nayī rāh milī hai mann mein (repeat)	I have found a new path in my mind
Naya gulsita banāoon	Let me make a new garden
Nayī duniyā main basāoon (repeat)	Let me establish a new world
refrain	*refrain*
Roshan karoon main jag ko	Let me light up the world
Koi raah meri na roko (repeat)	Let no one block my way
main hoon shakti main hoon nari	I am shakti. I am woman.
koi samajhe na bechāri (repeat)	Let no one see me as a pitiable girl
refrain	*refrain*

Listen to My Voice (*sunno sunno meri avāz*) by Anandmurti Gurumaa, trans.
Angela Rudert. (Used by permission of Anandmurti Gurumaa)

When Gurumaa sings from the narrative perspective of *shakti*, as the
Goddess Shakti, she gives this ancient theological concept voice in the contemporary world. And in this song, Shakti identifies herself as a power not
just accessible to male gods in trouble with demons, but also accessible and
already existing within the listener, male or female.[37] In both of Gurumaa's
early mixed gender audiences, girls were prominent among the listeners. The

Gurumaa Ashram. (Rishi Chaitanya Ashram)

first person voice, both as the *shakti* existing within and as its embodied form—the female guru—tells the second person to "listen!" (*suno suno*) and discover his or her own *shakti*.

Here in the song *Suno Suno* and elsewhere, Gurumaa points to herself as an embodiment of *shakti*. Both male and female gurus can be understood as embodiments of *shakti*. The female gurus, however, might be understood as "the classic embodiment[s] of shakti."[38] Gurumaa stresses that women, particularly, are embodiments of *shakti* because through their bodies they create life. When one recognizes *shakti* within herself, she gains strength. She must take "flight" (*parvāz*). She will create a "new world" (*nayī duniyā*) and she will not be seen as a "pitiable girl" (*becāri*). The first person singer of *Suno Suno* is both the empowered one—here, the guru—and the power that exists within the seeker's own form, within her own being. If the second person listener cannot yet recognize herself as *shakti*, then she might be able to see power reflected in the form of the guru or hear it in the guru's voice.

"A ROOM OF ONE'S OWN"[39]

Though it is obvious that Gurumaa intends to help underprivileged girls in India get their education and get empowered through that material means, she spends most of her time speaking to well-educated listeners—some of whom also become donors to the Shakti program—who may be empowered in some ways, but not in others.

Gurumaa attempts to awaken her listeners to the reality she teaches through her own body, that women can and do reach the highest state. She sings out "Listen! Listen! Listen! Listen to my voice . . . I am *shakti*. I am woman." Gurumaa is not shy. She is not necessarily even humble. She stands independently in her state, whatever that is and whatever people see it to be, exuding confidence in who she is and what she is and where she comes from. Some disciples see her as Durga, others see her as Radha, others see her as Krishna. One male Sikh devotee in Mohali, Punjab, once described her confident air to me: "When Gurumaa walks into the room, it's as if Guru Govind Singh himself has entered!" So for many, not surprisingly, her figure, her form—in addition to embodying "bliss" (*ānanda*), as her name suggests—denotes divine power (*shakti*).

In taking a room of her own in her parent's Amritsar home for spiritual practices (*sādhana*), Gurumaa sets an example that many of her followers have emulated or would like to emulate. For most, living in joint or nuclear family settings, extra space in a home is scarce. Setting aside quiet, private space for meditation (*dhyāna*) and other yogic practices like breathing exercises and postural yoga (*pranayāma* and *āsana*) has become an ideal for the modern (middle class) spiritual aspirant, espoused by a number of contemporary gurus, including Gurumaa. I met disciples of Gurumaa in six different cities who had established rooms or areas in their homes for yogic *sādhana*. Most of the time, the area could serve dual functions, both as a very private space for meditation or yoga *āsana* and as a communal space for the family's worship at the home-temple (*ghar mandir*)—a sacred space certainly not unknown to female religious expertise.[40]

In spring 2009 I visited Gurumaa's family home and saw what I call the "room of her own," preserved on the top floor to retain the atmosphere of those days when young Gurpreet returned to Amritsar as Swamiji. I was struck by the privacy and simplicity of the space. I learned from the disciple who accompanied me that during the time Swamiji was living in this room, a devotee might wait at the steps below for hours to be invited in, because in those years, having just returned from her quest, which we might consider to be her "flight," Swamiji spent much time in heightened states and private devotion. The family home sometimes became crowded with devotees waiting for Swamiji. In a recorded interview with Charpentier, Gurumaa explains, "I had my space. I always had my space because I know that we have to create our own space, so I was creating my space, always. But it was hard for them."[41]

Two days after seeing Gurumaa's Amritsar room, I visited a disciple in Jalandhar who proudly showed me her home-temple and meditation space, a small room added to the rooftop of her home. Adjacent to drying laundry, open air, and urban views, it struck me immediately that her space was very similar to Swamiji's Amritsar "cave" in its privacy and in its location at the top of the home. Similarly, the poised Jalandhar woman who kept the shrine and used this room often had recently informed her parents that she has no interest in marriage and, rather, needs the time and space for *sādhana*. Hers is a room available to all, but it is strictly preserved for spiritual practice; thus, most of the time it is a room of her own. Like Gurpreet, she has created her own space. Similar to the narrator of *Suno Suno*, this young woman in Jalandhar has "found a new path" (*nayī rāh milī hai*) and is not letting anyone—potential marriage prospects or, most particularly, her parents' interest in them—"block her way." Instead of moving permanently into the ashram, which she sometimes considers, she seeks to integrate her spiritual life with her life in the world, living with her family. She has created a flexible work life that earns for her and her family, allowing time for *sādhana* at home in Jalandhar and the freedom to make frequent trips to Gurumaa Ashram. In its own unique way, this Jalandhar devotee's narrative resonates with Gurumaa's story, not only in the creation of private space at the top of one's home but also in this seeker's determined intention toward the spiritual life and the integration of that life in the setting of her relationships.

Many disciples, both male and female, have answered my questions about what it means to have a female guru with words to the effect, "The guru is beyond gender." The answer did not surprise me; I had expected to encounter something like this and was nearly ready to drop the question altogether.[42] Sitting with three women and one man in Jaipur, all devotees of Gurumaa and self-described seekers (*sādhaks*), one of the women admitted that on one level, it does help her a great deal that Gurumaa is a woman. Because of this, she can go to her guru's ashram a lot and do so freely, without censure from her husband or family, who might otherwise have concerns for her vulnerability in spending copious time with a male guru who could be out to take her money or exploit her sexually. Other women in the room began to admit: "Yes, there is no way my husband would have let me go to that 30-day retreat in the ashram had my guru been a male. We were not even allowed to make phone calls!" or "Of course I get to spend more time with her because she's a woman!"[43] The reality for the women sitting in that small group nodding their heads—and for me—is that taking time away from domestic roles is not an easy thing to do, for householders generally and not least for women. Just integrating career responsibilities with domestic roles is challenging. Women give to their families. They give to their careers. But on the spiritual path, householder women give something to themselves. Many women might ask, "Can I take the time just for myself?" In her life example and in her words, Gurumaa says, "Yes, you can and you must!"

Householder women today are challenging and expanding so-called boundaries and expectations of their religious roles. In this regard, today's prominent and public female gurus—changing the master narrative—have broken a glass ceiling of sorts for female spiritual aspirants looking for a model. As women have entered the workplace, their domestic roles are already in flux, a tension in and of itself. Notwithstanding the need for *sādhana* in their lives, Gurumaa speaks about contemporary women who already work "second shifts" in their double roles as both provider and care-giver.[44] Now women also seek integration between these roles and their spiritual seeking and ensuing discipline. This classic tension, and challenge of integration, exists in the lives of seekers in general, and in this age, it exists poignantly for female seekers whose religiosity is expanding to include practices not originally designed by or for women, such as postural yoga (*āsana*) and other disciplines.

I met women in cities across North India who had incorporated yogic *sādhana* into their already busy lives, full of responsibilities to family and career, and the integration they sought and achieved came in numerous patterns. I met self-ascribed "housewives" engaged in *sādhana*. I met women whose children were already settled or away from home at school, leaving them more time. I met women whose husbands traveled and lived in far-off places for work, in the army or in the Middle East, leaving them open blocks of time for ashram visits. I met widows for whom *sādhana* has become the main focus of life. I met retired married couples engaging in *sādhana* together.[45] I met some women who were choosing not to marry, making their spiritual quest the higher priority in their lives, like Gurumaa's devotee in Jalandhar.

That Gurumaa is reaching a younger generation of educated women with her voice is evident in the number of educated women in their twenties living in Gurumaa Ashram as full-time residents, and others who visit regularly. Many of these women have just finished their education and are primed to work or marry or both, yet they choose to live a celibate, austere, and simple life focused on their goal. It is true also that some of these women come and go from the ashram, ultimately finding their place on the "outside" (*bahār*), choosing to struggle through the tensions inherent, yet seeking balance, in the householder life. Whether choosing to live a renouncer's life in an ashram or outside in the world, any true seeker, Gurumaa says, is a *sadhu*, one pointed straight at the goal.[46]

A female devotee's living history may or may not include narrative overlaps with that of her guru. And certainly not all gurus point to themselves as models. Even some of Gurumaa's devotees will utter statements like, "Oh she too high, too high!" indicating some self-doubt amidst the admiration. In this sense the guru becomes transcendent, extraordinary, and unreachable and thus the guru's life becomes the exception, not a model to be followed. With the voices of female gurus and their female students growing ever more powerful in the democratizing context of Internet technology, master narratives are indeed being reworked. Guruhood has been a boys' club, but it is no longer that. Female gurus in general, and Gurumaa among them, are creating a new space for women as specialists in 21st-century Indian spirituality.

CONCLUSION

Gurumaa's stage is a global platform upon which female religious leaders broadcast their voices and their embodied forms to those who will listen and see, utilizing not only internal websites but also social media. This "new age" is one in which a female guru's voice is not only heard but also broadcast throughout the globe. This is an age in which the voice of a woman from Amritsar, Punjab, can be heard by people from anywhere in the world at any time. This is a world in which a female spiritual leader can travel freely across boundaries and borders to places her mother and grandmother perhaps never dreamed of going. This is an age in which the *feminine voice's* potential audience is ever expanding through time and space.[47] Anandmurti Gurumaa also demonstrates that this is an age in which women's voices have the power not only to effect change but also to reclaim space in recorded history.

In this "new world," urban middle class women in India and around the globe are practicing spiritual arts and discipline not previously intended for them. It is a world in which a young woman can choose to live a celibate life in an ashram and then change her mind about it later. She can play basketball or become an engineer.[48] Gurumaa tells us it is a world where this young woman can choose whether or not to marry and has the "human right" to choose her partner. Gurumaa uses her voice, a "new instrument" enabled by *shakti*, as Shakti, to call out—to Indian girls in need of schooling, to potential donors, to ardent devotees, to casual listeners, to seekers. Gurumaa sings out "Listen, Listen!" offering hope that a new age is dawning as she seeks to "light up" a "new world." Offering narratives, visual and audible alike,[49] pointing to herself and then pointing to others, she invites her audience to do the same.

NOTES

1. Much appreciated financial support from FLAS and Fulbright-Hays enabled ethnographic fieldwork in India for 11 months in 2008 and 2009, during which I lived in Gurumaa's ashram and traveled to meet with devotees and to see Gurumaa's teaching presentations in various locations around India. I offer

my appreciation to Anandmurti Gurumaa and to many of her devotees who graciously participated in my study. My gratitude goes also to Ann Grodzins Gold, Marie-Thérèse Charpentier, and Juliana Finucane for their early readings of this chapter and to Zayn Kassam for encouragement and much valued editing. Much appreciation goes to Jishnu Shankar, who graciously offered advice on my translation of the song *Sunno Sunno*. This chapter also owes its current shape to helpful discussions of its earlier versions in Madison, Wisconsin, and in Syracuse, New York.

2. Gurumaa's free public discourses are called *Amrit Varsha* (lit. "rain of immortal nectar"). The TV show by the same name features recorded *Amrit Varsha* discourses given at various places throughout India and around the world. The word *aastha* means "faith," and the Aastha TV network hosts a number of TV gurus, mostly Hindu and mostly male.

3. Orsi, 2005, 110–145.

4. Ibid., 112.

5. For a thoughtful discussion of hagiography and how the process of biography—and hagiography—making occurs during the lifetimes of the contemporary female gurus she observes, see: Charpentier 2010, 51–55; 117–120.

6. Gurumaa feared that, in some cases, funds sent to families would get used up in drinking, gambling, or another purpose than a girl's education, and therefore, the program sends funds directly to schools.

7. In one case I know of, Gurumaa has made a tuition donation for the schooling of a young boy. He is an orphan cared for by grandparents and the sister of a "Shakti girl." She explained that it seemed the right thing not to discriminate against the brother just because he is not a girl.

8. In addition to education through 12th standard, the flagship program of Shakti, Gurumaa has begun offering tuition scholarships such as those at her alma mater, the S.R. Government College for Women, Amritsar, as well as to needy young women studying at other higher education and professional training institutions. Information here comes from an internal source: the Shakti NGO profile sheet used as a press release by Gurumaa Ashram.

9. Nagar and Sangtin Writers (Organization) 2006, 92–93.

10. Charpentier 2010, 257.

11. W.K. Mahony. (Audio recording) *Tantric Scholars Panel*, Yoga Journal Annual Convention, Estes Park, Colorado, 2008. In this recording, Mahony, in his role as a scholar-yogi, offers this perspective to a group of yoga teachers and practitioners in the United States.

12. Our conversation was specifically about the tuition program for school girls up to 12th standard; it was not about her college tuition program or other programs that now exist under the Shakti NGO umbrella.

13. Gurumaa explained to me that she and her ashramites taught martial arts and meditation instruction as well as other yogic bodily practices to "Shakti girls" (as they are referred to in the ashram). In 2010, I witnessed their

instruction in both meditation and postural yoga (yoga *āsana*) when "Shakti girls" were brought to the ashram.

14. Erndl 2000, 96.

15. See the following works entitled *Shakti*: Gurumaa 2006a, 2006b, 2008.

16. Gurumaa 2006a, 43–44. In spoken English, Gurumaa sometimes uses "salvation" to describe the state of "enlightenment".

17. Gurumaa (2006a, 2008).

18. Gurumaa (2006a, 43–53).

19. The video recordings of Gurumaa's large public *Amrit Varsha* programs such as these, with anywhere from 5,000 to 40,000 in attendance (location dependent), are utilized for Gurumaa's TV program by the same name (now also published on YouTube).

20. Anandmurti Gurumaa, *Amrit Varsha*, Nagpur, February 18, 2009, translated.

21. For more on Anandmurti Gurumaa's religious pluralism, see: Rudert 2014.

22. Pechilis 2004, 30.

23. Charpentier 2010; Pechilis 2004

24. The role of a spiritual teacher has been important in almost every religious tradition existing in India, including Hinduism, Buddhism, Jainism, and Sikhism, and also in Indian Christianity and Sufism.

25. Erndl 2004, 246.

26. Khandelwal 2004, 43. Khandelwal quotes and cites Sangari 1993, 867–882, 872.

27. It is worth noting here that Pechilis also points to the fact that female gurus whom scholars might call Hindu have the "tendency to avoid calling their paths 'Hinduism' in favor of a path of spirituality open to all." Pechilis, "Introduction," 35.

28. Pechilis 2004, 6.

29. Mirabai was said to have traveled from Rajasthan to Vrindavan and then to Dwarka in Gujarat, where she disappeared at Krishna's shrine. Contemporary South Indian female Hindu guru Karunamayi Ma also made a solitary journey in her spiritual quest. In the devotional biography on Karunamayi Ma's website, her parents are portrayed as having known from the very beginning of her life that she was special and would challenge norms of womanhood to become a great *yogini*. Charpentier 2010, 137–142, mentions Karunamayi Ma's journey in a section entitled "Going to the forest."

30. Anandmurti Gurumaa, *Amrit Varsha*, Kolkata, 30 January 2009.

31. I put the word "jungle" in quotations because the disciple-storyteller who shared this part of the narrative used it in her English telling. The word "jungle," a common Hindi-English word for forest (*jangal*), carries with it a connotation of being uncivilized. For instance, it can be used in a setting far from the forest to indicate an uncivilized (*jangli*) way of being. I understand my

storyteller's use of this word to indicate Gurumaa's parents' perspective of the Himalayan forest as a dangerous place for a young woman alone.

32. This Amritsar disciple-storyteller's own history with Gurumaa began shortly after this return.

33. Here I echo Gurumaa's own language. Gurumaa regularly refers to her spiritual attainment as her "treasure." Some of her own family members live "with her" in her ashram and others come to visit her there and support her mission and way of life. Some of her most senior householder disciples moved nearby so that they could remain "with her" and work in the ashram as paid workers. Gurumaa's senior-most disciple, a male contemporary from Amritsar, was "with her" before and after her solitary quest and remains close to her now, living in the ashram.

34. See Narayanan 1999. See also Hallstrom 1999, who points out that even though Anandamayi Ma initiated some women into renunciation, she never advised her female followers to imitate her, but, rather, often took the "do as I say, not as I do" tactic with her female disciples.

35. Pechilis 2004, 23.

36. Proper transliteration would be *Sunno Sunno*, but I use *Suno Suno*, to be consistent with Gurumaa's publishing house, *Gurumaa Vani*, and her record label, *Mystica Music*. Translation mine.

37. I reference here the *Devī Māhātmya,* a scriptural source in which the Great Goddess emerges from the collective fiery anger and force (*shakti*) of male gods as they impotently face demons too powerful. The Goddess handles the situation handily within the 579 verses extolling her glory.

38. Pechilis 2004, 34.

39. The subtitle of this section was adopted from Virginia Woolf's famous essay by the same title, where she asserted that in order for a woman to succeed as writer, she would need a room of her own and 500 (British) pounds. It seems an apt metaphor to use here since Gurumaa stresses the material needs of girls along with her own life's example of taking a room of her own.

40. Numerous scholars have written about women and domestic religious ritual in Hinduism, from the standpoint of women's "folk" traditions. See Wadley 1977, 127.

41. Charpentier 2010, 201.

42. See Khandelwal's reflections on gender and the "ungendered" soul: Khandelwal 1997.

43. The italicized words are paraphrased from field notes taken immediately after the conversation. Field notes January 25, 2009.

44. I heard this language in informal discourses in the ashram and in *Amrit Varsha*, Kolkata, 31 January 2009. See also *Soul Curry* (vol. 2.2, March–April 2008), 37.

45. I met one couple who live inside the ashram full-time, devoting their retirement years to full-time spiritual seeking, their own new version of *vānaprastha*.

46. *Sādhaka* (Hindi *sādhak*), *sādhu,* and *sādhana* all come from the same Sanskrit verbal root, *sadh*, to reach one's goal.

47. It is notable from a theological perspective that the name of a primary Vedic deity, *vāc*, means voice, or sound, and that the deity is feminine.

48. Gurumaa 2016.

49. Ibid.

CHAPTER 11

Storytelling for Change: Women's Activism and the Theater of Pritham Chakravarthy[1]

Kristen Rudisill

Pritham Chakravarthy, assistant professor of Dramaturgy and Film History at the Ramanaidu film institute in Hyderabad, has had a long, illustrious career as an actress, translator, and writer. She calls what she does now "Applied Theater," and while that unites all her work under a neat category, the genre, like her oeuvre, is considerably more complex than a simple label can convey. Theater scholar Helen Nicholson expresses her concerns that this convenient term may reduce "a rich diversity of theories and artistic practices to a single homogeneous discourse," noting that the primary binding characteristic of the genre is "intentionality—specifically an aspiration to use drama to improve the lives of individuals and create better societies."[2] Editors of the *Applied Theater Reader,* Tim Prentki and Sheila Preston, define the term as "a broad set of theatrical practices and creative processes that take participants and audiences beyond the scope of conventional, mainstream theater into the realm of a theatre that is responsive to ordinary people and their stories, local settings, and priorities" and "denotes the intention to employ theatre processes in the service of self-development, wellbeing and social change."[3] Chakravarthy's version involves the technique of storytelling added to a variety of applied theater approaches that make her work both effective and unique. While some of her goals involve being "transformative," as Philip Taylor describes applied theater, some of them are focused more directly on being "explorative" and "affirmative." All her work grapples with the politics of representation and issues of the body as she attempts to expand both her own and her audiences' points of understanding and experience as well as to benefit in some way the communities she is representing. Additionally, all her pieces, whether fictional or nonfictional, tell women's stories; through these stories, Chakravarthy emphasizes women's agency, choice, and power in an Indian context, whether they are found in educated and privileged circles or in the considerably more marginalized circles.

Growing up in an orthodox Brahmin family in Madras (Chennai) in the 1960s, Chakravarthy trained in classical dance and music, though her parents never thought of performance as a viable career option for her. These arts were popular among upper-caste communities during this time of heightened nationalism as they taught discipline as well as pride in Indian arts and familiarity with Indian stories. Most (if not all) of the veena music and bharatanatyam dance repertoire that Chakravarthy learned would have revolved around narratives of the Hindu gods. The Madras elite, as Lakshmi Subramanian shows, was greatly invested in classical music because of its versatility and ability to function as a marker of traits as diverse as tradition, modernity, spirituality, artistry, nation, and education.[4] Unlike most of her female cousins, who were content to perform for self-improvement and increased marriage potential purposes, Chakravarthy was determined to perform on stage, in front of audiences. There were a few avenues available for her to do this that would have been acceptable, but her maternal uncle Kamesh's involvement in Brahmin-oriented amateur theater led her in that direction. When she was six years old, he suggested that she perform a small part in a play for which he was producing music. Although her acting and her preferences of theatrical genre and method have changed over the years, once Pritham Chakravarthy got on stage, there was no getting her off.

She participated as a child actor in dramas put on by the sabha troupe Shanti Theatres, thanks to her family connections, but had to give it up when she finished her 10th standard. She says that she had to quit

> because my mom thought it wasn't appropriate if you are going to be devoting yourself to graduate study and then get married properly. It doesn't sound nice when you put in your matrimonial column: college educated, trained in Bharata Natyam and veena and cooking and housekeeping . . . and does stage plays. It was not possible for me to get a "good" Iyer maappillai [fiancé] if I put that as a qualification.[5]

For similar reasons, when she finished high school she was not allowed to apply to the National School of Drama in Delhi like she wanted to, so she ended up studying for a BCom degree at Madras Christian College, which had an active theater community. For Chakravarthy, college and activism started together: just a week after beginning college, she joined the Students Federation of India (SFI), the student wing of the CPM (Communist Party of India, Marxist), working as a translator for the Delhi-educated upper cadre who were having a hard time recruiting Tamil-speaking students.

She was excited to be involved in theater again, but the theater program at Madras Christian College was not that satisfying for her because it was primarily English-language theater, and she had a hard time understanding the relevance of Western plays to either her own life or the lives of others in the audience. It was, however, a shift away from the very Brahmin-oriented commercial genre of sabha theater that she had been part of as a child actress. Chakravarthy's dissatisfaction persisted, though she continued to participate by both acting and doing backstage work for college productions, until Professor Joseph James directed an English-language production of Bengali Badal Sircar's 1972 play *Procession*. This production was both innovative and relevant, even in translation, to Indian audiences in Chennai. Chakravarthy saw the play and said of it, "I did not know who Sircar was at that time, I only went for that play as an audience and I was blown off by the thought, by the entire form of that theatre itself."[6]

Sircar calls his work "third theater," designed to bridge the "unfortunate dichotomy between urban and rural life"[7] in modern India. Urban theater, as Pritham's experience with Madras Christian College demonstrates, was rooted in the English theatrical system and ran parallel to the traditional indigenous theater of the countryside. Sircar's project has been "to analyze both the theater forms to find the exact points of strength and weakness and their causes, and that may give us the clue for an attempt to create a Theatre of Synthesis—a Third Theatre."[8] He worked to take the popularity of the traditional and folk theaters and combine it with progressive action and the advanced ideas of the urban theater in order to produce plays that would connect people with "their own problems of emancipation—social, economic and cultural."[9] Thanks to a Jawaharlal Nehru Fellowship in the early 1970s, Sircar was able to travel and interview figures including Jerzy Grotowski, Richard Schechner, Julian Beck, and Judith Malina, who eschew the expensive, distancing proscenium theater productions that Sircar was having trouble connecting to the Indian experience. He writes of this trip: "What I found is that the theatre workers of the West are learning a lot from the Indian folk theatre and dance forms and are realizing the value of the use of the *live* performer and of *direct* communication, while we in our pride in city theater are neglecting what is there all round us."[10] From Grotowski,

Sircar borrowed something from the idea of "Poor Theater," where the performance is stripped of other art forms and techniques—music, lighting, sets, costumes—to focus on the body of the performer, but also took the idea of "poor" theater literally, trying to produce plays inexpensively and thereby create opportunities to both perform and view the productions. From Schechner, Sircar borrowed some of the principles of Environmental Theater as he tried to find new, non-proscenium style venues in which to perform. At Beck and Malina's Living Theater, Sircar recognized shared purpose in focusing on human consciousness and responsibility, and emulated their involvement and seriousness of approach to an openly political agenda. *Procession* gave Chakravarthy a vision of what a progressive, yet decidedly Indian, modern theater could be.

Chakravarthy's earliest work on social issues and performance, however, was not on a stage, but in a film studio. The lines between television, film, and theater are blurred in Chennai, and actors and writers very often cross between the media. Her aunt, Kamala Kamesh (who I interviewed in 2004 and who was married to the uncle who had first put Chakravarthy on stage at age six), was starring in an experimental film in Tamil, and "Kudisai" Jayabharathi, the director, a close friend of her aunt and uncle, asked Chakravarthy to play a small role in it. She was in her second year of college, and Jayabharathi put Chakravarthy in touch with Gnani Sankaran, who had started the alternative theater group Pareeksha in 1978, just the year before, in order "to present plays that 'are for the middle class.'"[11] Sankaran, too, was sensing the theater gap in India, where plays were either for the upper-class English-speaking elites or entertainment-based folk plays for more commercial audiences. By doing plays with progressive themes in Tamil on proscenium stages, Sankaran's work attempted to bridge that dichotomy. Sankaran founded Pareeksha when he left Koothu-p-pattarai, the revolutionary troupe he had founded in 1976 with N. Muthusamy.[12] He was with Koothu-p-pattarai for two years until he "had differences with the Koothu-p-pattarai regarding communication strategies . . . They thought that someday an audience would emerge that would understand their plays. This did not happen and the audience daubed all *avant garde* groups with the same brush. Also, more groups did not emerge, as expected, on the Tamil parallel theatre scene."[13]

When Chakravarthy read about Sankaran's new troupe and found out they performed plays by Indian writers like Sircar and Vijay Tendulkar, she says it was "Finished. I had already enrolled myself."[14] Having solicited the address from Jayabharathi, she sent a postcard to Sankaran that said, "Sir, I want to act in your troupe." He agreed, and she acted with him for nearly 20 years until 1997, developing a large body of work with Pareeksha, a troupe known for its progressive, experimental Tamil-language performances of plays by Brecht, Pinter, C. S. Lakshmi, Jeyanthan, Indira Parthasarathy, and many others. Chakravarthy describes Sankaran's theater as "really active, anti-establishment, everything that the Madras Christian College believed to be super theatre was what he did not believe in. So for me, it was great fun." Working with Pareeksha, especially such theater veterans as KPP, Dr. Rudhran, and Vaidheeswaran, placed Pritham Chakravarthy at the center of the parallel theater scene in Madras and trained her to work with sensitive and controversial topics, never expecting "claps or reviews."[15]

That training in sensitive topics served her well when in 1992–1993 she was awarded an Asoka Fellowship to work with an orphanage in Anna Nagar on the subject of sexual violence. She says of this period:

> That was very disturbing, very touching, something that which I would try to find a hundred excuses to keep myself away but I would force myself to be present there and do it. Because I always came home completely shattered . . . . How do you teach a child that is thirsting for touch that there is a good touch and a bad touch? You can't teach them. That child has had no touch. It's starving for a human hand to touch it and won't know whether or not it's a good touch or bad touch.[16]

She stayed with the project through 1996, with guidance from the feminist organizations Delhi Women and Sakshi, for whom she helped produce a booklet complete with theater exercises, movement exercises, and songs. A group of young feminists got together for a 10-day workshop in Bangalore, under the auspices of the National Institute of Mental Health and pooled ideas and experiences in order to create these materials.

Between this project and the work she did with Pareeksha, she became quite well known in Chennai theater circles as "Pareeksha Pritham." Ironically, however, it was a television program Sankaran directed in 1996 that pushed Chakravarthy toward the solo theater work she is now best known for. The show is called *Vergal,* and it celebrates 50 years of Indian independence (since 1947), including "vignettes of powerful stories of women who participated in the Freedom Movement in India."[17] Chakravarthy performed a four-minute dramatic piece on stigma that Sankaran had scripted based on recordings of Rathnabai, an early 19th-century middle-class widow. The experience of this performance, where she sat down and told the audience her life story, was when Chakravarthy began to move into her own as a performer and to develop the style that would stay with her through her career on stage. She identifies this performance as driving her toward doing more solo performances telling women's stories and reflecting her own progressive politics and activism, particularly advocating for women. She says that it was at this time that

> I kind of discovered this storyteller in me that was not necessarily a "once upon a time" storyteller. I used to do a lot of children's storytelling and they were very "long, long ago" that kind of story, so this was the first time I was telling a true story, and it happened quite—what do you say—not realistically . . . it was very clear it was a mediated event that was put across to you but I was doing it with far more ease and a connection with the audience, drawing the audience in.[18]

Her description of the experience sounds very like Philip Taylor's description of applied theater, which he says "becomes a medium through which storytellers can step into the perspectives of others and gain entry points to different worldviews . . . the art form is central to storytelling, to healing, to teaching, and to learning."[19] Ratnabai's story was a true one, but from an earlier time, and Chakravarthy was able to use her gift as a storyteller to help contemporary television audiences (including herself) connect to it. Telling the story of another, however, is always fraught with ethical problems for both the representer and the represented. In this particular case, the woman being represented was long dead and unable to speak for herself, but that is not true of most of Chakravarthy's performances, where there are negotiations that must take place between her, as playwright and storyteller, and the one whose story she is relating.

This performance, however, of a historical widow contemplating suicide, did have a very real effect on Chakravarthy's life. The episode of *Vergal* was very popular and thus recast on Doordarshan many times in the coming years. So even though Chakravarthy's part in it was only a few minutes, it both got her in trouble with her mother, who was distressed to see her inauspiciously dressed like a widow, and brought her to the attention of another local theater activist, Mangai Arasu. Arasu had just come back to Chennai following a Fulbright year at Tisch in New York, where she had a very active theatrical life. So when director Prasanna Ramasamy decided to develop a script based on C. S. Lakshmi's (aka Ambai's) short story, "Black Horse Square," about a custodial rape case of a Marxist woman in southern India, Pritham Chakravarthy's name immediately came to mind.

The three women enjoyed working on this project together so much that Chakravarthy and Ramasamy continued to work with Arasu and Mina Swaminathan, who had formed an interactive theater group called "Voicing Silence" through the M. S. Swaminathan Research Foundation. Voicing Silence focused especially on activism and women's issues with a goal of "evolving a distinctively female theatre idiom with a feminist slant."[20] It is important to note that Chakravarthy, Arasu, Ramasamy, and Swaminathan are all from a privileged class of educated Indian women, a fact that raises many questions. Sue Wilkinson and Celia Kitzinger have written eloquently about the problems of representing (and not representing) the Other. They restate the argument of many feminists that "we should speak only for ourselves, and eschew speaking for Others" because "Others have been too much spoken for and about already . . . it might be more appropriate to silence the cacophony of dominant voices busily regulating, explaining, justifying, exonerating or celebrating Others in favor of simply pointing to the silence of those Others and thereby helping to create a space for them to speak for themselves."[21] bell hooks, for one, would like to see all talk of "the Other" cease because often the very act of speaking about the Other erases and annihilates that Other:

> No need to hear your voice when I can talk about you better than you can speak about yourself. No need to hear your voice. Only tell me about your pain. I want to know your story. And then I will tell it back to you in a new way. Tell it back to you in such a way that it has become mine, my own. Re-writing you, I write myself anew. I am still author, authority. I am still the colonizer, the speaking subject, and you are now at the center of my talk.[22]

While this is, in some senses, both laudable and logical, it is also very often untenable. Sometimes the speech of Others may not be heard, particularly at international theater festivals, where someone like Chakravarthy would have the opportunity to make their stories known. And sometimes, as in the case of *Nirvanam,* which I'll discuss shortly, the Other may wish someone else to speak because they are too close and too affected by the stories. The effects of speaking only for ourselves, Wilkinson and Kitzinger argue, "are often the silencing of Others, the erasure of their experience, and the reinscription of power relations."[23] Chakravarthy faces these dilemmas on at least two fronts: she performs for both insider and outsider audiences whenever possible, and she performs the stories of women who come from a variety of power positions—mythological, historical, and contemporary.

Part of Chakravarthy's challenge with a style of solo performance that focuses on storytelling and narrative has been to create dramatic content and interest. With the performances of the widow and custodial rape victim, as with her first project with Voicing Silence, *Vellavi,* about a Dalit washerwoman, Chakravarthy had a narrative, a story told by a single woman, that she was dramatizing. Their stories, of course, resonated with larger groups of people (widows, custodial rape victims, Dalits), but there existed a single narrative thread to work with. Of her dilemma, she writes, "The narration is linear; there is nothing dramatic or dynamic. What is fascinating about an old Dhobi woman talking about her life and donkeys? How do you term this theater?"[24] In fact, Mangai had so many doubts about *Vellavi*'s entertainment potential that she decided at the last minute to add a chorus so that Chakravarthy would not have to carry the audience of 5,000 that they expected to attend at the Dalit festival in Madurai all by herself. All the performers, besides those from this group, were Dalits (aka untouchables, bottom of the caste system). At first, Chakravarthy says she was nervous and distracted by the chorus—so much so that she made a mistake in her lines. She notes,

> There was a pause, and I know that [one of them released] a giggle which was spreading in the audience. Until that point, on stage people were watching real Dalit bodies perform real Dalit stuff. And there was a part of me that was feeling extremely fraud[ulent] about it, you know, to go on stage to do this [perform an identity that wasn't hers]. And when the giggle spread it was like I didn't know what to do. I stopped at once and grabbed at one of the chorus who was passing me, stopped him, and I said, "Did I say mandai and talai [skull and head]? . . . If I made a mistake I am old. It's your business to tell me that I have forgotten something.". . . He said, "I thought you forgot your lines." I shot back, "Oh yeah? Am I telling your story as mine, that I forgot some lines?" The women in the first rows intervened, "Aatha, leave him. Tell us your story." I asked them, "Where did I leave?". . . they gave me the cue and I restarted. After this I forgot the chorus, the chorus couldn't do anything to benefit. It was happening with the audience and I was the one folding my clothes I was the one who was tying it up and now the audience was not looking at me as this fair-skinned person performing their story. They were looking at me as someone who's telling a story, doesn't matter if it wasn't my story or not, but it was a real person's story and they knew enough that this meant the same thing in their village . . . we were sharing common stories.[25]

After the performance, Chakravarthy joined the crowd to watch the following acts, and she relates that people came up to her, not noticing or caring that she was dressed in jeans, smoking, and sharing a beer with a male friend (none of which are generally acceptable for women), but wanting to know how she had developed her accent and if she had spoken to the dhobi woman herself. They commented over and over on the authenticity and power of the performance as well as the narrative. She had been self-conscious, before she started, about her light-skinned Brahmin body on that stage and was happy to have validation from the very people she was speaking for and to in the performance.

This interplay between subject and researcher/actor became more in depth with some of her later work, particularly the play *Nirvanam,* which I discuss in depth elsewhere,[26] and briefly in this chapter. The process is a vivid example of some of the best and most respectful practices that can be employed in speaking for others. Wilkinson and Kitzinger suggest that to develop dialogue it is important to "give representations back to the represented for comment, feedback, and evaluation."[27] While the dhobi woman herself may not have seen Pritham's performance, many women who are in similar situations did, and they sought her out to provide both validation and suggestions for improving the performance in the future. The other imperative is to emphasize *listening* to the Others before developing a script, and the corollary to this is that one's own subject position must then be relativized and problematized, especially when, as in Chakravarthy's case here, the performer is from a decidedly more privileged and powerful position than the marginalized Other she is representing. James Clifford argued in 1986 that "ethnographers should attempt to create a text within a context of collaborative story-making which celebrates dialogue over monologue, polyphony over monophonic authority."[28] It is this interplay that can lend the aura of authenticity and realism.

Storytelling is a technique that is often used by organizers to motivate and inspire people to work. Marshall Ganz has argued that stories are effective because they help the listener to contextualize information and translate values into a motivation to act. In contrast to an analytic argument, which convinces us, a narrative "engages us, captures our interest, and makes us pay attention" by helping listeners to identify with individual characters and through them experience "the emotional content of the story."[29] As a storyteller, Pritham Chakravarthy excels at encouraging listeners to enter into her stories, partly because she herself enters into them so completely. When she is telling a story, it is *her* story, *her* lived experiences, and this technique encourages others to either share their own stories or be moved to action on an issue. Ganz writes, "My story becomes 'our' story when its project is our project, its crisis is our crisis, or its resolution teaches a moral common to us all."[30] By engaging her viewers' emotions and drawing them into "her" stories, Chakravarthy motivates and inspires people, which can lead to political and/ or social action for the betterment of various populations, the goal of applied theater.

Vellavi, being a solo show, was an easy performance to produce, and therefore, it traveled quite a bit. All that was necessary was any kind of space—meeting halls, theaters, even slums—for Pritham Chakravarthy and her bundle of clothes. The power of the performance, in Chakravarthy's estimation, is that it starts conversations. Every time she performs it, she learns new stories, nuances, and gestures from her audience members and is able to deepen her identification and portrayal of the character. With *Vellavi*, though, there was a script based on an interview with one woman by a student of V. Arasu (Mangai's husband). I saw her perform this piece on a formal stage for an educated audience in 2004 at The Other Festival in Chetpet, Chennai, as did many others. The viewers who had the most effect on her future development as a storyteller, however, were the *aravanis*. *Aravanis* are also known as *hijras* or *alis*, transgenders, transsexuals, or members of the "third sex." Several saw her perform *Vellavi,* and when they ran into her at a neighborhood temple, they requested that Pritham "tell our story."

This request, for "our story," introduced another shift in Chakravarthy's style to something more resembling what Mangai Arasu calls "playback theatre." Now it was not just the story of one woman, reasonable to get a grasp on and memorize the lines directly from an interview in that woman's voice, but the story of a community made up of many people, each with a different story. She started ethnographic research in earnest, spending hours with six *aravanis* at the temple as well as at her home, and collected over 10 tapes of interviews, which she worked to combine into one, cohesive, believable, and yet somewhat anonymous narrative. The idea behind playback theatre is "to create both empathy and expression and to communicate the notion that learning to 'objectify' one's experiences, by allowing a group of actors to re-present them helped a person gain critical control over that experience . . . this sort of theatre demands a level of trust and understanding between the storyteller and the actor . . . it is important for the actor to reach into the core of what has been told to her or him and respond in a manner that does not damage the integrity of the teller's story."[31] As she developed her script, Chakravarthy called the Tamilnadu Aravani Association and told them about the ideas she was working with, focusing on abuse and exploitation, and they immediately said, "No. We want a strong story." By this they meant that a story of victimization was not what they wanted to see; rather, her performance should show their real daily lives and emphasize the power and agency displayed by those who choose to live this difficult *aravani* lifestyle.

In 2001, she debuted *Nirvanam,* then 10 minutes long, on the terrace at the Max Mueller Bhavan in Chennai and then at the International Human Rights Conference outside of Panchagni that included sessions on the rights of transgenders. The title refers to the surgery and the moment of transformation from woman-in-a-man's-body to woman that the individual undergoes to truly call herself *aravani*. At this moment, the option of returning to "normal" life as a man is no longer there. Chakravarthy performed on the second day of the conference immediately before the plenary session in the parking lot in front of the 600-seat hall where the session was to take place. It was not well advertised, so while people were milling around waiting for the plenary session, her young daughter sang a song to get people's attention;

then Chakravarthy started the performance. Most of the 70 or 80 people who saw the performance that morning did not understand Tamil and did not get a whole lot out of the play, but people were interested enough that the organizers asked her to do it again, morning and evening, for the remaining five days of the conference. And now that the word was out, the Tamil speakers made a point of attending and spreading themselves throughout the crowd to softly translate as she was speaking. There were transgenders in the audience from a number of countries, and they would come and tell her bits of their stories, until by the end of the week, after adding lines and details offered by these viewers, *Nirvanam* had doubled in length. It became popular with *aravani* groups, and they frequently requested her to stage it for their functions, continually adding to it until today's piece is a full hour and 10 minutes.

In 2007, Anjali Monteiro and K. P. Jayasankar released a film about the *aravani* community in Tamil Nadu called *Our Family*. This film "brings together excerpts from *Nirvanam,* a one-person performance by Pritham K. Chakravarthy, and the family of three generations of trans-gendered female subjects, who are bound together by ties of adoption."[32] The *aravanis*, especially the founder and president of the Tamilnadu Aravani Association and her daughter, son-in-law, and granddaughter, tell their stories, and Chakravarthy tells hers, too. One of the best things about the film is that after Chakravarthy's dramatic and disturbing depiction of a surgery, viewers get to see the reactions of real *aravanis* to the performance and hear a bit of discussion. So many theater projects done on this topic simply show the difficulties of the lifestyle without showing the grace, strength of character, affection, and dignity that are also a part of it. Chakravarthy's performance bears witness to some of the pain, abuse, and alienation, yes, but focuses on family, community, and self-discovery. This approach leaves non-*aravani* viewers not horrified and disturbed, but sympathetic and tolerant.

My choice of the phrase "bear witness" to describe Chakravarthy's work is deliberate. It is ordinarily used in reference to the holocaust or other "incomprehensible atrocities," as James Dawes, author of *That the World May Know: Bearing Witness to Atrocity,* calls them. Some of Chakravarthy's work does refer to atrocities against women, such as *Hit Me Not,* about domestic violence, and *Hands Off,* about a young girl who is sexually abused by her uncle, but that is not true of all of her performances. Some bear witness to more ordinary stories and the small everyday oppressions and restrictions on action that women face in their lives. I want to reclaim the phrase "bear witness" and separate it from its close link with trauma to remind us that *all* of our stories, however quotidian they may seem, are worth telling and remembering. *Aravanis* may have individual stories of traumatic events, but what Chakravarthy is able to approach is the idea of "insidious trauma" that Maria Root describes as "usually associated with the social status of an individual being devalued because a characteristic intrinsic to their identity is different from what is valued by those in power, for example, gender, sexual orientation, physical ability. As a result it is often present throughout a lifetime."[33] For many individuals, trauma is not an event they can pinpoint but a constant part of life that victims will often deny.[34] By performing the oral history of a Dalit laundry woman in rural Tamil Nadu (in *Vellavi*) or of a stigmatized film dancer (in *Mirror*, written and directed by her husband, Venkatesh Chakravarthy) or of an *aravani* is to take a narrative—which is not overly traumatic or eventful—and transform it into a story that the mostly caste-privileged, educated, middle-class intellectuals at The Other Festival or similar venues can relate to. This would be a feat in itself, but Pritham Chakravarthy's real innovation is to make these women's stories relatable and normal without exoticizing them or making them pitiable. Her characters are real women, with real strengths and strategies in the face of great oppression and adversary. Chakravarthy is able to tell these stories and leave audiences not with feelings of pity and revulsion but with respect, admiration, and hope.

Chakravarthy's intervention goes further. Because this is applied theater, she is very clear that *Nirvanam* is not *her* story. It never was. It is what the *aravanis* requested from her: *our* story. Thus far, they have not wished to perform it themselves, as Chakravarthy would prefer, but continue to ask her to do it for them. In *Our Family*, viewers are privy to *aravani* reactions to the play. One of them, Seetha's, first response to the performance is that "The turmoils that we've gone through, authentically, realistically, have been presented before us. It is really an achievement. I applaud Pritham . . . When I saw her performing, I got goose pimples." Her mother, Aasha, who is the president of the Tamilnadu Aravani Association, agreed, saying, "When I first saw the show, I couldn't bear it and tears came to my eyes. I didn't see Pritham there, but a fellow *aravani*. A fellow being's suffering that stayed in my mind." So having her do it feels authentic and real, negating the need for them to perform it themselves. But their role is not finished with simply viewing the performance. They are welcome to contribute to it by sharing their stories with Chakravarthy, and she states clearly that she finalized a script only after much discussion and suggestion from *aravanis*. But with this performance, like with the Dalit performance, her body and upbringing can get in the way of authenticity. She said to me,

> Sometimes I'd be performing, at the end of it they'd come and say "I was a Tayamma, my Tayamma did this for me . . ." Now this tale is one hour, 10 minutes because of them. And, they directed me. If they have one

real grouse about me about the show, it is that I'm not performing it in a sari. When they told me the story they would gather the sari, tuck it in and then tell me like this [she spreads her legs]. If you put me in a sari, I promptly become the Pritham whom Pritham's mother taught her how to wear a sari and that is one. So I'm very conscious in a sari. Two, there are several images which are ingrained into your mind through popular media on the use of sari in an Aravani story. So if the pallu [the piece of the sari that drapes over the shoulder] were to slip naturally, and I adjusted as the actor, anyone who is used to Tamil cinema will silently in their mind—oaahhhh [puts her right hand up by her armpit]—this is a typical aravani gesture in Tamil cinema. And talk this way [gestures with her hands], I avoided doing all that kind of, you know, those camp gestures and all that.[35]

So while it felt less authentic to *aravani* viewers, who would expect Chakravarthy to perform their story in a sari, she knows that it would actually be less so because of her own reflexes. She rarely wears a sari, and when she does, it brings back all of her orthodox Brahmin training and memories of her mother that would interfere with her ability to enter into character. Additionally, by deliberately avoiding the stereotypical *aravani* gestures and breaking the audience's expectations from their experience with Tamil cinema, she is able to keep the *aravani* whose story she tells from being a caricature and help to keep the encounter from feeling so much like a performance—even though it is.

Most of all, however, Pritham Chakravarthy's performances spark discussions within the community—as applied theater is supposed to. She asks several *aravanis* what the film *Our Family* should tell the outside world about their community, to which Selvam (Seetha's husband) responds, "The story . . . Like others, let them live." Seetha jumps in and says, "No. That is not the basic thing. Why should we ask them to let us live? . . . People should realize who an *aravani* is. People should know that we, too, have a life. They should learn to respect our feelings. Society should also accept us. If we're accepted, everything's fine." *Nirvanam* and *Our Family* open discussions about what the community most needs and wants from the outside world as well as gives a realistic window into their world and family for those who have never known an *aravani* or how to act with one.

ACKNOWLEDGMENTS

This chapter would not have been possible without the friendship and cooperation of Pritham Chakravarthy. She has been an invaluable resource to me over the past 15 years on various research projects, and it was a joy to finally focus on her very compelling theater work. I also need to thank Khani Begum and Zayn Kassam for suggesting and including me in this volume, Haripriya Narasimhan for reading the paper, and Sean Ahern for transcribing the interview tapes. Brandi Veneble and Tim Bavlnka invited me to present this paper for the Popular Culture Colloquium series at BGSU, where my colleagues and students provided useful feedback and asked me the hard questions, especially Marilyn Motz, Jeremy Wallach, and Sarah Rainey.

NOTES

1. Portions of this chapter have been adapted from Rudisill 2015, 535–554. Used by permission of The University of Hawaii Press.

2. Nicholson 2005, 3, 5.

3. Prentki and Preston 2009, 9, 14.

4. *Subramanian* 2006, 99–100.

5. Interview with Pritham Chakravarthy, September 2010.

6. Ibid.

7. Sircar 1978, 1.

8. Ibid., 2.

9. Ibid., 3.

10. Ibid., 24.

11. Santhanam 2008.

12. This troupe is still active, producing both stage and street theater productions in Chennai.

13. Santhanam 2008

14. Interview with Pritham Chakravarthy, September 2010.

15. Ibid.

16. Ibid.

17. "Chakravarthy, Pritham Blog," 2011

18. Interview with Pritham Chakravarthy, September 2010.

19. Taylor 2003, xviii.

20. Mangai 2015, 67.

21. Sue and Kitzinger 2009, 86.

22. Ibid., 84.

23. Ibid., 88.

24. Chakravarthy 2011.

25. Interview with Pritham Chakravarthy, September 2010.

26. Rudisill 2015, 535–554.

27. Wilkinson and Kitzinger 2009, 91.

28. Ibid., 92.

29. Ganz 2011, 11–12.

30. Ibid., 16.

31. Mangai 2015, 30.
32. Quote from dust jacket, Monteiro and Jayasankar 2007.
33. Root 1994, 240.
34. Mason 2010, 84.
35. Interview with Pritham Chakravarthy, September 2010.

CHAPTER 12

Women Living Buddhism in the West: Spiritual Practice and Daily Life

Leesa S. Davis

What does womanhood matter at all, when the mind is concentrated well, when knowledge flows on steadily as one sees correctly into Dhamma. One to whom it might occur, "I am a woman" or "I am a man" or "I'm anything at all" is fit for Mara [the Evil One] to address.
—Samyutta Nikaya 5.2

Over the past six decades, Buddhist spiritual traditions have been successfully transplanted into Western cultures attracting large numbers of committed students and establishing practice centers and temples. In this relatively short time, the Dalai Lama of Tibet has progressed from attracting small numbers of the devoted and the curious in the 1970s to more recent tours staged in large sporting arenas that attract audiences for traditional Buddhist teachings in the thousands or even tens of thousands. In an even shorter time span, from around the 1980s, a foundational Buddhist meditative practice, now known as "mindfulness," has been extracted from its traditional Buddhist contexts and has become a mainstay of the "well-being" industry. This "explosion" of interest in Buddhism coupled with the mainstreaming of traditional Buddhist meditative practices raises all sorts of complex and fascinating questions for the study of the transmission of Buddhism to the West, not the least being the challenges and adaptations of cross-cultural spiritual engagement and the reorientation(s) of the importance of gender roles.

In this chapter we want to explore some of these questions in the context of the experience of women practicing the *dharma* in modern, Western settings. By examining three case studies of long-term Buddhist practitioners, we can get a window on the impact of Buddhist practice on women's daily lives and isolate some key issues pertaining to gender and the status and roles of women in contemporary Buddhist communities. In addition to this, a focus on lived experience and the experiential impact of the practices allows us to catch a glimpse of some key Buddhist philosophical tenets "in action" both in the practice situation and in the ways that these tenets inform the worldviews of practitioners.

Thus, this chapter has a threefold aim:

1. To explore the impact of Buddhist practice on women's daily lives
2. To isolate some of the key reorientations of traditional Buddhist attitudes to women
3. To call attention to some foundational Buddhist philosophical tenets that underpin and inform practitioners' worldviews

Following Miranda Shaw, the discussion will primarily focus on the agency of women by concentrating on how women act and view themselves rather than how they are acted upon and viewed by the institution. This concept of agency fits very well with the practitioners interviewed below as none of them see themselves as being victims of institutional or doctrinal discrimination, yet they all recognize the tension that exists in Buddhism between what the scriptures state and how the institutions have developed. In effect, these women practitioners view themselves as independent agents that are capable of transforming not only themselves but also their respective traditions. In regard to the role and status of women in Buddhism, this is perhaps one of the key reorientations of Buddhist practice in the West.[1]

Traditionally, Buddhist meditative practice was undertaken by the ordained *sangha* (community of monks), but with the advent of the transmission of Buddhism to the West, the lines between monastic and lay practice increasingly intersect in ways that are not found in traditional Buddhism. In "modern"[2] Buddhism, lay female practitioners take on not only practices traditionally performed by the *sangha* but also institutional roles that were traditionally held by the monks. The blurring of the ordained/lay boundary also serves to weaken the structures of traditional, primarily male, monastic hierarchies in which monks were held to be spiritually superior to nuns. This shift is illustrative of Western ideas of a more egalitarian approach to institutional hierarchies and social roles.

The general Western emphasis on egalitarianism in terms of hierarchical structure is an operational factor in driving the changing roles of women within Western Buddhist institutional structures. This emphasis on egalitarianism not only opens up opportunities for the advancement of women in institutional roles but also grants credence to the full spiritual potential of women. The spiritual potential of women in Buddhism is a contentious issue that cannot be easily solved by turning to scripture. Buddhist scripture, in both the Theravāda and the Mahāyāna traditions, offers no consistent position on the status and spiritual potential of women.[3]

Claudia Romberg breaks these inconsistencies down into three general attitudes:

- That female rebirth is a result of negative karma accumulated in a past life.
- That Buddha was a male; therefore, a male rebirth or a sexual transformation is necessary for women.
- That gender is irrelevant for salvation in the sense that gender is one of the traits of the ego, which needs to be transcended.[4]

These three general attitudes well sum up the scriptural and institutional tensions that contemporary female practitioners face in the practice situation for, as Romberg goes on to state, "empirically all three stances are part of Buddhism."[5] However, there may be some "real-life" benefits for women practitioners in the seemingly ambivalent and contradictory attitudes to their roles and status in Buddhist discourse. According to Faure, "Like most clerical discourses, Buddhism is indeed relentlessly misogynist, but as far as misogynist discourses go, it is one of the most flexible and open to multiplicity and contradiction."[6] It is in the "gaps" of this flexibility and the subsequent emerging openness to challenge traditional hierarchies that contemporary Western female practitioners of the *dharma* find the space to transform traditional attitudes and to articulate more equitable gender roles both in the practice situation and in Western Buddhist institutional hierarchies.

The transformative possibilities of spiritual practice are not limited to subjective experiences in a formal practice context but are also apparent in the reported "flow over" into practitioners' daily lives and worldviews. Indeed, Buddhist traditions in the West emphasize the need for practice and daily life to inform each other.[7] Here, there is the emphasis "to be in the world," an orientation that links the key Buddhist ideas of compassion (*karuṇā*) and interconnectedness (*pratītyasamutpāda*) to broader action in the world.

INTERVIEW METHODOLOGY

The interviews with three long-term Buddhist practitioners were conducted with an interactive-relational methodology. This approach emphasizes the critical importance of both the interaction that takes place between an interviewer and interviewee and the relationship that develops between them. The interactive-relational approach or in-depth interviewing "is one of the central data-gathering planks of qualitative research strategy."[8] Furthermore, "a primary focus of in-depth interviewing is to understand the significance of human experience as described from the actor's point of view."[9]

We will unpack the interviews by first giving a brief outline of the subject's tradition followed by a description of her practice. The emphasis here will be on contemporary ideas of the role and status of women and any perceived differences pertaining to male and female practitioners. The discussion will then proceed by focusing on the impact on the subject's daily life. In the course of this analysis, key philosophical underpinnings will be highlighted.

INTERVIEW PL12

When women shine, their communities, society, and the future will shine as well.

—Daisaku Ikeda[10] (quoted by interviewee PL12)

Our first interviewee is an Australian woman who has spent most of her adult life in the United Kingdom. She has been a Nichiren Buddhist (Jap: *Hokke-kei Bukkyo*) practitioner for close to 30 years. Founded in 13th-century Japan by the charismatic reformer monk Nichiren Diashōnin (1222–1282), Nichiren practice centers around the chanting of the Japanese title of the Lotus Sūtra *myōhō-renge-kyō* (Sanskrit: *Saddharma-puṇḍarīka Sūtra*) with the addition of the honorific *nam* (homage); thus, practitioners chant: *nam-myōhō-renge-kyō* ("Homage to the Lotus of the Supreme Law"[11]) with the idea that the mantra (or *daimoku*) contains the full spiritual potency of the text and that chanting it with wholehearted devotion and focus activates or makes manifest one's intrinsic "Buddha nature." The chanting is supported by the daily practice of morning and evening *gongyo*, the recitation of two key chapters of the Lotus Sūtra[12] (the second, or *hoben*, chapter and the sixteenth, or *juryo*, chapter). Along with the title, these chapters are believed to contain the spiritual essence of the 28 chapters of the Sūtra.

Historically, Nichiren Buddhism is classified as part of the "new Buddhist movements" of the Kamakura period (1185–1313) that are "known for their emphasis on simple, widely accessible practices based on faith rather than doctrinal understanding or meditative insight."[13] Nichiren chanting practice shares some commonalities with all Buddhist meditative or contemplative practices. Like all Buddhist meditative practices, the chanting centers on a focusing of attention and concentrated intention with the cultivation of accompanying receptive awareness. The difference is that the Nichiren practitioner focuses on a question or a desire or a problem taken directly from daily life and applies their practice to this question.

According to our interviewee, by focusing on a personal life question, the need for taking on "any cultural baggage" is removed. She goes on to say that this serves to make Nichiren practice "deeply cross-cultural": "This practice does not involve taking on a whole lot of cultural trappings. It can be practiced within one's own culture and traditions—no special clothes, no name change, no special dietary habits and so on."[14]

Further, as a non-theistic practice, it is "human centric": "The practice is also non-theistic—it puts the human being at the center and attempts to describe the human condition and to give you steps to alleviate human suffering."[15] However, the focus in not solely on the individual, "it is also about our interaction with others, our care for other people and taking that care into our lives." Practitioners also extend their focus of concern for the individual to concern for the environment and "the planet": "we chant to see if [through] our actions we are changing the karma of the planet, working against warfare and destruction and ignorance of life." All this is in "very subtle ways" through "practicing every day with a very strong intention."[16]

Jacqueline Stone notes that "modern observers are often struck by the 'engaged' or even 'political' character of contemporary Nichiren movements"[17] such as the large-scale international Nichiren lay organization Sōka Gakkai International (SGI), in which our interviewee participates. The practice begins with the self, and through realizing the interconnectedness of all things, the focus extends to chanting for the benefit of all beings, and this intention is not considered as being separate from acting in the world. For practice, "transforms one's own inner world along with the way that you interact with others and view the world."[18]

NICHIREN PRACTICE

Practice is looking at ourselves in the most penetrating of mirrors.

—PL12, 2012

A common claim associated with Nichiren Buddhist practice is that if you practice "to the best of your ability, you will develop a state of life in which all your desires are fulfilled."[19] At first glance this claim appears to go against the standard Buddhist identification of craving or "desires" being the source of suffering as articulated in the Second Noble Truth.[20] However, according to our interviewee, the practice is not about fulfilling desires in the sense of "gaining anything" but rather by recognizing tendencies that fuel our desires: "Through chanting on a question we come to see our tendencies, things in ourselves that need to change, knots in our psyche, anger."

When asked "can you chant for things, to 'get' things or fulfill desires?" PL12 responds: "yes and no. Practice is not really about 'getting things' but through chanting on or for some 'thing' deeper insights are uncovered in the process. Practice is about uncovering or penetrating how we are and how reality is. We do chant about 'things'—about things in our life but 'things are' and we practice for the wisdom to see things as they are. In this process what we think we want changes."[21]

From this we can see that "every desire being fulfilled" is not necessarily "getting what one wants" but "seeing things for what they are." That is, seeing what causes or conditions "things"—emotions, desires, phenomena, and so on—arise from and what conditions shape them. This implies a much deeper penetration of wants and desires that doesn't focus on satisfying the desire in question but in recognizing the patterns and tendencies that underlie our desires and perhaps bring about more refined and less selfish wants and desires: "The practice brings out our inherent wisdom, through it we develop the wisdom to see the right approach to the question or issue that we are focusing our chanting on."[22] She elaborates:

> Everyone has problems—problems are inevitable but Buddhist practice gives me a personal sense of control [not in the sense of] controlling . . . but when something happens I can chant about it and . . . have some clarity on my emotional reactions and responses.[23]

When asked how this felt influence can "work," our practitioner responds with a fundamental Buddhist insight of the interrelatedness of all phenomena (*pratītyasamutpāda*): "Because all phenomena are connected and through my chanting I can have an influence on the interconnectedness [of things]." Interestingly, this process does not necessarily "get you the thing that you want": "For example I can be chanting for the bank manager's wisdom to make the right decision—the right decision may not be that he gives me the overdraft but . . . it might be the right decision in the larger sense"[24]—once again this insight is underpinned by the pivotal Buddhist insight of interconnectedness and the primary practice orientation of the cultivation of wisdom. Practice "is a very powerful force in my daily life and a best friend." It "intersects with and contains all aspects of life." Daily life and practice are mutually entailing or, as Buddhists would say, "co-conditioned": "You bring whatever happens in your daily life to your practice and you bring your practice to your daily life."[25]

When asked if there was any difference between women's experience of practicing Nichiren Buddhism and men's experience, our practitioner responded thus: "my first response is 'no'—but I think it's more complicated than that—both historically and in daily Buddhist practice, but not at the most profound spiritual level."[26] Here she is voicing the tensions inherent in Buddhist scriptural attitudes to women—historically and institutionally a female birth is not as auspicious as a male nor is there the same spiritual potential and status but

> at the deepest level, just as the practice [of chanting] is the same for both men and women—so are the effects the same, that is, wisdom, courage, compassion. But culturally . . . we all bring the baggage of sexism and societal attitudes inculcated into us to the practice. So each individual will in different ways process and transform this karma through their practice.[27]

The practice is transformative in the sense that it uncovers ingrained attitudes and prejudices and works to counter this with the cultivation of key Buddhist virtues: wisdom, courage, and compassion. The process of chanting both reveals and transforms innate conditioned tendencies: "[it] mines our layers of consciousness and conditioning, gradually transforming habitual tendencies"[28] and cultivates critical self-development: "At the same time chanting opens up self awareness and insight, enabling people to reflect on themselves, their unconscious or conscious motivations and patterns and thence the determination to create new more positive causes for the future."[29] In this process sexist cultural baggage and fixed ideas of gender are transformed: "So while men and women may sometimes be chanting about issues that have accretions of sexist cultural baggage the process of inner transformation through the resonance of chanting is the same. The practice is the same and so is the effect."[30]

According to PL12, "essentially all of our disease is the result of greed, anger and ignorance and we, both men and women, are blinded by these poisons"—the need and the process to see through these "poisons" and transform them through Buddhist practice are the same. Hence, for this practitioner gender is one of the traits of the ego, a trait that ultimately needs to be transcended through ongoing practice and action in the world.

Interview AL13

Being a mother is also a really good Buddhist practice—daily life is fierce and habits are horrible but it's how do you freshen things up—how you open the space again and again—how you trust and get the bigger picture that's really where the practice lies—where the accomplishment lies.

—AL13, 2013

Our second practitioner is a French woman of German descent who has practiced in the Nyingma[31] tradition of Tibetan Buddhism for over 25 years.

Although most scholars consider Tibetan Buddhism to be a branch of Mahāyāna Buddhism, there is a case for considering it as a separate school. Vajrayāna considers both the Pāli Canon of Theravāda Buddhism and the later Mahāyāna tradition as essential preliminary foundations for the practice, but the elaborate visualization practices and esoteric tantric texts are unique to Vajrayāna.[32] At the heart of Vajrayāna Buddhist practice is the central figure of the *lama* (teacher, guru) with the student-teacher relationship being all-important.

Vajrayāna Buddhism differs from other Mahāyāna forms of Buddhism primarily in the area of method—the elaborate tantric practices of the Vajrayāna (visualizations, rituals, and use of symbols) are believed to be more potent and effective than other Buddhist paths. Through these practices and devotion to the *lama,* the tantric practitioner is able to overcome delusion, afflictions, and obstacles and progress rapidly through to the state of Buddhahood in order to benefit others.[33]

Rita M. Gross notes that

> under Vajrayāna Buddhism, theoretical concepts about femininity and women . . . changed significantly. These changes correlated with changes about sexuality and the emotions. Rather than being dangerous territory that best be avoided, sexuality and the emotions are regarded as an extremely provocative working basis for enlightenment, provided that they are experienced with mindfulness and detachment.[34]

In Vajrayāna practice, symbolic rituals, textual study, and meditative concentration combine to train Buddhists "in a mindful, detached, and ultimately liberating approach to sexuality and the emotions, whether they be experienced in actual rituals or internally through visualizations."[35] Vajrayāna Buddhism is concerned with practices that aim to transform the relative, limited nature of our minds and to "tap into" the interconnected, dynamic nature of dualisms. In terms of the transformation and interconnection of female and male energies, we can describe one of the basic Vajrayāna practices thus:

> The masculine and feminine principles are symbolized by the ritual implements that the practitioner holds in the left and right hands—a bell in the left, feminine hand and the *vajra*, or ritual weapon or scepter in the right masculine hand. When the left and right hands holding the bell and the *vajra* are crossed in the ritual gesture (*mudrā*) of embracing, the feminine and masculine principles are united. When the hands form independent gestures, in correlation with each other, the masculine and feminine principles co-operate in constructing the world and seeking enlightenment.[36]

In tantric practice, male and female meditators are not limited to the traits that correspond to his or her physiological sex. "Women do not exemplify only the feminine principle, nor men the masculine. . . . Therefore, male and female initiates . . . both identify themselves with both masculine and feminine principles in order to develop their inherent enlightenment."[37] In other words, in this practice spiritual aspirants are not locked into one gendered principle; identification with both masculine and feminine principles is needed to activate inherent realization.

Our practitioner finds this reversing of gender identifications empowering: "women are very much empowered in Vajrayāna—many of the practices involve men visualizing themselves as female deities and women visualizing themselves as male deities—it's all about understanding transformation."[38] Understanding transformation is key to spiritual insight in the Vajrayāna, and this holds interesting possibilities for less adherence to solid fixed ideas of gender and status.

VAJRAYĀNA PRACTICE

Vajrayāna is the complete faith in all possibilities.

—AL13, 2013

After searching for a path and a teacher for many years (in Europe and Japan), AL13 found her "place" in Tibetan Buddhism. For our practitioner, "Vajrayāna has its basis in the Buddha's teachings—but there is a lot of generating things in the practice—visualizations of deities, Buddhas and so on." Importantly, "this practice needs to be completely and firmly established in emptiness (śūnyatā) and compassionate altruism (bodhicitta)" and focusing on these two key orientations must be done "every time you begin your practice."[39]

Hence, visualizations are not to be taken as substantial "realities" but rather as aids to realizing the limitless nature of mind and as experiential reminders that all things are "empty," that is, in dynamic process. Coupled with the need to ground practice in the dynamic emptiness of things is the need to cultivate compassion for all sentient beings and to work for both one's own liberation and the liberation of others. "[We practice] for all sentient beings—what you can see, what you can't see in this world and other worlds—Vajrayāna has a very broad idea of sentience."[40]

"Vajrayāna is focusing your mind and attention to particular things." Indeed for this practitioner, "practice is all about coming back to the nature of mind. It's about recognizing the moment when you turn the mind inside instead of turning the mind outwards with all its projections." The "turning inwards is the way the mind can recognize its own nature so the meditation is to perform this turning point where you can look inside rather than grasping the projections of the mind."[41]

According to our interviewee:

> We are limited because we think we are limited but if you really understand *śūnyatā* [emptiness] very profoundly you know that everything that arises—there is no limit to the arising—this is why the deities don't have any limit—there are thousands of deities because they all correspond to something in us—they are echoes of our inner states—it's not from outside it's from inside us—in essence they are all one.[42]

Further to this: "Vajrayāna practice is interacting with, penetrating, recognizing these kinds of myriad energies that are around us all the time or that *are* us."

AL13 admits that Vajrayāna practice can sound very esoteric but in effect what "you practice throughout the day is just trying to catch your emotions, trying to catch where you are. From practice I have some tools I can go back to my breathing [and] drop negative feelings or just see them for what they are—not make them bigger than they are."

In an echo of our first interviewee, AL13 links practice to being able to recognize and hence change one's perceptions and attitudes to things: "It doesn't mean that you don't take things seriously but it means that you see the space in which these things arise—they are just interdependent circumstances and circumstances can be changed—[the question is] how do you work around these differing sets of circumstances and how can you influence them?"[43]

Furthermore, "being able to step back gives you a different perspective that enables you to act more clearly rather than hanging on to something that you actually can't do anything about. Practice is a kind of training but there's no goal—you just learn to open."[44] To be open, "compassion and wisdom really have to come together and that's so important." Interestingly, this coming together of compassion and wisdom is not about knowing the nature of a limited individual, egocentric mind, but it depends on coming back to the nature of *the* mind: "the only idea is to come back to your own awareness—not to the nature of *your* mind but the nature of mind."[45]

Thus, for this practitioner, Vajrayāna practice is seeing "how you work with your emotions; how you work with your doubts; how you work with obstacles; how you build up trust; how you work together."[46]

Hence for her, "It is very easy to see the connections to everyday life—it's not separate—it's trying to be more aware, trying to be more focused, and opening all the time, not closing—with the basis of understanding emptiness and an understanding of impermanence and an understanding of the inter-connectedness of all things—and this is how to practice for all beings with compassion."[47]

On the importance of "opening all the time and not closing" and in one of the clearest statements of the connection between women's daily lives and the practice of Buddhism, our practitioner reflects on motherhood and the challenges it presents to Buddhist practice:

> What is different for women is in the case of motherhood—when I first began practicing I had kids and it's very hard to attend all the teachings with children. At the time I felt I was missing out—I was extremely unsat-isfied [sic] because I could neither practice and follow the teachings nor could I be a mother to my kids but it was when I relaxed and I just tried to be with my kids that I really took a long leap forward on the path.[48]

Buddhism teaches that attachment is one of the biggest impediments to insight, and being too attached to practice serves to solidify the path in the practitioner's mind and block insight into two key Buddhist tenets: imperma-nence and emptiness. The insight here is that when she relaxed her anxiety and let go of the wanting, then there was some insight into "how things are." She explains the process in this way: "It's a bit strange but in one way it's not that you leave the *dharma* but you have to allow yourself to be where you are and do what you have to do to really practice properly. If it starts to be a struggle then nobody benefits except when you release and then comes understanding."[49]

She concludes with a reflection on being a woman in the *dharma* and a prediction of a major shift:

> Personally I am not affected by being a woman in the practice—I have always felt completely accepted. Of course it is not always easy—we do have female deities—Tara and so on—and there are many accomplished female practitioners—legendary ones even—but thus far there are very few women teachers. Several *lamas* have been teaching that we are enter-ing the time of women, the age of women and it will be women that will carry on the *dharma*—it's a major shift that the *lamas* are predicting.[50]

INTERVIEW MP15

I think that women in the dharma are very powerful. The lamas say that women are the future. Now I think that the role of women is to inspire people because we have another way to connect.

—MP15, 2015

Our final interviewee is also a Vajrayāna Buddhist practitioner in the Nyingma tradition. At 24 years of age, she is younger than our other interviewees and has been seriously practicing Buddhism for approximately five years. However, in her words, she "was born in the *dharma.*" MP15 grew up in a Buddhist household in France very near her parents' *lama* and his main temple. After not being particularly interested in Buddhism in her childhood and early teenage years, she connected with the practice in her late teens. She describes her coming to practice thus:

> I am born in the *dharma* [sic]. I didn't come to the *dharma* because I had a bad thing in my life; it was always around me. I always heard the teachings whether I wanted to know or not—and through this I had something—afterwards I can see the difference between me and my other friends—I seemed to realize things that they didn't understand—I can look at things from different perspectives. One minute it was like—oh it's boring, I don't want to go but it changed and I began to feel something and no one made me [go] and I connected.[51]

As a second-generation Western female *dharma* practitioner, MP15 has very different attitudes to practice, to the status of women in the *dharma* and the importance of *dharma* in daily life. She sees no separation whatsoever: "practice is not only sitting [or] doing the prostrations and all that—it's all the life [sic] you put *dharma* into every activity everything for me is *dharma*—always try to create something positive—it's not about that you *should* practice—it's about that you are *always* practicing in whatever you do."[52]

Overall she exhibits a striking confidence that her *dharma* practice serves to empower her both in an interpersonal sense and in her life and career ambitions and aspirations. In terms of women practicing Buddhism, these attitudes and orientations represent a generational change in which women clearly feel empowered by Buddhist practice and in no way feel that gender is something to be overcome or somehow ignored in practice—rather being a woman is to be celebrated:

> The lamas say that women are the future. I've met so many powerful women. *Dharma* can go through women and it is more powerful—there are more female practitioners than men and a shift is building. We are not weak anymore we are independent and we have ambition—we want to participate.[53]

To be independent and to have ambition is key to this practitioner's aspirations—most of all she seeks to be inspired and to inspire: "Everyday

I want to be inspired by everything" and "I want to go out and help people to inspire them."[54]

To be compassionately active in the world and to inspire does not include any ambition to be ordained. In a major shift of attitude toward a "professional" spiritual life in the ordained *sangha,* our practitioner clearly views ordination as "a thing of the past":

> Before women had to become nuns but I think that now I can practice *dharma* and don't need to be ordained—our situation is not how they practiced the *dharma* in Tibet. They had different cultural conditions—but *dharma* is *dharma.* We can be authentic to the teaching, the lineage and everything but we live in this world so if we practice *dharma* in the right way we can change things—this is *dharma* in action, you can do retreats to reconnect with yourself but to be all your life in the temple—it's selfish! You have to go out and inspire others.[55]

Our practitioner has no need for the cultural trappings of her practice—what she sees as "authentic" practice is beyond that and very much rooted in where she is now and what she is doing in the world: "to live the teachings to apply the teachings we need to be in this world where we are." Furthermore, in what might be indicative of a generation shift in the *lama's* views on the importance of being in the temple, she goes on to say: "All the young masters say that it's not good to spend your whole life close to the temple—if you do that there is something that you haven't understood—it's an attachment."

VAJRAYĀNA PRACTICE

> I can look at a lot of things from different perspectives. If I can open then everything can change.
>
> —MP15, 2013

Continuing on an important theme in our previous interview, MP15 offers this observation on the nature of mind: "our minds are limitless—practice shows us that." For this practitioner, her way of "practicing the Vajrayāna is to be always full—always active. For her, "the world *is* how we interact with it." Once again there is the emphasis on recognizing negative emotions and not attaching: "Don't attach to things—recognize anger, negative emotions but don't hold them—pay attention to your body—realize how you hold tension—don't attach to good or bad—just take the present moment." Being in the present moment is a key Buddhist orientation indicative of the idea that reality is a process and not substance. If we try to "hold" things, that is, substantialize them, then we fall out of touch with reality, attach to things and don't "see things "as they are."

She elaborates on the key problem of attachment: "In the beginning you have to be attached to visualize the Buddha but later you realize that they are nothing—it's all just the nature of your mind. Buddha is not just a statue he is inside you—you already have everything."[56]

Further to this: "You don't only practice for yourself—you practice for everyone but it begins with yourself." She describes her approach to practice as very much being in the world—"if I can't always sit and practice—that's ok I go into the world. I'm more fluid, dynamic—it's really about the kind of attention that you give to things." Also "if you appreciate and are grateful for what you have then you don't focus on what you don't have."[57]

For MP15, "practicing *dharma* is being what you are. You don't have to believe in Buddha [like a God] Buddha is here [pointing to her heart]. Practice with joy and love and then you can inspire. Practicing Buddhism informs my entire life—it's everything."[58]

WOMEN LIVING BUDDHISM

For the three women *dharma* practitioners that we have interviewed here, there is no separation between formal Buddhist practice and daily life. All three see the teachings as pointers to moral and ethical guidelines and practical instructions for living. For our practitioners, the practice of Buddhism is a way to be in the world and operate with greater clarity of intention and compassionate purpose. The connection with a teacher, a practice, and a community is in no way an insular situation because the foundational Buddhist tenets of interconnectedness and the cultivation of discriminating wisdom and compassion underscore our responsibility to all sentient beings and the planet itself.

Buddhist practice is about "uncovering our innate wisdom" through knowing the "nature of mind." PL12 refers to practice as "polishing one's Buddhahood." AL13 says practice involves "turning the mind inward," and for MP15 "practice is really about the kind of attention that you give to things." For all our practitioners, once habitual patterns (in AL13's words "seeing where you are stuck") are recognized or identified, then the process of "seeing things as they are" begins. "Seeing things as they are," that is, impermanent, interconnected, and in constant interrelated flux, is crucial to the process of ongoing insight into self and phenomena that Buddhist practice generates.

Buddhist practice is thus not about gaining anything new, but it is a process of attention with a specific intention to focus on how our mind gets "caught up" in concepts and attachments and thus operates from a basis of ignorance rather than insight. For all our practitioners, the mind is limitless yet knowable, and ultimately, gender is not a factor in any spiritual insight or attainment. However, all three recognize the historical and institutional restrictions that female practitioners have faced and are aware that residues of discrimination are still subtly and unsubtly surfacing—but they generally believe that dedicated practice can undo and overcome this "cultural and conditioned baggage."

It is in the confidence and assurance of her place in the *dharma* that our youngest, second-generation Buddhist practitioner exhibits, that we see the possibility of women overcoming the three general scriptural attitudes to women with which we began this chapter. MP15 does not subscribe to the idea that a female birth is the result of negative karma nor does she feel that she needs to be reborn as a male to achieve liberation—the fact that the Buddha was male and most of her teachers are male does not lessen her sense of feeling empowered in a female body nor does it place any limits on her potential for spiritual insight. Paradoxically, our youngest practitioner actually feels that in some ways gender does matter as she feels it is the time for women to shine and that they can offer qualities—strength and energy for the dharma—that her male counterparts cannot.

NOTES

1. Shaw 1994, 12.

2. For the characteristics of "modern Buddhism" see Schedneck 2007, 57

3. To give a famous example in the positive, see the claims of Chapter 12 of the Mahāyāna Lotus Sūtra that liberation is accessible to all beings regardless of gender. Tsungunari and Akira 2007, 191–194. A contrasting view is the *Bahudhātuka-sutta*'s denial that women can become Buddhas. See Anālayo 2009, 135–190; Cabezón 1992, 3.

4. Romberg 2002, 161–170, 163.

5. Ibid.

6. Faure 2003, 3.

7. This is not to imply that the connection between practice and lay life is strictly an innovation of Western Buddhism—when Buddhism was transmitted to China around the first century of the Common Era, there was a shift toward the idea of enlightened action in lay life. This idea really flowered in the "enlightened layman" of Chan Buddhism (Jap: Zen) from around the fifth century.

8. Minichiello and Aroni 1990, 2.

9. Ibid., 8.

10. Daisaku Ikeda is the spiritual leader and president of the Nichiren Buddhist Sōka Gakkai International (SGI), a lay Buddhist organization.

11. Alternative translation: I devote myself to the Lotus Sūtra of the Wonderful Law.

12. Causton 1988, 13.

13. Stone 1998, 116–166, 116.

14. Interview PL12 2012.

15. Ibid.

16. Ibid.

17. Stone, "By Imperial Edict," 193.

18. Interview PL12, 2012.

19. Ibid.

20. The origin of suffering is craving or grasping (literally "thirst") *Dhamma-cakkappavattana Sutta SN 56.11*

21. Interview PL12, 2012.

22. Ibid.

23. Ibid.

24. Ibid.

25. Ibid.

26. Ibid.

27. Ibid.

28. Ibid.

29. Ibid.

30. Ibid.

31. The Nyingma order is the oldest of the Tibetan Buddhist traditions that advocates distinctive esoteric meditative practices designed to "cut through" appearances to reveal the true nature of mind. For a comprehensive history, see Powers 2007, 367–383.

32. Vajrayāna means Thunderbolt or Diamond vehicle and is also known as Tantric Buddhism.

33. Powers 2007, 257.

34. Gross 1996, 14.

35. Ibid., 13.

36. Ibid., 13–14.

37. Ibid., 14.

38. Interview AL13, 2013.

39. Ibid.

40. Ibid.

41. Ibid.

42. Interview AL13, 2013.

43. Interview AL13, 2013.

44. Ibid.

45. Ibid.

46. Ibid.

47. Ibid.

48. Ibid.

49. Ibid.

50. Ibid.
51. Interview MP15, 2015.
52. Ibid.
53. Ibid.
54. Ibid.
55. Ibid.
56. Ibid.
57. Ibid.
58. Ibid.

PART IV

Sexuality, Power, and Vulnerability

CHAPTER 13

Losing Faith, Gaining Empowerment: Changing Identities of Devadasis in Karnataka, India

Nicole Aaron[1]

The contemporary devadasi constitutes a small percentage of India's population, yet remains a highly contested group to people around the globe. Articles and books about the women continue to be published, and multiple documentaries are filmed every year, yet the image of the devadasi remains ambiguous. The 21st-century devadasi thrives in a few different regions throughout India, though her dominant presence is found in the South Indian states of Karnataka, Andhra Pradesh, and Maharashtra. In the postcolonial period, devadasi women have been viewed in a variety of ways, with the image of the women spanning from being empowered sex workers to exploited sex slaves. In Karnataka, devadasis are Dalit women, who also take on the role of priestesses, agricultural laborers, mothers, wives, and/or devotees. This chapter will explore the different embodiments that the contemporary devadasis of Karnataka may take and how their identities have changed through the influence of reform and rehabilitation schemes.

Kay Jordan has argued that these women were once empowered, but through the colonial gaze have become exploited prostitutes, stating that devadasis were "sacred servants" to Hindu deities until British colonial rule began.[2] From 1857 to 1945, the process of modernization and secularization in India resulted in the women becoming regarded as "profane prostitutes." However, as early as the 16th century, women were referred to as being "of loose character." Surveying documents written by missionaries and travelers to India as far back as the 16th century reveal that dancing women had a sexual role hundreds of years before British rule.[3] This sexual role has continued through to present day, with many (but not all) devadasis continuing to practice sex work. Jogan Shankar's sociological study in 1990 found that out of 85 devadasis, 39 were practicing prostitution, 34 of which were in brothels.[4] Although these statistics show evidence that more than half of the devadasis in Shankar's study were not practicing prostitution, he claims that girls are not dedicated to the goddess, but to urban brothels. While Shankar concludes that all dedications in his study were involuntary,[5] in 1991 K. C. Tarachand, who also advocates against the practice, observed that all dedications were voluntary.[6]

Ethnographic research by Lucinda Ramberg has demonstrated that some contemporary devadasis in South India maintain a religious significance in their communities, while others are sex workers.[7] Ramberg's nine months in a village in northern Karnataka reveals that the daily lives of devadasis continue to embody the goddess. Ramberg has found an element of the practice that other scholars have often disregarded: that of the religious. Treena Orchard has also undertaken research on the devadasis, revealing ways in which the women are empowered through their role, but her focus is primarily HIV/AIDS, and her target group was therefore devadasis practicing sex work.[8] Ramberg and Orchard argue that the contemporary devadasi displays agency through her dedication to the goddess. Shankar's research infers that the religious function of the women is virtually nonexistent, yet Ramberg's ethnography, 15 years later, concludes the opposite—religious practice is still very much a part of the everyday lives of these women. Such a varied array of conclusions about who devadasis are continues to confound scholars and laypeople alike, and the search continues to reveal who the "bona fide" devadasi is.

Devadasis in Karnataka are dedicated to the goddess Yellamma, and the image of these women that was presented to me in Karnataka is incontestably negative; devadasi women are understood by society to be nothing more than sex workers under the sanction of an ignorant and superstitious religious practice. While there were once a group of advocates who felt that the devadasi practice should continue because it had a religious importance, it is rare to find such individuals in today's society. Alternatively, there are those who advocate that there are no more devadasis; the women are believed to be temple dancers of an ancient tradition. Despite the devadasi practice becoming illegal in Karnataka in 1982, there are many devadasis who remain in villages of rural Karnataka today.

COLONIAL DEVADASIS: DANCING GIRLS AND PROSTITUTES

Literature on devadasis is problematic for two reasons. One is that there have been a multitude of temple women over the centuries, each carrying different roles, yet these women are now all understood to be the same women: religious prostitutes. While there is evidence from temple inscriptions that temple women once existed in Karnataka,[9] it is not a valid claim to say that the devadasis of Karnataka are related to the temple women found in the temple inscriptions. However, reform movements lumped all temple women and nautch dancers into the category of "devadasi" regardless of what their position was, or is today. Consequently, Karnataka devadasis are being approached in the same fashion that temple women in other states were reformed, though unlike in Tamil Nadu, where women were largely attached to the temples,[10] devadasis in Karnataka are more focused on sex work as a livelihood.[11] Eradicating the devadasi practice in Karnataka has therefore proven to be much more complex than it was in Tamil Nadu, where the practice has now been abolished.

As missionaries, travelers, and colonialists entered the Indian subcontinent, they began writing about the dancing women they found. Browsing through literature by Abbé Dubois, Edgar Thurston, Joep Bor, and John Shortt reveals that throughout the colonial period devadasis maintained a sexual role.[12] Many of these women were temple dancers, during an era when women who danced were also viewed as prostitutes. Thurston confirms that there were once seven different types of temple women, each carrying a different name and role within the temple and society.[13] Using "devadasi" as a blanket term to describe all of these different classes of women came about during the colonial period in order to simplify the complexity of (temple) women.[14] However, I would argue that creating a blanket term such as "devadasi" has not reduced or simplified any of the complexities that embody the devadasi practice. There are still multiple reasons why women become devadasis and multiple positions that the women may uphold (separately or all at once). There are different interpretations of the term "devadasi" in English, ranging from "god servant" to "slave of the god" to "sacred prostitute." Surveying literature and government archives from the 19th and early 20th centuries reveals that before the term "devadasi" was applied, "dancing girls" was the most frequently used term to refer to these women. However, today's devadasis in Karnataka are all Dalit women, whose history is unknown. It, therefore, may not be accurate to conclude that the reforms that took place during the colonial period took away the "sacred" element from the women of Karnataka, but rather that all temple women, some with sacred practices and some with more sexual practices, became known as "devadasis" at this time, in the midst of a class revolution and respectability movements.

THE MIDDLE CLASS AND "RESPECTABILITY" MOVEMENTS

The rise of the bourgeois feminist movement in India was fraught with patriarchal values of middle class Indian men who had been educated by the Western elite. The emergence of nationalism in the 19th century opened an avenue for introducing new conceptions of womanhood. Those who were part of the nationalist movement upheld the chaste and modest woman as the ideal in order to exemplify their own nationalist goals. This contributed to the underpinning of bourgeois notions of respectability that seeped into the social classes of the time.[15] A clear distinction was made between what admirable qualities constitute respectable middle class women and what lewd qualities lower class women possessed (with prostitutes being just one example of this).[16]

Using this framework, middle class women ousted devadasis from their role as dancers and temple servants in the name of respectability.[17] It was this middle class respectability movement that resulted in the practice being viewed as immoral, and these dancing women becoming understood as "nothing more than" prostitutes.[18] While it is evident that this was the effect of patriarchy on the middle class women at the time, Padma Anagol argues that placing blame on men (or patriarchy) takes away the acknowledgment that women have acted as agents of change throughout history. Rather, women had their own agenda in advocating for an end to the devadasi/dancing girl institution,

> [They were] . . . preventing men from engaging in the practice of keeping mistresses by making the practice socially unacceptable and improving the status of their own role as housewives by assuming attributes traditionally associated with [devadasis], such as the ability to sing or play musical instruments.[19]

The ability of lower class women to use their sexuality for pleasure and profit was seen as a threat by the middle class,[20] which led to the rise of a middle class movement of feminisms that further oppressed subordinate, low class women by advocating a married and domesticated life as the ideal for all women. These movements took away the rights of devadasis to put on nautch performances in order to create a new, more respectable image of dance, which middle class women named *bharatanatyam*, and began performing for the public, thereby "forcing [devadasis] into lesser-status occupations such as the theatre and urban prostitution."[21]

Dr. Muthulakshmi Reddy was one of the leading middle class women heading the abolition of devadasis in the early 20th century.[22] Reddy argued that the devadasi institution "was a great piece of injustice, a great wrong, a violation of human rights, a practice highly revolting to our higher nature to countenance, and to tolerate young innocent girls to be trained in the name of religion to lead an immoral life, to lead a life of promiscuity, a life leading to the disease of the mind and the body."[23] She established the Madras Hindu Religious Endowments Act of 1929. This was the first major step in Madras to abolish the devadasi system. Natarajan has suggested that Reddy used this sexual agency that devadasis had and reframed it as victimhood and helplessness. The ability of devadasis to have control over their sexual relations with men was interpreted as sexual exploitation in order to create a justification for rescuing the women and girls.[24]

In 1927, the South Indian Devadasi Association was launched in protest against Reddy's proposed bill of 1927 (formally accepted by the Council in 1929), intended to prevent future dedications.[25] However, with the support of the anti-nautch movement, by the 1930s Reddy had transformed the image of the devadasi to prostitute, and the women began to be policed under the Immoral Traffic Act of 1930.[26] It became visible that devadasi women did not agree with Reddy. Groups of women collaborated to fight for the right to continue their practice.[27] Devadasis wrote letters, arguing that they were temple servants, with the specialized practice of song and dance, and should not be degraded by being identified as prostitutes. Twelve devadasis from a temple of princely patronage wrote petitions in which they defended their position with religious texts and customs, believing that this "hereditary occupation" must be respected and protected.[28] Unfortunately, the association made between devadasis and prostitutes had gained recognition. As prostitutes, devadasis had no voice, and Reddy spoke for them, but not relaying the message they desperately tried to express.[29]

Reddy's solution for the women was marriage and a domesticated life. In 1947, with the implementation of the Madras Devadasi Prevention of Dedication Act, dedications to temples became illegal, and invalid, allowing devadasi women to enter legal marriages. This Act officially prohibited certain classes from participating in nautch dances. From this point forward, devadasis who participated in nautch dances were understood to have been dedicated to a life of prostitution.

According to Natarajan, the nationalists and middle class essentially hijacked the devadasi dance tradition in the name of respectability, which they claimed was located within the domestic sphere. Women who did not live up to the ideals of respectability were viewed as a threat to society (and thereby the nation and nationalist movement).[30] The men who were at the forefront of shaping India as a nation, whose values weighed heavily on what the British upheld as "moral," redefined the "good woman" as the domesticated wife while changing the image of devadasi into prostitute, and ultimately the "bad woman." While the focus of this movement targeted a different group of devadasis than those in Karnataka, these reform and abolition movements had a direct effect on the degradation of all temple women, including devadasis of Karnataka.

THE DIFFERENCE BETWEEN DEVADASIS AND SEX WORKERS

As a result of these movements, devadasis today face many challenges. Devadasi sex work remains more village based, though some may travel to brothels in bigger cities, especially during their younger years. The *mangala sutra* of the goddess (the *muttu*) is tied to the young girl by a priest or priestesses when she is dedicated to Yellamma and is viewed in society as a "license" to practice sex work. Though most women no longer wear their *muttu* in public, they will put it on when a client comes as reassurance of their devadasi status. With this license, devadasi women experience less physical attacks than commercial sex workers. Lakshmi[31] is a devadasi who practices sex work. She explained to me,

> I can say that I have the permission to do sex work because I have this *muttu* tied. I have the right . . . The sex workers would not have this value to what they do. They just do sex work. I have the right to tell anyone who asks me that I am here to do sex work, and it has been given to me by the society and the community . . . No one will talk rubbish about me if I have this *muttu*. No one will kick us or fight with us. If they fight I can beat him with my foot wear. I have the right to do what I do with my *muttu* round my neck.[32]

However, women also explained that because they take on the role of the eldest son within the family, they are financially responsible for their natal family. The expectation and requirement to provide for one's family result in women who are unable to do so or choose to focus their finances on their children, often being abandoned by their natal family. In this regard, devadasis may experience less financial independence than non-devadasi sex workers.

According to devadasis, the major difference between their tradition and sex work is that sex workers make the choice to practice sex work and devadasis do not. Sex workers who are not devadasis, and are therefore said by devadasis to have made the choice to practice sex work, are believed to be doing so only for the sake of money and materialism. Kasturi is a devadasi who continues to practice sex work. When I asked her what the difference is between a devadasi and a sex worker, she gave an answer that resonated through the opinions of multiple informants. She explained: "The women who do not have the *muttu* tied are different, madam. They are those with husbands. They would be doing this work for greed. They are different and we are different" (Kasturi, interviewed January 2013 in Bijapur district, Karnataka). Devadasis claim that they have been forced to practice because of poverty, while sex workers do it by choice for money. They often do not acknowledge that perhaps sex workers who are not devadasis are making this choice because they are also poor and, therefore, do not see it as a choice at all. Rasmani is an older woman, unsure of her age, but believes she is around 60 years old. She has been living in a government plot for devadasis since 1992. For most of her life, her maternal uncle was her only partner. He was married to another woman, and went back and forth between their homes. They had five children together, and he paid for all of their food and married off both of their daughters, before eventually leaving, at which point she never saw him again. It is unclear why he left, though she says that she continued having sex with him until a nongovernmental organization (NGO) came and told her what she was doing was "dirty," at which point she stopped. As we sat outside on her porch in the hot dry sun, she explained to me that some women get married and enjoy all of the "pleasures" that their husbands give them, until his alcoholism and abuse becomes a problem, at which point she leaves and goes to work as a sex worker in Mumbai. She clarifies, "They are not the devadasis. They are those who get married. Now there are no devadasis as such."[33]

ON THE IMPORTANCE OF MARRIAGE

The most recent law to ensure heterosexual marriage of devadasi women was the 1982 Karnataka Devadasis (Prohibition of Dedication) Act. This Act made it illegal for devadasis to marry the goddess, facing fines of up to 5,000 rupees and five years' imprisonment. With the introduction of this Act, the government began advocating for the marriage of devadasis to men and was initially offering money to men who would marry the women. However, most men who have married devadasi women still have another family with whom they spend the majority of their time. Therefore, even those who claim to be married are not in a monogamous relationship. In 1992 Chhaya Datar wrote, "The devadasis I met, wondered that after being married, will they be allowed by their husbands to sing and dance in public? If their husbands beat them, can they leave them as they are free to abandon their *zulwa*, the man they keep?[34] Their status of a concubine along with that as a ritual person offers them a different space in life, which many of them are not willing to trade off."[35] It could be argued that pushing devadasi women into monogamous heterosexual relationships not only breaks down the foundational ties of their marriage to the deity, but completely uproots their entire understanding of family and ways of functioning within the familial realm.[36]

In comparing my research to Datar's research, it appears that this is exactly what has now happened. Devadasi women I spoke to seem to have completely shifted their understanding of family, now believing that having a husband is the most respectable position they could be in, and not having a husband makes them a disgrace. In my own research, devadasis expressed desire for monogamous heterosexual relationships and wished the same for their children.

Though previous research suggested devadasis are empowered through their connection to the goddess and their role in the family and society, I found in my research that there is a huge sense of shame among these women when it comes to practicing sex work. They feel embarrassed to have to show their naked bodies to multiple men or a man that they are not married to. They consistently suggest marriage as an alternative. I sat with a group of devadasis who are all members of a *sangha* (self-help) group. As they told me they would prefer marriage to a man over marriage to the goddess, I asked them if they would prefer marriage even if their husband was an alcoholic, or abusive, to which they maintained their stance, that yes, marriage to a man is better. When I questioned them about their reasoning for preferring to live with a "bad" husband, one woman said that even if her husband killed her, she would still prefer this option over the life of a devadasi, because at least she would die a respectable married woman. I must have looked taken back by this statement, because multiple women then started chiming in, telling me that men in their village are generally "good" and beat their wives only when they have done something wrong. As having a husband is seen as more respectable than being a devadasi, many devadasi women resent that the choice was taken away from them to have a husband.

What is disregarded in arguing for heterosexual marriage is the reality that entering into this marriage in a patriarchal setting such as India may take away the woman's autonomy over her own body, as she relies completely on her husband for food and shelter and therefore must do as he says. In this regard, sex workers may be understood as more empowered than married women.[37] The conventional upholding of the normative family is so ingrained in Indian society that any single woman, be she a widow or a divorcee, is often rendered an outcast from her community. However, Mary John and Janaki Nair suggest a counter-approach to the feminist understanding, "it is clear that many of the feminist narratives fail to acknowledge the ways in which wife/non-wife are constituted by the same patriarchal authorities, so that they are structurally yoked in fundamental ways, making the securities and pleasures of one domain unavailable to the other."[38] In this regard, devadasis and sex workers present the "other" to the wife, which may be a threat to the normative family, though this does not necessarily mean that one is more empowering than the other. Each role, wife and non-wife, maintains characteristics that the women may find empowering and uplifting.

In reality, this spiritual dimension has typically been disregarded by reformers and rehabilitators, while the opposite message has been preached. By focusing on devadasi women as nothing more than exploited third-world prostitutes, NGOs have contributed to the changing identities of devadasi women, who now believe that having a husband is a better life and that sex work is "dirty" work. It is evident through previous research by Lucinda Ramberg, Treena Orchard, and Chhaya Datar that devadasi women valued their freedom and relationship to the goddess.[39] I did not find the same relationship. Devadasi women feel that having a husband gives them respect, in life and after life. Regardless of whether their husband is controlling or beats them, many of them long for societal respect and acceptance first and foremost, which they no longer get as devadasi women, and believe they would get if they had a husband. Believing that devadasis are exploited women, NGOs have set out to empower them. In reality, by making them believe that they are exploited and that heterosexual marriage will provide them with a more respectful life, I argue that in many respects they have disempowered these women.

THE VALUE OF DEDICATION FOR A FAMILY

Since devadasis are married to the goddess, it is difficult for them to marry a man, though legally they are now permitted to do so and it is not uncommon for women who have left the practice to marry Muslim men. However, because the majority of devadasis are not in a heterosexual marriage, men who father the children of devadasis have no financial obligation to the family. This leaves the children fatherless, usually carrying the names of their mothers. Devadasi women appreciate daughters, and some of them still dedicate their daughters (or the daughters may even dedicate themselves) to the goddess in order to keep them within the family to take care of them when they are older. This process of dedicating one's daughter in order to ensure economic security is what Lynda Epp calls "fertility economics" and what Lucinda Ramberg refers to as a "sexual economy."[40] As the women are not married to a man, their daughters help sustain the family. The *muttu* tied to the devadasi allows much more mobility than the *mangala sutra* tied to the bride by her husband, which implies a sense of control and dominance.

Lucinda Ramberg argues that the sacred marriage of devadasis and the crossing of gendered boundaries within it (with devadasis taking on the role of fathers and sons) increases the value of daughters.[41] My own field work revealed that this value depends strictly on the financial contribution the daughter is making to the family. If she ceases to give money to her parents, or shifts her priorities to educating her children, she loses value within the family, and in some cases her family no longer associates with her at all. When I asked devadasis if they feel that these "positives" outlined by Ramberg and Orchard are true of their own lives, many women felt it was irrelevant, and were not interested in implying in any way that there is any reason to value the devadasi practice. Some women did acknowledge that there are positive aspects of the practice: they enjoy that they have more freedom to roam around and control over their finances, but they feel that these positive characteristics do not outweigh the negatives, such as pressure from family to earn and abuse faced if they return home without any money from a day's work. While Ramberg and Orchard are accurate in their positive assessments of the practice, few women feel happy in their position as a devadasi. In my research, only two women told me that they would consider dedicating their own daughters as devadasis, if it became financially necessary. Nearly all women were adamantly against this suggestion.

CHANGING IDENTITIES OF DEVADASIS

The ban on dedications has also contributed to a loss of tradition and ritual. Many devadasi women used to have matted dreadlocks, and sometimes girls are dedicated because they are said to be born with this hair. NGOs have counseled women into understanding that such beliefs and practices are superstitious and ignorant. As sex outside of marriage is seen as dirty, any beliefs that may encourage such a practice are not viewed as honorable. As part of the government's plan to eradicate the practice, they began dismantling devadasi rituals and practice, initially by cutting off the matted dreadlocks of women.

However, despite the government's attempt to eradicate the practice, some devadasi women continue to claim that their beliefs in Yellamma are Truth. If they abandon their rituals, Yellamma creates problems for them, usually in the form of health and skin infections. They feel that the goddess calls them to this work and they must continue for her. Other women feel that as long as they do their work respectably, they should not be policed. As the government now claims that the devadasi practice is eradicated, there is not as much forceful action in trying to make women stop. It is believed that awareness has been given, and as long as no new dedications take place, the government is satisfied. However, women do continue to practice. Durgavva is a devadasi who continues to practice sex work. She maintains great faith in Yellamma, and while she does not support the continuation of devadasi dedications, she also refuses to stop practicing. She explained,

> She is our Goddess, Yellamma. We are dedicated in her name. You people tell us not to dedicate as per law. But she tells us to dedicate. The

government has tried to stop. There will be sores, and illnesses and infections. But at least in every village two to three dedications take place every year. Because the wounds and sores go away as soon as her *bhandara* (colored holy powder) is smeared. So they dedicate the girls as devadasis for our Goddess. It is all because of our faith and belief.[42]

Durgavva is not alone. Rema informed me, "All those things of people trying to make me stop have finished. They did try in the beginning and now they have stopped. I am continuing. They should not fight with us and we should also not rebel against them. We are doing this within the limits of decency."[43]

Though some women attempt to carry on the practice, police are now quite strict about ensuring that dedications do not take place. Women who are practicing sex work have the legal right to do so as long as they are not soliciting. However, for dedication purposes women have had to relocate to smaller temples, where they can perform dedications more secretly. Additionally, most devadasis do not want other young girls to have to experience the "sufferings" they have had and are adamant to ensure that no new dedications take place. If they see or hear of anybody dedicating or planning to dedicate their daughter, they will call the police and have them arrested.

Women from one particular NGO, who are part of *sangha* groups, were taught that matted dreadlocks are dirty and that this type of hairstyle has nothing to do with the goddess. The NGO had the women partake in forcibly cutting other devadasis' matted hair off and reporting them to the police. Devadasi women never questioned this approach, understanding that it was the correct thing to do: that it was necessary to eradicate the practice in order to ensure their children had a better livelihood, free of the sufferings from the life of a devadasi. The documentary *Sex, Death and the Gods* demonstrates how this was performed at the full moon festival at Saundatti Yellamma temple and clearly shows an older devadasi being very resistant to having her hair cut off, proclaiming that it is all she has left. However, the NGO feels that it is important for others to see that once the hair is cut off, nothing changes. In this regard, they are very proud to show the world they have entered into a sacred space and forcibly rid the premises of what some women consider to be sacred, as matted hair is an embodiment of the goddess. In the following excerpt, Indra, a devadasi who is no longer practicing sex work, and is far removed from tradition, describes how this process used to take place.

So the people from the organization used to shout at us and make us cut [the matted hair]. They would shout that; forget about your Yellamma and other goddesses, please cut off your dirty hair. Then they were given shampoo to wash and they would look very nice afterwards. Why should those knotted hairs be there? So it was cut off and they will not get

knotted again. When we used to go to the *jatre* (festival) we would catch
the women who used to have knotted hair and we would bring them to get
a haircut. Instead of watching the *jatre* we would be looking out to catch
such persons. We would bring them, cut their hair and scold them . . .
The police would say that they would arrest anyone who helps the women
to do these practices. They would take the women with knotted hair who
were taken by us and let us go. After they did all these procedures the
tying of *muttu* stopped. We used to go on "*Rundi Hunnime*" (full moon festival) and break the bangles. All that has stopped now. Now nobody can tie
muttu. (Indra, interviewed January 2013 in Belgaum district, Karnataka)

Working for advocates against their own tradition, reform, and rehabilitation
movements slowly shifted the way that devadasis identified with their auspicious status. It is undeniable that the influence of this NGO has had an
impact on the shifting identities and changing status of devadasi women.

Scholars and laypeople alike have typically applied the history of devadasis and dancing women in other regions of South India to Karnataka devadasis. Yet, it appears that devadasis in Karnataka never identified with this
history. An increasingly popular narrative of this comes through Chinmayee
Manjunath's article, where she recounts,

I bring up the topic of how devadasis used to be, hoping that it will ignite
memories. But I end up telling them their own history. The story of how
devadasis were once accepted in society, how their forms of dance like
sadir evolved into bharatnatyam and how their children inherited property
from benefactors. How they were sanctified prostitutes, traded by priests
and wealthy patrons. "We never knew that devadasis were even respected,"
gapes Rajeshwari. "People don't even talk to us in our village."[44]

Devadasis in Karnataka have now gone through two generations of people
recounting inapplicable histories to a group whose history was sadly lost long
ago. Through the introduction of the *sangha*, not only has the government
forced other women to stop practicing, but has also recreated the history of
devadasis through a story that justifies eradicating the practice. Below is an
example illustrating how the *sangha* has influenced the devadasis' understanding of their practice and contributed toward ending this tradition. The
following quote, by a devadasi who has had heavy involvement in *sangha*
groups, and now identifies as an "ex-devadasi," illustrates how *sangha* groups
have used a "historical" narrative, which no devadasi narrated as her own history, to persuade women to stop dedicating their daughters to this practice.

They tied the *muttu* earlier because there was poverty. So to make it convenient to the rich landowners of the village this devadasi system was

made. Because those rich farmers needed girls. They encouraged this practice among the poor families. I have heard about this. There is also this caste system, right? People of this caste are not aware and not intelligent. They have no education, they don't know how to progress. Because of poverty they would have taken loans. So those who lend money have to use the daughters of these families because of the loan. That is how this system prevails in the poor families. It is neither because of the parents nor because of God. It is just because of poverty. Because of poverty we would have taken loans from the farmers. We cannot return it as we are poor. They get repaid back by using the girls of the family. But their daughters cannot be used by the others. We learned this by the training they gave in [the] *sangha*.[45]

The second quote exhibits how the *sangha* forced women to stop their religious practices if they wanted to receive assistance from the NGO. It also reveals how women negotiate poverty and agency through their various positioning narratives. This explanation was given by a devadasi who continues to practice sex work and is a member of a sangha that is supported by the government, and seeks to empower sex workers, but does not support the devadasi system.

After I joined the *sangha* they told us not to follow the tradition. The office of the devadasis has told us not to do any devadasi customs; singing the *jogathi* songs and begging, or tying *muttu* etc . . . I stopped wearing [the *muttu*], when I joined the *sangha* . . . We take it off when those people come and we put it back when they go back. They forbid us from wearing the beads because we will beg if we have the beads. We should not wear those. That is the rule. They also confiscate our baskets and other articles of the rituals.[46]

Such lessons and legal enforcements from various organizations have contributed to the decline in devadasi dedications and, in turn, a change in devadasi tradition and identity. Those who felt that the devadasi practice was violent and exploitative told devadasi women their own opinions about the practice, persuaded them to stop, and used forceful methods to ensure it happened. Through the organization of *sangha* groups, government organizations and NGOs were able to raise awareness against the devadasi practice. They gave women training, but not in practical things like employable skills. Rather, they trained them to believe that they are doing dirty work and that their life would be much better once they stopped practicing. They connected the women to bank loans, lawyers, and government schemes so that they could leave this "dirty" practice and become aware and empowered. Having come to believe that what they were doing was wrong and not respectable, the women now have positive perceptions of how the NGO has influenced their practice. In many cases, they were much more excited to talk to us about these things than about their own personal stories.

My research assistant and I sat in Hollevva's one-room home with her and her sister, as they told us about their experience with NGOs. Like most women, they feel grateful that the NGO has brought them out of sex work. Hollevva told us about the initial approach by *sangha* leaders to train women into understanding that the devadasi system is wrong. "They used to ask in the *sangha*, 'Do you like doing this? Are you proud of having a *sangha* for yourselves?' . . . They told us to stop this work. They told that this was a dirty work which brought about many diseases" (Hollevva, interviewed January 2013 in Belgaum district, Karnataka). Nearby, we found Margavva busy working at her petty goods shop close to her home when we arrived. She took us to her house and sent her daughter to replace her at the shop. We sat down on the floor with her to discuss her relationship with NGOs seeking to rehabilitate devadasis, and hear her personal story. According to her, there was a teacher who went village to village to do a survey on devadasis and tell the women about the NGO. She explained to them that it was necessary to start *sangha* groups in order to save money, and they would organize the women to go to various festivals and watch for any dedications. The staff from the NGO gave the women a lot of "information and awareness" about their tradition, by telling them about the negatives of their own practice, which they had not realized before. They took this information and began telling the other devadasis what the NGO had taught them, and according to Margavva, they all started doing other work and sending their children to school once the NGO came along. Guralingavva, who is a devadasi no longer practicing, and a staff member for the same NGO, said, "Our life was going on in darkness till this [NGO] came to give us some light. If not for that organization we would have been dumped in the gutter . . . They told us, 'Devadasi is a horrible practice and that we should come out of that.' After that we became aware. If not our lives would have been in the dark. What else is there in our lives?"[47]

The message given by NGOs to practicing devadasis was very much one of colonial and patriarchal influence. Women came to believe that what they were doing was dirty, that they were not respectable, and that they would no longer be wanted by any other men now that they had practiced sex work. They were encouraged to leave sex work and carry on life as single women (the least respected position in Indian society). Devadasi women were made to believe that they had come to this practice because they are uneducated, lacking knowledge, and ignorant. They now degrade themselves and lack confidence to do any other kind of work. The NGO's approach implies that there is no respectable answer besides "No" when asked if the women enjoy what they do. They are shamed out of admitting that perhaps they enjoy the higher salary or, even more disgraceful (in the view of those seeking to rehabilitate the women), that they may actually enjoy the sex they get by doing sex work.

The problems that encompass the devadasi practice go far beyond the system itself, but are deeply rooted in a patriarchal morality that continues to thrive throughout India today. Though there are many qualities of the devadasi life that have the potential to be empowering, Indian culture understands the situation differently, labeling the women as dirty prostitutes, and devadasis have come to feel like some of the most oppressed and exploited women in society. In 1992, Chhaya Datar wrote, "As part of the process of integration, [the devadasi] is losing her traditional self image and feels humiliation at the hands of both the elite section of society, the men and also the reformers. She is confused at present, she is getting submerged in the cultural modernization."[48] Sadly, Datar predicted the future accurately. Women have been submerged into cultural modernization and feel humiliated by their devadasi status. Devadasi women are now left believing that practicing sex work is wrong. There is a larger percentage of women who have stopped practicing than women who continue, and there are few alternative livelihood options for either group. In reality, today's devadasi is arguably similar to any other rural Dalit woman, except that she receives a devadasi pension of Rs. 400 monthly (US$6.50) and is never eligible for a widow's pension.

NOTES

1. I am thankful to Douglas Hill, Will Sweetman, and Linda Zampol D'Ortia for comments on earlier drafts of this chapter, as well as to all the devadasi women who shared their stories with me and invited me into their homes to listen.

2. Jordan 2003, 8.

3. See Bor 2007.

4. Shankar 1990, 106.

5. Ibid., 162.

6. Tarachand 1991, 128.

7. Ramberg 2006.

NB: Throughout this chapter, I will use the term "sex workers" unless referring to an individual or organization who refers to the women as "prostitutes," in which case I will use "prostitute."

8. Orchard 2004.

9. Parasher and Naik 1986, 63–78.

10. See Orr 2000.

11. I say this in large part because it is how these women are portrayed in society. They do not have a connection to the temple, and most act as mistresses

rather than sex workers. However, sex out of marriage in India is considered prostitution, regardless of the situation.

12. Bor's chapter provides an overview of 16th-century travelers to India such as Portuguese trader Domingo Paes, Venetian jeweler Gasparo Balbi, and Dutch Calvinist Minister Abraham Rogerius, all of whom wrote about the sexual nature of devadasi women. He concludes that as early as the 16th century, these women were providing "sexual entertainment" to the elite class. See Bor 2007, 43.

In the 18th century, Abbé Dubois refers to temple women as "courtesans," "dancing-girls," "deva-dasis," and "prostitutes." He writes of the "shameful practices" of these women and remarks that "sacred temples" were often turned into "mere brothels." See Dubois 1906.

John Shortt speaks of two kinds of dancing girls: those attached to the pagodas and those who are simply prostitutes. See Shortt 1870, 182–194.

Edgar Thurston speaks of a group known as Asadis in Bellary district (now northern Karnataka) who were dedicated prostitutes and dancers who would also sing and chant the story of Yellamma. See Thurston 1906, 60.

13. Thurston 1906, 125.

14. See Jordan 2003.

15. For more on this, see Mosse 1985.

16. See Chatterjee 1993.

17. For more on this, see Anagol 2005; Natarajan 1997, 130.

18. Anagol 2005, 123.

19. Ibid., 126.

20. Natarajan 1997, 75–76.

21. Anagol 2008, 614.

22. Reddy 1964, 72.

23. Ibid., 64.

24. Natarajan 1997, 115–116.

25. Ibid., 107.

26. Ibid., 123.

27. For more on this see Jordan 2003, Hubel 2010, Natarajan 1997.

28. Nair 1994, 3162–63.

29. Natarajan cites one letter written by the South Indian Devadasi Association sent to the government in 1927: "Popularly our caste is styled by the name of dancing girl probably due to the reason that most of our caste women are experts in dancing and music. Such a hoary name is now unfortunately mingled up and associated with an immoral life. It would, we submit, be easily conceded by every one that the institution of dedicating one's life to a temple has nothing to do with prostitution. . . . Hence, we make bold to question the implied identification of Devadasis with prostitutes." Natarajan 1997, 124–125.

30. See Mosse, *Nationalism and Sexuality,* for more details on this.

31. All names have been changed to protect the identity of respondents.

32. Lakshmi, interviewed January 2013 in Bijapur district, Karnataka.

33. Rasmani, interviewed January 2013 in Bijapur district, Karnataka.

34. It is not uncommon for devadasis to have one man live with them for an extended amount of time, in their home, under their control. Often, these men may stay for a few months, a few years, or a lifetime, but will maintain a family of their own elsewhere, and therefore not take financial responsibility for the devadasi's family. They may buy her clothes or jewelry, or leave some money before departing.

35. Datar 1992, 88.

36. See Ramberg 2006, for a detailed account of ways in which devadasi mothers take on the role of husbands and fathers, while their daughters take on the role of sons.

37. This is discussed in more detail in Gangoli 2007, 21–39.

38. Nair and John 1998, 12.

39. See Ramberg 2006; Orchard 2004; Datar 1992.

40. For more on this, see Ramberg 2006; Epp 1996.

41. Ramberg 2006, 178.

42. Durgavva, interviewed March 2013 in Bagalkot district, Karnataka.

43. Rema, interviewed January 2013 in Bijapur district, Karnataka.

44. Chinmayee 2013.

45. Renuka, interviewed January 2013 in Belgaum district, Karnataka.

46. Ranavva, interviewed February 2013 in Bijapur district, Karnataka.

47. Guralingavva, interviewed February 2013 in Belgaum district, Karnataka.

48. Datar 1992, 91.

CHAPTER 14

A Politics of Empathy: Christianity and Women's Peace Activism in U.S. Military Prostitution in South Korea

Keun-Joo Christine Pae

INTRODUCTION

For more than six decades, the Korean War (1950–1953), which ended as a truce between North Korea and the United Nations, has traumatized Koreans' hearts and minds.[1] The war has not only divided the Korean Peninsula for an indefinite period, but also enabled the United States Armed Forces to stay in the heart of the sovereign country South Korea. America's military presence has provoked feelings of powerlessness among Koreans in terms of international politics and national security. As a result, the stories of more than 1 million Korean women who have sold sex to G.I.s have been systematically silenced.

Critically reflecting on the meanings of peace in the militarized world, this chapter analyzes Korean women's social activism in prostitution around U.S. military bases in South Korea. From a feminist theological perspective, this chapter particularly delineates the roles of Christian faith—rather than Christianity as an institutionalized religion—in peacemaking activism. More specifically, I will first historically examine the rise and fall and the aftermath of U.S. military prostitution in South Korea in order to contemplate how

Korean women activists contested and reconstructed the ideas and practices of peace, countering globalized militarism, militarized prostitution, and
gender-based military sexual violence; and how Korean women peacemakers
have practiced solidarity with the women working in military prostitution
beyond religious and national boundaries. These questions will further argue
what I call "a politics of empathy"—a Christian feminist ethic of antiwar
peacemaking.

Empathy is a key to understand feminist social activism in Korea. As Elli
Kim, a Korean feminist peace studies scholar argues, throughout the history
of Korean women's peace activism, "empathy with suffering human beings"
has been the vital force in pushing women to organize for peace.[2] From
the anti-nuclear power activism in the 1970s to the antiwar activism in the
2000s, "empathy" with those suffering from sociopolitical power structures
lies at the heart of Korean women's peace activism. Empathy leads women to
articulate interconnectedness among all living beings and to critically reflect
upon their own participation in oppressive political-economic systems. By
examining empathy as a social practice in U.S. camptown prostitution in
South Korea, this chapter attempts to construct an alternative idea of peace
with an emphasis on just human relations.

DEVELOPMENT OF MILITARIZED PROSTITUTION IN KOREA

It is no longer a secret that sex industries are "ubiquitous around the
military bases" and that soldiers have used women sexually "through rape,
kidnapping, and slave brothels that follow armies."[3] Military prostitution is
not a separate issue from military rape. The patriarchal assumption that soldiers have uncontrollable sexual drives leads [male] politicians to seek safe
and commercialized sex, allowing them to avoid the topic of military rape
and thus diplomatic conflict.[4]

Although the Asia Pacific–based organization International Women's
Network Against Militarism acknowledges militarized prostitution as wom-
en's shared experience of U.S. bases in Asia and the Pacific Islands, the systematically organized development of military prostitution might be found
only in South Korea.[5]

By the end of 1945, a few months after the arrival of U.S. military in
the newly independent South Korea from Japan, Bupyeong, a small town
between Seoul and Incheon, became the first "camptown" (*kijichon*) where
American soldiers sought out liquor and women for recreation.[6] Bupyeong
had public brothels around one of Imperial Japan's important military bases
for the Pacific War.[7] Since then, camptown prostitution has evolved in different stages: the early stage (1945–1949), the foundation of the rest and recreation business (1950s), the golden days (1960s), the systematic corporation

(1970s to mid-1980s), and the declining period (mid-1980s to present). These stages correspond to the changes in American foreign policy, the number of American soldiers stationed in South Korea, and the economic development of South Korea.[8] The Korean prostitutes, who cater to American soldiers, are pejoratively called *yang-gong-ju*, which can be translated into "Western princess." Western princess has since become the representative term for sexually loose and wanton women in Korea.

Prostitution around U.S. military camps in Korea is a continuation of Imperial Japan's system of public prostitution. The Japanese colonial government constructed red light districts and prohibited people from selling and buying sex outside of these districts. The Japanese colonial government monitored these brothels in order to effectively control the bodies and minds of colonized Koreans.[9] Imperial Japan's public prostitution was the backbone of militarized prostitution in modern Korea. Na-young Lee, a Korean feminist sociologist, stresses that American culture, American military occupation, poverty and military dictatorship augmented by the Korean War, and economic development were all built upon Imperial Japan's carefully installed system of public prostitution.[10] It was not a coincidence that Korean women's first organized movement after independence was to demand that the U.S. military government prohibit prostitution. Although public prostitution was banned in South Korea in 1947, private prostitution became popularized due to pandemic poverty. Moreover, service clubs and dance halls for American soldiers were quasi-public brothels where buying and selling sex were available and where the U.S. military monitored sex workers for the purpose of venereal disease control.[11]

On June 25, 1950, the Korean War broke out as North Korean troops crossed the 38th parallel. In response, the United States immediately called a meeting of the United Nation Security Council. While the former Soviet Union was absent, the members of the Security Council agreed to send out UN troops to South Korea in order to save innocent South Korean civilians. The Korean War was the first globalized war, as 31 countries from the five continents were either directly or indirectly involved.[12]

The Korean War was the most tragic event regarding prostitution in Korea.[13] Poverty-stricken girls and women, especially war widows who had multiple family members to support, were to sell their bodies for survival. It was also believed that both controlling UN soldiers' sexual desires by providing safe sex and protecting innocent Korean women from wild foreign soldiers were essential to win the war.[14] As a result, the U.S. military and the Korean government established 79 comfort stations and five dance halls for the UN soldiers in South Korea by the end of 1951.[15] Military authorities and private business owners collaborated with each other to effectively and safely run brothels for soldiers.[16]

After the war, the Korean government and the U.S. military systematically controlled Western princesses by bringing them into designated towns and by administering their encounters with American soldiers. For instance, in 1957, the South Korean Ministry of Public Health and the U.S. Eighth Army first gathered Western princesses at geographically marked places around the U.S. military bases so as to control venereal diseases; those who took regular medical checkups and obtained VD cards could officially cater to American soldiers.[17] While prostitution was illegal in Korea, by physically isolating entertaining camptowns from the rest of Korean society, the U.S. military and the Korean government successfully covered up state-sanctioned prostitution. At the same time, the particular needs of militarized prostitution have been normalized among Koreans.

Jung-Hee Park's military regime in the 1970s more systematically controlled Western princesses through the Camptown Cleanup Campaign. The campaign was in response to the Nixon Doctrine of 1969, which initiated the withdrawal of 20,000 American soldiers from South Korea by March 1971. The Park administration interpreted the reduction of the U.S. military forces as a risk for national security.[18] To prevent further reduction of American soldiers, the Korean government decided to modernize camptowns. Dictator Park first ordered the establishment of the Cleanup Campaign Committee, which would soon be officialized by the Korean government. The campaign arduously attempted to meet the U.S. military's needs, such as alleviating of racial tension among U.S. soldiers, reducing sexually transmitted diseases, and providing a safe environment for soldiers' recreation and relaxation.

The U.S. military police regularly visited bars and clubs and checked on whether they treated black and white soldiers equally. In addition, the Status of Forces of America in Korea (SOFA) subcommittee imposed off-limits restrictions on clubs and bars that did not cooperate with the decreasing of racial tensions or venereal diseases among sex workers.[19] However, racial tension between soldiers at clubs merely reflected the racial hierarchy inside the U.S. military. Even Western princesses were hierarchically divided, according to their associated soldiers' skin colors. Yon-ja Kim, the first Western princess activist, writes: "there are various forms of conflict . . . between women working for G.I.s and ordinary local women, between G.I. brides and Western princesses, between prostitutes for black soldiers and for white soldiers, between single mother prostitutes and those with no children."[20]

Western princesses must have regular medical checkups at the government-founded clinics in camptowns; those who were declared clean of venereal disease could obtain VD cards as the official sanction to sell their bodies. Otherwise, women were quarantined for the treatment's duration or had to pay the fines for no-VD cards. All Western princesses were registered with the local police station and wear nametags while working, so that American soldiers could easily name those who allegedly infected them with venereal disease. The VD cards created a camptown power structure between women with the cards and without cards, between pimps and Western princesses, and between people in camptown prostitution and those in law enforcement. Street workers without VD cards occupied the bottom of the camptown power structure and were most vulnerable to G.I. customers' violence.[21]

Governmental educators regularly gathered the prostitutes in order to indoctrinate them that their service for American soldiers was crucial for peace and security and that—by earning American dollars—they contributed to Korea's economic development.[22] Based on the success in the camptown sex industry, the military governments in Korea in the 1970s and 1980s utilized sex tourism in order to earn foreign currency.[23]

Since the late 1980s, U.S. camptown prostitution has declined, as the number of U.S. servicemen has decreased and South Korea's economy has dramatically developed. These days, foreign women from the former Soviet Union and the Philippines replace Korean prostitutes in camptowns who are too old now or have left for better economic opportunities.[24]

Western princesses' life in the U.S. military camptowns shows that the state is pimping and recruiting women into its war project. Hence, peace activism in camptowns or solidarity work with Western princesses first attempts to reveal militarized prostitution as state-sanctioned violence against women and gender-based military violence. It further aims to mainstream gender perspectives in analyzing the militarization of the world, so that alternative power relations in international politics will be created.

SOCIAL MOVEMENTS IN THE CAMPTOWNS: FAITH MATTERS

It has been difficult to organize a social movement in camptowns because prostitution there is interwoven with U.S. military imperialism, Korea's patriarchal nationalism, sexism, racism, classism, the division of Koreas, and commodified female bodies in global capitalism. Furthermore, until recently, women's movements in Korea had been considered peripheral to larger political-economic issues. These political realities discouraged women activists to identify themselves with Western princesses, the outcasts living outside the acceptable cultural and social norms of female sexuality.[25]

Nonetheless, social movements in the camptowns have been created by and for women, because the camptowns are gendered spaces where women's bodies are exploited and commodified as well as where the local economy depends on their sexualized labor. The feminist social movements in U.S. military camptowns in South Korea have roughly three phases. First, Western princesses take their own initiatives by directly confronting their employers, G.I. customers, or local authorities for their rights to earn fair wages and to work in a safe environment. Within given situations, Western princesses often used their autonomy to protect one another based on shared experiences of economic exploitation and violence. Their actions are mostly issue based and episodic; however, it is important to recognize how Western princesses use their own power to rectify injustice.

Yon-ja Kim, who had worked in camptown prostitution for 25 years, once transformed the self-governance organization of camptown sex workers (*ja-chi-hwi*), which had been originally installed by the Korean government. Siding with local political authorities, the leaders of the organization often collected membership dues and spied on their fellow Western princesses, thus participating in their exploitation. Kim attempted to reform her local chapter of the self-governance organization so that it would work to protect Western princesses from exploitation and violence. Later, Kim studied Christian theology and became a minister, which resulted in her opening a Christianity-based shelter for Western princesses and their children.[26] Christian faith helped Yon-ja Kim rediscover her invaluable dignity, heal her trauma, and courageously resist injustice. In her autobiographic writing, Kim states that what she truly wants to share with the world are not her experiences of exploitation, despair, and violence from working for G.I.s, but her sustaining hope and self-confidence gained though the camptown movements and Christian faith.[27] Yon-ja Kim's camptown activism is crucial to examine Western princesses' survival strategies, agency, and realities, as well as the obstacles in creating solidarity between Western princesses and outside activists. Western princesses are not merely the victims of militarism, but also active players able to resist the multiple layers of oppression through day-to-day struggle.

The second phase of the camptown movements is collaboration between activists and (former) Western princesses. In 1986, two Christian women, Fay Moon and Bok-nim You, founded Durebang, known as "My Sister's Place" to the English-speaking world. Durebang was unique at that time and multifaceted—a shelter for Western princesses and their children, advocacy group, educational center for both Western princesses and outsiders, job training center, healing center, and more. One of the founders, Fay Moon, is an American woman married to a well-known Korean *Minjung* theologian. While counseling Korean military brides in the United States' Eighth Army, Fay Moon learned about the realities of camptown prostitution.[28] The other founder, Bok-nim You of the Presbyterian Church in the Republic of Korea, was a feminist activist whose faith and social activism were rooted in *Minjung* theology, a Korean version of liberation theology. As the two women articulated, Durebang's mission was to help "Western princesses and interracially married military wives liberate themselves and live invaluable human life originally created by God."[29] Many women church leaders and feminist theologians participated in Durebang's early activities.

For more than 25 years, Durebang has connected the Uijeongbu camptown back to larger Korean society. Feminist activists and college students have interned with Durebang; in addition, domestic and international researchers and activists have visited Durebang to study local people' lives around U.S. bases. As the number of foreign sex workers has increased in the Uijeongbu area, Durebang has also been working for the human rights of these women.

In 1985, a group of Catholic nuns opened Magdalena House, a shelter for sex workers in Yongsan of Seoul; in the following year, they launched Hansori, an organization aiming to end prostitution and to support those who try to leave sex work.[30] Magdalena House theologically articulates that sex workers are the victims of the social system, and their humanity, created in God's image, must be recovered.[31]

Both Durebang and Hansori define prostitution as an unjust system that harms both sellers and buyers. Female prostitutes are the most oppressed victims of militarism and capitalism. Following the teachings of Jesus, Christians must work with prostitutes for their liberation from sexual and economic exploitation. These organizations' theological understanding of prostitutes' humanity having been created in Image of God (*Imago Dei*) is different from that of the mainline Korean church, which highly values female chastity and often condemns prostitutes as corrupted sinners who must repent before God.

Sunlit Center, nearby Camp K-6 in Anjungri of Pyeongtaek, is a similar organization that especially advocates for elderly women who used to cater sexually to American soldiers. Due to the negative social stigmas surrounding them, Western princesses do not leave the camptowns even after they can no longer serve G.I. customers. Sunlit Center's work is unique because the center brings feminist consciousness of ageism and prostitution together into the militarized world.

The third phase of the movements regards domestically and internationally working in solidarity. Due to the complexity of the issues in the camptowns, cooperation among diverse organizations is essential so as to protect Western princesses from gender-based militarized violence. In 2012, Durebang, Sunlit Center, Hansori, and the Korean Council for the Women Forcefully Drafted by Imperial Japan for Military Sexual Slavery launched the Solidarity Network for Human Rights in the Camptown (*Kijichon Inkwon Yondae*).

The empathetic understanding of diverse women living under the U.S. military power brings all these organizations together. This is because empathy does not simply mean taking a side with victims, but also recognizing gender as a power relation. By attempting to understand the gendered and militarized human life in the camptowns, outsiders can realize how their culture and society are militarized enough to condone the existence of militarized prostitution and why all human beings should also be liberated from militarism.

SUNLIT CENTER: THE NARRATIVES OF MILITARIZED PROSTITUTION AND POLITICAL APATHY[32]

In the summer of 2011, I had the opportunity to observe one of the Sunlit Center's important projects: Camptown Women Speak about Their Memories. The Sunlit Center and Choong-Ang University jointly collected the narratives of elderly women who had spent most of their lives in one camptown after another. As a participant-observer, I was allowed to attend the group meetings. Although it is impossible to generalize diverse stories from the women at Sunlit Center, I highlight three perspectives that may inform the meanings of peace and empathy in a concrete context.

First, Sunlit Center's elderly women are aware of the Korean government's and the U.S. military's involvement in camptown prostitution through VD cards, military curfew, imposition of off-limits on bars and clubs, education about reproductive health, legal marriage, and so forth. Some women's narratives also indicate that American soldiers' misconduct and superiority over Koreans reflected the unequal power relations between Korea and the United States. One elderly woman says, "When drunk, soldiers yelled at us, 'We are here to protect you from North Korean communists. In return, you should serve us well.'" The women's stories often describe their lives caught between the United States and South Korea, or between American men and Koreans. Their suffering caused by bar owners, pimps, and American soldiers is understood to have resulted from Korea's lack of military and economic power.

Second, many of the women's narratives indicate that both the Korean government and the U.S. military are unwilling to protect them from violence and exploitation. As a result, Western princesses are consistently exposed to physical, sexual, and psychological violence and are often caught in fights between soldiers. In fact, many military crimes such as systemic rape and sexual slavery happen when the state is incapable or unwilling to protect the victims or when the state denies the occurrence of sexual crimes against women.

Several women said that soldiers fought over them, but that they themselves were blamed for the fight when police arrived; after the soldiers' fights, some women were not allowed to work. When raped and physically attacked by G.I. customers or by club owners, Western princesses can hardly expect the law enforcement to protect them or to punish the perpetrators. In fact, Western princesses are treated as criminals in South Korea, where prostitution is illegal. The Status of Forces of America in Korea (SOFA) does not give the Korean law enforcement power to investigate G.I. crime, unless the perpetrator is caught when the crime happens and the crime is bad enough to be punished. According to the Korean-U.S. SOFA, if American soldiers commit sexual crimes, they should be investigated and punished at the Korean court. However, both the U.S. military and the Korean authority question whether Western princesses can be sexually assaulted if they are selling sex.[33] Sexual violence against Western princesses is unknown to the public, unless the victim is murdered. Furthermore, SOFAs usually guard American soldiers' privileges and rights abroad rather than protecting the local victims of G.I. crimes and pursuing legally fair judgment of the crime.[34] This is why Korean organizations such as the National Campaign for Eradication of Crimes by U.S. Troops argue for the urgency to revise the Korean-U.S. SOFA in order to protect Korean civilians.

Third, some narratives exemplify how the absence of a social-security net after armed conflict can harm women for an indefinite period of time. The concept of so-called postconflict does not apply to many women's lives, as various postwar statistics show the increase in diverse forms of male violence against women. One such example of this is K, a woman in her sixties, who entered Yongsan camptown prostitution at the age of 16 after being sexually abused at an orphanage. As a Korean War orphan without a birth certificate, K was unable to obtain a citizenship card due to a simple lack of information on how an orphan could obtain one. The club owners took advantage of her status by charging her for a fake identification card and stealing her cash savings. Sharing her story, K expressed the love-and-hate relationship with the United States and with South Korea. K refused the dichotomy between Western princesses as victims and American soldiers as perpetrators, because both parties were victims and perpetrators at the same time. Her story points to the patriarchal war and military system that disrupt ordinary people's pursuit of happiness and reproduce unequal power relations between both countries and between the peoples.

Sunlit Center and Durebang publish the narratives of Western princesses. Countering the official history or record of war, the two organizations have utilized a feminist storytelling method in order to create empathy between Western princesses and activists, as well as between Western princesses and global citizens. The power of the narratives is not based on whether these women tell facts, but on whether storytellers, readers, and listeners are altogether able to find certain truths about military brutality. Military brutality does not simply harm the downtrodden such as Western princesses, but also sustains callous capitalism and commodifies female bodies for national wealth and security. In addition, it further disables human capability to be empathetic with suffering beings and implants political apathy in human hearts.

The stories from Sunlit Center have the power to break down political "apathy." Dorothee Soelle, a German feminist theologian, defines apathy as "a form of the inability to suffer" or a social condition in which "people are so dominated by the goal of avoiding suffering that it becomes a goal to avoid human relationships and contact altogether."[35] Mainstream Christian theology has also participated in the process of socially conditioned apathy by separating God from politics and by depicting God as the almighty, the most powerful, or the supreme who does not need any relationships.[36]

As mentioned earlier, the Korean government and the U.S. military physically isolated the camptowns from the rest of Korean society. The state power has intentionally made its people apathetic regarding those who struggle to survive in camptowns. At the same time, the majority of Koreans participate in political apathy by consciously forgetting about camptown prostitution. Political apathy further numbs Koreans' capability to question, challenge, and criticize the state military project. Women's narratives from Sunlit Center show how the state misuses its power, especially over economically vulnerable women, unless its members scrutinize and monitor it.

Grace Cho, a Korean American scholar, compares the Western princess to a ghost. The Western princess, as the embodiment of Koreans' collective trauma caused by colonialism, war, and shame, experiences "epistemic violence" through the erasure of her presence in the modern Korean history.[37] In essence, because the Western princesses' presence is too traumatic for Koreans, Korean society avoids the relationship with her in order to avoid suffering. However, the "ghost" always shadows people's minds and provokes fear and deep wounds that must be revealed, faced, and healed.[38] Analyzed through the lens of Cho's study, Sunlit Center's project first resists epistemic violence by making the ghostly Western princess visible, by recognizing her full humanity, and by letting her speak. When society recognizes this ghost, social members can overcome apathy and embark on a journey toward healing as a whole.

Politics of Empathy Countering Transnationalized Militarism

Transnationalized militarism has accelerated the militarization of women's life on a global level. Yet the transnational military powers, especially America's global network of bases, force people to be apathetic to international politics, war, and armed conflict. How can we, who envision alternative peace with an emphasis on just human relations, resist political apathy?

How can feminism generate human power to resist transnationalized militarism that sustains camptown prostitution? What roles can religion play in contributing to creating peace that is based on shared power relations, as opposed to feeding militarism?

First of all, as Elli Kim suggests, Korean feminist peace activists do not necessarily define what feminist peace should be.[39] Peace should embrace both women and men indiscriminately, and peacemaking activism requires engaged dialogue beyond the gender dichotomy. Feminist consciousness has led Korean women activists to take effective actions to diverse issues. For this reason, peace is not a theory or concept to be defined but rather an active practice based on the critical analysis of the issue. The analysis of militarized prostitution motivates Korean women to see their conscious and unconscious participation in the militarized culture, international relations, and patriarchal assumptions of male and female sexuality. These women become attentive to and empathetic with the real women of flesh and blood living inside the system of military prostitution.

In order to resist transnationalized militarism, we should envision and practice a new form of politics that is sensitive to human suffering. As a Christian feminist ethicist, I suggest a "politics of empathy," reflecting on my encountering of Korean women activists in the camptowns who have crossed the boundaries of the "sacred" and the "secular," and the "domestic" and the "transnational." My proposed politics of empathy are threefold.

First, increasing global interdependence encourages any peacemakers to search for global solidarity, even though their works are grounded in their respective local communities and their perspectives on war and militarization are diverse. In other words, it is empathy—not military bases—that should be transnationalized. Several local organizations in South Korea are networking among themselves while actively seeking global solidarity with other antimilitary organizations. Through international conferences and Internet communications, these organizations share their peacebuilding strategies and information about the U.S. military's impact on women's lives in diverse regions, supporting one another's political activism. Together, they articulate that the U.S. military is not being held accountable for peace or global security.

Through the International Women's Network Against Militarism, solidarity work among women in Puerto Rico and the U.S.–Asia Pacific regions (United States, Hawaii, Guam, Saipan, Okinawa, Philippines, Korea) has been remarkable. In 2011 these women's organizations collaboratively made a documentary film, *Women Living along the Fence Line,* in order to educate the general public about real women affected by the global network of U.S. military bases—from ecological destruction to military prostitution.[40]

Religious faith often empowers women activists to resist the militarization of the Pacific. A leading narrator from the film, the Reverend Debbi Lee from Women for Genuine Security, said, "Although we do not theologize what we are doing for peace, religion is an important part, depending on how you define religion. For example, peace is spirituality for Hawaiians. Protecting nature from militarization is an active spiritual practice. My faith in a Christian God has also taught me that militarism goes against every Christian teaching—it destroys life, the sacred."[41]

In addition, Sunlit Center is working with the transnationally active Korean Council for the Women Drafted for Sexual Slavery by Japan during World War II. A couple of months before my visit at the Sunlit Center in 2011, the elderly women at the center started attending the Korean Council's Wednesday protest in front of the Japanese consulate. Every Wednesday for the last 11 years, the survivors of the Japanese military "comfort women" system and their allies have protested, demanding that the Japanese government officially recognize and apologize for the military's sexual slavery during World War II. Western princesses and the survivors of this sexual slavery used to differentiate themselves from one another: while the (innocent) women were forced, drafted, and kidnapped into the Japanese military "comfort women" system, U.S. military sex workers did so voluntarily. The more they meet and protest together, though, the more they understand the connection between the two: both systems were sustained by the government and military authorities in order to support the patriarchal heterosexist male bonding within the military system. Through solidarity work, the two different groups of women now empower each other and understand their experiences more analytically and critically.

Second, military prostitution suggests the necessity of a robust and critical gender analysis of transnationalized militarism and international politics. A robust analysis is the first step to practice true empathy, beyond mere sympathy with sufferers or anger at massive injustice. Sunlit Center's project suggests one method of analyzing a militarized world and international politics—a bottom-up storytelling method. By listening to Western princesses, we can learn new perspectives on international politics as seen through women's everyday life. British feminist sociologist Cynthia Cockburn reminds us that every aspect of international politics and military policy is about everyday human relations.[42] Therefore, when mainstream discourse on international politics dismisses the importance of everyday human life, feminists must work to resist this form of knowledge production. The analysis and transformation of women's everyday life is as important as the so-called big pictures in international politics, such as nuclear policy, military deployment, and international treaties.

Elli Kim accentuates, "Peace activism is the most radical social movement because it questions what human life truly means." She continues to argue that peace demands radical changes in every part of human life—within the nation-state, human relations, gender relations, power structures, and so forth.[43] Therefore, feminist peace activism must inquire about how everyday human life is militarized—for example, how casually we use military language, how our culture praises military values, and how our society normalizes military masculinity. Peace activism does not solely mean organized movement, but also necessitates that every individual should scrutinize her or his own involvement in militarized culture and consciously resist it. Here, empathy can play an important role in everyday peace activism. For instance, if we truly empathize with Western princesses, we may see how our own lives have been militarized enough to sustain camptown sex industries and thus take an action to resist militarization both on an individual and on a collective level.

Third, a politics of empathy should include courageously embracing human suffering, overcoming fear, healing the victims and the perpetrators, and peace that counters militarism every day. It also requires one's critical self-reflection that is powerful enough to dismantle the dichotomy between us (i.e., good people) and them (i.e., enemies), between men and women, and between victims and perpetrators.

Consciously resisting a militarized human life can be made stronger through the Christian language of mysticism, just as how Dorothee Soelle articulates mysticism as a power for the resistance of violence, militarism, status quo, and political apathy to suffering. For her, deep contemplation on the sacredness of life or living in mystical union with God turns the triviality of everyday life into wonder, joy, and astonishment. This mystical experience leads one to empathetically embrace others' suffering and will sustain their life in the midst of darkness, confusion, and exhaustion.[44] Mysticism can energize peace as everyday feminist practice. Everyday feminism is political activism that leads one to consciously see that the personal is internationally political. This practice will further enable one to make conscious choices in everyday life in order to transform unequal power relations on every level of human interactions. By the same coin, spiritual practice is a conscious effort to change both individual and communal ways of living so that we may ultimately arrive at peace with ourselves and with the world. This peace is possible when we see the roots of human suffering, responsibly face those roots, consciously eradicate them, and resist a delusional peace that the militarized world may promise.

CONCLUSION

The camptowns are arbitrarily created borderlands between South Korea and the United States resulting from the Korean War. Living in these borderlands, Western princesses have been able to see America's military imperialism, South Korea's desire to be like the powerful United States, and examples of racism, sexism, classism, and much more. In fact, the narratives from places like the Sunlit Center show the multiple layers of injustice in the U.S.–South Korea relations marked with militarism. The camptowns are also powerful places where feminist consciousness challenges patriarchal militarism, military-based security, and patriarchal gender ideologies. This chapter attempts to show how Western princesses and their allies for justice, peace, and liberation have worked domestically and internationally together in order to debunk the myth of militarized peace and security and to construct an alternative vision of peace based on just human relations in every part of human society. Empathy is understood as a politically, theologically, and spiritually important practice to sustain solidarity between camptown prostitutes and their allies.

Being truly empathetic with the victims of gender-based military violence such as Western princesses requires Korean women activists critically to analyze the political and economic structures in which Western princesses have lived. However, empathy does not necessarily lead ordinary people to resist transnationalized militarism or to work for justice in camptown prostitution. In order to avoid romanticizing empathy, feminist consciousness should lead us critically to reflect on several issues, including whether we define and objectify the victims, whether we only listen to certain experiences of Western princesses, and whether we force or impose empathy on all women by erasing power differentials among diverse groups of women in peace activism.

Epilogue

Various people have participated in the Sunlit Center women's healing journey. Among them, Yang-gu Lee, a playwright, wrote *The Village of Seven Houses* based on the collected narratives from the Sunlit Center.[45] His goal was to bring the Anjungri camptown to the world so that the distance between the two would disappear little by little. In preparing the play, actors and actresses had visited Anjungri and become friends with elderly women at the Sunlit Center so that they could empathize with the women. Writer Lee says of the experience,

> I witnessed a former Western princess's lonely death at Anjungri. Her death tells me certain truth about human life. In my play, a dying elderly woman, who used to prostitute herself with American soldiers, asks Hana from the United States who researches the camptown for her doctoral dissertation to pray for her. As Hana hesitates, the dying woman says,

"When you pray for me, my tears flow into your eyes, and your tears into God's eyes. God is the one whose eyes are full of tears." I wish everyone in audience shares tears with Western princesses, and will see the teary eyes of God.[46]

Closing this chapter, I have the same hope. A God whose eyes are full of tears will surely liberate us from fear, anger, war, and suffering. Women at the Sunlit Center are liberating themselves little by little and are truly inviting others to participate in this liberating project from their own social locations.

NOTES

1. In this chapter, Korea usually refers to "South Korea" or the "Republic of Korea," unless it is specified. Koreans generally means those who live in South Korea.

2. Kim 2005, 190–191.

3. Brock and Thisthlethwaite 1996, xviii.

4. Enloe 2004, 119.

5. The International Women's Network Against Militarism, www.iwnm.org.

6. From the end of World War II in the Pacific in 1945 through 1948, General John Hodge's U.S. military unit deployed from Okinawa had governed South Korea. The Korean War broke out a few months after the Atchison Line excluded South Korea from America's military defense system in Asia.

7. Lee 2010, 176 (Korean).

8. Moon 1997, 24–32.

9. Hong 2007, 82–83 (Korean).

10. Lee 2010, 171.

11. Gang 1999, 263–265 (Korean).

12. Edwards 2006, 512–528.

13. Gang 2012, 48 (Korean).

14. The majority of the UN soldiers were Americans. Although Korean soldiers outnumbered UN soldiers, they were considered the allies of the United Nations because South Korea was not a UN member country at the time of the Korean War. Edwards 2006, 514.

15. Yi 2004, 130 (Korean).

16. Yuh 2004, 233.

17. Yi 2004, 232–233.

18. In 1969, American military servicemen counted 52,580 in South Korea and the number decreased to 33,250 in 1971. Bae 1999, 22 (Korean).

19. Moon 1999, 75–81.

20. Kim 2005, 99 (Korean).

21. Ibid., 98–99.

22. Moon 1999, 89–91.

23. Gang 2012, 86–88. During the 1970s, the Korean military government utilized prostitution as the state-controlled exporting business and military business. In the 1980s, Doo-hwan Jun, the military dictator who succeeded Jung-hee Park, used the same tactic concerning prostitution. In public, the government continued antiprostitution law but secretly sustained prostitution.

24. Durebang 2009, 16–17 (Korean). Durebang is the oldest advocacy group for the camptown sex workers and located next to Camp Stanley in Uijeongbu city.

25. Jung 2005, 301 (Korean).

26. Ibid., 309–314.

27. Kim 2005, 273.

28. Ibid., 313.

29. Ibid., 314.

30. The U.S. Yongsan garrison is arguably the biggest U.S. military facility located in the center of a foreign country's capital. Around the Yongsan garrison camptown was constructed, and the sex industry for American soldiers, foreign tourists, and Korean men has spread since the Korean War. Yongsan, which is now a special tourist district, had been a well-known red light district until the Korean government recently announced its will to shut it down and to gentrify the area. The land occupied by the Yongsan garrison will be returned to the Korean government and the headquarters of the U.S. Armed Forces in Korea will move to Dae-chu-ri of Pyeongtaek, the southern satellite city of Seoul.

31. Magdalena House, http://www.magdalena.or.kr/php/english/english01.htm.

32. A part of my participant observation at the Sunlit Center was presented at the 2011 Annual Meeting of the American Academy of Religion.

33. National Campaign for Eradication of Crimes by U.S. Troops in Korea 2008, 40–42 (Korean).

34. Hohn and Moon 2010, 15.

35. Soelle 1984, 36.

36. Ibid., 42–43.

37. Cho 2008, 32.

38. Ibid., 41.

39. Elli Kim, interview with the author in Korean, Soul, Korea (July 2013).

40. This film was screened at the 2011 Annual Meeting of American Academy of Religion.

41. Debbie Lee, interview with the author in English, Berkeley, California (March 2012).

42. Cockburn 2007, 232.

43. Elli Kim, interview with the author in Korean, Seoul, Korea (July 2013).

44. Soelle 2001, 195–207.

45. The old name of Anjungri.

46. Yang-Gu Lee, interview with the author in Korean, Seoul, Korea (July 2013).

CHAPTER 15

Transforming Trauma: From Partition Hauntings to Post 9/11 Angst in South Asian Cinema

Khani Begum

In the wake of the September 11, 2001, terrorist attacks on the World Trade Center, the question "why do they hate us?" echoed around many an office, school, and home seeking a rational explanation for an irrational event. While media punditry attempted answers, the cinema industry provided no "real" or "fantasmatic" solutions in the following months. Despite this being the most documented event of our time, filmic responses in its immediate aftermath were slow to emerge; critics noted the 9/11 attacks had smashed Hollywood's monopoly on myth making. This silence expressing respect for the nation's need to mourn also points to confusion over how to represent this national tragedy that has visually bested the best of the disaster film genre. Drawing on Karen Engle's discussion of how "the imbrication of the visual with mourning" is tied to the making of history,[1] I explore how the Indian subcontinent's 1947 Partition haunts South Asian filmic responses from post-Partition trauma through 9/11 and the war on terror era. Responding to the World Trade Center attacks and the effects of the war on terror on Pakistanis and Indians at home and in the diaspora, these films recall Partition trauma by engaging with discourses of terrorism, religion, gender, and nation. Transgressing and transforming relationships between men and women, between nations, and between Islam and the rest of the world, they articulate new ways of belonging in the post 9/11 era.

During World War II, filmic representations of national trauma patriotically justified war, purporting a masculine, nationalistic rhetoric with women playing supportive roles as spouse or mother, willingly sending men to fight moral wars on foreign shores. Most media at the time were influenced or controlled by the government through censorship or funding. While more independent of government influences since then, immediately after 9/11, Hollywood hesitated making films that could impair bringing perpetrators of the tragedy to justice. Not only were Hollywood films late responders to the 9/11 attacks, but productions including terrorists or blown buildings were canceled or delayed. Television programs with hijacking or bio-terrorism plots suffered a similar fate.[2] Slavoj Zizek finds "the fact that many "blockbuster" movies with scenes which bear a resemblance to the WTC collapse . . . were postponed (or the films were shelved) should thus be read as the "repression" of the fantasmatic background responsible for the impact of the WTC collapse."[3] This reticence in mainstream Hollywood productions is related not just to films addressing the 9/11 attacks directly, but also to films offering culturally alternative perspectives. Such self-censoring for public good by Hollywood can also be interpreted in more sinister terms given how at this time, as Hoberman puts it, Hollywood was "drafted" by the government:

> Just days after the terror attacks, the Pentagon-funded Institute for Creative Technologies at the University of Southern California convened several meetings with filmmakers—including screenwriter Steven E. De Souza (*Die Hard, Die Hard 2*), director Joseph Zito (*Delta Force One, Missing in Action*), and wackier creative types like directors David Fincher, Spike Jonze, and Mary Lambert. The proceedings were chaired by Brigadier General Kenneth Berquist; the idea was for the talent to "brainstorm" possible terrorist scenarios and then offer solutions.[4]

Zizek, remarking on 9/11's association with Hollywood disaster movies, finds the "ultimate twist in the link between Hollywood and the "war against terrorism" occurred when the Pentagon decided to solicit the help of Hollywood . . . with the aim of imagining possible scenarios for terrorist attacks and how to fight them."[5]

Examining terrorism and counterterrorism policies since the Reagan era, Robert Merrill finds "the study of terrorism takes us into the world of the hyperreal where "real" murder and violence occur on a huge scale but do not register even the slightest notice on the mediascape, public consciousness, or government policy."[6] I find Merrill's analysis of the "hyperreal" resonates in Zizek's discussion of the "real" and the "fantasmatic" when "the Real itself, in order to be sustained, has to be perceived as a nightmarish unreal spectre."[7] The "de-realization" of the attack on the World Trade Center occurs, says Zizek, with the citing of the number of victims repeatedly with no visual realization for we see "little of the actual carnage we see no dismembered bodies, no blood, no desperate faces of dying people."[8] Lack of visual imagery of victims and absence of corpse photographs in the news are noted by foreign correspondents at Ground Zero. Engle, citing from Reporters Without Borders (2001), ascribes this lack partly "to an inconsistency in American journalistic policy—'western media . . . don't hesitate to show massacres when they happen in Rwanda'"[9] and partly to the desire to limit images of defeat. Zizek also connects de-realization of the events to how the West views global traumas whose images of death and devastation are broadcast endlessly as long as it is occurring elsewhere. He perceives this lack of visual representations of trauma victims as "further proof of how even in this tragic moment, the distance which separates Us from Them, from their reality, is maintained: the real horror happens *there*, not *here*?"[10] Prohibition over photographing and filming details of trauma experience is driven by the desire to protect the public and respect victims and the suffering of their families. In the controversy over Associated Press photographer Richard Drew's image of an as-yet-unidentified man jumping from one of the towers to immanent death, titled *Falling Man*, Engle claims even though photography serves as an important medium of witness, in this case the morality of viewing led to the image being removed from public view—"*Falling man* was pulled in the interest of common decency, as an attempt to protect viewers from any further visual trauma."[11]

Merrill's analysis of the "hyperreality" of terrorism maintains that simulations of terror express "how the hyperreality of terrorism is the process of stimulating the imaginations of Americans with certain kinds of images in order to ground a certain kind of social structure and governmental policy."[12] Today this has led to having

> a different relationship between people, one grounded on the model of policing. The same holds true for nations. What we are aiming toward is a period of re-colonization. First the re-colonization of minds and then the re-colonization of the third world.[13]

This parallels the Bush administration's determination to change "hearts and minds" and bring democracy and freedom to those enslaved by fundamentalist regimes and ideologies. It also furthers Zizek's notion of government's use of the us versus them rhetoric, for it is *their* minds that have to be changed and *their* hearts won; even the winning of hearts and minds has to happen *there* and not *here* in order to ensure that terrorism does not find its way *here*.

The recolonization Merrill refers to, I argue, took place in parts of the global South through globalization prior to the declaration of the war on terror. What remains debatable, however, is to what extent hearts and minds are changed, desired results achieved, and whether the war on terror continues to fuel the process of recolonization through U.S. intervention in Afghanistan and Iraq, thereby possibly generating an activist backlash leading to a post-recolonization?

Once the impact of 9/11 and the war on terror was felt on diasporan Indians and Pakistanis, it was not long before these cinemas, with their history of filmic depictions of internal terrorism, started to go beyond domestic border tensions between Indians and Pakistanis and indigenous tribal conflicts to mediate a space for a South Asian filmic perspective within global discourses of terrorism. In order to reframe the rhetoric of "Indianness" and "Pakistaniness" for a global audience, they dialog innovatively with discourses of gender, religion, race, and nation. This move can be interpreted as a form and function of mourning and re-remembering Partition in its parallels to how in the 9/11 era too, religious and national allegiances of contemporary Indians and Pakistanis in the homeland and the diaspora were once again in question. Belonging on the wrong side could easily become a matter of life or death. Between 2001 and 2010 several South Asian films, exploring the impact of 9/11 on Indian and Pakistani men and women in their homelands and in the diaspora, are haunted by the trauma of Partition. These films, offering perspectives of Indians and Pakistanis not seen in Western films or media, at times humanize the characters of terrorists and suspects and at others voice the angst of diasporan Indian and Pakistani men and women in the United States and the United Kingdom caught in the crossfire of the rhetoric of the war on terror.

Pakistani and Indian cinemas are no novices at representing terrorism in film given their national histories are intertwined with communal violence and indigenous tribal and cross-border conflicts since the 1947 Partition. In its immediate aftermath, however, they too exercised restraint by shying away from direct representations of violence and bloodshed.[14] Bhaskar Sarkar sees the immediate post-Partition cinema's deafening silence and deliberate amnesia over Partition trauma as symptomatic of the process of mourning, which can unfold unpredictably. Sarkar, arguing for a hermeneutics of mourning, finds:

> Depictions of trauma, dispersed as they are over the years and across film genres, do compromise a before/after temporarily, an early phase temporality demarcated from a later one, in which similar modes of representation take on very different functions in relation to the tasks of memorialization and mourning.[15]

Similarly, the memorialization of the World Trade Center collapse through cinematic depictions of post 9/11 trauma gets dispersed across film genres over the years as the films take on different forms and functions of mourning. South Asian films that explore the tragedy's effects from the perspectives of their citizens frame their response through the experience of Partition trauma and thereby effectively mourn and memorialize it yet anew.

M. S. Sathyu's 1974 film, *Garam Hawa*, the first serious attempt to memorialize post-Partition trauma through experiences of a Muslim businessman and his family who decide to remain in India after independence, traces their endurance of hostilities and injustices meted out by former Hindu friends and neighbors, making life impossible in the wake of escalating Hindu/Muslim tensions. Sathyu, a traditional Brahmin, documents these tensions nostalgically, evoking memories of pre-Partition times when Hindus and Muslims lived in peace and harmony. This quiet film, an act of memorialization, mourns a nation that once was united and now is split. By the mid-1970s changing political realities between the two countries and popular taste for action films led to more violent productions like Ramesh Sippy's wildly popular *Sholay* (1975). Once this floodgate for representations of violence opened, pastoral and nostalgic films of the early Partition period took a backseat to plots deploying visceral imagery of burning buildings and shootouts. Partition trauma continues to underlie the plots of this period's violent political films even though none present real or fictional depictions of Partition's bloody riots. This turn toward unrestrained violence, Sarkar calls "the return of the repressed."[16]

Between the 1970s and 1990s, border disputes, local terrorism, and communal riots provided real and imagined plots for both cinemas replete with explicit representations of violence in images of death, bodies, and carnage. Despite this engagement with violent depictions, none represented the violent reality of Partition until 1998, when the first two films to depict post-Partition riots realistically were released. In Pamela Rook's *Train to Pakistan* and Deepa Mehta's *Earth 1947*, the chaos of Partition is presented in scenes of Hindus and Muslims attacking each other in cities and villages in Punjab while bloodied trains arrive from across the border with passengers hacked to death. These scenes present historical facts,[17] and while their graphic visuality may shock viewers, their contextual dialogic engagement with Partition trauma makes them relevant and necessary. Traversing a fine line between documenting violent events and calling for a cessation of hostilities between the newly separate nations of Pakistan and India, these films iterate connections between Hindus, Muslims, and Sikhs.

Sumita S. Chakravarty claims that South Asian films of the 1990s focus on the disaffected Other within the nation rather than express national unity found in films made during the immediate post-Partition period. Her argument draws upon prevailing images of terrorism in Hollywood films that show how "both internal and external forces threaten the lives of ordinary Americans and that American National identity . . . can no longer be taken as a given."[18] Similarly, Indian and Pakistani films continue to address the "fragmented nation" in ongoing issues relating to communal nationalism in Kashmir and Tamil Nadu into the 21st century. In the year 2000, Vidhu Vinod Chopra's *Mission Kashmir* addresses terrorist issues in Kashmir through the metaphor of a fragmented family. In 1999, Santosh Shivan's *The Terrorist*, focusing on the psychology of the female terrorist, explores her single-minded dedication to the cause of Tamil Nadu while the fragmentation of the nation, although implied in the plot to assassinate a politician against Tamil Nadu nationalism, remains secondary.[19]

Both films mentioned above that depict Partition trauma, *Train to Pakistan* and *Earth 1947*, along with Yash Chopra's 2004 *Veer Zara,* use the figure of "Woman" to deploy the discourse of national belonging. "Woman" in these films symbolizes the nation for whom men are willing to make the ultimate sacrifice or commit the most heinous crime. Indian films have consistently used the figure of "Woman" as symbol for nation, best illustrated in Mehboob Khan's *Mother India*, India's first Academy Award nomination in 1957 in the Best Foreign Language Film category. A response to Katherine Mayo's 1927 book of the same name that disparaged Indian culture, the film is a remake of Khan's earlier 1940 film *Aurat (Woman)*. Containing several allusions to Hindu mythology, *Mother India* exudes a strong sense of nationalism and nation building through its representation of a morally honest female protagonist, a poor Hindu village woman. Her self-sacrifice and dedication in raising her sons in the face of natural disasters, ruthless landlords, and banking systems inspire citizens in the wake of independence to persevere through the growing pains of a new nation. This tradition of *Mother India's* metaphorical representation of "Woman" as "Nation" reasserts itself again when the nation is threatened of fragmentation in times of tribal and/or communal conflict. During the 1990s, when Hindu/Muslim tensions and tribal communal unrest in various parts of India (Kashmir, Bengal, Maharashtra, and Tamil Nadu) were escalating, Tamil filmmaker Mani Ratnam rose to prominence. Problematizing the metaphoric representation of "Woman" as "Nation" in his terrorism trilogy he explores how women from tribal and/or Muslim cultures can or cannot be integrated into the rhetoric of nationalism. His films *Roja* (1992), *Bombay* (1995), and *Dil Se* (1998), while still focusing on the figure of "Woman" as central to the discourse of either national or communal identity and solidarity, also exoticize alterity whether female, Muslim, insurgent, and/or terrorist—in *Bombay* this exotic Other is a Muslim woman in the midst of Hindu riots, and in *Roja* and *Dil Se* it is women insurgents—all of whose agendas run counter to the national narrative. "Woman," on the one hand, is essential in building the nation/community, and on the other hand, poses the threat of fragmentation if she represents ideological, religious, and communal positions antithetical to the national narrative. Chakravarty, referring to the historical representation of the Indian nation visible in immediate post-Partition films where the nation is imagined as a united family of Hindus, Muslims, and Christians, finds Ratnam's terrorism trilogy playing out Z. Bauman's notion of "the stranger" and how the stranger is "an anomaly, and fits no schema"[20]—as these females, one Muslim and two insurgents from tribal cultures exemplify. The Muslim woman and the female insurgents inadvertently seduce the male protagonist, who becomes attracted by their exoticism, otherness, and their religion/tribe/caste, thus making "Woman" the "stranger"—that which once signified nation now becomes that which is outside the nation. The desire to locate the stranger takes over the male protagonist striving to bring the Other, the "stranger," into the nation's fold through love or marriage. In *Dil Se*, the hero, failing to dissuade the woman from executing her suicide mission, willingly sacrifices himself by choosing to be with her in death when being with her in life becomes unrealizable. Through his decision to follow the female "stranger" in insurgence against the nation, he commits treason. The film presents this sacrifice/treason as romantic courage through its incendiary final scene in which the two lovers lock in a passionate embrace as an enormous fireball engulfs them. The nation becomes irrelevant in this Romeo and Juliet–like ending that privileges love between a man and a woman from different classes and different religions over national or religious allegiance. *Dil Se,* presenting its protagonists' suicide in visually exotic and romantic scenes against an evocative music soundtrack, romanticizes this final incendiary act of terrorism against the nation. The film performing extremely well at home and among diasporans[21] is critiqued for its disengagement from a national aesthetic. Dr. Uma Vangal points out that despite his origins in Chennai's flourishing Tamil cinema, Ratnam is chastised by Tamil Nadu nationalists in Chennai for moving away from serious political engagement with Tamil Nadu nationalism.[22] *Dil Se,* more than his other films, exemplifies this disconnection that is attributed to the influence of Mumbai's Hindi film industry for this film is closer to Bollywood's filmmaking style than to Chennai's Tamil style with which Ratnam began his filmmaking career before moving to Mumbai.

Gender in colonial and postcolonial national histories and its linkage with terrorism—Algeria's and India's histories being particularly pertinent examples—has been addressed by scholars in past years. Rosalind C. Morris, tracing the rise of pan-Islamism and European and Eastern discourses around war and how colonial violence operates, finds parallels with post 9/11 discourses around gender and terrorism:

Our current belief that the war on terrorism is a war to liberate women is a misrecognition of this historical fact, whose origins are to be found less in any indigenous oppression of women (though there is indigenous oppression of women, whose overturning can yet be supported) than in the histories of colonialism to which the United States is heir.[23]

Historically, colonial cultures justify initiatives under the guise of protecting or improving conditions of women in cultures they colonize. In a documentary on the history of Afghan women's movements, Afghan women activists and spokespersons for WAW (Women for Afghan Women)—among them cofounder Suraya Parlika—remark on the hypocrisy of nations claiming to fight for the rights of Afghan women as an excuse for their continued intervention and military presence in the country.[24] This applies not only to the United States' presence and support for the mujahideen who terrorized the Afghan people (making the United States indirectly instrumental in eradicating rights Afghan women enjoyed in prior regimes), but also to politically motivated interventions of Saudi Arabia, Pakistan, and Russia over past decades. Morris's discussion is worth noting in light of the recent interest in literature and films from Islamic cultures and by Muslim women and an increase in college and university courses on Islam, women in Islam, and the Middle East especially during the years following President Bush's declaration of the global war on terror. This support of Muslim women's writing is seen as liberating them in general, for celebrating the few who speak to us can be empowering for those who cannot. Many women writers from Muslim countries and/or Muslim backgrounds living in the West rose to prominence quickly during this period,[25] and works like Azar Nafisi's *Reading Lolita in Tehran* and Marjane Satrapi's *Persepolis* suddenly became indispensable to Women's Studies courses. Predictably, most women writers celebrated in the West during this period are also the ones who take a Western worldview in representing Islamic cultures.[26]

The following discussion of Shoab Mansoor's 9/11-themed Pakistani film, *Khuda ke Liye (In the Name of God)* (2007), dialogues postcolonial, trauma, and exilic film theories, to explicate how, through engaging with discourses of gender, religion, and nation, the film documents and reflects on world-changing events in the wake of 9/11.[27] Exploring changing realities of national belonging, this film transcends local ideological, political, geographical, and cultural concerns to deconstruct binary narratives of us versus them and East versus West. Its multi-dimensional response to 9/11 and the war on terror, by recalling and re-remembering Partition trauma, its colonial experience with Great Britain, and its relations with Afghanistan, is therapeutic for both filmmaker and audience as it takes on the form and function of national mourning. This process leads to derailments, disruptions, and rearticulations of discourses of nationalism, transnationalism, gender, religion, and postco-lonialism, making this film illustrative of "cinematic transvergence." Design theorist Marcos Novak's concept of "transvergence," derived from architec-tural science, is employed by Will Higbee, Michael Goddard, and Pietari Kaapi to explore transcultural Maghrebian cinema. Novak, using the term in reference to a nonlinear or trans-linear relation between two or more systems, claims "while convergence and divergence are simple linear extrapolations that proceed by strategies of alignment, transvergence advances translin-early through tactics of derailment."[28] I argue that nonlinear and translinear "derailments" of idealized conceptions of nationhood, patriotism, religion, gender, and cultural heritage question current ideologies driving these dis-courses today. The film's "tactics of derailment" disconnect notions of stable identities, calling for new ways of belonging. It engages in de-westernizing processes to reframe nationalist discourses and express multidimensional perspectives through the personal conflicts of its three protagonists set in motion by 9/11. In the same way that the United Kingdom's post 9/11 films draw upon Britain's history with terrorism and fear around immigration, this film draws upon Pakistan's nationalist struggles, recollections of 1947 Parti-tion trauma, and its internal conflicts with Islamic fundamentalism.

A critical and box office success in India and Pakistan, *Khuda ke Liye*, whose storyline spans three countries, the United Kingdom, Pakistan, and the United States, engages with issues of women's rights in Islam, debates on Islamic law, and the rise in Islamic fundamentalism. It critiques the manipu-lation of religion by religious bigots, their influence on impressionable youth, as well as the misrepresentations of Islamic culture and practice in Western media. Despite its concern with such meaty philosophical, religious, and political arguments, the film handles interpersonal relationships between Western and Pakistani characters effectively to reveal shifting understanding of what it means to be a diasporan Pakistani citizen in the United Kingdom and the United States pre and post 9/11. Like other contemporary South Asian films, it is made with domestic and international audiences in mind even though its target audiences are Pakistanis and Indians at home and in the diaspora. South Asian cinema's popularity in the Middle East, Africa, and other non-Western countries is immense despite their distinctly South Asian worldview. Their concerns, no matter where their characters travel or live, are embedded within their own cultural, political, and historical con-texts and preoccupations, which in post 9/11 films are reconfigured to reflect the changing transnational relations between East and West. To satisfy its diverse audience demographics, the iconography in *Khuda ke Liye*'s publicity posters for internal versus external release differs significantly. The poster for its 2007 Pakistani release targets religious conservative segments within Pakistan showing the chief mullah in traditional garb fronting an extremely long beard with the film's original title[29] in large Urdu script followed by its English translation in smaller script. The 2008 poster for its international release exudes less religious and nationalist fervor featuring instead diasporic and cosmopolitan characters against a muted background echoing orientalist longings in its distant minarets against a tropical sunset. Arabic or Urdu characters have vanished and the text lists in English the film's international awards alongside characters' images with a stamp proclaiming it a "World Hit."

During an interview with Shalini Singh, when asked what triggered him to focus his first feature on religious and political issues, Shoab Mansoor replies it was no single incident, but rather

> It was thousands of wrong doings by people of my faith and others, which cultivated enormous anger in me over the years. Every faith and religion is full of its followers who interpret it in the most illogical and unworthy ways. Islam is no exception. Majority of the Muslims have been full of complaints on the subject but since they are tolerant and silent, people outside the Islamic faith never really knew about it. After the 9/11 incident unfortunately, the silent and tolerant majority faced the major brunt and their lives became extremely difficult and just bearing a Muslim name became a crime. Extremism and rigid interpretations of religion had always bothered me but the post 9/11 scenario triggered the writer inside me.[30]

He critiques Muslims in his own community as well as Western governments and media for their treatment of innocent Muslims after 9/11. Wanting to give moderate Muslims a voice, he does not hesitate to chastise them for their lack of decisive action. Critical of the fundamentalist factions for hijacking religious doctrine for their own ends, he still holds liberal and cosmopolitan Pakistanis responsible for not proactively resisting them. Such irresponsibility has led to a situation where "there is a war going on between the Fundamentalists and the Liberal Muslims. This situation is creating a drift not only between the western world and the Muslims but also within the Muslim community."[31] As a result, terrorist activity has increased globally with the main casualties of this "difficult situation" being women, whose rights are trampled and Quranic law subverted. Shoab Mansoor shows liberal Muslims have failed to stand up against fundamentalist mullahs through depictions of the conflict between moderates and fundamentalists. He documents this climate of dissent in Pakistani society through stories of two brothers, one residing in Pakistan with his wife and two sons, and the other in England with his Pakistani daughter and longtime English girlfriend.

The lives of the three young cousins are not terribly different before the 9/11 attacks, for these "liberal Muslims," educated and proud of their national and religious heritage, see themselves as cosmopolitan citizens of the world. Mary has grown up in the United Kingdom with her Muslim Pakistani father Hussein Shah and his English girlfriend who is more of a real mother to her than her father a parent. Having lived most of his adult life in England, Hussein has lost touch with his religion and culture. Now in a climate of increasing Islamization of British Pakistani neighborhoods, he decides it is time Mary knows her heritage. He talks her into visiting Pakistan before committing to her English boyfriend, Dave; however, once in Pakistan, he marries her against her wishes to her cousin, Sarmad. Having recently come under the spell of the fundamentalist mullah, Maulana Tahiri, Sarmad has rejected his own earlier westernization. His older brother, Mansoor, departs for Chicago to study music around the time Mary is forcibly married to Sarmad in an Afghan village where he now lives in obeisance to Maulana Tahiri.

The characters that experience extreme negative repercussions after the 9/11 attacks are Mary and Mansoor—one who grew up in the West travels to Pakistan, the other who grew up westernized in Pakistan travels to the United States. Both survive their ordeals, one at the hands of Muslim fundamentalists and the other at the hands of the CIA. While Mary is stripped of her rights and becomes a prisoner in an Afghan outpost away from civilization, Mansoor, living in one of the centers of modern civilization, Chicago, is arrested, detained, and tortured as a suspected terrorist. His arrest arises out of an example of Partition haunting experienced by his Sikh neighbor who prior to 9/11 had been cordial with Mansoor. This Sikh's Partition memories are revived by "the first 9/11 backlash fatality" on September 15, 2001, when his friend, a fellow Sikh, is shot and killed in Arizona:

> [Balbir Singh Sodi's] assailant, Frank Roque, wanted to "kill a Muslim" in retaliation for the terrorist attacks. He selected Mr. Sodhi simply because he had a beard and wore a turban in accordance with his Sikh faith. Mr. Roque shot at Mr. Sodhi three times, then shot at another service station owned by a Lebanese American, and finally shot at a home of a family of Afghan descent.[32]

During Partition riots many Sikhs had suffered similar or worse fates at the hands of Muslims when marked by their traditional attire as non-Muslims. Angry that Sikhs now in the wake of 9/11 are being targeted as Muslim terrorists, his latent memory of Partition atrocities Sikhs suffered is aroused, leading him verbally to vent his anger at Mansoor, holding him responsible for the unjust profiling of his community by virtue of Mansoor's being a Muslim. A neighbor overhearing their altercation calls the authorities—a citizen responding in fear and to official calls to all Americans: "if you see anything, say something."

Khuda ke Liye's scenes addressing the treatment of Pakistanis who are profiled, arrested, and undergo torture are extremely disturbing. To date only a handful of documentaries address "enhanced interrogation techniques":[33] *Road to Guantanamo* (2006) by Michael Winterbottom from the United Kingdom and *Taxi to the Dark Side* (2007) independently produced by American documentarian Alex Gibney, Eva Orner, and Susanna Shipman. It wasn't until 2013 that Hollywood portrayed the use of torture on 9/11 suspects in any substantive way in Katherine Bigelow's *Zero Dark Thirty*. It lost the Oscar that year to Ben Affleck's *Argo* (2012), possibly because of its torture scenes that came under criticism. Considered the best film of the year by many, *Zero Dark Thirty* is still perceived by critics as bordering on the "politically and morally reprehensible."[34] *The Guardian*, taking the position that "the film takes a pro-torture stance," describes it as "pernicious propaganda" that "presents torture as its CIA proponents and administrators see it: a dirty, ugly business that is necessary to protect America."[35] Bigelow, on *The Late Show with David Lettermen* and other TV appearances, defends the water boarding scenes as a small part of the film, not integral to the plot, and merely one of many strategies used in the real CIA search for Osama bin Laden. The torture scenes in *Khuda ke Liye* and other South Asian films, on the other hand, are distinctly central to plot and significantly shape why and how characters and their lives change, as well as show long-term effects of torture of detainees on transnational relations.

After months of detainment and torture, Mansoor is eventually released, partly because of the protests organized by his white American wife and liberal Americans who protest his detention with marches and speeches and partly because no evidence of terrorist connections is found. By depicting protests by average Americans in Chicago, Shoab Mansoor emphasizes his critique is directed not at American people but rather at the United States government's treatment of innocent Muslims during this period. Sadly, the torture leaves Mansoor mentally and physically disabled. Upon returning home, in the film's closing scenes in Karachi, he is shown with his family barely aware of his surroundings. When his favorite music starts to play, the camera focuses on Mansoor's hands, and we see his fingers keeping time with the beat hinting at a possible recovery in the fold of his loving family.

Mary stands out as a beacon of hope for the future of Pakistani and Afghani women finding a way to maintain her sanity by engaging with Afghan women in the outpost and remaining hopeful by smuggling a letter to Dave in England. Even after giving birth, she continues teaching the children and women to read and write English. In a series of court scenes during her divorce proceedings, Shaob Mansoor deploys a debate over how Quranic law has been misinterpreted by fundamentalists anxious to cause a rift between East and West. The film is a wake-up call to moderate Muslims and their clergy through the use of the character of the rational Maulana Wali, renowned Islamic scholar, whom Mary persuades to testify at her divorce proceedings after chastising him for being wrapped up in scholarly pursuits and prayers and ignoring needs of people suffering injustice. While the fundamentalist mullahs adamantly hold to their conservative views, Maulana Wali refers the judge to relevant texts revealing actual words from the Hadith by quoting book, chapter, and verse. When asked by the defense lawyer, "and Islam permits a girl to marry a man of her choice?" Maulana Wali responds vehemently: "Permits! It is her right. It is her birthright. Open the book of Hadith. Take Nisa Vol 2 Chapter—The Book on Marriage page 403."[36] After he testifies that Islamic law also gives women the right to a speedy divorce, the trial ends. Not only is Mary's divorce granted, the courtroom and audience come away realizing the fundamentalist mullahs have misled them. The court scenes emphasize how the Qur'ān treats women as equal citizens, granting them individual rights before and after marriage.

Mansoor's and Sarmad's parents (Shoab Mansoor's moderate Muslims) throughout the turmoil of the past months are depicted as powerless to change the tide of events and as impotent in protecting their sons and niece from the escalating effects of fundamentalism, implying that the future direction of Pakistan lies with the next generation. Mansoor and Sarmad held promise, but while one is damaged the other succumbs to the fundamentalists (a warning how easily this can happen to impressionable Muslim youth, even those not disaffected). During Mary's divorce trial, Sarmad comes to his senses realizing Maulana Tahiri has misled him. Back at his beloved job singing the call to prayer at the mosque where he first encountered Tahiri, he is seen in the final scenes in jeans and a baseball cap turned backward—attire he wore prior to his indoctrination. His defiant return to what he loves upon his own terms expresses he now integrates his heritage and personal Islamic faith within the contemporary context of his life.

Once released from her marriage, Mary, free to go back to England with her child, changes her mind and decides to return to the village to continue educating Afghan women. When her stepmother asks why she would go back, especially now that everything is fine, Mary responds: "Everything is not fine, it never will be. I am not the Mary Dave loved. He deserves better." One of my American male students considers this a confession of shame on Mary's part as "damaged goods," calling it a disappointing statement from a feminist standpoint.[37] A female student, on the other hand, reads Mary's decision as "pragmatic." The majority of the students in this class expressed disappointment because Mary doesn't return to David, love, and marriage in Britain. Their need for closure arises out of desiring romantic endings; at another level, it speaks to how Western viewers, finding the Other's rejection of egalitarian/democratic Western values incomprehensible, cannot embrace an alternative choice as culturally and politically empowering. Such responses recall Gayatri Spivak's famous, often misinterpreted quote, critiquing British initiatives to end Suttee (or Sati; widow suicide) in colonial India—"white men are saving brown women from brown men."[38] Spivak's position on the West's desire to protect "othered" women from their own cultures is echoed by Muslim feminists responding to the contemporary turn toward colonialist discourse during the era of the war on terror. Sherene Rezack finds "[g]lobally, while Muslim men have been the target of an intense policing, Muslim women have been singled out as needing protection from their violent hyperpatriarchal men."[39]

I argue, despite David's (the white man's) role in Mary's release, she rejects the idea of going back to Dave and her life in England because of her realization of her own identity as a Muslim woman. In England she would always be a colonial trophy, the subaltern woman given voice by the white man and Britain's intervention. Instead, she chooses to stay not out of shame, but because she has found her mission and sense of purpose—a sense of purpose she lacked while growing up in Britain oblivious to the conditions her Muslim sisters endure—conditions created by not just the radical Islamists, but also American, Russian, and British interventions in the region over decades. Ironically, through her extreme experience, she becomes decolonized, recognizing that her generation of Muslims, with their knowledge of the West, privileged by education and material wealth, can and should empower their own people. Just as the ordeals of the protagonist of the iconic film *Mother India* inspire the 1950s' generation of Indians with nationalistic zeal and their Hindu identity, so too does Mary inspire a renewed sense of allegiance to Islamic culture, Pakistan, and Afghanistan. She returns to the Afghan village as a single mother taking on the responsibility of raising her daughter on her own. Her arrival at the village is met with quiet joy for she is welcomed back as one of their own by men and women hungry to learn. Mary's choice empowers Afghan and all Muslim women often led to believe they are powerless to change the world, let alone their own situation. Her insistence on the importance of education in empowering women echoes Spivak's 2013 work addressing the role of humanities education in an era of globalization.[40] How education can empower women to enact change is illustrated further in the real life example of Pakistani Afghan Malala Yousafzai.[41] Like Malala, Mary is the modern female face of Islam and its future. The film ends hopefully precisely because she chooses to stay over abandoning her culture and faith for a comfortable existence in England separated from her roots. Here she can help build the educational infrastructure that will make it possible for Afghani subalterns to have a voice. She embodies how modern and traditional values can coexist, representing what it means to be a contemporary Muslim, Pakistani, and Afghan.

Through her efforts she will ensure fundamentalist ideologies are not easily accepted by the next generation, the generation that can bridge the gap between East and West, further women's rights in their corner of the Islamic world, and make it possible for Pakistan to be one with this world and still continue to be true to its culture and Islamic faith.

NOTES

1. Engle 2009, 7.

2. Warner Brothers delayed the release of Andrew Davis's *Collateral Damage* (2002), Fox dropped *Deadline*, and Jerry Bruckheimer decided against making *World War III*, a film about nuclear attacks. *Nose Bleed,* in which Jackie Chan, plays a window washer, was scheduled to film on top of one of the towers and the shoot was delayed because of a late script. When interviewed for Hong Kong's *Oriental Daily News*, Chan says "Filming was scheduled to have taken place at 7 am last Tuesday morning . . . As I had to be on top of one of the Towers I would probably have died. Well, I guess my time is not up yet." http://www.theguardian.com/film/2001/sep/20/september11.usa "Late script saved Chan from New York attack" (Accessed online August 17, 2015). Tim Allen's *Big Trouble,* scheduled for release on September 21, 2001, was held back till April 2002 because its plotline involved a nuclear device and gun being smuggled on an airplane.

3. Zizek 2013, 19.

4. Hoberman 2013, 52.

5. Zizek 2013, 18.

6. Merrill 2005, [171–184], 174.

7. Zizek 2013, 23.

8. Ibid., 15.

9. Engle 2009, 32.

10. Zizek 2013, 15.

11. Engle 2009, 30.

12. Merrill 2005, 180.

13. Ibid., 184.

14. Films during the first few years following Indian and Pakistani independence avoided representations of Partition by focusing instead on an urban/rural dialectic where the pastoral/rural untainted life was presented as essentially Indian and/or Pakistani with the urban life as contaminated by crime and greed. The experience of colonization, though elided, was referenced indirectly in the West's influence in urban spaces and on urbanites. The true Indian, it seemed, resided in unpolluted rural spaces even when those were often centers of poverty and deprivation—a legacy of colonization. Many of this era's films including Raj Kapoor's, while celebratory in tone over the country's freedom, were socialist statements often critical of the newly independent nation's economic initiatives.

These include, among others, *Awaara* (1952), *Shree 420* (1955), *Mr. and Mrs. 55* (1957), *Mother India* (1957), *Madhumati* (1958), and *Jis Desh Mein Ganga Behti Hai* (1963).

15. Sarker 2009, 33.

16. Ibid., 2.

17. While exact figures are contested, most documents conservatively estimate that at least 1 million people died with over 12 million being displaced from ancestral homes during the Partition riots.

18. Chakravarty 2006 [232–247], 233.

19. *The Terrorist* was inspired by the assassination of Rajiv Gandhi during his campaign stop in Tamil Nadu in May 1991 by a female suicide bomber working for the Liberation Tigers of Tamil Eelam.

20. Chakravarty 2006, 244.

21. It was the first Indian film to get in the top 10 of the United Kingdom's box office hits, and A. R. Rahman's soundtrack, especially the song "Chhaiyya Chhaiyya," played incessantly in Indian streets. In a 2002 international BBC poll it was placed at #9 of the top 10 songs of all time. www.bbc.co.uk/worldservice /us/features/topten/profiles/index.shtml. Accessed on July 14, 2016.

22. Dr. Uma Vangal provided this perspective when I asked her about the reception of Mani Ratnam's films in Tamil Nadu following her presentation, "Fan Club Culture in Tamil Nadu, India: Religion and Politics Come Full Circle." She was invited to deliver the Annual Colloquium Lecture organized by the Popular Culture Studies Association at Bowling Green State University on September 24, 2015. Dr. Vangal was a visiting professor of Film at Kenyon College, Ohio, for Fall 2015. She is a filmmaker, critic, freelance journalist, and full-time professor and head of Media and Entertainment Department of LV Prasad Film and TV Academy in Chennai, India.

23. Morris 2005 [297–320], 311.

24. Foster 2007.

25. These include women writers Marjane Satrapi, Azar Nafisi, Farzaneh Milani, Persis Karim, and Ayaan Hirsi Ali, whose memoir, *Nomad: From Islam to America a Personal Journey through the Clash of Civilizations*, by reiterating an "us versus them" rhetoric, helps further the divide between Islam and the West.

26. I address the reception in the West of Muslim women's writing and film in "The Dialogics of the New Orientalist Discourse: Telling Tales of Iranian Womanhood" in *Women and Islam (Women and Religion Series)* (Begum 2010, 263–288).

27. This analysis is part of my larger discussion of South Asian films that deploy Partition trauma through responses to 9/11. Here, I focus on Shoab Mansoor's *Khuda ke Liye* (2007).

28. Novak 2002, 4–7.

29. The direct translation of the original Urdu title, *Khuda Ke Liye*, would be either "For God's Sake" or "For the Sake of God," yet the English translation

used for distribution and the DVD is *In the Name of God*—possibly because it resonates more readily with Western audiences?

30. http://www.paklinks.com/gs/showbiz-pakistan/276193-shoaib-man soor-talkscontroversial-movie-khuda-ke-liye.html. Accessed September 3, 2015.

31. This is the description on the DVD cover of the film. Shoab Mansoor, *Khuda ke Liye [In the Name of God]* (2007).

32. http://saldef.org/issues/balbir-singh-sodhi/#.Vfxkv-kUbak. Accessed September 14, 2015.

33. This is a euphemism for the CIA's use of systematic torture in prying key information from detainees on terrorist activities. At "black sites" such as Bagram, Guantanamo Bay, and Abu Ghraib, these techniques were authorized by the Bush administration. In December 2014, the Senate made available a small portion of the Senate Intelligence Committee Report on the CIA's use of these techniques unofficially referred to as "The Torture Report" in the media. The torture used is similar to what French forces employed during the Algerian Revolution from 1955 to 1962, such as water boarding, sensory deprivation, and forced feeding of pork products to prisoners of the Islamic faith, which are documented in Gillo Pontecorvo's *The Battle of Algiers* (1966), a film that continues to be used for training purposes by the CIA.

34. "Does Zero Dark Thirty endorse Torture" 2012.

35. Greenwald 2015.

36. Shoab Mansoor, *Khuda ke Liye [In the Name of God]* (2007).

37. These responses are from students in an online summer graduate course I taught on post 9/11 film and literature in 2014.

38. Spivak 1994, 93.

39. Razack 2008, 4.

40. Spivak 2013.

41. Malala Yousafzai, shot in the head by a Taliban in 2012 on a bus in Pakistan at the age of 15 for demanding an education for girls, survived the attack to become the youngest recipient of the Nobel Peace Prize in 2014. She continues to advocate for women's education through speaking engagements and activist initiatives. The Malala Fund raised enough money to build a school for Syrian refugee women in Lebanon's Bekaa Valley in 2015. Celebrating her 18th birthday at the school's opening, Malala "called on world leaders to invest in 'books not bullets.'" See "Nobel Winner Malala Opens School for Syrian Refugee Girls" 2016.

Part V

Women, Worldview, and Religious Practice

CHAPTER 16

The Virtuous Life of a Thai Buddhist Nun

Petcharat Lovichakorntikul, Phramaha Min Putthithanasombat, and John Walsh

INTRODUCTION

Thai society continues to view women as the "rear legs of the elephant" who should follow and support their husbands who are the front legs. Yet this traditional lifestyle has been challenged by the spread of capitalism through globalization and has been transformed, particularly in urban areas. The expectations and aspirations of women have been significantly altered, as have their ability and willingness to work outside the house, both of which have had clear impacts upon their duties within families and households. This changing role for women is matched by their increased importance, particularly in Bangkok. In the meantime, although Thai Buddhist society does not recognize Bhikkuni, or female monk status, it does accept women becoming nuns and following the eight precepts. One such woman who followed this route and founded the Wat Phra Dhammakaya ("wat" means temple) is Khun Yai Chand (or Grandmother Chand) Khonnokyoong (1909–2000), who lived a long and virtuous life that in many ways parallels the changes in Buddhist women's status in Thailand as the country entered the modern age. Born into a middle class agricultural family, she received no formal education according to Thai tradition. She rejected familial claims to become a maid in a rich household

Phra Dhammakaya Temple. (Dhammakaya Foundation)

in Bangkok and left in order to dedicate herself to meditation as a means of making merit for her father and family, and ultimately she devoted her life to being a nun at the age of 29. In 1970, with just $91 (at present value, which was equivalent to $160 at that time), she was able to establish her own temple, which has become an extremely successful organization aimed at uniting the sentiments and ideas of the past with the present. Her career combines traditional values with the modern means of bringing them about, thereby indicating the role that technology has had in freeing women from domestic labor and enabling them to follow other pursuits. Within 20 years, her followers were spreading her teaching around the world, and now there are over 700 temples or branches that are the training center for the male ordination program of the original Wat Phra Dhammakaya nationwide and 160 temples or meditation centers around the world. Further, she focuses on spiritual development and the purification of the mind and body. More than 50,000 teenagers have joined programs to avoid drugs, alcohol, and gambling as well as to volunteer for public service on a regular basis because of her influence. Some 3,000 monks and 1,600 Ubasokas and Ubasikas (male and female laypeople) devote their lives to Buddhism working as full-time staff at her temple. On Buddhist holidays, as many as 50,000–100,000 people come together to meditate in silence and to attend the religious ceremonies.

KHONNOKYOONG'S LIFE HISTORY

HER CHILDHOOD

Khonnokyoong was born on January 19, 1909. She was the fifth out of nine children in her family. Mr. Ploy and Mrs. Phan were her parents living in Nakhonchaisri district, Nakhonpathom Province. It was a rural municipality of central part of Thailand. Her first name was "Chand," which means "moon," and her last name was "Khonnokyoong," which means "the peacock's feather." Born in a middle class farming family, she did not attend formal schooling, as was the norm with other young Thai girls in those days. Due to the strong Thai old customs, people adored males more than females. Therefore, men were the leaders in every facet of life. Ladies were meant to be good followers walking behind men. Moreover, schools were located at the temples, where Buddhist monks resided. Thai women only stayed at home taking care of family members and doing chores.

Consequently, Khonnokyoong never ever learned how to read and write. Her duties were helping her parents on household tasks and rice farming. The farmer's life had trained her to be responsible, industrious, and persistent. She would get up around 3–4 o'clock every morning and go straight to the rice field before sunrise, plowing, cutting grass, and cultivating rice seeds until harvest, year after year. Her rice field did not have even one stem of grass since she paid attention to it thoroughly. With her diligence, her family maintained good financial status without any debts and liabilities, which was different from other farmers. In addition, she felt gratitude toward her family, especially to her parents, and for being loved by all family members.

Khonnokyoong was disciplined on being punctual. Since she started working early every morning, she took a break for lunch at 11:00 A.M., which was also the time for offering meals to monks. They would stop working during the luncheons. The buffalos could get some rest and Khonnokyoong continued to work again in the afternoon until returning home at sunset. Due to her hard work, the local people in that community called her "An Iron-shin Chand."

Before sunset, at the rice field, Khonnokyoong always looked upon at the sun in the sky. She dreamed that she could reach out there one day. She had a happy time watching over the sun and kept asking herself, "Why were we born, and what is the ultimate goal in our life?"[1] Although at that time she received no reply, she was still happy looking at the bright round sun before it went down at the horizon.

Once she grew up into a teenager, she never paid attention to marriage. She preferred to be alone and lead a monastic life, in contrast to expectations for young women during those times. In Thai culture, most women would get married before they turned 20. However, Khonnokyoong was content to help her family with the farming.

A TURNING POINT

Although Khonnokyoong's father was a good family man, he was addicted to alcohol. One day he got extremely drunk and was sleeping in his house (a Thai house in the past always had two stories, the first floor being a multi-purpose open-air area without walls to protect from flooding and the second floor used for living). In sleep, he was mumbling and her mother felt annoyed by his loud voice, leading her to shout at him saying, "A sparrow who lives in another's nest." This authority was a result of her higher financial status than her husband. When he heard his wife's impertinence, he got very angry and asked his children whether or not anyone had heard their mother insulting him. All the children kept quiet except Khonnokyoong, who did not want her parents to continue fighting, so she said, "Mom did not insult Dad." In anger, her father cursed Khonnokyoong to be deaf for 500 lifetimes.

It was a Thai belief that the parents' words are sacred and holy and will come true, whether they are good or bad. If the parents give blessings, comfort, and warm words to their children, then they will become true for their children and vice versa. Therefore, Khonnokyoong was so worried about this event that she intended to ask for her father's forgiveness some day before he passed away to convey her pure intention of not seeking any revenge against each other as doing so might stop the effects of *kamma* (karma) for both the father and the daughter.

Unfortunately, on the day that her father passed away, Khonnokyoong was still working in the rice field. She did not get a chance to apologize to her father. And this was one thing that disrupted her mind always. Most Thai people have faith in reincarnation. At that time, since she was only 12, Khonnokyoong worried that she might be born as a deaf person for 500 lifetimes due to her father's curse.

After her father's death, Khonnokyoong still lived with her family and worked at the rice field until she was 18. To her great relief, she heard that there was one great master who could teach people to go to see the realm of afterlife including heaven and hells and to attain *nibbana* (nirvana). The great master monk was Phramongkolthepmuni (1885–1959), the abbot of Wat Paknam Bhasicharoen, Bangkok. As a result, she strongly committed to herself to study *dhamma* (Pali; Sanskrit *dharma*) with Phramongkolthepmuni so that she could see her father, but she did not know where the temple was.

Finally, in 1935 Khonnokyoong left her home when she was 26 years old. She appropriately arranged the family's property before she left. Henceforward, she decided to abandon all her heritage and even her beloved family despite their grief. It was such a big decision in her life especially for a tiny single woman. With merely THB 2 (equal to $0.05), she went directly to Bangkok to stay with her relative. Afterward, she learned that Madam Liab was one of the benefactors of Wat Paknam Bhasicharoen. At her house, Mrs. Thongsuk Samdaengpan, one of the great disciples of Phramongkol-thepmuni, came to teach meditation regularly. Khonnokyoong was hired to work as a maid in this house. She was honest, hardworking, and responsible. Madam Liab loved Khonnokyoong very much and entrusted her over her children with the keys for her safe box.

Her intention became true when Samdaengpan realized how deeply Khonnokyoong desired searching for her father after his death. Samdaeng-pan asked Madam Liab for permission to let Khonnokyoong study and practice meditation. After finishing her undertaking, she arranged herself to meditate every day at the deck of that house sitting quietly and happily on her own for two years. Eventually, she came to attain the inner wisdom and experiences called the "Dhammakaya Knowledge." It was a state of tran-quility of mind and absorption in meditation where the mind becomes one and the same with the inner Body of Enlightenment. This insightful wisdom leads individuals to penetrate through all greed, anger, and delusion and gain enlightenment into the reality of life, *dhamma* knowledge, and the worldly knowledge that is different from formal education at a school, and also a state of peaceful mind reaching its height of mental consciousness. It is a method of training minds and developing spirits. With the Dhammakaya Knowledge and Samdaengpan's guidance, Khonnokyoong finally could help release her father from realms of hell due to his drinking habit when he was alive. Eventually, she was able to ask for his forgiveness as well.[2]

MEETING WITH HER GREAT MASTER

In attaining the Dhammakaya Knowledge, Khonnokyoong realized that dhamma was her utmost life destiny. In 1938, she decided to ordain as a Buddhist nun at the age of 29, which was the same as the age when Lord Buddha had left his palace to search for dhamma. Khonnokyoong shaved her head, wore white clothes, and observed the eight percepts for her whole life. Thai Buddhism does not have female monks anymore. Thus, being a nun is the highest status for a woman. Later, Samdaengpan made Khon-nokyoong meet with the great master dhamma teacher Phramongkolthep-muni at Wat Paknam Bhasicharoen, Bangkok. Without doubt and hesitation, Phramongkolthepmuni accepted her as his disciple, allowing her to join the super-advanced meditation workshop for the most accomplished meditators. Normally, everyone must pass and be trained for a long time until their skill-fulness in advanced meditation was approved by the great master. However, when Phramongkolthepmuni first met her, he said, "you came here so late," a comment that Khonnokyoong could not understand completely at that time.

With her endurance, humility, and respect to her great master dhamma teacher, Khonnokyoong would not give up or feel tired of practicing in the supreme advanced class. She often was mistreated by meditative peers who were jealous and looked down upon her. On the contrary, she taught herself that she was here to study the profound dhamma. If she did good deeds, she would get good in return, while others would get based on their good or bad actions. Because she was one of Phramongkolthepmuni's disciples, she committed herself strictly to follow his teachings no matter what would happen.

At the super-advanced meditation workshop, they had a 24-hour meditation class daily divided into four sessions and each session was six hours long without interruption, meaning that each person meditated during the day time for six hours and at the night time for six hours. This workshop was only for the highly advanced meditators and Khonnokyoong was one of them. She came to her class 30 minutes before her session and stayed for an extra 30 minutes. During her break, she also practiced on her own by meditating all the time and did not pay attention to trivial things. Consequently, she was appointed the head of her session and became one of the great master's most outstanding disciples. Phramongkolthepmuni publicly observed that

Khonnokyoong ordained as a Thai Buddhist nun. (Dhammakaya Foundation)

"Daughter Chand is second to none," because she could attain the profound Dhammakaya Knowledge with her inner skills of self-realization.

In 1954, Phramongkolthepmuni called a meeting among his disciples to help spread the Dhammakaya Knowledge worldwide and to alert them that he was going to pass away in five years. Additionally, he told Khonnokyoong to stay at Wat Paknam Bhasicharoen until the time she meets her followers, after which she will build a new temple. Five years later, his foresight came true. Phramongkolthepmuni passed away on February 3, 1959.

Waiting for and Meeting with Her Followers

Khonnokyoong followed her great master dhamma teacher by continuing to teach dhamma and staying at Wat Paknam Bhasicharoen until one day in October 1963 she met a young man, 19, named Mr. Chaiyaboon Suddhipol (currently Phrathepyanmahamuni, the abbot of Wat Phra Dhammakaya), who was searching for a dhamma practice. At that time, Khonnokyoong was 54 and also known as "Khun Yai Chand" by younger students. Suddhipol became one of her students. He had just graduated from high school and was going to study economics at Kasetsart University. Khonnokyoong taught him meditation and Dhammakaya Knowledge until he achieved a high level in meditation practice. Khonnokyoong assigned him to teach meditation to others, and he realized that he would like to be ordained as a Buddhist monk and did not prefer to study any further. However, Khonnokyoong persuaded him to finish his graduate-level studies before entering monkhood, to forestall criticism that Suddhipol could not live in the worldly realm and was grasping at Buddhism as a refuge. Suddhipol became a Buddhist monk on August 27, 1969, after his graduation.

At Kasetsart University, Suddhipol also encouraged his college friends to study meditation with Khonnokyoong at Wat Paknam Bhasicharoen. Mr. Padej Pongsawat (currently Phrarajbhavanajarn, the vice abbot of Wat Phra Dhammakaya) was one of the group members, and later he ordained as a Buddhist monk on December 19, 1970. Both of them played a crucial role in all Khonnokyoong's dhamma projects and were the supporters behind Khonnokyoong's success.

After the ordination of Suddhipol, Khonnokyoong tried to find a place for building a Buddhist temple where they could teach mediation to a larger group of participants and propagate Dhammakaya Knowledge to all human beings worldwide. In fact, during that time Khonnokyoong had only THB 3,200 ($160 in 1970 and approximately $91 currently) in savings. At the age of 61, when most working persons are beginning their retirement, Khonnokyoong got started on building a Buddhist temple. She once asked Pongsawat how much needed to be invested to get a good man (to support her in her work). Pongsawat replied, "Although we give out THB 100 million, no one can ensure that we will get a good man." Then, Khonnokyoong said that she had assets over THB 1,000 million because she had more than 10 people who observed the five precepts regularly, practiced meditation daily, had the same goal, and devoted their lives to Buddhism. Therefore, she was quite strongly confident that the temple would be finished completely. She, however, warned that while the group might disagree with each other, they should not get angry when working together to build the temple.

Eventually, Wat Phra Dhammakaya was officially established on February 20, 1970, which fell on the Magha Puja Day. This land located in Pathumthani Province was donated by Lady Prayad Prattayapongsa Visudhadhipbodi on her birthday; she gave the entire 78.4 acres of her property to this temple. The gift was considered a miracle since they did not have enough money to buy even a piece of land. With her optimistic thinking, Khonnokyoong attributed it to the power of merit and the unity of the team members to make this mission possible.

HER LAST STEP

Finally the main chapel was completed in 1982 by laypeople ranging from little children, teenagers, students, and adults to the elderly giving their hands and donation. In comparison with other traditional Thai temples, the chapel style of Wat Phra Dhammakaya looked architecturally different, but they still preserved the important parts of a Thai chapel. The main objective in the construction of Wat Phra Dhammakaya was to be "the thriftiest in cost, the utmost in utility." They did not want to waste their budget on maintenance so their styles were characterized by simplicity and magnificence. Donations received on any projects were efficiently implemented to ensure that they were utilized entirely to cultivate and support Buddhism to their full value. Khonnokyoong and her team leaders embodied this philosophy and method of financial management in temple construction with their first establishment.

The three main purposes of this temple were (1) to make ordinary people virtuous; (2) to make ordinary monks virtuous; and (3) to make an ordinary temple into a great temple. The monks concentrated on teaching dhamma and training laypeople in ethics and morality. Starting from hundreds of participants and ultimately reaching hundreds of thousands, the monks started expanding their property to 1,000 acres in 1985. Phrathepyanmahamuni informed that he expanded the temple because there were so many laypeople coming to study meditation and Buddhism. This was the reason why he had to think big and do the best he could. The first assembly hall held only 500 persons in 1980; then the second one was built in 1985 with a palm-leaf roof with the capacity to hold 10,000 people but there still was not enough room for meditators. Finally, the Dhammakaya Assembly Hall was constructed in 1997 for 200,000 people. Although it was not completely finished, it is being used to the present day on a monthly basis and for holy Buddhist memorial events.

The Great Dhammakaya Cetiya (or pagoda), which is the world's largest Buddhist monument, consists of 1 million Buddha statues, of which 300,000 Buddha images are enshrined on the exterior dome and 700,000 on the interior dome. This remarkable pagoda will last for the next 1,000 years for the next generations who will come to study Buddhism and Dhammakaya Knowledge. It was completed in 2000 and can hold 1 million people together. A grand opening ceremony was held on April 22, 2000, when Khonnokyoong was 91. It was the first celebration of Wat Phra Dhammakaya gathering hundreds of thousands of Buddhists from around the world to offer alms, observe the precepts, and practice meditation in silence together. Since then this place has become an astonishing world Buddhist center. Over 1 million Buddhists gather at the Great Dhammakaya Cetiya during important Buddhist events held not only for Thai people but also for people around the world regardless of gender, age, and faith. Due to Wat Phra Dhammakaya's mission statement, "World Peace through Inner Peace," they are open to anyone who would like to create "peace" in one's mind and in this world.

Khonnokyoong passed away on September 10, 2000, at the age of 91. Her legacy on dhamma teachings and meditation will be kept alive in her

The Great Dhammakaya Cetiya, Pathumthani, Thailand. (Dhammakaya Foundation)

One million Buddha statues, the Great Dhammakaya Cetiya. (Dhammakaya Foundation)

students' and followers' hearts. Her life was pure, chaste, and virtuous, making her a role model for those who would like to train and uplift themselves to be better in all aspects. It does not matter what knowledge or degree levels an individual holds but one's true and inner wisdom is the most important enlightenment in one's life. At Khonnokyoong's cremation ceremony, on February 3, 2002, 100,000 Buddhist monks from 30,000 temples nationwide including senior monks from 20 countries and hundreds of thousands of laypeople from around the world came to pay their final respects.

Vorasubin et al. state:

> Like the story in a fairy tale:
> A tiny little farmer girl, completely illiterate, took a journey on a spiritual quest, found a Great Master, learned the great Knowledge from the Master, went on to build a great temple, produced many true monks and virtuous people, and brought goodness to mankind.[3]

KHONNOKYOONG'S NOBLE WORKS

TO MAKE ORDINARY PEOPLE VIRTUOUS

This was Khonnokyoong's first objective in building her own temple. To build a virtuous person is the most important issue, more than constructing a building. Once she attained inner peace and true happiness within herself, she wished to spread this knowledge and method to others with the support of her two students, Phrathepyanmahamuni and Phrarajbhavanajarn. Khonnokyoong's team members accumulated to a bigger group. They could cultivate good habits and better characteristics in themselves changing their drinking and smoking habits to be people who followed the five precepts and meditated every day. Normally, people think if they do not harm others, they are good, but Khonnokyoong taught them to be aware that they might misleadingly harm themselves by ruining their health from intoxicants and drugs. Because of her teachings, many college students changed their mind and behaviors as well as followed in her footsteps. As a result, they became devotees of Buddhism.

Several training programs were provided, ranging from those for kindergarten students to college students, from youngsters to adults, from operational employees to top executive levels, for example, the Path of Progress, the World-PEC, the Mass Ordination, Peace Revolution, and Peace-in and Peace-out. These projects intended to promote dhamma teachings and to encourage all walks of life to study Buddhism.

In Buddhism, the three key elements to gain more merits are donation, taking precepts, and meditation. All the programs listed above are based on these foundations and were initiated during Khonnokyoong's lifetime. However, Phrathepyanmahamuni is a proactive spiritual leader and also applies the methodology of doing good deeds "inside-out" to public, for example, "The National Alms Offering to Two Million Buddhist Monks" program started in 2004. Over millions of people joined in this program, and it was the new revolution of alms offering to the monks. Also the alms were offered to the Buddhist monks, military, policemen, school teachers in the southern part of Thailand (currently there is a conflict and violent issue), as well as the needy and victims from natural disasters.

TO MAKE ORDINARY MONKS VIRTUOUS

Khonnokyoong did not teach her students only to be virtuous laypeople but supported anyone who wished to become a Buddhist monk. Buddhism has four factor communities: Buddhist Bhikkus, Buddhist Bhikkunis, Ubasokas, and Ubasikas. To strengthen and prolong Buddhism, individuals should support these four communities. In Thailand there are no Buddhist Bhikkunis; hence, Buddhists Bhikkus or monks are the dhamma teachers whom Buddhists should respect and help support in learning dhamma scriptures and Pali language and attaining relevant education. This was why, according to the vision of Khonnokyoong and the team leaders, the monks at Wat Phra Dhammakaya were required to study both dhamma theories and practices.

Thus, Wat Phra Dhammakaya has originated training programs for Buddhist monks all over Thailand to get together to share and discuss dhamma principles, practice meditation, and motivate each other. The most important issue was to encourage them to quit smoking, which was part of the old Thai tradition to offer cigarettes to monks in the countryside. Consequently, Wat Phra Dhammakaya tried to create a new concept for Thai Buddhist monks.

Moreover, "The Walking Meditation and Dhutanga" program was arranged after the mass ordination to walk around and preach dhamma to laypeople. In this event, they would make alms offering to all Buddhist monks as well. Recently, Phrathepyanmahamuni brought back this approach of propagating dhamma to people living in large cities like Bangkok because they are getting away from Buddhist practices and also to comfort them after the disastrous flooding in 2012.

To Make Ordinary Temples into Great Temples

With her two bare hands and a small amount of initial funding, Khonnokyoong, who could not read and write, was able to build Wat Phra Dhammakaya, the largest Buddhist temple in the world. According to her mental acuity and insightful wisdom, she inspired millions of people around the world to follow her teachings and dhamma practices.

Phrathepyanmahamuni expanded Khonnokyoong's original idea to build great temples by preserving empty temples that no longer had Buddhist monks staying there. This method was integrated with the "To Build Ordinary Monks to be Virtuous Monks" program since the increase in the number of monastic members required temples nationwide at which Buddhist monks could reside.

Dhamma from Khonnokyoong's Teachings

The Ways to Pursue Good Deeds in Our Life

Khonnokyoong imparted valuable teachings to her students and followers since she was at Wat Paknam Bhasicharoen, Bangkok, until she settled up Wat Phra Dhammakaya in 1970. The two core crucial teachings that she emphasized to her students were the "Four Basic Good Habits," which comprise cleanliness, orderliness, politeness, and punctuality, and the "Three Basic Moralities," which consist of discipline, respect, and endurance. Accordingly, she realized that these two frameworks would form the ethical infrastructure of each person and would be of benefit to those individuals who could cultivate these moral principles and apply them to their everyday lives, generating good deeds and merit.

Khonnokyoong taught her students to be present, not to think about the past since it has already happened and cannot be changed, and not to worry about the future as it has not yet occurred. She thought she would do her best and be responsible for her duties only in the moment and nothing could interrupt her. With this reason, when she practiced meditation, she could stop her thoughts and peacefully still her mind.

MERITS AND SINS

Khonnokyoong emphasized that all living beings born under the umbrella of Buddhism are very fortunate and must accumulate more merit in order to get rid of suffering. Profession and wealth do not matter because we cannot change anything in the past, and our present is a result of our past actions. From now on, we can create our own new life by doing good deeds. Everyone will die one day and we do not know when death will come toward us. We can bring only merits with ourselves. Once we start meditating, we will earn further merits and all the sins will go away from us. Khonnokyoong compared accumulating merit to drops of water filling up the water jar over time. Even during illness, the merits will soothe us and help us from suffering. Notwithstanding, we should occupy our mind with the merits we have been performing and do so in the future as well.

She also taught that merit supports all aspects of our life in terms of success in living and working, for there is no escape from our own acts, whether meritorious or sinful, as these are recorded at the center of our body. Visiting the temple is one of the methods of acquiring merit. Further, she taught that good deeds should be done for the sake of good deeds without concern for what others think, for good deeds open up the possibility of going to heaven and attaining nibbana.

After we do good deeds for ourselves, we should do good deeds for others as well. If we can do so, we will be proud of ourselves that our lives are worth living. Before going to sleep each night, Khonnokyoong strongly suggested, we should reflect on our actions and consider how much merit we gained on that day and what bad actions we should omit and not take with us even overnight, reminding ourselves later not to do it again.

MEDITATION

Khonnokyoong paid the most respect to meditation and dhamma. She agreed that to practice meditation is the most important thing in life and to attain inner dhamma is the ultimate goal of life. She had noticed that each person has one's own specialty; whatever we do, we should love that particular thing. She loved meditation; therefore, her inner dhamma experiences developed precisely, profoundly, and powerfully, leading to her advancement in meditation. Not only did she practice meditation every day, she also encouraged her students to do so. With increased meditation, defilements cannot penetrate into our mind; further, if we meditate habitually, all good things and merits will find their way to us. Meditation is the method to cultivate good mindfulness and gain new merit; it is as assured as hitting the ground with your fist, you never miss.

She preached that dhamma is in us, for if we can stop our mind we will reach dhamma within; if not, we cannot reach our inner happiness either. Once we still our minds, then our body, speech, and mind will become pure. And we will earn the most merit.

Finally, she observed that she had meditated a great deal in her previous existences until her accumulated merit gave rise to the knowledge and wisdom that enabled her to teach herself.

SPIRITUAL AND ETHICAL DEVELOPMENT

"Standing on our own feet" was also one of Khonnokyoong's principles, since she lectured her students that she had nothing, not even any property apart from the accumulation of merit. We use our merit by making a good wish for ourselves to cultivate good thoughts and acquire self-development. We have to help ourselves; not even all the people in the entire world or universe can help us.

Khonnokyoong taught that every single person is successful due to faithful determination and perseverance. Even though she could not read and write nor held any educational degrees, she could build a large temple with her team members. With a "true" intention and a strong will, one can accomplish one's goal, and it should begin in this lifetime with training and developing oneself.

Most people came to the temple to get some comfort or encouragement and needed someone to help relieve their sufferings. Khonnokyoong told her followers that first of all we have to understand ourselves, and then we can understand others. Keeping our mind at the center in the merit status with a mercy mind when talking with them is essential; additionally, if we can attain the profound meditation, we can easily help them out.

ANALYSIS OF KHONNOKYOONG'S TEACHINGS

Khonnokyoong had not received a formal education but learned by practicing meditation until she reached the inner wisdom, in contrast to Lord Buddha, who had graduated in 18 subjects by the age of 16 years. After that Lord Buddha searched for inner wisdom to look into oneself, learning about the world's nature and living beings till reaching the stillness point and seeing the law of truth that was the inner life of each person. While formal education teaches us to know how to take good care of our health and to earn our living through a career, informal education teaches us mindfulness, spiritual development, morality, and the truth of life.

Practically, when we calm our minds successfully, our minds will expand limitlessly to cover our houses, community, the country, the whole world, the universe, and the galaxy at large. Our minds will develop gradually starting from brightened mind, expanded mind, and mind power.

Phrabhavanaviriyakhun (2012) shared that Khonnokyoong taught and trained herself in the "Four Basic Good Habits" plus wisdom meditation, which was called the "Universal Goodness 5," or "UG 5." In this regard, she could generate her inner wisdom and expand her mind to cover the universe and she thought that she would like to help every single human find a way out from all sufferings. She attained the deepest of happiness within and also wanted to help other people reach that stage. In fact, inner happiness is different from outer happiness. For example, inner happiness comprises a peaceful mind, tranquility, and freshness, whereas outer happiness comes about from having delicious food, luxurious clothes, traveling to nice places, and so on. Those who have deeply practiced dhamma can differentiate the level of their mind's tenderness. At this point, not only will their mind be soft, but also their bodily performances and polite speeches will be delivered to nearby persons as well. Rudeness, impoliteness, harsh words, and curse will be uprooted from their minds eventually.

Not only did Khonnokyoong impart such teachings to her students and followers, but she also put her teachings into action. Hence, she was a role model for her disciples as well.

FOUR BASIC GOOD HABITS

Cleanliness

Khonnokyoong's conspicuous cleanliness was the good habit she had formed since she was young. Once she noted that no one, not even her father or mother, taught her on this score. She was very different from her siblings. When she cleaned up her house, she mopped every angle of the stairs—the top surface and underneath, and her siblings asked her "Why don't you just mop the top surface?" She replied, "I don't know but I want to make them all clean. And I feel good doing so."[4] Again, when she worked at Madam Liab's house, she also did the same thing. This practice helped her when she practiced meditation. She could attain the clear and clean mind and gain inner wisdom to teach her own self and others.

When she moved to stay at Wat Paknam Bhasicharoen, she was given the oldest bed with bedbugs and an old, dirty, and worn-out mosquito net. Although she was mistreated by her peers, she did not complain of anything. She cleaned up everything until they all became spotless. She said she loved cleanliness and orderliness and she had been like this since childhood. This was the way she taught herself everything as well.[5]

On October 25, 1981, Khonnokyoong once said the following about her love of cleanliness:

> My love of cleanliness has been a part of me for as long as I can remember, I have fought for a long time to keep cleanliness wherever I go. Cleanliness has become a symbol of this temple. It has contributed to the faith, confidence, and respect of the people who come here. They see this place as a sanctuary and as a serene place to practice meditation. Please do not abandon the way of cleanliness that I have worked so hard to maintain.[6]

Therefore, it was the first impression of laypeople when they first visited Wat Phra Dhammakaya, particularly the cleanliness of the temple's restrooms. According to a survey, more than 90 percent of visitors were

To cultivate moral principles and apply to daily life. (Dhammakaya Foundation)

impressed with the cleanliness of its place. Basically, they felt comfortable and touched; next they could further study on Buddhism and dhamma as well as practice meditation. This strategy encouraged them to come to Wat Phra Dhammakaya again. Moreover, Khonnokyoong persuaded laypeople to wear white when they came to the temple although she got resistance at first or when someone did not understand why, but she prevailed for the sake of cleanliness and orderliness, and this method worked out well in helping to calm down minds quickly for meditation.

Orderliness

This was the second priority of Khonnokyoong's teaching. It is also the way that we will be admired by humans and angels, she cited. Khonnokyoong claimed that upon seeing some brooms laying around haphazardly, she would order them to be put back neatly. She said we must learn how to keep everything neat and tidy. After we finish using something, we should put that thing back in its own proper place. Try to maintain cleanliness and tidiness always. Keeping this habit will help us find orderliness in everything that we do in every lifetime especially when we practice meditation.

At Wat Phra Dhammakaya, Khonnokyoong set the rule of separating males from females sitting for meditation for orderliness and to avoid sexual attraction.

Politeness

Khonnokyoong reflected that she was not an ambitious person. This has been her characteristic for a long time. She taught her students to be neither blindly ambitious nor greedy. Indeed, she told us to learn modesty and contentment. If we kept our minds pure and clean, and accumulated enough merit, then our desires would become true without the need for ruthlessness. Further, she encouraged us to live a simple life and make use of our possessions prudently.

When she welcomed her students and disciples, she always put her palms together in a gesture to greet them all although she was older than them. When foreigners came to visit her temple, Khonnokyoong greeted them in Thai and let them have some meals before leaving. They all were impressed by her polite body language and manners even though they did not understand the Thai language.

Punctuality

With self-discipline in dealing with time, she would not only be on time for the super-advanced meditation class at Wat Paknam Bhasicharoen but she also attended 30 minutes prior to the start of class and also stayed longer after the class. That was why she could achieve the enlightened state of mind and also strengthen the purity of her mind.

Khonnokyoong suggested us to learn how to divide our time for meditation every day. She confirmed that life is short and we do not know when our final day will come. Days and nights pass by quickly. With each sunset our life becomes one day shorter. We should build up merit and know how to maintain merit by using the merit as wisely as we would spend our money.

In addition, she valued time since it waits for no one. Time passes by day, week, month, and year. So she proffered to do only good deeds by doing them now and doing them well.

THREE BASIC MORALITIES

Discipline

Khonnokyoong never infringed upon any temple rules and regulations, although she was the founder of her temple. And later on, her student became the abbot of Wat Phra Dhammakaya, but she never ever thought that she was his teacher. On the contrary, she abided by all restrictions and also paid high respect to the abbot.

In her real life, even though she faced many obstacles due to spite or jealousy, especially when she first joined the advanced meditation class at Wat Paknam Bhasicharoen, no one could find fault with her since she never violated any rules or regulations. She knew how to manage her timetable and how to handle her tasks according to cleanliness, orderliness, and discipline. She believed that we should abide by the rules and regulations of the places where we live. She paid faithful respect to the abbot of Wat Paknam Bhasicharoen until he passed away in 1959 and even after his death. She also maintained the same self-discipline and encouraged everyone to do so.

Respect

Khonnokyoong's behavior since she was young is instructive with regard to respect. Whenever a beggar came to her home asking for rice, she gave him rice. If he asked for grain, she gave him grain. She said that she never looked down upon anyone, whether they were poor, middle class, or wealthy. She gave respect to everyone and thought that we all were equally human. Thus, she taught her students to use kind words to everyone especially to the temple's volunteers since they came to help out with the temple's tasks. She believed kind speech creates respect and cooperation from the persons we are speaking to, for then we will accomplish our work and they will also gain more merit from volunteering at the temple.

Khonnokyoong not only paid respect to people but also honored the donations received. She exhorted that one be cognizant of the fact that money is not easy to come by. We must appreciate the value of money. We must understand how difficult it is to make each dollar that we spend. The supporters make their own living assiduously; they have full faith in the temple and make their donations to support Buddhism. It is wise to learn how to spend minimum money for maximum benefit.

The highest respect that Khonnokyoong evinced all her life was in how she admired the master's teachings and strictly followed them. And this was her determination, "To my elders, I pay the deepest respect by showing my humility, honesty, and truthfulness. In doing so, I have earned their highest trust." Showing humility, she did not brag and not show off at all.

Endurance

Khonnokyoong warned the temple staff members that everyone devoted oneself to helping Buddhism grow and to cultivate goodness in one self, and therefore, one should have more patience and try to get rid of bad habits. She always herself did this every day. We should carry good habits along with us to the next life; if we cannot do in this life time, then in the next life time we have to do it. Consequently, we should adjust and correct ourselves to be the best person we can be. In order to accomplish this, we should have endurance, self-consciousness, wisdom, and purity and give up recklessness.

Khonnokyoong modeled patience. She said she would like to gain more merit so she could tolerate everything and everyone no matter how hard it was because she preferred every single person to attain more merit. She fought to be silent to perform more good deeds. For the sake of harmony and merit, everyone should have a give-and-take attitude when working together. With patience and coalition, the task becomes easier and the merit benefits all.

When she established Wat Phra Dhammakaya, she set her mind to the ultimate goal of making the place clean and pure where laypeople could come to practice meditation and achieve purity. As a result, she devoted her life and worked so hard that she became severely sick due to malnourishment and nearly died. With her strong patience and taking refuge in her merit, she survived eventually. She knew what was what since she had meditated immensely, and relied on her inner dhamma to give her the strength to endure and the ability to survive.

In conclusion, before Khonnokyoong passed away, her parting words to her beloved students Phrathepyanmahamuni and Phrarajbhavanajarn were,

For my whole life, I've always trained myself and I found out that meditation is the best thing to do in our life. If anyone loves me, please deeply meditate until you could study the Dhammakaya Knowledge and work as a good teamwork to propagate it to the whole world because I've committed to Phramongkolthepmuni. With this knowledge, it will help all living beings from sufferings and could get out of the Samsara.[7]

Khonnokyoong's teachings identified the moral principles for training ourselves: (1) The principle of taking precepts is cleanliness for body, speech, and mind, which will lead us to strictly observe the precepts; (2) The principle of meditation is the brightness of mind. If we practice meditation until our mind becomes brightened, we can see things clearly and correctly; and (3) The principle of wisdom is tranquility. Inner wisdom will create a peaceful mind and generate mind power.

Furthermore, Khonnokyoong was also the foremost female leader in Buddhist society in Thailand who devoted herself to Buddhism and gave an opportunity to female laypeople by following her path and dedicating their life to Buddhism. She was a role model not only for female laypeople but also for the Buddhist monks and male laypeople in terms of how to train themselves to be a better person.

Chandra Khonnokyoong, the founder of Dhammakaya temple, Thailand. (Dhammakaya Foundation)

NOTES

1. Trianusorn 2001, 3.
2. Ibid., 25.
3. Vorasubin et al. 2012, 41.
4. Ibid., 48.
5. Ibid., 49–50.
6. Ibid., 201.
7. Phrabhavanaviriyakhun 2004, 11–12.

CHAPTER 17

Women in Contemporary Japanese Religious Civil Society Groups

Paola Cavaliere

Religious organizations in Japan have historically been engaged in social work and activities for community well-being: they contribute with educational facilities (vocational training centers, schools, universities, museums); social welfare activities in hospitals; homes for orphans, the elderly and the disabled; nurseries; dormitories for houseless families; and disaster relief and rebuilding efforts.

Women constitute the majority of members in most Japanese religious organizations and have been extensively involved in religious civil society organizations (RCSOs) with volunteer activities devoted to social welfare services, post-disaster management, reconstruction, and relief. They respond to disasters by organizing fund-raising campaigns, supporting people in the affected areas, sending and distributing goods, and providing relief and emotional care. The Great East Japan Earthquake of 2011 and the Kumamoto earthquake of 2016 mobilized a massive volunteer response, and religious organizations quickly organized their support and reconstruction activities.[1] Many women members of religious organizations have been contributing to the reconstruction and relief activities by working together with lay and state-funded groups and institutions.[2] In the aftermath of the parallel disaster at the Fukushima nuclear plant in 2011, many of them have also joined grassroots movements supporting antinuclear protest and citizens' groups.[3]

The literature on volunteering regards religion and gender as two important components facilitating civic engagement, which in turn is believed to foster citizenship and democratization.[4] Through their volunteer activities, women members of religious organizations engage in open public debate on a range of common public concerns and issues. In this respect, the expansion of RCSOs in Japan has important implications for understanding the role of religious civil societies in enhancing women's participatory democracy and the implications for empowerment and gender equality.

However, a rooted resistance toward gender concerns in the Japanese religious context hinders the development of studies discussing religious civil society from a gender perspective.[5] By essentializing religiosity, investigations have largely neglected the varied and often subtle ways in which an agency may manifest in women's lives, thus overlooking the social significance of women's active participation in those volunteer groups. This study avoids any facile assumption that religion is merely a tool for oppressing women and evaluates carefully the normative role of gender socialization in channeling Japanese women into certain volunteer domains. Rather than looking at how religion and socialization provide identities to these women, the exploration focuses on women's volunteering in religious civil society groups as women's agency, thus shifting the question to what women do *with* religion.

The emphasis on the binding role of practice is especially significant in view of the strategies and approaches women develop to increase the degree of autonomy and self determination that is essential for an expanded participation across all sectors of social and economic life. In order to test the empowerment thesis, this chapter will evaluate what characteristics and customized practices may be congenial for the empowerment of Japanese women through religious-based civic engagement and how and to what extent women's participation in RCSOs might be a vehicle for empowerment and participatory democracy in practice.

The factual information offered in this chapter is drawn upon a survey of 82 women the author conducted in Japan from 2009 to 2012 in the greater Tokyo area and Saitama Prefecture. The respondents of this survey are members of three religious organizations: two Buddhist-related new religious movements (Risshō kōseikai and Shinnyoen) and members of one Christian denomination, the Roman Catholic Church of Japan.

WOMEN IN JAPANESE RELIGIOUS-BASED VOLUNTEER GROUPS: A DEFINITION

In many ways, the public benefit; the public nature and social contribution activities of religious civil society groups make them overlap with community-based volunteer groups. In view of these facts, it is difficult to give a clear definition of what constitutes a religious civil society group. Literature tends to define them as groups characterized by the presence of staff and volunteers coming from a specific religious group and with a philanthropic endeavor rooted in a particular religious ideology.[6] Other scholars consider groups with an institutional connection to religion as faith-related organizations[7] or groups that publicly acknowledge a relationship to a religious group.[8] For the Japanese case, this study suggests a definition of religious civil society groups as those volunteer groups that are often ethically inspired by a philanthropic project of a particular religious organization, although the groups are not necessarily of a religious character, nor are its members exclusively religious affiliates.

In Japan, religious-based volunteer groups operating at grassroots level are generally characterized by small-scale community-based groups, not formally incorporated as nonprofit organizations and not dependent upon the sponsoring religious organization for managing and running their activities and projects. They are typically initiated by members of a religious organization living in the same community where they become aware of problems and needs, to which they respond through their everyday volunteering, mostly dealing with social issues of large public interest: eldercare, childcare, and unemployment. They present a typical proposal style in responding to local needs, relating with institutions and working with the local government.

There is an overall lack of empirical data of both women members and the gender ratio in community-based religious civil society groups. This makes it difficult to specify the number of women engaged in them and the type of activities in which they are involved. The *Religion Yearbook* published every year by the Bunkachō (Japanese Agency for Cultural Affairs) reports the total membership of each registered religious organization and the number of specialized members (those holding the position of a teacher or higher in the religious organizations). The latter is divided by gender, which helps produce estimates of the gender ratio in the membership of two religious organizations targeted in this study, Shinnyoen and Risshō kōseikai, where the overall proportion between male and female teachers is roughly 1:3.[9] The Catholic Bishops' Conference of Japan in 2010 informed that the Movement of Lay Catholics, which engages in several social activities including care services and social work, counts 174,804 men and 265,497 women.[10] These facts suggest that membership in the religious organizations may be similarly characterized by a higher proportion of women. In summary, this study argues for an estimated prevalence of women members in the three targeted organizations, which in turn may suggest a higher presence of women engaged in volunteer activities sponsored by the religious organizations. Empirical evidence of grassroots religious-based volunteer groups in this study confirmed the estimates of the gender trends discussed here.

The Fieldsites

The five surveyed religious civil society groups are the Itabashi Church Social Welfare Association and Kawagoe Church Volunteers, sponsored by Risshō kōseikai; the Shinnyoen Social Contribution Department—Youth Division and Univers Volunteers, a nonprofit organization (NPO) sponsored by Shinnyoen; and Yotsuya Onigiri Nakama, sponsored by the Roman Catholic Church in Japan.

The Risshō kōseikai–sponsored Itabashi Church Social Welfare Association (*Itabashi kyōkai shakai fukushi iinkai*) and the Kawagoe Church Volunteer Group (*Kawagoe kyōkai borantia*) run similar activities: women members regularly volunteer in homes for the elderly and disabled, usually helping professional staff with care-giving work and visiting the recipients at home. The Itabashi Church Social Welfare Association was established in 1999 and counts about 50 women (including eight non–Risshō kōseikai members) regularly engaged with home visits, *yūai hōmon,* giving assistance to aged people living on their own, helping the staff during lunchtime, bathing, and organizing recreational activities. The Kawagoe Church Volunteer Group, established in 1978, is formed solely by Risshō kōseikai *ippan kaiin* (single women members under 39) and members of the *fujinbu* (women's division). It counts 130 women members. Most Risshō kōseikai community volunteering is carried out in cooperation with the local government, local welfare organizations, and other lay volunteer groups. It is not uncommon for Risshō kōseikai female volunteers to receive a request of services for the elderly from the local neighborhood association, the local social welfare agency, other local eldercare facilities, or directly from family members (very often non–Risshō kōseikai members). Similarly, volunteers tend to refer to the local social welfare office whenever a specific case needs further assistance.

The Shinnyoen-sponsored volunteer group called the Shinnyoen Social Contribution Department—Youth Association (*shinnyoen shakai kōken seinenbu*) is composed of 144 members (34 men and 110 women) under the age of 35 years. They engage in environmental protection, disaster relief training, local community service assisting the elderly and disabled people, and fund collection to be donated to international organizations with which Shinnyoen cooperates. They also hold training courses for members on how to care for people in the event of a disaster. These latter activities are organized by the Shinnyoen-sponsored NPO "Shinnyoen Relief Volunteers," which covers specifically disaster prevention and support, and has been contributing to several reconstruction projects in the Tohoku hit area since the 2011 Great East Japan Earthquake and in Kumamoto area since 2016.

The second Shinnyoen group targeted for this study is the Univers Volunteers Tokyo, a branch of the Shinnyoen-sponsored NPO Univers Foundation.

The NPO offers community-based activities supporting the elderly organizing community gatherings, recreational activities, and home visits providing emotional care and support. The surveyed Univers Volunteers Tokyo has 18 male and 105 female volunteers,[11] with two men and one woman employed as permanent staff.[12]

The Catholic church–sponsored volunteer group is Yotsuya Onigiri Nakama, founded in April 2000 by five students at Sophia University. About 40 people participate in this group, the majority regularly volunteering three times a week. In terms of gender ratio, during the fieldwork a large majority of women were recorded as regular participants, usually a proportion of five women to one man. The group supplies freshly made *onigiri* (rice ball) to the homeless in central Tokyo. However, the volunteers' main purpose is to give them assistance, support, and emotional care. Over the years, the group has successfully built connections with several institutions, government agencies, social welfare officers, and NPOs serving the homeless and unemployed. Volunteers meet directly with local public officials and leaders to advocate for the rights of marginalized groups, conduct evidence-based research for advocacy campaigns in cooperation with antipoverty NPOs, speak out through letter writing to national newspapers, and build tent villages for the homeless in central Tokyo where also doctors, nurses, and lawyers volunteer. In this way members of Yotsuya Onigiri Nakama advocate changes in relationships between people from different strata of society and try to become influential in local politics.

WOMEN IN JAPANESE RELIGIOUS CIVIL SOCIETY GROUPS: CULTURAL IDEAL AND SOCIAL MODELS

In order to understand the social impact of the lived experience of grassroots faith-based volunteering, it is important to understand women's motivations toward preferences for religious volunteering as well as how government discourses and policies and gender socialization processes exercise an influence on women's prosocial choices.

Japanese femininity has been historically closely associated to women's role in the family.[13] In Imperial Japan, the catchphrase *ryōsai kenbo* (good wife, wise mother) exemplified the feminine ideal prescribed by the Meiji state (1868–1912), which reinforced the reproductive role of women who were expected to perform self-sacrifice, obedience, and family-centered duty.[14] The postwar political-economic system similarly enforced a structural gender stratification by requiring virtuous strength from women in order to support and develop the national economy through the domestic responsibilities of full-time housewives.[15] Since the economic downturn in the 1990s, a trend has been consolidating, mainly channeling female labor into part-time or temporary jobs as a supplement to the household budget rather than integrating with the wage for a full-time job.[16] In fact, a part-time job seems the dominant option for women who need to balance family and work.[17] On the other hand, Japan's shrinking and aging population has reiterated the feminine ideal and the intrinsic value of its reproductive role, largely promoted by government and media discourses, tax systems, and policies that regulate women's reproduction choices, lifecycle perspectives, and economic conditions.[18] Government moves and economic policies have channeled women's role so that they would be caring for children and the elderly, while contributing to the economy whenever possible, that is, when they are not caring for their family.

At the same time, as a byproduct of the massive volunteer response that occurred in 1995 in the aftermath of the Hanshin-Awaji earthquake and in 2011 after the Great East Japan Earthquake, a well-defined volunteer narrative has developed and established. The government has introduced a law (the NPO Law, 1998), policies, and directives to regulate people's prosocial choices and behavior, while largely supporting and encouraging the population to devote their time and energy to others also in the name of new liberal democratic ideals of independence, self-realization, self-development, and individual compassion beyond blood relationships as the word "volunteer" conveys. In this view, women's engagement in volunteer activities outside the family is valued as it represents the kind of realization of those ideals as embedded in the volunteer narrative. Moreover, women's unpaid care work and volunteer work have been largely valued as they express the sort of altruism, flexibility, and nurturance mainly attributed to Japanese women in the face of their family responsibilities and gender socialization. The 2010 White Paper on Gender Equality emphasizes the need to promote women's active participation in volunteer activities at the local level because it would be effective in promoting economic growth and the realization of related gender-equal policies.[19]

This volunteer role shaped upon conservative views of family and women's expected roles has been backed up by the majority of Japanese religious organizations. They have been encouraging and supporting women's engagement in volunteer activities by offering human and financial resources, training courses, and infrastructures to favor an increased engagement in activities covering care services (mainly eldercare and childcare), life safety, *machi tsukuri* (revitalize the locality), conserving the environment, and disaster relief. Women in their late thirties and forties, an age that matches the valley in the M-shaped curve of Japanese female labor-force participation made of those who drop out of the labor force for childrearing and child education, are still the majority participating in those activities.[20]

Given the above contextual factors, it comes as no surprise that the volunteer narrative expected of women, with or without religious affiliation, favors mainly a caring role toward the elderly and children: women's volunteering seems to be accepted as long as it complies with women's feminine ideal, those of wife and mother. The tendency to favor gender-specific goals reveals the extent to which gendered roles have been incorporated into women's everyday practices and how they are reiterated by religious institutions and religious-based volunteer activities.

WOMEN, RELIGION, AND PROSOCIAL BEHAVIOR

Sociology of religion tends to understand religiosity as giving individuals a stable, core identity that signifies the person in all social settings.[21] However, only a small number of informants surveyed in this study talked about religion as the main reason for their social commitment. The results from the questionnaire data indicate that many respondents were already interested or already involved in volunteering before engaging in religiosity. This finding was further confirmed during the interviews where respondents said they took advantage of the extant volunteer activities organized by the religious organization in order to become socially engaged without the stress of searching for opportunities by themselves. They also drew upon the shared symbolism to signify their commitment according to the worldview offered by their religion, because it was a ready-at-hand philanthropic image they could use when explaining their volunteer endeavor to their families, friends, and acquaintances. Moreover, the sponsoring religious organization gives several opportunities such as seminars, training courses, and conferences through which staff, volunteers, and members can acquire the skills and knowledge needed for the type of volunteer service they are giving. In doing so, the organization offers its members a better organized way—often free of charge—to gain the sort of ad-hoc vocational education volunteers need to respond suitably to the community's local needs.

From this point of view, religious civil society groups and NPOs offer women adherents a better organized environment, as compared with other secular organizations, to accomplish the sort of active participation envisaged by government discourses and policy-making moves. They express their prosocial endeavor and perform the active participation and revitalization of economy and society that is suggested by Prime Minister Shinzo Abe government's vision of a society where "all women shine."[22] In relating religiosity with her volunteer commitment, Y-san, one Univers Volunteers Tokyo respondent, said *"tama tama Shinnyoen datta"* (it just happened to be Shinnyoen):[23] this statement implies that religiosity did not function as the rationale for her social engagement, but just as the gateway to express it.

The majority of interviewees claimed they *used* belief as a source of spiritual strength and support. Members of Shinnyoen Social Contribution Department—Youth Division drew upon a well-defined and highly self-integrating group identity anchored in the religious organization and could earn confidence by reproducing patterns of peer-to-peer and top-down interactions borrowed from the religious group's customs. Risshō kōseikai members emphasized the interpersonal relationships customized within the religious organization to make them feel part of a community of individuals who shared a worldview and wanted to improve it. The Catholic-based Yot-suya Onigiri Nakama volunteers used the social thought promoted by the church to generate a critical understanding of social-structural conditions obfuscating social divides.

On a micro-level, respondents' stories illustrate how religion provided a vehicle to think critically about their '"role to play" and a "place to belong" suggested by the 2010 White Paper,[24] their relationship with the social world, and their own purposes. In this parlance, religion has provided these actors with a greater variety of ways to develop strategies and cultivate resources, knowledge, and skills necessary to attain common goals and social change, as well as reflect on and learn from those experiences. This reveals the nature of religion in this context: for the surveyed women, belief was but one of the components in the course of a self-exploratory journey, generating further reflection while testing the social setting, including their own religious organization. By volunteering for the homeless with members of the Catholic group Yotsuya Onigiri Nakama, the respondent M-san became accustomed to the practice of self-reflection and social criticism. She discusses the role and the power of institutions and government in informing and shaping individuals' lives and counts the religious institution as one of those offering narratives that can be used resourcefully or wasted completely.

WOMEN'S VOLUNTEER AGENCY AND ITS IMPACT

In view of the expansion of RCSOs in Japan, the focus on what women *do with* religion, rather than what religion makes them do, becomes both a timely and necessary way to situate questions regarding the effects of faith in real-life situations. It allows for two important points of analysis: (1) the effects of women's actions performed on behalf of the religious institution and (2) the impact of faith-based volunteering on women's social steward-ship and entrepreneurship.

WORKING ON BEHALF OF THE RELIGIOUS ORGANIZATION: MASTERING SYMBOLIC CAPITAL

The Religious Corporation Law enacted in 1951 and the following amendments, the latest one made in 1997, prescribes that Japanese religious organizations cannot exercise political authority and religious groups are not endorsed with the legitimacy to carry out roles such as cooperating with the government in discussing solutions for social issues.

However, many respondents expressed the idea that the true value of religion lies in its capacity to mobilize human, physical, and financial resources to contribute to the society's well-being. They also maintained that volunteering for a religious-based group meant, to some degree at least, working in society on behalf of their religious organization, which proves the public benefit of religion. For this reason respondents felt responsible for performing their services in the best way possible, by matching efficiently resources to needs. From the point of view of the religious organization, members who succeed are valued as success demonstrates their ability to integrate their religious organization with the community. Such a process may play an important function in giving religious institutions broader recognition and acceptance.

In this parlance, while Japanese religions offer their adherents worldviews and formal belief systems with which to identify, the adherents' participation in concrete, everyday life projects gives the religious institutions more civic responsibility than they had before. By removing debris, sorting relief supplies, offering emotional care, and providing help to the elderly and people in need, female volunteers enable themselves and their groups to interact with multiple actors and agencies. From this point of view, by exercising their role as citizens in religious civil society groups, women become the gateway for the religious organization to participate in the social contract, thus reinforcing indirectly the role of religious organizations in society at large. At the same time, women act vicariously for the religious organization, thereby achieving the role of negotiator among power structures and institutions on behalf of the religious organization. The more women recognize themselves in this role, the more they acquire awareness of secular discourses and resources. In Bourdieu's terms, mastering the "symbolic capital"[25] of the public discourses and resources helps them to organize disparate experiences into relatively coherent structures that allow styles and roles belonging to fields of "collective practice"[26] beyond the one they are sourcing.

The customs of Risshō kōseikai and St. Ignatius Church volunteer groups were the most potentially successful in favoring the integration of the religious organization in the community and their cooperation with local state agencies, thus favoring an expanded social role. However, women were not primarily interested in expanding a positive image of their religious institution. Therefore, if any integration happened, it occurred as an indirect consequence of women's actions.

RELIGIOUS-BASED VOLUNTEERING: DEVELOPING WOMEN'S SOCIAL ENTREPRENEURSHIP

Although the number of Japanese women working after marriage or reentering the labor market after childbirth is increasing, the anticipated family responsibilities and the burden of childrearing still make them prone to part-time or fixed-term jobs. In these terms, by engaging in everyday volunteer work addressing issues of public interest, religious-based volunteer groups and NPOs become a big pool for the differently skilled women who share skills and knowledge in order to develop strategies and projects to cope with the difficult circumstances of everyday life. Female volunteers we may find in those groups are full time employed women, or those who have never entered the labor market, or have withdrawn from it for personal or family commitments. Religious-based volunteer groups offer occasions for experienced and inexperienced women to meet up and work together, exchange knowledge, share interests, and build communal goals. They also offer opportunities for those who have not trained yet for an occupation-specific branch of the labor market to gain social and task-specific skills. Volunteer groups and NPOs, therefore, are sites for work-like experiences where women broaden their awareness in terms of socioeconomic structures. They are also sources of work-like opportunities offering flexibility and autonomy with regard to working hours according to family and private commitments, thus enhancing work-family compatibility.

Furthermore, the findings of this study show that women's experience in the religious-based volunteer groups fostered an enterprising approach to their initiatives and roles by strengthening entrepreneurial skills through their capacity to build and train resources and establishing business-like initiatives. The outcomes of such entrepreneurial development are seen in the cases of several respondents who have initiated cooperative and private enterprises by sourcing from the volunteer experience.

When Risshō kōseikai member O-san (29 years old) started looking for an alternative to both religious-based and community children's groups, she found the Japan Nature Game Association, a lay NPO that promotes activities in the nature for children. After volunteering for the NPO for a few years, in 2007 she eventually established a private enterprise offering Nature Game trainings to schoolteachers and public workers. She now manages four employees and cooperates with the local board of education in organizing extra-curricular activities. She cooperates with several homes for the elderly organizing nature events for the elderly and disabled and offers guided walks for companies so that employees can join the company trip with their families.

In 2008 F-san, a 58-year-old member of Univers Volunteers Tokyo, founded with other women an NPO called *Gurūpu ōkina ki* (the Big Tree Group). The mission of F-san's NPO mirrors Univers volunteers' motivations and goals where F-san had been volunteering for several years: improving current facilities so that the next generations of senior citizens, including themselves, will enjoy a more comfortable late stage life. Nowadays, the

Big Tree Group works in cooperation with the local social welfare agencies and supplies several caring services for the elderly living in Yokohama and Kanazawa.

E-san, a 22-year-old woman toward the end of her university course in social welfare studies, was one of the Yotsuya Onigiri Nakama volunteers helping to build the tent village for the homeless in Hibiya Park central Tokyo in December 2008. Since she joined the Yotsuya Onigiri Nakama, she has developed a tension between the path of the student in social welfare studies and the activist against discrimination toward the urban underclass. By the time she joined the survey, E-san's narrative identity of a student in social welfare studies had been already undermined by her engagement in volunteering for the homeless: encountering the urban underclass shifted her concern from the values of caring for others to the values of social equality and justice. After graduation E-san was employed by the antipoverty NPO she used to volunteer for as a member of Yotsuya Onigiri Nakama. Part of her job is meeting directly with local public officials and leaders to advocate for the rights of marginalized groups and conduct evidence-based research for advocacy campaigns in cooperation with antipoverty NPOs.

These are just a few examples of those surveyed in this study. They clearly inform us that despite structural, ideological, and socioeconomic components channeling women into social roles providing volunteer attitudes and practices, women are able to create new orientations and new customs and develop an enterprising approach that gives them the opportunity of social entrepreneurship.

Although it is difficult to generalize on prominent trends within the specific forms of organizations surveyed in this study, three elements facilitating new customs and developing an enterprising approach seem to characterize the volunteer groups. First, all surveyed groups showed an entrepreneurial way of thinking, driving the organization's operational style. The volunteer groups shaped their organizational model upon the various initiatives they offered. At the same time they kept reshaping their organizational and operational styles through the new responses to community needs they initiated. This trend favored flexibility in the organizational structure, interchangeable roles, and transferable and task-specific skills. Moreover, volunteers were constantly urged to gain new skills and credentials in order to meet the requirements for new tasks and roles, while cultivating a form of self-entrepreneurship: women who were surveyed tended to perceive their personal achievements as a success of the entire group and counted needs arising from personal experiences as a source for ideas for organized response favoring all members' and community living conditions.

Second, all groups conveyed a strong relational culture not characterized by strong ties and long-term personal relationships. Volunteering in a loosely

connected network allowed participants to create brief interpersonal relationships, while sharing resources and experiences. While "social capital"[27]
would regard as crucial regular relationships in which people are doing things
with others, most connections witnessed in this study represented weak
ties[28] occurring while doing things *for* others. Surveyed volunteers valued
the "relational goods," that is, the social and human capital that relationships
and ties could offer in helping to achieve their volunteer goals. The routine
of interacting with others helped in developing a habit of respect outside the
small circle and the situated occasions of the volunteer group. Relationships
built through civic participation counterbalanced the "natural" inclination to
the private and individualistic pursuits found in mainstream society.

Third, beyond differences in size and structure, all surveyed groups
seemed to lack hierarchical structure, which results in a trend toward a par-
ticipative model and an emphasis on equality. The prevalence of flextime
arrangements, self-managed tasks, and transferable skills offered female volunteers the work-like environment that better matched women's life course
and lifestyle.

The above are important characteristics, and women who can take
advantage of those experiences increase their participation in the society
and economy of contemporary Japan, as the cases reported show. In these
terms, religious civil society groups and NPOs become basins of training and
trained individuals who may establish private enterprises, find employment
opportunities, or may be able to perform working roles in the labor market
with the sort of flexibility that changing economic conditions require.

CONCLUSION

The relationship between religion, gender, and civil society is complex,
changing, and sometimes conflicting with the actual life choices of an individual. In this chapter the opportunities, potentialities, constraints, and
expectations have been discussed, evaluating the extent to which women's
everyday interactions and agency in religious civil society help in increasing
their social participation and promoting women entrepreneurs in Japanese
informal and formal economy.

The results show that religious civil society groups exert four main functions in women's everyday life. First, they give women the opportunity of
transforming private concerns into public issues. Their effort to address their
private concern often leads to the emergence of a civic group, which takes
on the task of organizing local activities that often successfully develops
into a well-established organization. Second, the religious-based volunteer
group allows its members to transfer the knowledge they have gained to others, including public institutions with which they interact. The solutions

and alternatives to various issues in the community are developed from the knowledge participants acquire in their daily lives. In this way, when participating in the religious-based volunteer group, women prioritize certain types of activities and suggest alternatives to extant modalities according to their own needs and those of the recipients of the local community. Third, women acquire social awareness through developing an understanding of the multifaceted socio-structural conditions in the surrounding environment, which fostered them to think critically about their actions and the resources and conditions of the community. Fourth, it trains women through occupation-specific tasks and provides them with the sort of social and task-specific skills they may use to revitalize society and economy.

Testing these functions with the empowerment thesis,[29] it is found that they all belong to the dynamics of the process of empowerment in social work that the literature suggests. However, the respondents in this study did not engage in volunteering to empower themselves. Rather, an amelioration of their status, as claimed by most of respondents, came as a byproduct of their everyday volunteer practice where they engaged in interpersonal relationships, problem-solving discourses interfacing with institutions, and building individual confidence and capacity that they could contribute to their community's well-being. In these terms, from the respondents' perspective, religion offered an environment that provided well-organized resources and opportunities that they favored as compared with other secular ones. Adherents used their belief to cultivate their citizenship, gain knowledge and skills they can use in the labor market, and become empowered and trace new trajectories.

The above arguments bring us to an interpretation of Japanese women's religious-based volunteering as a form of women's agency taking place in the community, beyond the specific ideological drive of a religious belief or the opportunities informed by institutional channels. Religious civil society groups are training sites of new forms of democratic participation where Japanese women learn how to better match their lifecycle perspective vis-à-vis living and economic conditions. They may become flourishing resources providing women with the kind of skills, qualities, and flexible and interchangeable attitudes that inclusive society requires.

This makes religious volunteering overlap with other aspects of social life, which may imply a form of politicized action. If a religious community is a vehicle for establishing a basis for social participation, women' expanding grassroots activities in everyday life projects may give their actions a political nuance. The lasting impact of Japanese women's increased engagement in religious civil society groups will ultimately be seen in the broader participation in the democratic discourse and good governance that reflects the needs and concerns of many Japanese citizens.

NOTES

1. Keishin 2016, 43–59.
2. Information collected at the sites in 2011 and 2016 by the author.
3. Fujiyama 2016.
4. See Wilson and Janoski 1995, 137–52; Becker and Dhingra 2001, 316–35; Brown and Ferguson 1995, 145–72; Taniguchi 2006.
5. Kawahashi 2006, 323–35.
6. Wilson 1974.
7. Chaves 1994, 794–75.
8. O'Connor and Netting 2009, 17.
9. Bunkachō [Japanese Agency for Cultural Affairs] 2009, 67 and 75.
10. Catholic Bishops' Conference of Japan 2010.
11. Eight male and 153 female volunteers are registered at Univers Volunteers Kobe, while Univers Volunteers Niigata has 4 male and 50 female volunteers. Information supplied by permanent staff of Univers Foundation Tokyo (January 2010).
12. Two women are employed at Univers Volunteers Kobe, while Univers Volunteers Niigata is managed by one woman.
13. Takeda 2011, 46–64.
14. Fujita 1989, 67–91, 72; Kanbayashi and Miura 2003, 97–142, 104.
15. Takeda 2005, 100.
16. Kanbayashi and Miura 2003, 100.
17. Naikakufu 2016.
18. Takeda 2015.
19. Naikakufu, Danjō kyōdōsankaku kyoku 2010, 1.
20. Naikakufu, Danjō kyōdōsankaku kyoku 2008, 16.
21. Ammerman, 'Religious Identities and Religious Institutions', 209.
22. Takeda 2015, 1.
23. Interview 21.12.2009.
24. Naikakufu, Danjo kyōdō sankaku kyoku 2010, 12.
25. Bourdieu [1980] 1990, 112–21.
26. Ibid., 141.
27. Putnam 2000, 116–7.
28. Granovetter 1973, 1360–80.
29. Gutierrez et al., 1998.

CHAPTER 18

From the Old Lady of the Grove to *Ekatmika Bhava*: Women's Mysticism, Devotion, and Possession Trance in Popular Bengali Shaktism

June McDaniel

There are many ways that religion impacts the lives of women in West Bengal, India. For women of tribal or *adivasi* groups, gods and goddesses live in nature or exist in supernatural worlds, and they can possess people and allow them to bless, to curse, and to predict the future. They are linked to place and are thus regional—different adivasi groups will have different deities and ancestral spirits. In rural areas with local Hindu deities, women perform *bratas* or ritual vows as ways to link themselves with gods and goddesses. These rituals teach girls cultural values: they learn to be helpful, obedient, reverent toward the deities, and less selfish and greedy. In urban areas with strong traditions of yoga and tantra, we find women who are renunciants, variously called *stri gurus, sadhikas, tantrikas,* and occasionally *sannyasinis* and *yoginis*. These are women dedicated to religious lives, who often have disciples. There are also urban women who follow the *bhakti* or devotional tradition, who have their identities linked by love with their chosen deities. In this chapter we shall look briefly at each of these categories.

WOMEN AND RELIGION AMONG THE ADIVASIS

Among the Indian tribals, or *adivasis* (those who first lived on the land), we find many understandings of deities. They are generally not "high" gods and goddesses, as we see in the pan-Indian brahmanical forms of Hinduism, but rather they are regional deities, intimately associated with the members of the tribe. Supernatural entities who are given offerings and are worshipped include ghosts, ancestresses, water and plant essences, guardian spirits, and disease controllers. We see some overlap of tribal deities in the village gods, or *gramadevatas,* of village Hinduism. There is no sharp differentiation between the gods and goddesses of the adivasis and those of folk Hinduism. Rather than a polarity, we see a continuum, for both traditions worship many deities in common. Thus, I include tribal deities as a part of Bengali Shaktism.

Such deities are associated with specific places, temples, fields, and streams. The Kali of one village is not the same as that of the next village. One Chandi gives good hunting, while another Chandi cures disease. These gods and goddesses are not pan-Indian; they are specific to a person's tribal or caste group, extended family, village, or neighborhood. Worship is for a specific end: fertility, good harvest, good weather, and cures for diseases. If local goddesses are not worshiped, it is well known that they may get irritable, especially when they get hungry.

Among adivasi groups, women usually worship goddesses, and men worship gods. Tribal goddesses tend to have human personalities, with both negative and positive sides. They may be impatient, ill-tempered, impulsive, lustful, greedy, and angry, as well as merciful and benevolent to their worshipers. Sometimes they are jealous, and get angry if they are neglected or if their devotees show more attention to other deities. Goddesses can be shape shifters, appearing as natural objects at one time and as human beings at another. One's grandmother may be human, or she may be a goddess in disguise. Supernatural power appears in various figures: nature spirits, ghosts, ancestors. Gods and goddesses are not limited to spiritual entities ritually incarnated in statues or appearing spontaneously in nature.

Among the Santal tribal group, for instance, we have women's groups of singers and dancers, as well as herbal healers. Men's religion is separate, and women who try to practice men's religion and worship gods may be accused of being witches. Santal men have traditionally justified their exclusion of women from the supernatural world by their claims of women's greater powers and the tendency for women with religious power to become evil. As Chaudhuri states of the Santal *mahans* (witch finders):

> The mahans do not see anything wrong in forbidding the womenfolk from worship of the Gods or Bongas. In their reckoning, women are more

powerful in matters of mantras . . . than men, and in the event of their being allowed to worship the Gods or Bongas, they would acquire unwarranted "power," and everybody knows that women can do harm on account of jealousy, a very strong motive-force in women.[1]

This myth of women's greater power that must be kept in check is pan-Indian. The Santals have an interesting origin myth about witches and women's power, dealing with the high god Marang Buru. It also explains why magic is good if performed by men and bad if performed by women. According to the story:

> In the beginning, the tribal women dominated the men. The men resented this, and decided at a meeting that they should seek the blessings of Marang Buru and learn magic (*jadu*) so that they would be able to control the women. They sought Marang Buru, and asked him to teach them magic. Marang Buru agreed on one condition: each man must give him a Sal leaf marked with his own blood. The men did not like this idea, and told Marang Buru that they would discuss it and return the following evening. They did not know that the women had followed them, and overheard the conversation.
>
> Back at the village, the women indulged the men, served them with good food and large amounts of rice beer, and made them comfortable at night and throughout the following day. The men decided that there was no need to go to Marang Buru, as the women seemed to have found their proper place simply by the god's grace.
>
> However, that evening the women gathered together, and decided to go to Marang Buru and learn magic themselves. Since he had promised magical teachings to the men, they would disguise themselves as men to go to him, and they put on beards and moustaches made of goat's hair as well as male dress. The women were willing to give him leaves marked with their blood, and Marang Buru taught them about magic. They returned home to the men, and again took up their dominant position.
>
> The unhappy men returned to Marang Buru, and they told him that they had never returned to learn magic from him. Marang Buru realized that he had been tricked, and told the men that the women had gained his knowledge by deceit. Therefore, he would teach men the ability to find witches, and the Jans (witch-finders) would be able to find the Dans (witches) by this method. Because the women had learned magical knowledge by deceit, it became destructive if a woman used it.[2]

According to a variant of this story, the men had become lazy and spent their time drinking and feasting, and left the burden of running the family on the women. The women became angry and lost respect for the men, so the men sought a way to control the women. For this reason they went to Marang Buru.[3]

Thus, women have been forbidden from learning men's forms of religion and magic out of fear of women's power. However, while Santal women cannot worship the gods, they can worship the goddesses. Jaher Era is the most important goddess of the Santal pantheon, the Lady of the Sacred Grove. Her name signifies "fertile area," and she is often called a mother goddess or ancestress (Jaher Budhi).[4] She is a goddess dwelling in nature and as such has no statue in which she lives or is ritually placed. Like the Hindu forms of the goddess Chandi, she will sometimes stay in a stone on a square altar, anointed with oil and vermilion. She is worshipped for good crops and for happiness and health. She possesses Santal women at certain ritual times, such as the Erok Sim festival after the spring New Year's feast, when women go to the sacred grove (*Jaher Than*) and sing songs to Jaher Era.

While most adivasi people worship the deities of their own tribal groups, some include the deities of others. According to one Santal informant interviewed, Parvati Soren, Hindu goddesses can come and call women in dreams to be priestesses and devotees. Parvati grew up in her village in Birbhum worshipping the Santal deities, or *bongas*. However, several Hindu goddesses called her in dreams and visions to be their worshipper. She struggled against their desires, but she would be punished with illness and bad luck when she resisted them. She now performs ritual worship to the snake goddess Manasa as well as other deities such as Kali and Durga. She is a Santal healer and priestess with long matted hair and a tribal woman who has incorporated Hindu deities into her worship. She learned to give medicines and blessings from revelations that came during trance states.[5] She is valued in the neighboring villages for her healing skills with roots and plants.

Adivasi goddesses too may call for worshippers, and they may be old or young. In Midnapore, we see many adivasi and Hindu folk goddesses who are called Budi Ma or Buri Ma. In modern Bengali, *budi* means "old woman," but the adivasi or tribal meaning of the term is "ancestress," a woman who is old because she originated the group. She is not merely old, but ancient, and revered for her age and power. Some of these older goddesses are associated with trees (such as Vana Durga or Durga of the forests, and Budi Ma or Rupasi, who dwells in the *sheora* tree).

Nanimadhab Chaudhuri calls the Old Lady's worship "the cult of a tribal clan deity" and mentions as examples Buri Thakurani, Burhia Mata, and Burhi Mai.[6] Hathi-dhara-Buri, the Old Lady who catches elephants with her hands, is said to have cleared the Midnapore jungle for her tribal followers by killing and chasing away the wild elephants. Sometimes the Old Lady is worshiped along with her consort, the Old Man, in the cult of Bura-Buri, especially in West Bengal, Bihar, and Assam. Chaudhuri notes several aspects as important in the worship of the Buri, including the absence of any statue of the deity (she is worshiped as present in nature) and the use of an outdoor shrine *(than)*.[7] She may be worshipped by the *deyashi* (a non-brahmanical priest) or the *deyashini* (a priestess). The Old Lady may be located in a tree, in groups of plants with offerings of hibiscus flowers and vermilion, or in a rock in the shrine. As the Old Lady goddess is respected in many groups, so are older women seen as sources of knowledge. The Old Woman of the adivasis has the knowledge that she has gained through age, and she shows an increase of both knowledge and years.

This contrasts with the image of the mainstream Hindu goddess, who is generally young and beautiful. She may enter nature, but her home is elsewhere, and she takes on the form that represents her power: the face of a 16-year-old girl and the breasts of a nursing mother. She thus combines the powers of eternal youth, beauty, and immortality with the symbols of nurturing and motherhood. Her power is not in her wisdom gained in years of survival, but is a part of her essential nature. The major Bengali Hindu goddesses—Kali, Durga, Lakshmi, and Sarasvati—are generally shown as young and attractive. Even the goddess Kali, whose images in other regions of India are emaciated and ugly, is frequently shown as beautiful and voluptuous in West Bengal. It is the youth of the Hindu goddess that shows her power, as it is the age of the adivasi goddess that shows her wisdom.

The Old Lady goddess can possess women both young and old. Among the tribal Oraons, the Old Lady of the Grove (known as Jair Budhi or Sarna Burhi) jumps from one dancer to another, uniting them in a shared divine identity. Such events usually occur at the Sarna Darma, or sacred grove, in the spring, during the Sarhul festival, when the *sal* trees are in blossom. The Old Lady of the Grove is said to have her long white hair reflected in the white blossoms of the *sal* trees, and the dancing of girls and women while possessed is believed to motivate the goddess to bring rain and good crops. Group possession is usually marked by a heightened sense of group unity and happiness among the women. The groups of men and women dance separately, and the goddess usually possesses one group of dancers at a time.[8]

There are many forms of adivasi religion in West Bengal, with at least 40 scheduled or accepted tribal groups. The largest are Santal and Oraon groups, which are described here. While there are similarities between the lives and rituals of tribal and rural Hindu women, we also see many differences in their belief and practice.

WOMEN AND HINDUISM IN VILLAGE BENGAL

One of the most popular rituals for rural Hindu women is the performance of *bratas* (or *vratas*). The term refers to a disciplined religious practice intended to help the practitioner or another person. It usually involves a vow, with the observance of certain restrictions for a prescribed period, such as avoiding certain foods or actions, sleeping on the floor, or creating models of desired events—as well as hearing or reading a story that tells the meaning and origin of the practice (*brata-katha*). They may be practiced on certain days of the week, months, or dark or light fortnights of the moon. While men can perform *bratas,* and are described in many older texts as doing so, in modern rural Bengal it is women who are the primary performers of *brata* rituals.

In *brata* stories, women are often the heroines—they save their families from danger and motivate gods to help the souls of their selfish and unworthy husbands escape from the hell worlds. Some *bratas* derive from classical brahmanical sources, the Vedas and puranas and epics and dharmashastra texts. Others are handed down by oral tradition and performed by village women. These tend to come from folktales, in which goddesses come down in a vision to reveal rituals to help people who are in trouble.

A popular theme is the story of a person who accidentally or deliberately offends a goddess, who then comes down to show her anger to the offender. The story then shows the plight of the proud or ignorant person, and the ways that the behavior can be forgiven and harmony can be restored. These revealed teachings become the bases of the *brata*.

Generally, married women instruct young girls about *brata* rituals. From the age of five years, girls are taught to pick flowers, sculpt small statues, and draw *alpana* pictures on the floor or entrance to the house. Each *brata* has its own *alpana* design or pattern, which is usually drawn in white clay and rice powder. Some *alpana* pictures give protection from danger, others give blessings, yet others symbolize a desired goal. Many are decorated, and a small pot (with water and a twig) may be placed at the center of the design to represent the presence of the deity.

While more brahmanical *bratas* hand down teachings that are understood as eternal, folk *bratas* are often stories of direct revelation, usually from a goddess to a girl or woman. While brahmanical *bratas* require a brahmin priest, and he requires payment, folk *bratas* do not require a priest's presence. The married woman is the *brata* priestess or *aye* of her household or village.

The rituals and fasts use imagery of plants and animals and familiar objects to show the girl how to be a virtuous woman, and good and evil people are contrasted and rewarded and punished by the goddesses in the stories. They are an alternative sort of schooling for girls who may not have much formal education.

Such *bratas* encourage community among girls and women, and demonstrate respect for young girls, married women, and old women. The different stages of life are shown to be valuable in different ways. The rituals encourage artistic creativity in drawing *alpana* pictures, and modern versions of the pictures may include social and political commentary. *Bratas* encourage respect for nature, with rituals that involve creating lakes and ponds, feeding hungry animals, and caring for miniature forests and groves. *Bratas* encourage concern for family members, especially for the husband and children. They show girls who overcome difficulties, and who recount tales of suffering, which they overcome by the practice of virtue. Some *bratas* articulate tensions and power struggles that are a part of daily life and give strategies for responding to them and insight into shared concerns. While *bratas* start out as a sort of play for children, other aspects become important as the girl grows up into a woman.

Village *bratas* are usually learned and practiced in all-female groups, while those performed in urban India are often done individually. *Bratas* tend to become more brahmanical as they enter the cities—they are performed to more male gods and often taught to girls by male priests. Urban areas have more influence of institutional Hinduism—and more availability of texts, including those of yoga and tantra.

WOMEN AND SHAKTA TANTRA

Though most tantric texts are written from a male perspective, the texts do include three major roles for women: as ritual incarnations of the goddess, as ritual consort for sexual *sadhana* (spiritual practice), and as female gurus. However, women's roles in actual tantric practice are much more diverse than these three roles. We see female *tantrikas* who are holy women of various types: the woman who has renounced worldly life (*sannyasini*); the woman who is dedicated to celibacy, service, and obedience to a tradition (*brahmacarini*); the woman who practices yoga, especially kundalini yoga (*yogini*); and the woman who has married but has left her husband to pursue a spiritual life (*grihi sadhika*). A holy woman may be a devotee of Kali or Tara, and worship the goddess with tantric mantras, or she may get possessed by Kali as a vocation. The female tantrika may also be a wife who practices tantric sexual ritual as a part of her marriage, in obedience to her husband and guru, or a professional ritual partner in tantric sexual practice. She may be a female teacher (*stri-guru*), usually celibate and head of a group of devotees or an ashram. She may also be a widow or celibate wife, whose practice involves ritual tantric worship (*puja*) or a mixture of devotional love of a goddess (*bhakti*) and tantric ritual.

The roles for women described in tantric texts often appear exaggerated—the images of women are strongly sexual or idealized or both. One does not often get the sense of real women used as models for textual ritual. Rather, these women are "perfect" in various ways (beautiful, graceful, happy, quiet, obedient), or they are imaginary women, also beautiful and graceful but dwelling on lotuses wearing silk and jewels, shining with light or sometimes having a frightening demeanor. Women in tantric texts tend to be described primarily in terms of their ritual actions—the male tantrika finds a suitable woman (according to a long list of qualifications), and then performs various rituals with her. The *Kularnava Tantra* states that the woman must be beautiful, young, pious, devoted to her guru and god, always smiling, pleasing, and without jealousy, among other qualities.[9] A *kula* woman cannot be unattractive or old or sleepy, and she cannot feel desire or argue with her partner—these disqualify her from tantric practice, even if she has been initiated.[10]

Some tantric texts say that women can be tantric gurus and that a practitioner's mother makes the best guru (this is different from brahmanical Hinduism, in which male gurus are either required or preferred). A woman may be knowledgeable as a tantric consort, whether she is the tantrika's wife or the wife of another man, a courtesan or laundrywoman, a dancer or fisherwoman, a woman who sells meat or works with leather. Some tantras encourage the worship of goddesses within living women and girls, for women may incarnate Shakti. Some tantras say that one must never harm a woman or look down upon her, or even hit her with a flower.

When a woman is chosen to be an incarnation of the goddess, she is offered ritual worship. Sometimes a young girl is worshiped (in *kumari puja*), and sometimes a mature woman is the object of worship (in *stri puja* or *sakti puja*). *Kumari puja* is popularly performed during the annual holiday of Durga Puja; young girls are brought to the altar and given candy, jewelry, and new clothing, and people sing hymns to them.

As well as being within the woman, the goddess may be located in food, wine, fish, red cloth, red flowers, and a red sun. Goddesses may ritually dwell almost anywhere—from trees to corpses. However, because the human woman has her own feminine power or *sakti,* she is an especially appropriate place for a goddess to dwell.

There are also female tantric gurus, inspired by the goddess, and they may teach men ritual practices under certain circumstances. Such women are rarely mentioned in the texts; the greater emphasis is upon male teachers.

Tantric sexual practice is called *lata sadhana,* the spiritual exercise in which the woman is like a vine (*lata*) growing around the man. *Lata sadhana* is an individual practice, with a single couple practicing mantras, breath control, and other forms of meditation in a ritual context. The *kula cakra* is a group practice, where men and women sit in a circle (*cakra*) in couples and perform the ritual of the *pancatattva*, taking the five forbidden things, of which one is intercourse.

Among human practitioners, we see these textual roles, but they are lived out in more complex fashion, and women are not limited to such roles.

The living female *tantrikas* whom I have interviewed tended to fall into five categories:

Celibate tantric yoginis. These women, whose status was the highest among women interviewed, were lifelong celibates. Many were gurus with disciples, and some headed temples, ashrams or tantric study circles. Tantra for them is a dedicated practice involving mantras, visualizations, austerities, worship (*puja*) and ritual actions (*kriya*); the goal of tantra was to gain Shakti, both as the goddess and as power.

Holy women who had been married (*grhi sadhika*), but left their husbands and families. These women had lower status, but some had disciples. Some would wander, practicing tantric meditation and worship, and live at temples or ashrams. Some holy women would go into states of possession by the goddess Kali, inducing by chanting tantric *bija* mantras or singing hymns to the goddess. Tantra for them is ritual action, worship and possession, usually in response to a call by the goddess.

Tantric wives. These women performed tantric ritual sex and worship as part of devotional action towards their husbands and gurus. The woman is often initiated by the same guru as her husband, and follows his teachings. Tantra is a form of service, involving obedience and following a woman's marital obligations (*stri-dharma*). The goal of tantra was to please the husband and fulfill social obligations.

Professional consorts. These women performed ritual sex and worship as a way to make a living, and the consort (as well as any children) was generally supported by the man who was her ritual partner. Often, the woman moves from one sadhu to another, depending on who will shelter and support her. Tantra here is sexual practice, and a subcategory of prostitution. The goal of tantra was to make money, and possibly get a home and a male protector.[11]

Celibate wives and widows. These women incorporate tantric meditative practice as an aspect of devotion to the Goddess. Tantra is a form of ritual devotion, especially in combination with *bhakti yoga*. Retirement in India often includes celibacy, and many celibate wives are older and their children are grown. The goal of tantra here is to please the goddess while living a spiritual family life.

Most female *tantrikas* interviewed were not only celibate, but insistently so. Several said that tantric meditation involves purity and concentration, and that desire would be a distraction and would cause them to fall. I interviewed three women in depth who were female gurus, initiated into Shakta tantric lineages. Two of them practiced tantric rituals themselves, and the third belonged to the Shakta universalist perspective, who knew several practicing women *tantrikas*. All of these women were highly respected, and all of them were celibate. In fact, the highest status *tantrikas* that I met, male or female, were all celibate.

Shakta widows hold an unusual role. The householder widow who spends her life in religious ritual and pilgrimage is often respected as a family authority. I have seen Bengali Shakta religious widow-matriarchs, who are called *sadhikas* by members of the extended family, who domineer both their households and the brahmin priests called in to perform rituals. They literally hold the keys to the household and to the moneybox as well. I observed one widow who kept correcting both household males and brahmin priests who she said were doing their rituals incorrectly—and they listened to her and changed their behavior. However, this household dominance of widows seems to be limited to Shakta households.[12] In other households, widows are viewed as unlucky and have little say in their own lives and the lives of others.

The popular notion of a tantrika in the United States is not a person performing austerities or a householder worshipping a goddess, but rather a person seeking pleasure—preferably in a group. This is not an accurate picture for Bengali understandings of tantra. Most Shakta *tantrikas* tend to be loners, and they rarely get together for rituals. Most Shakta *tantrikas* that I interviewed could not identify other Shakta *tantrikas* in the vicinity—or even at a distance.

Much literature on tantra has sensationalized the sexual aspects of tantra, making it the one necessary thing. However, sexual ritual is clearly not necessary, or even common, among *tantrikas*. Women *tantrikas* spoke of it as unimportant. Most said it was rarely practiced, and some said that such practices were almost never performed, like the large Vedic sacrifices performed by kings long ago. Some women *tantrikas* have told me that the individual sexual ritual is really only for men, who have difficulty controlling their instincts, and that it is rarely useful or necessary for women. Because of the way Indian girls are brought up, it is rare to find any who cannot control their instincts; Indian sons are indulged and petted, while Indian daughters are taught to give the best food and toys to their brothers. Indian women thus learn to sacrifice their desires at an early age. Sexual ritual is basically for people who are weak rather than strong—and such people do not belong doing rituals at the burning ground.

The issue is not that the people performing sexual practices are sinful, but rather that they are weak and are spending their time at the lower end of practice rather than the higher end. Some female *tantrikas* implied that men were generally weaker than women in this area and more compulsive about the need for sexuality. As the guru Gauri Ma stated,

Most women have no need of sexual ritual (*lata sadhana*). It is for men, who are bound by lust (*kama*), and need to overcome it. Then they take a consort. In women, lust is not so strong. *Tantra sadhana* for women is meditation (*kriya*) and worship (*puja*).[13]

No female *tantrikas* said that *lata sadhana* was evil, or sinful, or scandalous. They did not appear to be hiding their secret, forbidden practices. They simply said it was rare and unnecessary. Some female *tantrikas* were outspoken, saying that no man was going to take away the *shakti* they had gained by hard austerities and long recitation of mantras (it was understood by many female *tantrikas* that the merit gained from difficult spiritual practices could be transferred during intercourse, generally from the woman to the man).

In tantric practice, women are ritually united with the goddess Shakti. The great goddess is without birth or death, eternal, independent, the soul of the universe. She is greater than the universe, yet at the same time smaller than an atom. She may be visualized in yoga and tantra, or loved in the devotional or *bhakti* tradition.

WOMEN AND DEVOTION TO THE GODDESS

Devotion to the goddess, or emotional Shakta bhakti, became popular in West Bengal toward the end of the 18th century. Tantric goddesses became more kind and benevolent, and the relationship between the goddess and the devotee became close and intense. Devotion may be shown in both group and individual styles.

While Bengali Vaishnavas tend to have five relational styles, or *bhavas,* to the god Krishna, in goddess devotion, we see four major relationships. The goddess is majestic in her Great Goddess role, the Mother of the Universe, and in relation to her the devotee is the child or servant. The goddess may also be loved as a young girl, the daughter of the household adored by her parents. This role includes sorrow, as they know that the daughter must leave in her teens to marry into another household. In some cases the goddess may be the divine lover, and there is an erotic relationship with her (this is seen primarily in male devotees). And in modern Shaktism, the goddess is also the Ocean of Consciousness, loved as both finite and infinite, dwelling in the heart of the devotee. This is the state of *mahabhava*, the state of mystical perfection, which combines devotion and union with the Mother as *brahman*. The fifth role, the friend *bhava*, is rarely seen in Hindu Shaktism, though it is popular in the goddess worship of the adivasis.

The goddess as a daughter has been traditionally worshipped by groups of women singing *agamani* and *vijaya* songs, the songs of welcome and farewell sung at Durga Puja. This holiday welcomes the goddess Durga on her visit to earth, and devotees sing farewell as she leaves to return to her husband Shiva in their heavenly home. The songs are full of love and sorrow, for the goddess loves the earth and her parents and friends there, but it is her duty to be with her husband.

There is also individual devotion, which may involve possession and mystical union. There are degrees of respectability in such states, with higher and lower levels.

The lower level involves the state of *bhar,* in which the goddess will come down to her devotee to help solve some problem. In this case, possession can become a career track. These women become specialists, getting possessed once a week and having a group of devotees and an audience who pays by donation.[14] It is understood to be a difficult career to enter, for the inner presence of a goddess is not easily accepted psychologically, and there are often trances, breakdowns, periods of madness, and mood swings in the person's life. It is believed by Shaktas that such states cannot be generated by human will; they are a gift of the goddess.

There is usually a set model for possession: the person receives a call from a god or goddess, who wants to be worshiped, and if the person will not perform the worship, the god or goddess then possesses the reluctant devotee. The person is pursued psychologically by the deity until he or she gives in and is willing to form a relationship with the deity. Unless the person is chosen by the deity, this is not a possible career.

Such possession is generally described by the persons involved as pleasurable or like a dream-state. There is often no memory of events, or only a hazy memory (as one holy woman said, "Don't ask me what happens when I get possessed, I never know—ask my disciples, they keep track of such things.") Another woman who often became possessed spoke of the goddess as a "quiet darkness" that descended upon her, removing all pain. Her ordinary personality fell asleep or watched what went on from a distance.

The higher form of trance is called *bhava,* and it is found more frequently in practitioners of devotional or bhakti yoga. The colloquial term *bhava* is short for *devabhava* (a general term for divine state or state of unity with a deity) or *bhavavesa* (the state of being overwhelmed or possessed by *bhava*). *Bhava* combines possession and devotional love, allowing the possessed person to retain consciousness in the midst of the goddess's power and presence. It shows intense love of a deity and a person's humility and willingness to submit to the goddess.

Informants who had experienced this state described it as a penetration of the *atma* rather than the *jiva,* the divine soul rather than the human personality. The goddess's presence or power enters the soul, filling it with light and bliss during the time of the possession, bringing greater strength, concentration, and energy than the person had normally. The ordinary personality stayed in place, as did the person's memory, but the soul was filled with the goddess's presence. The person's ordinary language, ideas, and memory remained, but the motivation, energy, and will belonged to the goddess.

This state was often temporary, but I spoke with two holy women, Jayashri Ma and Archanapuri Ma, who had been in this state of altered *atma* for a long time. Both of these women had undergone ascetic training (one as a tantrika and the other as a *sannyasini,* or female renunciant), and had strong powers of concentration. They called this state *ekatmika bhava,* or the state of unified *atma.* It is a state in which the person's *atma* becomes united with the deity's personality and essence. In one case, the holy woman had her *atma* fused with the goddess Kali. In the other it was fused with the spirit of her guru, who had died many years ago. He was a devotee of Kali, who had his own soul fused with the goddess after a vision. In both cases, this was understood as a permanent fusion of souls, brought about by meditation and the will of the goddess or guru.

Despite the notion of one shared *atma,* there was a strong component of devotional love in both women. The shared essence seemed to generate strong love in the individual personality and a continual focus upon the goddess or guru as the object of that love. Though both women were well educated and familiar with the categories of mind from Samkhya philosophy, they spoke of their own experience in the language of Vedanta: as a transformation of *jiva* and *atma.*[15] Though this state resembles possession trance in many ways, it might be better described as a form of mystical union through love, for the individual self remains present and fully conscious. This *bhava* is a highly respected state.

According to the *sadhika* Jayashri Ma, the types of trance are dependent on the relationship of the *jiva* and the *atma.* The self is a two-part entity; it consists of the "lower" personal self or ego, the *jiva,* and the "higher" divine self, the *atma.* When the goddess comes down, she puts the *jiva* to sleep, and her personality takes over for the *jiva* and is able to speak with other people. This is ordinary possession (*bhar*), in which the individual self is eclipsed, and the deity's personality is superimposed.[16] This is why there is generally no memory of the events—the individual self is understood to have been elsewhere, possibly asleep or unconscious. However, in the higher state of *bhava,* the *jiva* stays conscious and is fused with the *atma,* so it is aware of all that occurs. Women who enter the state of goddess possession (*devi bhava*) do not forget the events, and their souls are strong enough to be aware of the goddess's presence. Sometimes this is a fusion of love, in which two separate identities remain, and sometimes it is a full merger, in which the identity of the goddess is the true identity for both.

CONCLUSION

This range of religious experiences of women in rural and urban West Bengal shows a variety of possible relationships between the goddess and the female worshipper. Women may praise the goddess at a distance or the goddess may be recognized as a part of the worshipper, and such relationships may occur both individually and in groups.

One question that has interested observers of women's religious experiences is the role of goddess worship in the social environment. Are women treated differently if they worship goddesses rather than gods? Is there any advantage for them in this type of worship? Do they gain greater social status and respect if the deity is a female?

In the situation of Bengali Shaktism, possession primarily occurs when women worship goddesses—there is very little cross-gender possession trance (unlike South India, where this is often seen). Whether women gain greater respect through goddess worship is really a question of the local understanding of *shakti*.

The term *"shakti"* refers to both women and power. A person who is active, creative, and strong is said to possess *shakti*, and in such cases the person is valuable and respected. Both men and women may possess *shakti* in the sense of power, but men are not said to have the creative feminine *shakti*, which gives birth to the universe and to living beings. Untamed *shakti*, which may be wild and destructive, is feared. A woman is respected for the degree and type of *shakti* she is understood to possess.

Women may worship a goddess as a distant entity, who is given offerings in hopes of blessings. When the goddess is distant from the woman, her social standing is generally not much affected by the gender of the deity, for she will not participate in the *shakti* of the goddess. Worship at a distance will not affect social status—issues like dowry or brideprice will be much more important.[17]

However, if the woman becomes close to the goddess, or merges with her, then she is understood to participate in the goddess's power, or *shakti*, and she is then generally respected and treated in a special way. This is the case with holy women of various sorts, but it is also seen in the houses of Shakta devotees. As one Shakta housewife in Kolkata told me, "*Shakti* is in my body, it is the way I speak and move my hands. It is the same *shakti* that moves the universe. All women express that *shakti*, that is why they are like the goddess."[18]

Simply worshipping a goddess has little social impact in West Bengal. But when women experience that worship intensely and can analyze and express their relationship to the goddess of the community in clear and impressive ways, it can transform both their status and their lives.

NOTES

1. Chaudhuri 1987, 67.
2. Ibid., 100–102.
3. Troisi 1979, Volume 1, 396.
4. While the Bengali understanding of *budhi* or *budi* is "old woman," the tribal understanding is "ancestress," a woman not merely old but ancient and venerable.
5. McDaniel 2004, 54–58.
6. Chaudhuri 1939, 417–418.
7. Ibid., 419.
8. McDaniel 2004, 47.
9. *Kularnava Tantra*, 1383/1976, VII: 47–49. Henceforth KT. My translation.
10. Ibid., VII: 49–51. My translation.
11. Note: I did not find any of these women for interviews; my informants refused to introduce me to any of them. The reasons for their refusal to help me get in touch were varied. Some said that they didn't know any, some said that if I wrote about them it would give West Bengal a bad reputation, some said that I would be corrupted by them, and some said that it was not a suitable topic for research. Even those who defended them, largely by the argument from pity, said that it would be unsuitable for me to interview them. Thus, my information is second-hand.
12. Widows are viewed in a variety of ways in India. Sometimes they are blamed for the deaths of their husbands, having brought bad luck into the house, and then they are treated badly. I have seen widows ignored and pushed aside by others in their households; they must act humbly and have their heads shaved. Men, even their own Vaishnava gurus, look down on them. I should note that I have not seen this attitude of scorn toward widows in Shakta families. The Shakta widows that I have seen were strong women who were respected. They did not shave their heads and often lived a householder's life much like the situation of women whose husbands were alive.
13. Interview, Gauri Ma, *sadhika* and ashram head, Bakreshwar, 1994.
14. See the biographies of several such holy women in my McDaniel 1989, Chapter Five.
15. Interviews, *sadhikas* Archanapuri Ma, Calcutta, 1994; Jayashri Ma, Suri, 1994.
16. Interview, *sadhika* Jayashri Ma, Birbhum, 1994.

17. Dowry and brideprice are the ways that Hindu families fund newly-weds. In the dowry system, money and gifts go from the bride's family to the groom's family—thus having a daughter means the family will lose much wealth. In the brideprice system, the money goes from the groom's family to that of the bride. Under the dowry system, sons are desired; under the brideprice system, daughters are more valuable and desired than sons. Dowry is the dominant practice in West Bengal, but brideprice can be found in rural areas, such as Purulia district.

18. Interview, Mrs. A. Sinha, 1994.

CHAPTER 19

The Rise of Female *Vipassanā* Meditation Teachers in Southeast Asia

Brooke Schedneck

Whether lay or ordained, female meditation teachers are becoming more and more prominent in the global Buddhist landscape.[1] This can be seen in American and other forms of "Western" Buddhism where the equality of women is an important issue.[2] Another significant example of the rise of female meditation teachers has taken place in Southeast Asia. A significant avenue through which much of the development in this region is occurring is the modern institution of the *vipassanā* meditation center. While full participation in monastic institutions is often contested within the Theravāda Buddhist lineages of Southeast Asia, female participation in *vipassanā* meditation is not.[3] Monks still predominate the role of meditation teachers; however, female practitioners, as lay Buddhists, fully ordained *bhikkhunī*,[4] or precept nuns,[5] are able to enact Buddhist roles in more diverse ways through the emergence of this institution.

It has been argued that the proliferation of the *vipassanā* meditation centers allows more spaces for lay participation,[6] and I argue this can also be extended to specifically female involvement. Through contrasting traditional individualized meditation methods that employ close student-teacher relationships, I show how the rationalized, structured practices of the meditation center, meant for mass audiences, have created spaces of legitimacy for Buddhist women. In much of the information that follows, Thai and, to a

313

lesser extent, Burmese women are discussed. This is because much scholarship has been done in these countries, which also contain a large number of
meditation centers. Contrarily, in Laos and Cambodia, the other two Southeast Asian Theravāda Buddhist countries discussed here, there is compara-
tively less scholarship available and a small number of meditation centers.
Because of political and economic devastations in Laos and Cambodia, a
large number of Buddhist institutions have not yet been able to develop.

AVENUES OF LEGITIMACY AND SUPPORT

Four significant ways Theravāda female practitioners can gain legitimation are through scholasticism, social engagement, supernatural powers, and
meditation practice. Studies of Theravāda Buddhist women have noted the
essential importance of education, which generates recognition, respect, and
patrons. There has been a longstanding prestige associated with the study of
Pāli and the words of the Buddha among monastics, and a tension between
the path of practice and that of study. Education has been a key factor in gar-
nering respect and support among Buddhist communities for precept nuns;
however, this is not always accessible. Despite a historic lack of access, Buddhist education has been a significant feature of *mae chees*'s[7] involvement
in religious roles and their legitimacy as monastics.[8] Monica Lindberg Falk
reports on the national Thai Mae Chee's Institute, which provides education and has established a number of schools and colleges providing access
to Buddhist, secondary and higher, education for *mae chees*.[9] Kelly Meister
describes another institution, the Abhidhamma-Jotika College in Bangkok
with branches at temples throughout Thailand. These institutions often consist of *mae chee* and lay female teachers and students, thus affording acces-
sibility to and teaching opportunities for this Buddhist philosophical text
for Thai Buddhist women.[10] Besides, Steven Collins and Justin McDaniel
highlight Thai *mae chee* who teach Pāli language and Abhidhamma in institutions of monastic education in Bangkok.[11] These educational opportunities
as teachers and students are important developments toward increasing the
respect and prestige directed toward Buddhist women in Southeast Asia,
especially precept nuns.

In Myanmar, studying the Pāli scriptures and pursuing a scholastic
career has contributed significantly to making nuns, or *thilashin*,[12] worthy
of lay support. Hiroko Kawanami has, for several decades, studied the educational opportunities and lives of *thilashin*, especially in the Sagaing Hills
area outside of Mandalay city.[13] Young Burmese nuns who join the order
before marriage are usually more educated in the Buddhist scriptures. This
category commands greater respect from the laity than those nuns who had
been householders and pursue meditation in their elder years. Because these

young nuns have more access and opportunities for education, the most influential Burmese nuns come from this category.[14] In Cambodia, nuns called *daun ji* or *yeay chi*, who are equivalent to Thai *mae chee*,[15] are currently rising in number. Especially important within this group are young nuns who are serious about learning the Buddha's teachings. They have found sponsorship through the Khmer-Buddhist Educational Assistance Project (KEAP),[16] who offer books and facilitate study groups so that women can preach and provide counseling. In all of these cases, education is necessary not only so that women can be of assistance in local communities, but also so that they can be seen as authorities of Buddhism and create legitimation for themselves. Through these institutions and educational opportunities, this particular avenue of legitimacy is gradually improving and opening spaces for women in Southeast Asia.

A more recent source of enacting Buddhist roles for female leaders is through social engagement projects. Social engagement, as with meditation, has been a contested activity among some for ordained persons. Only recently have critics who argue that monastic involvement in social engagement should be a lay occupation been quieted by the rise in international support and global networks of engaged Buddhists. The idea that monastics should solely be concerned with their own and others' spiritual development has given way in modernity to a proliferation of projects by monastics in Theravāda societies and much support from laity. This role has perhaps been enacted most famously among Thai Buddhist women by Mae Chee Sansanee and her Sathira-Dhammasathan,[17] in Bangkok, Thailand. Established in 1987, Mae Chee Sansanee's center is a place of learning for the community with meditation and dhamma courses as well as projects helping all types of disadvantaged populations.

In Chiangmai, northern Thailand, Ouyporn Khuankaew leads women's retreats and workshops for dealing with domestic violence and offers leadership training for nuns drawing from both Buddhist teachings and feminism. She hopes to bring Buddhist values into practice by developing programs for Buddhist peacebuilding, nonviolent resistance, and social change for women through her organization founded in 2002, called the International Women's Partnership for Peace and Justice.[18] This organization emphasizes empowerment of women through working with a female population of activists, refugees, and abused women from throughout Asia.[19] Venerable Dhammananda Bhikkhunī, one of the few fully ordained women in Thailand,[20] has been outspoken about the potential positive effects of female ordination in Thailand.[21] She believes this will give more opportunities for women in Thai society.[22] Löschmann discusses the creation of the Association of Nuns and Laywomen of Cambodia, which hosted a successful conference for Cambodian nuns in 1995 and has as its mission improvement of the status of these women in Cambodian society.[23] They encourage leadership, counseling, education, and networking throughout Cambodia and are funded through the Heinrich Böll Foundation.[24] In Battambang, Cambodia, Wat Poveal nun's center, head nun Dy SaVy is working to establish a home for underprivileged children in the area so that they can receive an education in the nearby primary school and dhamma instruction from the nuns.[25] These women demonstrate that leadership roles within Southeast Asian societies are possible for lay and ordained Buddhist females and there is some support and institutional backing for these projects.

Additionally, Rachelle Scott reminds us of another historically important avenue of support, that of supernatural abilities, or *iddhi* in Pāli.[26] Through these powers, exemplary females have been able to establish their authority as religious teachers and healers. In the modern period, perhaps Mae Chee Thosaphon is the most well known in this regard in Thailand. She is a best-selling author and popular television personality who can view others' past karma and read minds. She uses this ability to help others find ways to heal the bad karma they have created in the past.[27] Another example of female spiritual abilities is demonstrated by Mae Bunruean Tongbuntoem (1895–1964). Martin Seeger describes how her amulets and other objects related to her magically protective powers continue to be venerated decades after her death.[28]

Another avenue for women to enact Buddhist roles, and the one most considered here, is the practice of meditation, where there have historically been fewer barriers. Because of the high status accorded to scholasticism as a pursuit for Buddhist monks historically, meditation practice has been more available to women than educational opportunities. Isolated cases of female Buddhist meditation adepts have been recorded as well as the prominence of this practice among older precept nuns throughout the Theravāda world. However, neither of these instances has created significant social legitimation for Buddhist female meditators. There have been exceptional women of the forest lineage such as Mae Chee Kaew, which specifically attest to the great respect possible for female meditators. However, for the average precept nun in Southeast Asia, meditation practice within a temple is not enough to increase their esteem among the laity.[29] Many Thai nuns then do not have access to education, and their skill in meditation does not garner enough legitimacy. A similar problem has been identified in Myanmar. Because young nuns have recently been able to capitalize on educational pursuits, meditation has become the default vocation for older women.[30] All avenues of legitimation, therefore, have been significant for Buddhist women; however, none of them provides a large-scale institutional structure for practice as the meditation center does. This new institution has begun to change and has the possibility to continue altering the perception of the vocation of meditation among Theravāda Buddhist women.

RISE OF THE *VIPASSANĀ* MEDITATION CENTER

Vipassanā meditation has become one of the most significant pathways to communicate Buddhist teachings to a large, popular audience. Traditionally, *vipassanā* meditation had been taught exclusively within monastic institutions. Within its modern history, the practice has spread to Buddhist laity and, most recently, further expanded to reach an international audience of non-Buddhists. The replicable methods used in the large facilities of meditation centers can be transmitted to many disciples and even to international centers abroad. Through the proliferation of meditation centers throughout the Theravāda world, especially in Myanmar and Thailand, this institution opens spaces for female practice more than premodern possibilities.

Historically, meditation monks were scarce because it was believed that over time the Buddha's teaching would decline and the chances for liberation would be so low that *nibbana* would not be a reasonable goal even for monks.[31] When meditation was practiced in the premodern period before the rise of the meditation center, it was taught individually between a teacher and a student, usually both monks, who had established a relationship. Following the *Visuddhimagga*, which lists 40 meditation objects, a "Good Friend" (*kalyana-mitra*), or meditation teacher who knows the student well, would be asked to assign one of these objects,[32] which would combat the defilements of that particular person.[33] Each meditation student needed to search for the right teacher who could select the correct method for that student's character, considering the student's past experiences with meditation and his temperament.[34] This personalized relationship contrasts greatly with the rationalized, one-size-fits-all approach of large urban lay meditation centers meant for the masses.

Vipassanā meditation underwent a process of laicization that ultimately opened the cultural sphere so that it became accessible to Buddhist laity as well as "spiritual travelers" from abroad. Offering *vipassanā* meditation to laity on a large scale transformed the relationship of monastics to their lay students. Through these transfigurations, laity undertake steps toward liberation without taking up the vocation of a renouncer.[35] This has reconfigured Buddhist practice in Theravāda Southeast Asia as well as created openings for female meditators and teachers.

Theravāda *vipassanā* reform movements, above all, emphasized the importance of meditation and offered this practice and its goal of *nibbana* as a possibility for both laity and monastics. The ability for laity to undertake meditation practice could not occur without the new institution of the urban lay meditation center. The meditation center is different from any other Buddhist institution in history.[36] This is because the center is not a monastery but a place where both monks and laity practice meditation together.[37] This is a new type of institution in that it is preoccupied with a universalizing ideal about the possibility of enlightenment for anyone, whether Buddhist or not, ordained or lay, female or male. This institution is designed for temporary meditation practice usually for large numbers of people. In addition to the core buildings of any monastery, the meditation center has ample facilities for the temporary resident meditators such as accommodation, assembly halls, dining halls, kitchens, administrative offices, and so on.[38] The large administrative complex needed to coordinate the large turnover of meditators on a daily basis is not normally needed for routine monastic life.[39] The daily routine of the meditation center is extremely regimented and revolves almost exclusively around the practice of meditation.[40]

This new institution began in Myanmar and transformed the laity's relationship with Buddhist practice. The Burmese meditation center model and meditation methods spread to Thailand and beyond. Today, there are countless meditation centers in Thailand and Myanmar, and fewer in the less-developed Theravāda countries Laos and Cambodia. This institution constitutes a reinterpretation of *vipassanā* meditation, which led not only to lay Buddhist practice, but also to opportunities for a number of groups not traditionally associated with meditation teaching such as Buddhist women.

THE ROLE OF MEDITATION CENTERS FOR FEMALE BUDDHISTS

Isolated cases of meditation teachers during the premodern period do not fully support the widespread availability and opportunities for enacting Buddhist roles among women as the institution of the meditation center does. Individual meditation teachers can act as models for others—but meditation centers provide an institutional structure for lay and ordained teachers to continue their work beyond one individual's capability. Through the rise of *vipassanā* meditation centers, the practice is no longer seen as the occupation of a certain type of monk but for all, and this has had implications for female roles. This institution therefore signals a significant change for Theravāda Buddhist countries of Southeast Asia, creating an influential movement evidenced especially in Thailand and Myanmar. This creates opportunities for women of various backgrounds to practice and take leadership roles within these institutions. Women now have a large-scale institution in which to practice as lay Buddhists, precept nuns, or fully ordained *bhikkhunī*, with the possibility of access to *nibbana*, as verified by monastic teachers.[41]

This idea about the possibility of *nibbana* has generated new, more participatory roles for women. Within the role of the temporary meditation center
practitioner, realization could be obtained without formal status within the
monastic hierarchy. In Thailand, *mae chees* can garner prestige and embody
monasticism through their practice and teaching roles in meditation centers
throughout the country.[42] International meditation centers follow this trend
by creating roles for English-speaking Thai *mae chees*, international female
monastics, and lay female meditation teachers. The rise in the popularity of
meditation practice and the international meditation center is, therefore,
opening new spaces and alternative forms of authority for women and laity
within Buddhism. Therefore, a diverse array of women has taken inspiration
from the meditation center institution and its democratizing forces. These
opportunities are created by the proliferation of these centers, but it is the
specific meditative practices, behaviors, and comportments that generate
prestige and respect from Buddhist communities.

FEMALE MEDITATORS

Some Buddhist women have become nationally known meditation
teachers and some have been considered to have attained or to be close to
attaining *nibbana,* the ultimate goal of Buddhism. Isolated cases from Thailand include Mae Chee Kaew, Ajan Naeb Mahaniranon, Upasika Ki Nanayon, Upasika Ranjuan Indarakamhaeng, Khun Yai Chandra, and Mae Chee
Brigitte. These women have made their own choices to remain lay or ordain
as precept nuns, but all are recognized publicly for their meditation skills and
have helped to shape female roles in meditation centers to varying extents.
In order to illuminate the importance and relevance of the meditation center institution, in this section I offer five specific cases of exemplary female
meditators. These cases demonstrate the extraordinary nature of these figures and how the widespread institution of the meditation center has led to
more opportunities for leadership and involvement for female meditators.

Mae Chee Kaew (1901–1991) is considered to be an *arahant* by the
well-known Thai monk Luangda Mahabua (1913–2011). Her biography is
written by an American disciple of Luangda Mahabua, Bhikkhu Silaratano.[43]
This account follows her life in rural northeast Thailand chronologically to
her death and the turning of her bones into relics as the final proof of her
attainment. In her youth, Mae Chee Kaew yearned to ordain, but was prohibited due to her duties toward her family. However, after some time when
her husband remarried and her child had a new family, Mae Chee Kaew
finally had an opportunity to pursue her quest for enlightenment. After ordination, her practice reached a plateau until meeting her teacher, Luangda
Mahabua. His stern council shifted her practice to the point where she

was able to attain the highest dhamma. Since that time until her death she guided and taught many nuns and laypeople about the Buddhist path and meditation. An important recognition of her attainment is a *chedi* (stupa), called the Mae Chee Kaew Memorial Stupa, built in her honor in 2006 in her hometown of Mukdahan, Northeast Thailand.[44] Although she was able to teach those in her community, this example is not generalizable and does not allow for large-scale participation of many meditators. Seeger writes that she was little known outside of her local area and the forest tradition. Only when Luangda Mahabua confirmed her *arahant*ship and her remains were believed to become crystallized and become relics did her reputation grow.[45] Her life, however, demonstrates the possible achievements of female meditators and provides a model of a female meditation teacher.

Ajaan Naeb Mahaniranonda (1897–1983) is another example of an extraordinary female meditator. A Thai laywoman, she had a deep experience of no self at the age of 34. She sought out someone who could teach her *vipassanā* meditation. She practiced under Ajan Pathunta U Visala, a Burmese teacher at Wat Prog in Bangkok. She then studied the Abhidhamma[46] and taught meditation and Buddhist philosophy in Thailand for many years. She is also associated most famously with Wat Sraket in Bangkok, where she created the Buddhist Research and Mental Welfare Association.[47] For 40 years she lectured on and taught *vipassanā* at these centers, most notably the Boonkanjanaram Meditation Center near Pattaya, Chonburi Province.[48] After her retirement, her lineage continues through her students, who are mostly monks, at Boonkanjanaram and her other centers.[49] Although Ajahn Naeb is part of the institution of meditation centers, her method and institutional network has not become extensive in Thai Buddhism. However, through her available teachings and centers, Ajahn Naeb has created a model that is easier for female Buddhists to emulate. Nevertheless, we must keep in mind that a major reason for her following was her high level of education and ability to explicate and understand the Abhidhamma. Therefore, she points to the possibility of a meditation lineage and meditation centers created by an accomplished female meditator.

Upasika[50] Ki Nanayon (1901–1978), who is also known as K. Khao-suan-luang, is a highly respected lay renunciant who established a meditation center for women in Ratchaburi, in central Thailand.[51] Growing up in this region with her large family, she felt an aversion to marriage and childbirth. Her dream was to save enough money to devote herself to the practice of dhamma. In 1945 she enacted this vision by living in her aunt and uncle's small home that was to become Upasika Kee Nanayon's women's practice center. When the center became well established, Upasika Kee Nanayon met with her students every day for group meditation, discussion, and chanting. During these meetings Upasika Kee Nanayon gave talks on important issues that were discussed by her disciples. Many of these talks have become part of her large number of publications that have attracted followers and have been translated into English.[52] Her teachings were influenced by Buddhadasa Bhikkhu;[53] however, she adapted his concepts to her own experience and for her audience. After her passing, the center has been run by her younger sister, Upasika Wan, and upon her death, by a committee. The women at her center continue to listen to her speeches and make her teachings known through continued printing and publishing of her books for widespread and free distribution.[54] Upasika Kee Nanayon did not establish a widespread meditation practice model with institutionalized structures; however, she created both opportunities for female meditators through establishing her women's practice center and a nationally recognized model of a female meditation teacher.

Upasika Ranjuan Indarakamhaeng is also a student of Buddhadasa Bhikkhu and, according to Martine Batchelor,[55] progressed quickly in her meditation practice. After listening to a dhamma talk in a forest monastery, Ajahn Ranjuan continued to practice meditation while working full-time at a university. Over time she decided that meditation should be her exclusive practice, and after a year studying and practicing with Buddhadasa Bhikkhu, he encouraged her to teach.[56] She remains a well-respected meditation teacher and her association with the internationally known Buddhadasa Bhikkhu has helped her to garner prestige in Thailand and demonstrate the possibilities of female meditation teachers who are disciples of famous monks.

Khun Yai Chand (1909–2000) is another example of a female disciple of a famous monk. Her teacher was Luang Por Sot Chandassaro (1885–1959), the well-known abbot of Wat Paknam, near Bangkok. This famous monk is believed by his followers to have discovered the *Dhammakaya* meditation technique, which Khun Yai Chand, having reached the highest levels of this practice, propagated after his death. She is believed to have attained supernatural powers through this meditation technique. Leaving Wat Paknam in 1970, she began a new project with two of her male followers who would later become the leaders of the largest temple in Thailand, Wat Dhammakaya.[57] After her death, the abbot and co-abbot of Wat Dhammakaya built a memorial monument in her honor at this monastery outside of Bangkok in Pathum Thani. She was known as a highly accomplished meditator as evidenced by her memorial hall and remains a model for those within the Dhammakaya movement as well as of the possible attainments and leadership abilities of female meditators and teachers.[58]

A long-time teacher of foreigners in Thailand, Mae Chee Brigitte Schrottenbacher (1962 to present), most recently of Wat Prayong Gittavararam, is another example of a female meditation teacher. Although she is an Austrian, she has been a part of the Thai Buddhist *sangha* for most of her adult life. Mae Chee Brigitte was married with children while in her twenties, but because of a strong fear of death that emerged following the birth of her children, she started to explore ways to cope with this. She discovered meditation and completed her first two-month intensive retreat in 1989. She eventually decided to leave her children with her husband after they lived with her for a short time in Thailand because she did not want to disrobe. Even though it was very difficult, she felt it was the best decision for her life and her family. Since that time she has devoted her life to meditation and being a nun. She stresses mindfulness, the applicability of meditation for daily life and for all religious and nonreligious people.[59] Mae Chee Brigitte's path demonstrates a kind of model for many Thai or foreigners interested in meditation. Her teaching in Thailand and Europe displays the audience available for female meditation teachers and the possibility of this role for precept nuns of the Theravāda sangha.

These exemplary female meditation teachers represent possible paths for learning and teaching meditation within contemporary Buddhism. The widespread replicable methods of *vipassanā* meditation centers spread this further, creating large-scale opportunities for lay and monastic practice. Because of the large population that participates in retreats in these centers, opportunities for female participation have also increased. I witnessed this in my research on international meditation centers (August 2009–September 2011). At the meditation centers of Wat Chom Tong and Wat Rampoeng in Chiangmai, and Wat Mahathat in Bangkok, *mae chees* especially are tasked with demonstrating and teaching the fundamentals of the meditation technique taught at these temples. They have significant roles as teachers and models of meditation practice within the centers. These along with other recognized women cannot all be discussed here. Above I have provided illuminating examples and models of female meditation teachers that have created opportunities and inspired others.[60] A significant way that females are able to gain attention as accomplished practitioners is through their performance of the meditative lifestyle.

PRACTICES OF THE SELF

In order to understand meditation's role in helping women enact Buddhist roles, it is important to discuss the concept of "practices of the self." This refers to bodily actions and performances, which can be traced to early Greco-Roman philosophy. These practices are intended to create a change in the behavior and character of those who enact them. External practices working on the body make one fit for spiritual development and eventual transformation into the state of ethical perfection.[61] Female meditators, through embodying Buddhist practices and doctrines in their external expression, mindful movements, and general care of the self, can enact Buddhist roles obvious to their communities. Bodily acts conducted during a meditation retreat such as eating, walking, and teaching others demonstrate to Buddhist communities the extent to which practitioners have brought themselves into alignment with Buddhist doctrines.

Female lay Buddhists and precept nuns in Southeast Asia exhibit this daily within meditation centers in ways that can be more significant for them than for fully ordained monastics. Because neither female lay Buddhists nor precept nuns contain the strict rules of the *vinaya* that fully ordained persons abide by, female performance as a meditation practitioner is a crucial expression of their understanding, renunciation, and embodiment of the principles of meditation. Some of the meditation teachers highlighted above, Ajahn Naeb, Upasika Ki Nanayon, and Ajahn Ranjuan, did not seek *mae chee* ordination. Instead, as laywomen they shaved their heads, followed the eight precepts, and wore a white shirt and black skirt as opposed to the white robes of a *mae chee*.[62] A common reasoning and one expressed by Ajahn Ranjuan is that the way one practices is the most important—not the status of ordained or lay, and to ordain on the inside, from the heart, is the ideal. Ajahn Ranjuan in this way does not see a difference between the status of lay or precept nun as long as one's lifestyle helps one to be aware.[63]

Vipassanā is intended to bring about a change in perception in the meditator consistent with Buddhist ethical principles. In this way, through *vipassanā* meditation, practitioners make themselves moral Buddhist subjects.[64] Female meditators engage in specific practices in order to change their experiences in relation to religious concepts, so that religious tenets become embodied and visible. Joanna Cook has observed this in her study of *mae chees* in a northern Thai meditation temple. She argues that with the rise of lay *vipassanā* meditation, a significant way *mae chees* can embody the monastic ideal is through teaching meditation.[65] International meditation centers, with foreign meditators who need instruction in English, in particular follow this trend by creating roles for English-speaking Thai *mae chees*, international female precept nuns, and lay female meditation teachers. Through this embodiment, women can enact Buddhist roles in demonstrable ways within meditation centers. These practices garner respect and support from Theravāda communities within both roles of practitioners and teachers. The communal aspects of the meditation center and practice of meditation express one's capabilities and embodiment of the tradition to supporters and monastics. Without this institution this opportunity would not be as readily available to Buddhist women.

CONCLUSION

The rise in popularity of meditation practice and the international meditation center is opening new spaces and alternative forms of authority for women and laity within Buddhism. Given this history of meditation in

Theravāda communities and the ways the practice can be embodied through the proliferation of meditation centers, precept nuns, fully ordained *bhikkhunī*, and lay women have sought and continue to seek out ways to participate in these institutions. These centers create new roles for women through their abundance and institutional structure. Meditation centers are enthusiastically patronized by women at all levels and this is a positive development. Models for female Buddhist religiosity have included older nuns, young scholar nuns, lay practitioners, and extraordinary meditation nuns—but now there are more opportunities for women to practice and enact Buddhist roles through widespread participation in meditation centers and embodying *vipassanā* through practices of the self.

Notes

1. Sections of this chapter are derived from a conference paper written for the 13th Sakyadhita Conference titled "Enacting Female Buddhist Roles Through *Vipassanā* Meditation Centers", Vaishali, India, January 8, 2013, and Chapter 3 from my dissertation titled "Constructing Religious Modernities: Hybridity, Reinterpretation, and Adaptation in Thailand's International Meditation Centers", Arizona State University, PhD Dissertation, 2012.

2. Schedneck 2009, 229–246.

3. *Vipassanā* meditation, usually translated as insight meditation, Buddhists hold, leads to enlightenment and the disappearance of defilements, through being aware of everything occurring around and inside the body and mind during the present moment. It is essential for insight meditation that one lets go of wandering thoughts. In this type of meditation, the meditator is aware through direct experience. The point of *vipassanā* meditation exercises is to comprehend the nature of *dukkha* (suffering), *anicca* (impermanence), and *anattā* (nonself). This is accomplished through awareness of one's reality; through applications of mindfulness to body, feelings, mind, and mind objects, one comes to perceive directly these characteristics of reality.

4. For important studies regarding the controversy of *bhikkhunī* ordination in Thailand, see Ito 2012, 55–76; Seeger 2006, 155–183.

5. Because Buddhist women in Southeast Asia do not have the support of the full ordination lineage (fully ordained women are called *bhikkhunī* in Pali), a compromised role of the precept nun has emerged. In each Theravāda Buddhist country, the vernacular titles and particular circumstances of precept nuns vary. However, they usually undertake either 8 or 10 precepts, shave their heads, and wear renunciant robes. In this way these precept nuns hold an ambiguous position between an ordained and a lay person. In this chapter I will mainly discuss precept nuns as they are much more numerous within Southeast Asia than fully ordained *bhikkhunīs*. Secondly, *bhikkhunīs* have distinct issues of legitimacy, given their monastic status, which cannot be fully treated in this chapter.

6. Jordt 2007.

7. *Mae chee* are white-robed Thai Buddhist nuns. Because females cannot be fully ordained within the Thai sangha, the status of *mae chee* creates for the female renunciant a lifestyle that is more disciplined than that of a lay person but does not adhere to as many behavioral rules as that of a fully ordained monastic. *Mae Chees* usually keep eight precepts.

8. Falk 2007, 2.

9. Ibid., 193.

10. Meister 2009, 549–565, 557.

11. Collins and Justin 2010, 1373–1408.

12. *Thilashin,* when translated from Burmese, means one who upholds morality, or keeper of moral discipline. *Thilashin* are female practitioners who are initiated into a renunciant lifestyle where they maintain eight precepts. Kawanami 2013, 29–30.

13. See Kawanami 2013.

14. Kawanami 2000, 159–171, 160.

15. In Cambodia *yeay chi* keep five or eight precepts and wear long black skirts, while *daun chi* wear white robes and keep ten precepts. Jacobsen 2013, 75–87.

16. See the organization's website: http://www.keap-net.org/project/educa tion.htm.

17. The Sathira Dhammasathan's website in Thai can be found at: http:// www.sdsweb.org/sdsweb/.

18. For more information on Ouyporn KhuanKaew and her organization see: http://womenforpeaceandjustice.org.

19. King 2009, 173.

20. A *bhikkhunī* lineage never existed in Southeast Asia; instead, each Theravāda country's nuns follow 8 or 10 precepts. Although there have been nuns in Thailand who received ordination from Taiwan and Sri Lanka, monastic hierarchies of Thailand and Myanmar resist the reinstitution of the *bhikkhunī* ordination. As the ordination ceremony of a *bhikkhunī* must involve the participation of existing *bhikkhunīs,* some see it as impossible to restart the Theravāda *bhikkhunī* ordination line once it has lapsed.

21. For more information on Venerable Dhammananda Bhikkhunī, see her website: http://www.thaibhikkhunīs.org/eng/.

22. Both of these women's stories are highlighted in the 2007 documentary film *What Harm Is It to Be a Woman?,* directed by Attie & Goldwater productions. For more information see: http://www.religiousconsultation.org/what_ harm_to_be_a_woman_DVD.htm.

23. Löschmann 2000, 91–95, 91–92.

24. This organization funds socially engaged Buddhist activities in Thailand and Cambodia. See http://www.boell.org.

25. This information comes from the January 2012 circular of KEAP located at: http://www.keap-net.org/updates/documents/2011missionReportv.2a.pdf.

26. Scott 2011, 489–511.

27. Ibid., 500–503.

28. Seeger 2013, 1488–1519.

29. Falk 2007, 195.

30. Kawanami 2000

31. This decline in the availability of the Buddha's teachings is asserted in one of the Pāli suttas (Cakkavatti-Sihanada Sutta DN 26). This sutta declares that there will be a future where the Buddha's teachings and practices have become so degenerate that *nibbāna* will no longer be possible.

32. Some examples of these 40 objects are: the four elements of earth, water, fire, and air; the four colors of blue, yellow, red, and white; 10 kinds of bodily decay such as different kinds of corpses; and 10 recollections including the Buddha, Dharma, Sangha, virtue, generosity, mindfulness of death, mindfulness of the body, and mindfulness of breathing.

33. Shankman 2008, 59.

34. Kornfield 2010, 276.

35. Jordt 2007, 18.

36. Ibid., 15.

37. Mixing of monastics and laity is not as strict in meditation centers as in temple environments. Temples are places for monastics to study and observe the *Vinaya* while living with other monastics. The modern institution of the meditation centers is meant for lay people.

38. This is in contrast to solitary meditation locations within huts and caves.

39. The meditation center can be contrasted with the typical monastery in many ways. Monasteries provide for the residence of a limited number of monks. Some have spare accommodation available but few possess the large number of facilities of meditation centers. The monastery serves many functions and so there is more freedom within the daily schedule. Besides the morning alms-round, morning and evening chanting, and meals, monastics carry out a number of duties. Novices have to memorize passages and carry out duties like sweeping the floors, cleaning, and preparing offerings at the Buddha statue. More senior monks often conduct ceremonies away from the temple or for visitors to the monastery.

40. For descriptions of meditation centers in Myanmar, see Houtman 1990; Jordt 2007. For centers in Thailand, see Cook 2010.

41. Jordt 2005.

42. Cook 2010.

43. Silaratano 2012.

44. Ibid., 227–229.

45. Martin 2010, 555–595, 583.

46. The Abhidhamma is the section of the Pāli Canon that presents a scholastic and detailed analysis of physical and mental processes.

47. Kornfield 2010, 131.

48. For her meditation teachings, see: Naeb 1982.

49. Irons 2008, 354.

50. *Upasika* are devout lay devotees. They maintain usually eight precepts but are not formally ordained in any way as precept nuns. These women wear white clothing or white top and black bottom but not robes and sometimes shave their heads. The reason for becoming an *upasika* varies but often includes seeking more independence than the life of a precept nun or *bhikkhunī* would offer.

51. Falk 2007, 14–15.

52. For translations of her dhamma talks, see Thanissaro Bhikkhu's translations on the Access to Insight website: http://www.accesstoinsight.org/lib /thai/kee/index.html. The most famous of these translations is *Pure & Simple* (2003), found at http://www.accesstoinsight.org/lib/thai/kee/pureandsimple.html accessed 8/19/2015.

53. Buddhadāsa Bhikkhu (1906–1993) was a famous Buddhist scholar and philosopher whose English writings cover many shelves on subjects such as comparative religion and Buddhist teachings for daily life. He has many more publications available in Thai, and he is well known among this audience for his interpretation of Buddhist teachings.

54. Thanissaro 2010.

55. Martine 2000, 156–158, 156.

56. Ibid., 156–158.

57. Falk 2007, 181–182.

58. See Chapter 16 in this volume for a full discussion of Khun Yai Chand's life.

59. Mae Chee Brigitte's story is taken from her website Meditation Thailand (http://www.meditationthailand.com) as well as personal interviews from March 9–11, 2010.

60. A significant indicator of important work by Buddhist women is the United Nations' list of Outstanding Buddhist Women. These awards have occurred annually since 2002 and recognize a number of women each year for their charitable activities and spreading the dhamma. The award ceremony takes place in Thailand through the International Women's Meditation Center Foundation. For more information see: http://www.iwmcf.org.

61. Foucault 1988, 16–49, 21.

62. Falk 2007, 29.

63. Batchelor 2000, 157.

64. Cook 2010, 95.

65. Ibid., 2.

Abbreviations

AMDF	*Al Mujadilah* Development Foundation
ANLWC	Association of Nuns and Laywomen of Cambodia
ANR	assisted natural regeneration
ARMA	Agung Rai Museum of Art
ARMM	Autonomous Region of Muslim Mindanao
ART	artificial reproduction therapies
BE	Bengali Era, follows the Gregorian calendar by 593 years, 3 months, and 14 days
BWFPD	Bangsamoro Women's Foundation for Peace and Development
CAR	Cordillera Administrative Region
CEDAW	Convention on the Elimination of all Forms of Discrimination against Women
CMPL	Code of Muslim Personal Laws
CSR	child sex ratio
DEVAW	Declaration on the Elimination of Violence against Women
FAB	Framework of Agreement for the Bangsamoro
GI	Soldiers of the United States Army, include air and marine forces
KAPWR	Kaohsiung Association for the Promotion of Women's Rights
KEAP	Khmer-Buddhist Educational Assistance Project
LTTE	Liberation Tigers of the Tamil Homeland
MILF	Moro Islamic Liberation Front
MNLF	Moro National Liberation Front
MTP	medical termination of pregnancy
NGO	nongovernmental organization
NPO	nonprofit organization
PCID	Philippine Center for Islam and Democracy

PKK	*Pembinaan Kesejahteraan Keluarga*
RCSO	Religious Civil Society Organization
Rs	Indian Rupees, currency of India
SC/ST	Scheduled Castes and Tribes
SeRV	Shinnyoen Relief Volunteers
SOFA	Status of Forces of America
TGEEA	Taiwan Gender Equity Education Association
THB	Thai Baht, currency of Thailand
UG	universal goodness
USAID	United States' Agency for International Development
USD	United States Dollars, currency of the United States of America
VD	Venereal Disease
VIP	very important person
World-PEC	World Peace Ethics Conference
WWJD	What Would Jesus Do?

Glossary

abaya	Islamic clothing; a cloak or loose overgarment
abhayamudrā	raising the right hand
abhayavāṇī	assurance
adat	cultural customs
adhikār	right
adivasi	tribal
agamani	songs of welcome
akshar	letters
alpana	motifs, art, or painting on a horizontal surface
ānanda	bliss
ananku	powerful magical force that works against evil
anattā	nonself
anicca	impermanence
anito	ancestor
arahant	"perfected person," or one who has attained nibbana/nirvana
aravani	transgenders, transsexuals, or members of the "third sex"
āsan	seat
āsana	postural yoga
atma	the divine soul
atman	soul
aṭṭahāsi	peal of laughter
avant garde	experimental or radical innovation in art and culture
bābu	men of substance
bāgdī	brigand

bago	new Christian communities
bahār	outside
bal	strength
Balik Islam	return to Islam
Bangsamoro	Moro nation
banjar	family associations
bapak	father
becāri	pitiable girl
bhadralok	gentlemanly
bhadramahilā	lady
bhairavī	a female practitioner of *tantra*
bhakti	devotion
bhālobāsār atyācar	persecutions of adoration
bhandara	colored holy powder
bhar	state (of possession) in which the goddess will come down to her devotee to help solve some problem
bharat kī gārī	vehicle of India
bhava	relational style
bhavavesa	the state of being overwhelmed or possessed by *bhava*
bhay	fear
bhikhāri honā	a life of voluntary poverty
bhikkhunī	fully ordained Buddhist women
bija	one-syllable seed sounds that activate the chakras when said aloud
bodhicitta	altruism; enlightenment mind
bonga	Santal deity
brahmacāriṇī	female initiate
brahmacarini	a woman dedicated to celibacy, service, and obedience to a tradition
bratas	ritual vows
buana agung	macrocosm
buana alit	microcosm
budi/budhi	an old woman
cabhutra	platform
caturmās	spiritual retreat performed often during the rainy season
chedi	stupa
chop suey	Chinese dish made with chopped meat and vegetables
chotalok	commoners

cudail	witches
daimoku	mantra
ḍākāt bābā	robber-father
dans	witches
dar	fear
darśan	vision of the holy; seeing
daśa	ten
devabhava	a general term for divine state or state of unity with a deity
devadasi	sex worker
devi bhava	state of goddess possession
deyashi	non-brahmanical priest
deyashini	priestess
dhamma	dharma
dharma	(Buddhism) teaching or religion of the Buddha
dharma wanita	women's duty
dhūnī	sacred site
dhuturā	datura, or angel's trumpets, a species of vespertine flowering plants
dhyāna	meditation
dīkṣā	initiation
dukkha	suffering
ekānt	solitude and isolation
ekatmika bhava	the state of unified *atma*
ema	votive amulet
ensho	product of local causes and conditions
fujinbu	women's division
gakoku mura	foreign village (Japan)
gamba	male, war-related spirits
gamelan	music and dance ensembles in Southeast Asia
garbha	womb
ghar mandir	home-temple
ghomṭā	veil
ghṛṇā	hatred, malice, ill-will
ghuṅṭé	cow dung cakes
gongyo	recitation
gramadevata	village god
grhi sadhika	a woman who has married but has left her husband to pursue a spiritual life
gudiya	female rag doll

guṇḍas	thieves
guru	spiritual preceptor
guru-bhakti	guru devotion
gurubhai	brother monk
gurudaksina	repayment/donation to one's teacher
hijra/ali	trans-women (male to female)
hoben	second
hukum karma	retribution of deeds in past and present lives
ibu	mother
ibuism	constructions of women's roles that sanction women's behaviors when tied to motherhood, domesticity, a company, or the state without expectation of personal power or prestige
iddhi	supernatural abilities
Imago Dei	image of God
imitatio dei	imitating the deity
ippan kaiin	a single woman
iṣṭadevatā	chosen ideal; lit. favored or chosen deity
itarjan	lower orders
iyer maappillai	fiancé
izzat	honor
ja-chi-hwi	(camptown) sex workers
jadu	magic
jaher than	sacred grove
jans	witch-finders
japa	silent repetition of sacred words
jāt	caste
jaṭā	matted hair
jatre	festival
jiva	the human personality
jogathi	devadasi; female follower of the goddess Yellamma
junglī	wild
juryo	16th
jyānta Durgā	the living *Durgā*
kain/kebaya	traditional Balinese dress consisting of unstitched cotton material wrapped around the waist (*kain*) and a blouse (*kebaya*)
kalyana-mitra	"Good Friend" or meditation teacher
kama	lust
kāminī-kāñcana	woman and gold (wealth)

kamisama	Japanese word for deity
kamma	karma
kamsya	bronze
kaṇakāmparam	firecracker flower native to South India and Sri Lanka
karpu	purity
karuṇā	compassion
kathoey	Thai term referring to effeminate men
kepala keluarga	heads of households
khalifah	Allah's Vicegerents
kijichon	camptown
kodrat	intrinsic nature; identifying men under Indonesian New Order as providers and women as mothers and wives
kriya	meditation or ritual actions
kula	one who follows Kula Tantra
kula cakra	a group practice, where men and women sit in a circle (*cakra*) in couples, and perform the ritual of the *pancatattva*, taking the five forbidden things
kumari puja	when a young girl is worshiped
la original	the original
la peregrine	the pilgrim
la viajera	the traveler
lajja	shame
lakh	one hundred thousand, a unit in the Indian numbering system
lama	teacher, guru
lata sadhana	spiritual exercise in which the woman is like a vine (*lata*) growing around the man; sexual ritual
machi tsukuri	revitalize the locality
madaris	Islamic religious school, the Philippines
madhura bhava	the "sweet mood" of Rādhā, restive in Kṛṣṇa's absence
mae chee	white-robed Thai Buddhist nuns (*daun ji* or *yeay chi* in Cambodia)
mahabhava	state of mystical perfection
mahan	witch-finder
mandadawak	priestess who invokes the spirits
mandai	skull

mangala sutra	"auspicious thread" or necklace tied around a woman's neck by the groom upon marriage
mantra	word or sound recited repeatedly during meditation
mastî	desire
māyā	web of illusion
mepamit	ceremonial leave taking
moksha	unity with God
mudrā	ritual hand gesture
mumbaki	priestess
muttu	sacred pendant
nautch	an anglicized version of *nāc* (Hindi), dance or dancing
nayī duniyā	new world
nibbana	nirvana
niqab	Islamic clothing; a full-body covering including the face, leaving the eyes open to view
obiter dicta	incidental remark
onigiri	rice ball
orang biasa	commoners
pallu	the piece of the sari that drapes over the shoulder
paṇḍit	Hindu scholar/priest
paniyu	taboos
paramahamsa	lit. "the supreme swan"; one who relies only on divine grace
pareśāni	troubles
parvāz	flight
pāṭh	group recitation
pati	husband
pendanping suami	standing by the husband's side
peran ganda	dual/multiple roles
pisī	auntie
prakṛti	nature, primal matter
praṇām	salutation
pranayama	breathing exercises
prapattibhakti	single-minded devotion to God and total dedication to God's service
prasādam	holy leavings from the ritual food offered to the deity
pratītyasamutpāda	interconnectedness; codependent origination
pravāchan	discourses

puja	ritual worship
puṇya	merit
puranas	lit. "ancient"; refers to Sanskrit religious texts containing myths, legends, and folklore, the earliest of which dates to the fourth century of the common era
rasaddār	supplier of victuals
reformasi	reformation
rudrākṣa	lit. "Rudra's Teardrops"; seed traditionally used for prayer beads
ryōsai kenbo	good wife, wise mother
sabha	a genre of Tamil-language comedy theater
sādhak	self-described seeker
sādhanā	disciplinary practices as a means of accomplishing a goal; a spiritual regimen
sadhavā	a married woman whose husband is alive
sadhu	holy person; one pointed straight at the (spiritual) goal
śaīr	body
Śakti	meaning power; the primordial cosmic energy often personified as divine feminine creative power
sālo	bastards
salwar kameez	tunic and trousers worn primarily in the Indian subcontinent
samādhi	final stage (of union with the divine)
sang yang widi wasa	supreme God
sangha	community of monks; also self-help group
sanghajananī	mother of the Order
sannyās	renunciation
sannyāsin	world renouncer
sannyasini	a woman who has renounced worldly life
sansār	separation from the world
sār	essential knowledge
sārī	six yards of fabric draped around the waist and upper torso to create elegant folds and a train; South Asian women's dress
śarīr	body
sarvadevīsvarūpiṇī	representation of all goddesses
saya tidak berani	"I don't have the courage"
sepak takraw	a ball game played mostly among men
shad	six

shakti bhavan	electrical transformer or power station
śmaśān	cremation ground
Ṣoḍaśī Pūjā	"virgin worship," supposedly a *tāntrika* ritual
Śrīmā	Holy Mother
stri-guru	female teacher
stri/sakti puja	when a mature woman is the object of worship
strīdharma	duties of a married woman
śuddha-buddha-muktātmā	pure, enlightened, and liberated soul
suno suno	listen!
śūnyatā	emptiness
svadharma	personal duties
Svāmī	Hindu male religious teacher
svarūpa	true identity
tākat	strength
talai	head
tang-ki	spiritual medium
tantra	system of beliefs that utilizes meditation and rituals to channel divine energy into the human being to attain enlightenment and liberation from the cycle of birth, death, and rebirth
tāntrika	pertaining to *tantra*; a practitioner of *tantra*
tapas	penance; heat
tapuy	rice wine
tawḥīd	divine unicity
tej	sharp, mentally agile
tejasvin	renouncer
tema paku	foreign country theme park (Japan)
than	outdoor shrine
thaṇḍā	cool
thilashin	female Buddhist practitioners initiated into a renunciant lifestyle
tom	Thai term referring to masculine women
tri hita karana	the three traditional principles of well-being in Bali, invoking harmony among people, with nature or environment, and with divinity
ulama	Islamic clerics
upasika	devout Buddhist lay devotees
vaibhav	glory
vairāgy	detachment
vajra	ritual weapon or scepter
vātsalya bhava	spiritual state in the mood of a child

vedantist	one who is well versed in the philosophical doctrines of the Vedanta, which denote "the end of the Vedas," that is, the Upaniṣads
veena	plucked musical instrument originating in India
vijaya	songs of farewell
vinaya	Buddhist regulatory framework
vipassanā	meditation that provides insight into the true nature of things
vrata	penance
wat	temple
yagnaphala	the fruits of sacrificial or devotional rituals
yoga	spiritual discipline consisting of meditation, bodily postures, and breath control
yūai hōmon	home visits
zār	malevolent spirits
zulwa	kept man

Bibliography

Chapter 1

Ariani, I.G. Ayu Agung, and Sara L. Kindon. "Women, Gender and Sustainable Development in Bali." In *Bali: Balancing Environment, Economy and Culture,* edited by Sugeng Martopo and Bruce Miller, 507–519. Waterloo: University of Waterloo Press, Department of Geography, 1995.

Ariani, A.A. Oka. In *Bali Sustainable Development Project: Summary of the Gender and Development Workshops,* edited by Kevin Boehmer, May 27, 1991, Yogyakarta, Java; June 6, 1991, Sanur, Bali. Waterloo: University Consortium and the Environment Publication Series, 1992.

Aripurnami, Sita. "Whiny, Finicky, Bitchy, Stupid and 'Revealing': Images of Women in Indonesian Films." In *Indonesian Women: The Journey Continues*, edited by Mayling Oey-Gardiner and Carla Bianpoen, 50–65. Canberra: RSPAS Publishing, 2000.

Belo, Jane. *Trance in Bali*. New York: Columbia University Press, 1960.

Blackburn, Susan. *Women and the State in Modern Indonesia*. Cambridge: Cambridge University Press, 2004.

Bond, Kevin. "Forcing the Immovable One to the Ground: Revisioning a Major Deity in Early Modern Japan." PhD dissertation, McMaster University, Hamilton, Ontario, 2009.

Brooks, A. and Theresa Devasahayam, eds. *Gender, Emotions and Labor Markets: Asian and Western Perspectives*. London: Routledge. Taylor & Francis e-library, 2011. Accessed December 15, 2011. http://lib.myilibrary.com /Open.aspx?id=304169.

Coast, John. *Dancing Out of Bali*. Singapore: Periplus Editions, 1954.

Connor, Linda, Patsy Asch, and Timothy Asch. *Jero Tapakan: Balinese Healer an Ethnographic Film Monograph,* 268. New York: Cambridge University Press, 1986.

Creese, Helen. "Reading the Bali Post: Women and Representation in Post-Suharto Bali." *Intersections: Gender, History and Culture in the Asian Context*, no. 10 (August 2004): 61–65. Accessed September 28, 2011. http://www.sshe.murdoch.edu.au/intersections/issue10/kellar.html.

Cukier, Judie. "Tourism Employment Issues in Development Countries: Examples from Indonesia." In *Tourism and Development. Concepts and Issues*, edited by Richard Sharpley and David Telfer, 165–201. Bristol: Multilingual Matters Limited, 2002.

Cukier, Judie, Joanne Norris, and Geoffrey Wall. "The Involvement of Women in the Tourism Industry of Bali, Indonesia." *Journal of Development Studies* 33, no. 2 (1996): 248–270.

Dibia, I. Wayan. *Kecak. The Vocal Chant of Bali*. Denpasar, Bali: Hartanto Art Books Bali, 1996.

Gouda, Frances. "Teaching Indonesian Girls in Java and Bali, 1900–42. Dutch Progressives, the Infatuation with 'Oriental' Refinement, and Western Ideas about Proper Womanhood." *Women's History Review* 4, no. 1 (1995): 1–36.

Hendry, Joe. "Foreign Country Theme Parks: A New Theme or an Old Japanese Pattern?" *Social Science Japan Journal* 3, no. 2 (2000): 207–220.

Jennaway, Megan. "Displacing desire: Sex and Sickness in North Bali." *Culture, Health & Sexuality* 5, no. 3 (May–June 2003): 185–201.

Long, Veronica and Kindon Sara L. "Gender and Tourism Development in Balinese Villages." In *Gender, Work and Tourism*, edited by Thea Sinclair, 91–119. New York: Routledge, 1997.

Oey-Gardiner, Maeyling. "And the Winner Is . . . Indonesian Women in Public Life." In *Women in Indonesia: Gender Equity and Development*, edited by Kathryn Robinson and Sharon Bessell, 100–112. Singapore: Institute of Southeast Asian Studies, Seng Lee Press, 2002.

Ong, Aihwa. *Spirits of Resistance and Capitalist Discipline: Factory Women in Malaysia*. Albany: State University of New York Press, 1987.

Ortner, Sherry. "Specifying Agency: The Comaroffs and their Critics." *Interventions* 3, no. 1 (2001): 76–84.

Osteria, Trinidad. *Gender Equality and Development*. Fifth Asian and Pacific Population Conference. Selected Papers. New York: United Nations, 2003.

Parker, Lyn (Lynnete), ed. Introduction to *The Agency of Women in Asia*, 1–26. Singapore: Marshall Cavendish Academic, 2005.

Parker, Lyn (Lynnete). *From Subjects to Citizens. Balinese Villagers in the Indonesian Nation-State*. DEMOCRACY in Asia Series #9, 178–183. London: Taylor & Francis, 2003.

Pratt, Mary Louise. Por qué la Virgen de Zapopan Fue a Los Angeles? Algunas Reflexiones Sobre la Movilidad y la Globalidad [Why the Virgin of Zapopan Went to Los Angeles? Reflections on Mobility and Globality]. *A Contra Corriente* 3, no. 2 (Winter 2006): 1–33.

Robinson, Geoffrey. *The Dark Side of Paradise: Political Violence in Bali*. Ithaca, NY: Cornell University Press, 1995.

Sears, Laurie J., ed. *Fantasizing the Feminine in Indonesia*. Durham, NC: Duke University Press, 1996.

Sullivan, Norma. "Gender and Politics in Indonesia." In *Why Gender Matters in Southeast Asian Politics*, edited by Norma Sullivan, 61–86. Monash Papers on Southeast Asia no. 23. Glen Waverly, Australia: Aristoc Press, 1991.

Suryakusuma, Julia I. "The State and Sexuality in New Order Indonesia." In *Fantasizing the Feminine in Indonesia*, edited by Laurie J. Sears, 92–119. Durham, NC: Duke University Press, 1996.

Suryani, Luh Ketut. "Balinese Women in a Changing Society." *Journal of the American Academy of Psychoanalysis and Dynamic Psychiatry* (Special Issue Women and Society) 32, no. 1 (Spring 2004): 213–230.

Suryani, Luh Ketut. "Peran Ganda Wanita Bali-Hindu." In *Rahasia Pembangunan Bali*, edited by D. Tifa and Sugriwa, 211–229. S. Jakarta: Gita Budaya, 1993.

Talamantes, Maria. "The Cultural Politics of Performance: Women, Dance Ritual and the Transnational Tourism Industry in Bali." PhD dissertation, University of California, Riverside, 2004.

Talamantes, Maria. "Performance of Identity: The *Pelegongan* Andir of Tista, Bali." *Asian Theater Journal* 23, no. 2 (Fall 2006): 256–373.

Van Der Molen, Willem. "A Token of My Longing: A Rhetorical Analysis of Sita's Letter to Rama Old Javanese *Ramayana* 11.22–32." *Indonesia and the Malay World* 31, no. 91 (2003): 339–355.

Wieringa, Saskia. "The Birth of the New Order State in Indonesia: Sexual Politics and Nationalism." *Journal of Women's History* 15, no. 1 (Spring 2003): 70–91.

Wieringa, Saskia. "Ibu or the Beast: Gender Interests in two Indonesian Women's Organizations." *Feminist Review* 41 (Summer 1992): 98–113.

Wikan, Unni. *Managing Turbulent Hearts: A Balinese Formula for Living*. Chicago: University Chicago Press, 1990.

Williams, Catharina P. *Maiden Voyages. Eastern Indonesian Women on the Move*. The Netherlands: KITLV Press, 2007.

CHAPTER 2

[Note: B.E. indicates Bengali Era, that is, Bengali calendar that follows the Gregorian calendar by 593 years, 3 months, and 14 days.]

Abjajananda, Svāmī. *Prakṛtiṁ Paramām* [To the Transcendent Feminine]. 2 vols. in 1. Kalikata: Sri Krishna Nath Basu, 1397 B.E.

Akṣaycaitanya, Brahmacārī. *Śrīśrīsāradādevī*. Calcutta: Calcutta Book House Private Limited, 1396 B.E.

Archanapuri, Śrī. "Jananī Sāradeśvarī" [The Divine Mother Sarada]. In *Śatarūpé Sāradā* [Many Faces of Sarada], edited by Svāmī Lokeshvarananda, 1–13. Golpark: Ramakrishna Mission Institute of Culture, 1989.

Banerjee, Ranendranath. Personal interview (September 17, 1997), Calcutta.

Banerjee, Sumanta. "Marginalization of Women's Popular Culture in Nineteenth Century Bengal." In *Recasting Women: Essays in Indian Colonial History*, edited by Kumkum Sangari and Sudaish Vaid, 127–179. New Brunswick, NJ: Rutgers University Press, [1989] 1990.

Bhumananda, Svāmī. *Śrīśrīmāyer Jīvan-Kathā* [A Life of the Twice-blessed Mother]. Kalikata: Śrī Ramakrishna-Sarada Math, 1986.

Bodhananda, Svāmī. Reminiscences in *Mātṛdarśan* [A View of the Mother]. Kalikata: Udbodhana Kāryālaya, 1397 B.E., 14–17.

Bose, Mandrakranta, ed. *Faces of the Feminine in Ancient, Medieval, and Modern India*. New York: Oxford University Press, 2000.

Bynum, Caroline W. *Holy Feast and Holy Fast: The Religious Significance of Food to Medieval Women*. Berkeley: University of California Press, 1987.

Canetti, Elias. *Crowds and Power*. Trans. Carol Stewart. New York: Viking Press, 1962.

Chakravarti, Nilkanta. "Udbodhané." In *Mātṛdarśan* [A View of the Mother], 225–232. Kalikata: Udbodhana Kāryālaya, 1397 B.E.

Datta, Chandramohan. "Puṇyasmṛti" [Holy Remembrance]. In *Śrīśrīmāyer Padaprānté* (At the Feet of the Twice-blessed Mother), edited by Svāmī Purnatmananda, I: 109–134. 3 vols. Kalikata: Udbodhana Kāryālaya, 1994–1997.

Datta, Ramchandra. *Śrīśrīrāmakṛṣṇa Paramahaṁsadever Jīvanbṛttānta* [The Life of the Twice-blessed Ramakrishna]. 8th edition. 1950. Rpt. Kalikata: Udbodhana Kāryālaya, 1995.

Davis, Elizabeth G. *The First Sex*. New York: G.P. Putnam's Sons, 1971.

Denton, Lynn T. "Varieties of Hindu Female Asceticism." In *Roles and Rituals for Hindu Women*, edited by Julia Leslie, 211–231. Rutherford, NJ: Fairleigh Dickinson University Press, 1991.

Devi, Sridurgapuri. *Sāradā-Rāmakṛṣṇa*. Kalikata: Śrīśrīsāradeśvarī Āśram, n.d.

Gambhirananda, Svāmī. *Holy Mother Sri Sarada Devi*. Madras: Sri Ramakrishna Math, 1977.

Ganesh, Kamala. "Mother Who Is Not a Mother: In Search of the Great Indian Goddess." *Economic and Political Weekly* XXV, no. 42–43 (October 20–27, 1990): 58–64.

Ghanananda, Svāmī and J. Stewart-Wallace, eds. *Women Saints of East and West: Shri Sarada Devi (The Holy Mother Birth Centenary Memorial 1955)*. London: The Ramakrishna Vedanta Centre, 1972.

Gupta, Sanjukta. "The Goddess, Women, and Their Rituals in Hinduism." In *Faces of the Feminine in Ancient, Medieval, and Modern India*, edited by Mandrakanta Bose, 87–106. New York: Oxford University Press, 1999.

Gupta, Sanjukta. "Women in Shiva/Shakta Ethos." In *Roles and Rituals for Hindu Women*, edited by Julia Leslie, 193–210. Delhi: Motilal Banarsidass, 1992.

Her Devotee-Children. *The Gospel of the Holy Mother Sri Sarada Devi*. Madras: Sri Ramakrishna Math, 1984.

Hiranmayananda, Svāmī. "The Holy Mother Ideal." *Prabuddha Bharata*, XC (March 1985): 105–110.

Ishanananda, Svāmī. *Mātṛsānnidhye* [In Mother's Company]. Kalikata: Udbodhana Kāryālaya, 1396 B.E.

Jagadishvarananda, *Svāmī. Śrīrāmakṛṣṇapārṣadprasaṅga* [The Divine Play of the Blessed Ramakrishna]. First published 1357 B.E. Rpt. Belur: Śrīrāmakṛṣṇa Dharmacakra, 1398 B.E.

Kinsley, David. *Hindu Goddesses.* Berkeley, CA: University of California Press, 1988.

Kinsley, David. *Hindu Goddesses: Vision of the Divine Feminine in the Hindu Religious Tradition.* Delhi: Motilal Banarsidass, 2005.

Kinsley, David. *Tantric Visions of the Divine Feminine: The Ten Mahavidyas.* Berkeley: University of California Press, 1997.

Chitadatmanda, Swami. *Life of Sri Ramakrishna Compiled from Various Authentic Sources.* 2nd edition. Calcutta: Advaita Ashrama, 1928.

Mātṛdarśan [A View of the Mother]. Kalikata: Udbodhana Kāryālaya, 1397 B.E.

McDaniel, June. *Madness of the Saints: Ecstatic Religion in Bengal.* Chicago: University of Chicago Press, 1989.

Mitra, Ashutosh. "Śrīmā" [The Blessed Mother]. In *Śrīśrīmāyer Padaprānté* (At the Feet of the Twice-blessed Mother), edited by *Svāmī* Purnatmananda. 3 vols. II: 271–475. Kalikata: Udbodhana Kāryālaya, 1994–1997.

Nikhilananda, Svāmī. *Holy Mother: Being the Life of Sri Sarada Devi Wife of Ramakrishna and Helpmate in His Mission.* New York: Ramakrishna-Vivekananda Center, 1982.

Ojha, Catherine. "Feminine Asceticism in Hinduism: Its Traditions and Present Condition." *Man in India,* 61–63 (September 1981): 254–285.

Pavitrananda, Svāmī. *A Short Life of the Holy Mother.* Calcutta: Advaita Ashrama, 2000.

Prabhananda, Svāmī. *Śrīśrī Sāradā Mahimā* [Glory of the Twice-blessed Sarada]. Kalikata: Udbodhana Kāryālaya, 1403 B.E.

Prabhananda, Svāmī. "Swami Vivekananda and His 'Only Mother.'" *Prabuddha Bharata,* LXXXIX (January 1984), 10–20.

Purnatmananda, Svāmī. *Cirantanī Sāradā* [Eternal Sarada]. Kalikata: Udbodhana Kāryālaya, 1997.

Ray, Sarayu. "Kalkātāy 'Māyer Bāḍīté' Mā ké Pratham Dekhi" [My First Meeting with the Mother at the 'Mother's Home'"]. In *Śrīśrīmāyer Padaprānté* (At the Feet of the Twice-blessed Mother), edited by Svāmī Purnatmananda. 3 vols. I: 84–88. Kalikata: Udbodhana Kāryālaya, 1994–1997.

Śatarūpé Sāradā [Many Faces of Sarada], edited by Svāmī Lokeshvarananda. Golpark: Ramakrishna Mission Institute of Culture, 1989.

Satsvarupananda, Svāmī. "Karuṇāmayī" [The Compassionate Mother]. In *Śrīśrīmāyer Padaprānté* (At the Feet of the Twice-blessed Mother), edited by Svāmī Purnatmananda. 3 vols. I: 62–67. Kalikata: Udbodhana Kāryālaya, 1994–1997.

Sengupta, Achintyakumar. *Paramāprakṛti Śrīśrīsāradāmaṇi* [Supreme Womanhood of the Twice-blessed Saradamani]. 14th edition. Calcutta: Signet Press, 1394 B.E.

Sepaniants, Marietta T. "The Image of Woman in Religious Consciousness: Past, Present, and Future." *Philosophy East and West*, XLII (1992): 239–247.

Sil, Narasingha P. *Crazy in Love of God: Ramakrishna's Caritas Divina*. Selinsgrove: Susquehanna University Press, 2009.

Sil, Narasingha P. "Saradamani the Holy Mother: The Making of a Madonna." *Asian Culture*, XXI:2 (Summer 1993): 71–81.

Śrīśrīmāyer Kathā [Tales of the Twice-blessed Mother], compiled by Svāmī Arupananda. 1369 B.E. Kalikata: Udbodhana Kāryālaya, 1398 B.E.

Śrīśrīmāyer Padaprānté (At the Feet of the Twice-blessed Mother), edited by Svāmī Purnatmananda. 3 vols. Kalikata: Udbodhana Kāryālaya, 1994–1997.

Śrīśrīrāmakrṣṇakathāmrta [The Nectar of the Talks of the Twice-blessed Ramakrishna], compiled by *Śrī* Mahendranath Gupta, 5 *bhāgas* [parts] (1308–39 B.E.). Rpt. Kalikata: Kathāmṛta Bhavan, 1394 B.E.

Śrīśrīrāmakrṣṇalīlāprasaṅga [The Divine Play of the Twice-blessed Ramakrishna]. 5 parts in 2 vols. (Each part with separate pagination). Kalikata: Udbodhana Kāryālaya, 1398 B.E.

Tapasyananda, *Sri Sarada Devi the Holy Mother: Life and Teachings*. Madras: Sri Ramakrishna Math, 1982, 37–47.

Vishuddhananda, Svāmī. "Reminiscences." In *Mātṛdarśan* [A View of the Mother], 18–23. Kalikata: Udbodhana Kāryālaya, 1397 B.E.

Vivekananda, Svāmī. *The Complete Works of Swami Vivekananda*. 8 vols. Calcutta: Advaita Ashrama, 1990.

Vivekananda, Svāmī. *Patrāvalī* [Letters]. Kalikata: Udbodhana Kāryālaya, 1394 B.E.

CHAPTER 3

Bacigalupo, Ana Mariella. "Ritual Gendered Relationships: Kinship, Marriage, Mastery, and Machi Modes of Personhood." *Journal of Anthropological Research* 60, no. 2 (2004): 203–229.

Bourguignon, Erika. "Identity and the Constant Self." *The Psychoanalytic Study of Society* 9 (1994): 181–212.

Bourguignon, Erika. "Suffering and Healing, Subordination and Power: Women and Possession Trance." *Ethos* 32, no. 4 (2004): 557–574.

De la Perriere, Benedicte Brac. "'Nats' Wives' or 'Children of Nats': From Spirit Possession to Transmission among the Ritual Specialists of the Cult of the Thirty-Seven Lords." *Asian Ethnology* 68, no. 2 (2009): 283–305.

Dow, J. "Universal Aspects of Symbolic Healing: A Theoretical Synthesis." *American Anthropologist* 88, no. 1 (1986): 56–69.

Endres, Kirsten W. "Fate, Memory, and the Postcolonial Construction of the Self: The Life-Narrative of a Vietnamese Spirit Medium." *Journal of Vietnamese Studies* 3, no. 2 (2008): 34–65.

Geiger, Susan N. G. "Women's Life Histories: Method and Content." *Signs: Journal of Women in Culture and Society* 11 (1986): 334–351.

Gomm, Roger. "Bargaining from Weakness: Spirit Possession on the South Kenya Coast." *Man* 10, no. 4 (1975): 530–543.

Goodson, Ivor. "The Story of Life History: Origins of the Life History Method in Sociology." *Identity* 1, no. 2 (2001): 129–142.

Graham, Elspeth, and Lucy P. Jordan. "Migrant Parents and the Psychological Well-Being of Left-Behind Children in Southeast Asia." *Journal of Marriage and Family* 73, no. 4 (2011): 763–787.

Hayami, Yoko. "Introduction: The Family in Flux in Southeast Asia." In *The Family in Flux in Southeast Asia*, edited by Yoko Hayami, Junko Koizumi, Chalidaporn Songsamphan, and Ratana Tosakul, 1–26. Chiang Mai: Kyoto University Press and Silkworm Books, 2012.

Igreja, Victor, Beatrice Dias-Lambranca, and Annemiek Richters. "Gamba Spirits, Gender Relations, and Healing in Post-Civil War Gorongosa, Mozambique." *The Journal of the Royal Anthropological Institute* 14, no. 2 (2008): 353–371.

Kapferer, Bruce. *A Celebration of Demons: Exorcism and the Aesthetics of Healing in Sri Lanka*. Bloomington: Indiana University Press, 1983.

Kawamura, Kunimitsu. "A Female Shaman's Mind and Body, and Possession." *Asian Folklore Studies* 62, no. 2 (2003): 257–289.

Kehoe, A. B. "Women's Preponderance in Possession Cults: The Calcium-Deficiency Hypothesis Extended." *American Anthropologist* 83, no. 3 (1981): 549–561.

Kendall, Laurel. "Initiating Performance: The Story of Chini, a Korean Shaman." In *The Performance of Healing*, edited by C. Laderman and M. Roseman, 17–58. New York: Routledge, 1996.

Kendall, Laurel. *Shamans, Housewives, and Other Restless Spirits*. Honolulu: University of Hawaii Press, 1985.

Kleinman, Arthur. "'Everything That Really Matters': Social Suffering, Subjectivity, and the Remaking of Human Experience in a Disordering World." *Harvard Theological Review* 90, no. 3 (1997): 315–336.

Kleinman, Arthur, Veena Das, and Margaret M. Lock. *Social Suffering*. Berkeley: University of California Press, 1997.

Lewis, I. M. *Ecstatic Religion: An Anthropological Study of Spirit Possession and Shamanism*: London: Penguin, 1975.

Masquelier, Adeline. "From Hostage to Host: Confessions of a Spirit Medium in Niger." *Ethos* 30, no. 1/2 (2002): 49–76.

Mazzucato, Valentina and Djamila Schans. "Transnational Families and the Well-Being of Children: Conceptual and Methodological Challenges." *Journal of Marriage and Family* 73, no. 4 (2011): 704–712.

Nabokov, Isabelle. "Expel the Lover, Recover the Wife: Symbolic Analysis of a South Indian Exorcism." *The Journal of the Royal Anthropological Institute* 3, no. 2 (1997): 297–316.

Norton, B. "'Hot-Tempered' Women and 'Effeminate' Men: The Performance of Music and Gender in Vietnamese Mediumship." In *Possessed by the Spirits:*

Mediumship in Contemporary Vietnamese Communities, edited by Karen Fjelstad and Nguyen Thi Hien, 55–76. Ithaca, NY: Southeast Asia Program, Cornell Univeristy, 2006.

Ong, Aihwa. "The Production of Possession: Spirits and the Multinational Corporation in Malaysia." *American Ethnologist* 15, no. 1 (1988): 28–42.

Parrenas, R. S. *Children of Global Migration: Transnational Families and Gender Woes*. Standford, CA: Standford University Press, 2005.

Peacock, James L. and Dorothy C. Holland. "The Narrated Self: Life Stories in Process." *Ethos* 21, no. 4 (1993): 367–383.

Pinthongvijayakul, Visisya. "'I Am Not Your Mother! I Am Phaengsri, the Goddess!': A Medium's Failure To Be a Good Daughter and Her Reconstruction of the Self." *Rian Thai: The International Journal of Thai Studies* (May 2012): 275–292.

Sangree, Walter H. "Going Home to Mother: Traditional Marriage among the Irigwe of Benue-Plateau State, Nigeria." *American Anthropologist* 71, no. 6 (1969): 1046–1057.

Snodgrass, Jeffrey G. "A Tale of Goddesses, Money, and Other Terribly Wonderful Things: Spirit Possession, Commodity Fetishism, and the Narrative of Capitalism in Rajasthan, India." *American Ethnologist* 29, no. 3 (2002): 602–636.

Spiro, Melford E. *Burmese supernaturalism*. Philadelphia: Philadelphia Institute for the Study of Human Issues, 1978.

Statistical Report for 2011 Overseas Employment. *Statistical Report for 2011 Overseas Employment* 2012 [cited December 8, 2012]. Available from http://www.overseas.doe.go.th/.

Chapter 4

Agarwal, Bina. "Gender and Land Rights Revisited: Exploring New Prospects via the State, Family and Market." *Journal of Agrarian Change* 3, no. 1/2 (January 2003): 184–224.

Amin, Sajeda. "The Effect of Women's Status on Sex Differentials in Infant and Child Mortality in South Asia." *Genus*, 46, no. 3–4 (1990): 55–69.

Arya, Lakshmi. "The Uniform Civil Code: The Politics of the Universal in Postcolonial India." *Feminist Legal Studies* 14, no. 3 (October 2006): 293–328.

Bahadur, Gaiutra. "India's Missing Women." *Nation* 299, no. 1/2 (July 7, 2014): 35–39.

Banerjee, Paula. "The Acts and Facts of Women's Autonomy in India." *Diogenes* 53, no. 4 (November 2006): 85–101.

Berry, Kim. "Disowning Dependence: Single Women's Collective Struggle for Independence and Land Rights in Northwestern India." *Feminist Review no.* 98 (June 2011): 136–152.

Bhattacharya. Swasti. *Magical Progeny and Biotechnology: Toward a Hindu Reproductive Bioethics*. Albany: State University of New York Press, 2006.

Chang, Mina. "Womb for Rent." *Harvard International Review* 31, no. 1 (2009): 11–12.

Das, Rahul Peter. *The Origin of the Life of a Human Being: Conception and the Female According to Ancient Indian Medical and Sexological Literature.* New Delhi: Motilal Banarsidass, 2003.

Doniger, Wendy. "Put a Bag over Her Head: Beheading Mythologies of Women." In *Off with Her Head: The Denial of Women's Identity in Myth, Religion and Culture,* edited by Howard Eilberg-Schwartz and Wendy Doniger, 15–32. Berkeley: University of California Press, 2002.

Frederick Pargiter, trans. *Markandeya Purana.* Calcutta: Royal Asiatic Society, 1923.

Gill, Roopan, and Donna E. Stewart. "Relevance of Gender-Sensitive Policies and General Health Indicators to Compare the Status of South Asian Women's Health." *Women's Health Issues* 21, no. 1 (2011): 12–18.

Ghosh, Rohini and Premananda Bharati. "Women's Status and Health of Two Ethnic Groups Inhabiting a Periurban Habitat of Kolkata City, India: A Micro-Level Study." *Health Care for Women International* 26, no. 3 (2005): 194–211.

Government of India, Department of Social Welfare, Ministry of Education and Social Welfare. *Towards Equality: Report of the Committee on the Status of Women in India.* New Delhi: Government of India, 1974.

Halder, Debarati and K. Jaishankar. "Property Rights of Hindu Women: A Feminist Review of Succession Laws of Ancient, Medieval, and Modern India." *Journal of Law & Religion* 24, no. 2 (October 2008): 663–687.

Hume, Robert, trans. *Brihadaranyka Upanishad.* Oxford: Oxford University Press, 1921.

Indian Council of Social Sciences Research. *Status of Women in India: Synopsis of the Report of the National Committee on the Status of Women.* New Delhi: Allied Publishers, 1975.

Jain, Pannalal, ed. and trans. *Harivamsapurana of Punnata Jinasena.* Kashi: Jnanapita Murtidevi Granthamala, 1962.

Kanojia, R. "Rights of An Unborn Baby Versus the Social and Legal Constraints of Parents: Birth of a New Debate," Editorial. *Journal of Indian Association of Pediatric Surgeons* 13 (2008): 92–93.

Kapani, Lakshmi. "Note on Garbha Upanishad." In *Fragments for a History of Human Body Part 3,* edited by Michel Feher, Ramona Naddaff, and Nadia Tazi, 181–196. New York: Zone Books, 1989.

Kaur, J. "The Role of Litigation in Ensuring Women's Reproductive Rights: An Analysis of the Shanti Devi Judgement in India." *Reproductive Health Matters* 20, no. 39 (2012): 21–30.

Klaveren, Maarten van, Kea Tijdens, Melanie Hughie-Williams, and Nuria Ramos Martin. *An Overview of Women's Work and Employment in India: Decisions for Life MDG3 Project Country Report No. 13.* Institute of Advanced Labor Studies, University of Amsterdam, Amsterdam, Netherlands,

2010. Accessed September 23, 2016. http://www.paycheck.in/root_files/An-Overview-of-Womens-Work-and-Employment-in-India.pdf.

Kumar, Radha. *The History of Doing: An Illustrated Account of Movements for Women's Rights and Feminism in India, 1800–1900*. New Delhi: Kali for Women, 1993.

Mahr, Krista, Nilanjana Bowmak, and Sanjaya Sharma. "India's Shame." *Time Magazine*, January 14, 2013: 12.

Malhotra, A. and R. Malhotra. "All Aboard for the Fertility Express." *Commonwealth Law Bulletin*, 38, no. 1 (2012): 31–41.

Mishra, P. (2009). Surrogate Mother Hood in India: A Legal Vacuum. *Vidhigya: The Journal of Legal Awareness*, 4, no. 1 (2009): 9–14.

Mukherjee, Sucharita Sinha. "Women's Empowerment and Gender Bias in the Birth and Survival of Girls in Urban India." *Feminist Economics* 19, no. 1 (2013): 1–28.

Parks, Jennifer. "Care Ethics and the Global Practice of Commercial Surrogacy." *Bioethics* 24 (2010): 333–340.

Patel, Reena. "Hindu Women's Property Rights in India: A Critical Appraisal." *Third World Quarterly* 27, no. 7 (October 2006): 1255–1268.

Rimm, J. "Booming Baby Business: Regulating Commercial Surrogacy in India." *University of Pennsylvania Journal of International Law*, 30, no. 4 (2009): 1429–1462.

Ross-Sheriff, F. "Transnational Cross-Racial Surrogacy: Issues and Concerns." *Affilia: Journal of Women & Social Work*, 27, no. 2 (2012): 125–128.

Selby, Ann. "Narratives of Conception, Gestation, and Labour in Sanskrit Ayurvedic Texts." *Asian Medicine: Tradition and Modernity* 1, no. 2 (2005): 254–275.

Shastri, J. L. and G. P. Bhatt, eds. and trans. *Brahma Purana*. 3 vols. New Delhi: Motilal Banarsidass, 1985.

Smerdon, U. R. "Birth Registration and Citizenship Rights of Surrogate Babies Born in India." *Contemporary South Asia*, 20, no. 3 (2012): 341–358.

Suktankar, V.S., ed. *Mahabharata: Adi Parva*. Poona: Bhandarkar Oriental Research Institute, 1933.

Unnithan, Maya. "Thinking Through Surrogacy Legislation in India: Reflections on Relational Consent and Infertile Women." *Journal of Legal Anthropology* 1, no. 3 (2013): 287–313.

Vaidya, P. L., ed. and trans. *Harivamsapurana*. 2 vols. Poona: Bhandarkar Oriental Research Institute, 1969–1971.

Vanaja, G. "Women Parliamentarians in India." *Golden Research Thoughts* 1, no. 10 (April 2012): 1–3.

CHAPTER 5

Abuza, Z. *Militant Islam in Southeast Asia: Crucible of Terror*. Boulder, CO: Lynne Reinner, 2003.

Al Mujadilah Development Foundation (AMDF). https://www.facebook.com/pages/Al-Mujadilah-Development-Foundation-Inc-AMDF/100454010027972?sk=info&tab=page_info.

Angeles, V. SM. "Moros in the Media and Beyond: Representations of Philippine Muslims, *Contemporary Islam*, 4 (2010), 48.

Angeles, V. SM. "The State, the Moro National Liberation Front (MNLF) and Islamic Resurgence in the Philippines." In *Religious Fundamentalism in Developing Countries*, edited by Santosh Saha and Thomas Carr, 184–200. Westport, CT: Greenwood Press, 2001.

Angeles, V. SM. "Women and Revolution: Philippine Muslim Women's Participation in the Moro National Liberation Front." *Muslim World*, 86 (1996): 130–147.

Alojamiento, S. B. "Feminism in Philippine Activist Politics: The Case of Mindanao." *Tambara*, 21 (2004): 161–174.

Banes, M. D. "Young Muslim Professional Advocate 'Halal Lifestyle.'" *Business World Online*. May 6, 2011. Accessed August 21, 2015. http://www.bworldonline.com/content.php?section=Nation&title=Young-Muslim-professionals-advocate-%91halal-lifestyle%92&id=30894.

Barawid, R. C. "In the Name of Religious Freedom." *Manila Bulletin* August 23, 2012: E1.

Barlaan, K. A. and C. Cardiente, "Breaking Traditions." *The Standard*, October 16, 2016. Accessed June 14, 2016. http://thestandard.com.ph/mobile/article/101889.

Berkeley Center. "A Discussion with Amina Rasul Bernardo, Lead Convenor, Philippine Council for Islam and Democracy." Berkeley Center for Religion, Peace and World Affairs. July 8, 2010. Accessed August 22, 2015. http://berkleycenter.georgetown.edu/interviews/a-discussion-with-amina-rasul-bernardo-lead-convenor-philippine-council-for-islam-and-democracy.

Bonifacio, G. T. *Pinay on the Prairies: Filipina women and Transnational Identities*. Vancouver: University of British Columbia Press, 2013.

Brecht-Drouart, B. *Between Re-traditionalization and Islamic Resurgence: The Influence of the National Question and the Revival of Tradition on Gender Issues Among the Maranaos in Southern Philippines*. Doctoral dissertation, University of Frankfurt 2011.

Catada, R. "Maranao Woman Activist Speaks on Gender and Inequality." Oxfam in the Philippines, January 21, 2015. Accessed June 14, 2016. http://www.oxfamblogs.org/philippines/maranao-woman-activist-speaks-on-gender-and-inequality.htm.

Choy, C. *Empire of Care: Nursing and Migration in Filipino-American History*. Durham, NC: Duke University Press, 2003.

Congress Adjourns, Fails to Pass BBL, *Philippine Daily Inquirer*, February 4, 2016. Accessed June 14, 2016. http://newsinfo.inquirer.net/761319/congress-adjourns-fails-to-pass-bbl.

Constitution of the Republic of the Philippines 1987. Accessed August 20, 2015. http://www.gov.ph/constitutions/1987-constitution/#article-x.

Coronel-Ferrer, M. "Women at the Talks." *Kababaihan at Kapayapaan* 1 (2014): 3–7.

Dwyer, L. and R. Cagoco-Guiam. *Gender and conflict in Mindanao*. Washington, DC: Asia Foundation, 2012.

Francisco, K. "Race to the Senate: The Women Who Want Your Vote in 2016." Accessed June 14, 2016. http://www.rappler.com/nation/politics/elections /2016/114685-women-senatorial-candidates-2016-elections.

Gutoc, S. "Mindanao YSpeak, Upping the Peace Antenna." SGV Hall, AIM Conference Center Manila, 2009. Accessed August 20, 2015. http://www .theaimblog.com/promoting-peace/.

Hilsdon, A. "Invisible Bodies: Gender, Conflict and Peace in Mindanao." *Asian Studies Review*, 33, no. 3 (2009): 349–365.

Lacar, L. Q. "Philippine Muslim Women: Their Emerging Role in a Rapidly Changing Society." In *Mindanao: Land of Unfulfilled Promise*, edited by Mark Turner, R. J. May, and Lulu Rospall Turner, 109–125. Quezon City: New Day Publishers, 1992.

Mahmoud, S. *Politics of Piety: The Islamic Revival and the Feminist Subject*. Princeton, NJ: Princeton University Press, 2005.

Mangahas, F. B. and Llaguno, J. R., eds. *Centennial Crossings: Readings on Baba-ylan Feminism in the Philippines*. Quezon City: C & E Publishing, 2006.

McKenna, T. *Muslim Rulers and Rebels: Everyday Politics and Armed Separatism in Southern Philippines*. Berkeley: University of California Press, 1998.

Misuari, N. *The Rise and Fall of Moro Statehood* (MNLF policy paper, 1974), *Philippine Development Forum* 6, no. 2 (1992), 1–41.

Moro National Liberation Front. *Rise and fall of Moro Statehood*. n.p., 1974.

Parrenas, R. *Servants of Globalization: Women, Migration and Domestic Work*. Stanford: Stanford University Press, 2001.

Philippine Government (GPH) and Moro Islamic Liberation Front (MILF). *Framework of Agreement on the Bangsamoro*. 2012. Accessed August 20, 2015. http://www.c-r.org/downloads/2012%20Framework%20Agreement %20on%20the%20Bangsamoro.pdf.

"Philippine School Bans Hijab." August 5, 2012. Accessed August 20, 2015. http://newsinfo.inquirer.net/243069/philippine-school-bans-muslim-hijab.

Rallonza, M. L. "Yasmin Busran-Lao: Peace Building from the Grassroots to the Peace Table and Back." *Kababaihan at Kapayapaan,* 1 (2014): 8–9.

Rasul, A. B. "Moro Women Second to None." *The Moro Times* (a monthly supplement *of the Manila Times*). March 28, 2008. Accessed August 18, 2015. Also available at: http://www.mindanews.com/top-stories/2008/03/29/moro-women-second-to-none/.

Republic of the Philippines. Executive order No. 209 as amended by executive order no. 227. 1988. *The New Family Code of the Philippines*.

Republic of the Philippines. *Presidential Decree no. 1083*. (A decree to ordain and promulgate a code recognizing the system of Filipino Muslim laws, cod-ifying Muslim personal laws, and providing for its administration and for other purposes). 1976.

Republic of the Philippines. *Republic Act. No. 7192* (An Act Promoting the Integration of Women as Full and Equal Partners of Men in Development and Nation Building and for other Purposes). 1988.

Roces, M. "Rethinking the 'Filipino woman': A Century of Women's Activism in the Philippines, 1905–2006." In *Women's Movements in Asia: Feminisms and*

Transnational Activism, edited by Mina Roces and Louise Edwards, 34–52. London: Routledge, 2010.

Santiago, P. (Director). *Perlas ng silangan (Pearl of the Orient)* [Film]. Manila: FPJ Productions, 1969.

Sarip, L. H. "A Profile of Economic Activities of Maranao Women in Molundo, Marantao and the Islamic city of Marawi, Lanao del Sur." *Dansalan Quarterly* 7, no. 1–2 (1985–1986): 7–8.

Siapno, J. "Gender Relations and Islamic Resurgence in Mindanao, Southern Philippines." In *Muslim Women's Choices: Religious Belief and Social Reality*, edited by Camillia Fawzi El-Solh and Judy Mabro, 184–201. Oxford: Berg Publishers, 1994.

Simpal, Esmie. Personal interview. August 2011.

Sobritchea, Carolyn I., ed. *Gender, Culture & Society: Selected Readings in Women's Studies in the Philippines*. Seoul: Ewha University Women's Press, 2004.

Tan, S. K. *Internationalization of the Bangsamoro Struggle*. Quezon City: University of the Philippines Center for Integrative and Development Studies, 2003.

United States Department of State. U.S. Government Projects in the Philippines: Human Rights, Democracy and Labor. 2010. Accessed August 20, 2015. http://photos.state.gov/libraries/manila/19452/pdfs/USG_Grants_to_Promote_DHRL_Philippines.pdf.

Usodan-Sumagayan, A. "The Changing role of Maranao Women in a Maranao Rural Society." *Dansalan Quarterly* 9, no. 4 (1988): 165–228.

Vitug, M. and G. Gloria. *Under the Crescent Moon: Rebellion in Mindanao*. Quezon City: Ateneo de Manila University Press, 2000.

CHAPTER 6

DeNapoli, Antoinette. *"Real Sadhus Sing to God": Gender, Asceticism, and Vernacular Religion in Rajasthan*. Oxford: Oxford University Press, 2014.

Flueckiger, Joyce. *Gender and Genre in the Folklore of Middle India*. Ithaca, NY: Cornell University Press, 1996.

Flueckiger, Joyce. *In Amma's Healing Room: Gender and Vernacular Islam in South India*. Bloomington: Indiana University Press, 2006.

Gardner, Katy. *Age, Narrative and Migration: The Life Course and Life Histories of Bengali Elders in London*. New York: Berg, 2002.

Jackson, Michael. *Lifeworlds: Essays in Existential Anthropology*. Chicago: University of Chicago Press, 2013.

Khandelwal, Meena. *Women in Ochre Robes: Gendering Hindu Renunciation*. New York: State University of New York Press, 2004.

Lamb, Sarah. *White Saris and Sweet Mangoes: Aging, Gender, and Body in North India*. Berkeley: University of California Press, 2000.

McGregor, R. S., ed. *Oxford Hindi-English Dictionary*. Oxford: Oxford University Press, 1993.

Olivelle, Patrick, trans. "On the Road. The Religious Significance of Walking." In *Theatrum Mirabiliorum Indiae Orientalis: A Volume to Celebrate the*

70th Birthday of Professor Maria Krzysztof Byrski, Rocznik Orientalistyczny, 173–187. Warszawa: Dom Wydawniczy Elipsa, 2007.

Olivelle, Patrick, trans. *Saṃnyāsa Upaniṣads*. Oxford: Oxford University Press, 1992.

Olivelle, Patrick, trans. *Upaniṣads*. Oxford: Oxford University Press, 1996.

CHAPTER 7

Blackburn, Stuart H., et al. *Oral Epics in India*. Berkeley: University of California Press, 1989.

Bloom, Mia. "Female Suicide Bombers: A Global Trend." *Daedalus* 136, no. 1 (Winter 2007): 94–102, 97.

Dominik Guss, C., Ma. Teresa Tuason, and Vanessa B. Teixeira. "A Cultural-Psychological Theory of Contemporary Islamic Martyrdom." *Journal for the Theory of Social Behaviour* 37, no. 4 (2007): 415–445.

Hart, George. "Woman and the Sacred in Ancient Tamilnad." *Journal of Asian Studies* 32, no. 2 (February, 1973): 233–251.

Hawley, John S. *Sati, the Blessing and the Curse: The Burning of Wives in India*. New York: Oxford University Press, 1994.

Ilankovadigal. *Cilappatikaaram*. Tirunelveli: Tenintiya Saivasittanta Nurpatippu Kalakam, 1973.

Inden, Ronald and Ralph Nicholas. *Kinship in Bengali Culture*. Chicago: The University of Chicago Press, 1977.

Raj, Selva and William Harman. *Dealing with Deities. The Ritual Vow in South Asia*. Albany: State University of New York Press, 2006.

Rajam, V. S. "Ananku: A Term Semantically Reduced to Signify Female Sacred Power." *Journal of the American Oriental Society* 106 no. 2 (April—June, 1986): 257–272.

Roberts, Michael. "Killing Rajiv Gandhi: Dhanu's Sacrificial Metamorphosis in Death." *South Asian History and Culture* 1, no. 1 (2009): 25–41.

Obeyesekere, Gananath. *The Cult of the Goddess Pattini*. Chicago: University of Chicago Press, 1984.

Schalk, Peter. "Women Fighters of the Liberation Tigers in Tamil Ilam: The Martial Feminism of Atel Placinkam." *South Asia Research* 14, no. 2 (1994): 163–183.

Tambiah, Stanley. *Sri Lanka: Ethnic Fratricide and the Dismantling of Democracy*. Chicago: University of Chicago Press, 1986.

CHAPTER 8

Barton, R. F. "Ifugao Law." *American Archaeology and Ethnology* 15, no. 1 (1919): 1–33.

Conklin, Harold. *Ethnographic Atlas of Ifugao: A Study of Environment, Culture, and Society in Northern Luzon*. New Haven, CT: Yale University Press, 1980.

Cordillera Schools Group Inc. *Ethnography of the Major Ethnolinguistic Groups in the Cordillera*. Quezon City: New Day Publishers, 2003.

Dacawi, R. "The Ifugao Way of Forest Conservation." *Philippine Upland World* 1 no. 2 (1982): 14–15.

Dulawan, Lourdes. "Singing HudHud in Ifugao." In *Literature of Voice: Epics in the Philippines*, edited by N. Revel, 115–125. Manila: Ateneo de Manila University, 2005.

Florendo, Maria Nela B. "Ethnic History (Cordillera)." Republic of the Philippines: National Commission for Culture and the Arts, 2011. Accessed October 2, 2016. http://ncca.gov.ph/subcommissions/subcommission-on-cultural-heritagesch/historical-research/ethnic-history-cordillera/.

Jang, Jae Woo. "The Promotion of Human Dignity as Manifest in the Ifugao Familial and Socio-Political Structure and Oral Traditions as Primary Factors in Developing a Sustainable and Peaceful Community." *Eubios Journal of Asian and International Bioethics* 22 (September 2012): 169.

Jang, Jae Woo and Scott Salcedo. "The Socio-political Structure that Regulates Ifugao Terracing and Land Maintenance System as a Model for Water Conservation, Management and Sustainability." Working paper, National Innovation Conference on Education. Laguna, Philippines: National Association of the UNESCO Club Philippines, January 2013.

Krutak, Lars. *"The Last Kalinga Tattoo Artist of the Philippines."* Accessed March 17, 2017. http://www.larskrutak.com/the-last-kalinga-tattoo-artist-of-the-philippines/.

National Statistical Coordination Board. *Cordillera Administrative Region*. Baguio City: National Statistical Coordination Board, 2010.

Pyer-Pereira, Tlana. "Telling Tales: Memory, Culture and the Hudhud Chants." Master's Thesis, Swarthmore College. Accessed July 13, 2015. http://triceratops.brynmawr.edu/dspace/bitstream/handle/10066/10200/Pyer-Pereira_thesis_2007.pdf?sequence=1.

Reid, Lawrence. "Who are the Indigenous?" *The Cordillera Review* 1, no. 1 (2009): 3–26.

Shedden, Rikardo. "Ameliorating Uncertainty and Rebalancing Human/Spirit-World relations: A Look at Ritual Practice in the Uplands of Northern Luzon." Master's thesis, Department of Anthropology, Australian National University, 2010.

Sianghio, Christina. *"Ifugao," Tripod* (blog). Accessed March 8, 2013. http://litera1no4.tripod.com/ifugao_frame.html.

Stephen, Acabado. "The Archaeology of the Ifugao Agricultural Terraces: Antiquity and Social Organization." PhD Thesis, University of Hawaii, 2010.

Chapter 9

Chien-ling, Su and Chao-chun Hsiao, eds. *Danianchuyi hui niangchia (Going Back to My Mother's House on New Year's Day: Culture, Customs, and Gender Equity Education)*. Taipei: Fembooks, 2005.

Harrell, Stevan. "Men, Women, and Ghosts in Taiwanese Folk Religion." In *Gender and Religions*, edited by Caroline Walker Bynum, Stevan Harrell, and Paula Richman, 97–116. Boston: Beacon Press, 1986.

Harrell, Stevan. "When a Ghost Becomes a God." In *Religion and Ritual in Chinese Society*, edited by Arthur Wolf, 193–206. Stanford: Stanford University Press, 1974.

Hsun, Chang. "Funu shengqian yu sihou diwei" (Chinese Women's Kinship Status: Adopted Daughters and Adopted Daughters-in-Law Reconsidered). *Kaogu renlei xuekan* 56 (2000): 15–43.

Jordan, David. *Gods, Ghosts, and Ancestors*. Berkeley: University of California Press, 1972.

Lee, Anru. *In the Name of Harmony and Prosperity: Labor and Gender Politics in Taiwan's Economic Restructuring*. Albany: State University of New York Press, 2004.

Lee, Anru. "Shaping One's Own Destiny: Global Economy, Family, and Women's Struggle in the Taiwanese Context." *Women's Studies International Forum* 32, no. 2 (2009): 120–129.

Lee, Anru. "Women of the Sisters' Hall: Religion and the Making of Women's Alternative Space in Taiwan's Economic Restructuring." *Gender, Place and Culture* 15, no. 4 (2008): 373–393.

Lee, Anru and Wen-hui Anna Tang. "The Twenty-Five Maiden Ladies' Tomb and Predicaments of the Feminist Movement in Taiwan." *Journal of Current Chinese Affairs* 39, no. 3 (2010): 23–49.

Lin, Wei-ping. "Conceptualizing Gods through Statues: A Study of Personification and Localization in Taiwan." *Comparative Studies in Society and History* 50, no. 2 (2008): 454–477.

Martin, Emily. *The Cult of the Dead in a Chinese Village*. Stanford: Stanford University Press, 1973.

Shih, Fang-long. "Generation of a New Space: A Maiden Temple in the Chinese Religious Culture of Taiwan." *Culture and Religion* 8, no. 1 (2007): 89–104.

Tang, Wen-hui, "Constructing and Practicing Feminist Pedagogy in Taiwan Using a Field Study of the Twenty-Five Ladies' Tomb." *Gender, Place & Culture* 20, no. 6 (2013): 811–826.

Tang, Wen-hui and Ying-Yao Cheng. "Xingbie pingdeng tongshi jiaoyu kecheng de jiangou yu shishi: Yi 'xingbie yu shehui' wei li" (The Construction and Practice of Gender Equality Curriculum: The Case of the 'Gender and Society' Course). *Jiaoyu xuekan* 34 (2010): 33–67.

Wang, Hsiu-yun. "'Ershiwu shunu mu jingguan zhengjian ji mingming tianye fangtan jihua' chengguo baogaoshu" (The Final Report of the 'Twenty-five Maiden Ladies' Tomb Renovation and Name Rectification' Field Interview Project). Unpublished report. Kaohsiung: Kaohsiung City Bureau of Labor, 2006.

Weller, Robert. "Capitalism, Community, and the Rise of Amoral Cults in Taiwan." In *Asian Visions of Authority*, edited by Charles F. Keyes, Laurel Kendall, and Helen Hardacre. Honolulu: University of Hawaii Press, 1994.

Wolf, Arthur P. "Gods, Ghosts, and Ancestors." In *Studies in Chinese Societies*, edited by Arthur P. Wolf, 131–182. Stanford: Stanford University Press, 1978.

Wolf, Margery. *Women and the Family in Rural Taiwan*. Stanford: Stanford University Press, 1972.

CHAPTER 10

Bose, Mandakranta. *Faces of the Feminine in Ancient, Medieval, and Modern India*. New York: Oxford University Press, 2000.

Charpentier, Marie-Thérèse. *Indian Female Gurus in Contemporary Hinduism: A Study of Central Aspects and Expressions of Their Religious Leadership*. Abo, Finland: Abo Akademi University Press, 2010.

Erndl, Kathleen M. "Afterword." In *The Graceful Guru: Hindu Female Gurus in India and the United States*, edited by Karen Pechilis, 245–250. New York: Oxford University Press, 2004.

Erndl, Kathleen M. "Is Shakti Empowering for Women: Reflections on Feminism and the Hindu Goddess. In Is the Goddess a Feminist?" In *The Politics of South Asian Goddesses*, edited by Alf Hiltebeitel and Kathleen M. Erndl, 91–103. New York: New York University Press, 2000.

Falk, Nancy Auer and Rita M. Gross, eds. *Unspoken Worlds: Women's Religious Lives*. San Francisco: Harper and Row, 1980.

Gross, Rita M. *Feminism and Religion: An Introduction*. Boston: Beacon Press, 1996.

Gupta, Samjukta Gombrich. "The Goddess, Women and Their Rituals in Hinduism." In *Faces of the Feminine in Ancient, Medieval, and Modern India*, edited by Mandrakanta Bose, 87–106. New York: Oxford University Press, 2000.

Gurumaa, Anandmurti. *Shakti*. New Delhi: Guru Maa Vani, 2006a.

Gurumaa, Anandmurti. *In Quest of Sadguru: An Ultimate Guide for the Seekers in Search of a True Master*. Delhi: Gurumaa Vani, 2011.

Gurumaa, Anandmurti. *Shakti: The Feminine Energy*. Revised edition. Delhi: Gurumaa Vani, 2008.

Gurumaa, Anandmurti. *Shakti: An Ode to Women* (Video). VCD. New Delhi: Gurumaa Vani, 2006b.

Gurumaa, Anandmurti. "Suno Suno Meri Aawaaz by Anandmurti Gurumaa" (Music Video). Accessed September 26, 2016. https://www.youtube.com /watch?v=vmqt-2SEvxU.

Hallstrom, Lisa Lassell. *Mother of Bliss: Anandamayi Ma (1896–1982)*. New York: Oxford University Press, 1999.

Hallstrom, Lisa Lassell. "Anandamayi Ma, the Bliss-Filled Divine Mother." In *The Graceful Guru: Hindu Female Gurus in India and the United States*, edited by Karen Pechilis, 85–118. New York: Oxford University Press, 2004.

Khandelwal, Meena. "Ungendered Atma, Masculine Virility and Feminine Compassion: Ambiguities in Renunciant Discourses on Gender." *Contributions to Indian Sociology* 31, no. 1 (1997): 79–107.

Khandelwal, Meena. *Women in Ochre Robes: Gendering Hindu Renunciation*. Albany: State University of New York Press, 2004.

Khandelwal, Meena, Sondra L. Hausner, and Ann Grodzins Gold, eds. *Women's Renunciation in South Asia: Nuns, Yoginis, Saints, and Singers*. New York: Palgrave Macmillan, 2006.

Kieckhefer, Richard and George Doherty Bond, eds. *Sainthood: Its Manifestations in World Religions*. Berkeley: University of California Press, 1988.

Mackenzie, Vicki. *Cave in the Snow: A Western Woman's Quest for Enlightenment*. London: Bloomsbury, 1998.

McDaniel, June. *Making Virtuous Daughters and Wives: An Introduction to Women's Brata Rituals in Bengali Folk Religion*. New York: State University of New York Press, 2003.

Menon, Kalyani Devaki. "Passionate Renouncers: Hindu Nationalist Renouncers and the Politics of Hindutva." In *Women's Renunciation in South Asia: Nuns, Yoginis, Saints, and Singers*, edited by Meena Khandelwal, Sondra L. Hausner, and Ann Grodzins Gold, 141–169. New York: Palgrave Macmillan, 2005.

Nagar, Richa and Sangtin Writers (Organization). *Playing with Fire: Feminist Thought and Activism through Seven Lives in India*. Minneapolis: University of Minnesota Press, 2006.

Narayan, Kirin. *Storytellers, Saints and Scoundrels: Folk Narrative in Hindu Religious Teaching*. Philadelphia: University of Pennsylvania Press, 1989.

Narayanan, Vasudha. "Brimming with Bhakti, Embodiments of Shakti: Devotees, Deities, Performers, Reformers, and Other Women of Power in the Hindu Tradition." In *Feminism and World Religions*, edited by Arvind Sharma and Katherine K. Young, 25–77. Albany: State University of New York Press, 1999.

Nhat Hanh, Thich. *Old Path, White Clouds: Walking in the Footsteps of the Buddha*. Berkeley, CA: Parallax Press, 1991.

Orsi, Robert A. "Two Aspects of One Life: Saint Gemma Galgani and My Grandmother in the Wound between Devotion and History, the Natural and the Supernatural." In *Between Heaven and Earth: The Religious Worlds People Make and the Scholars Who Study Them*. Princeton, NJ: Princeton University Press, 2005.

Osho. *A New Vision of Women's Liberation*. New Delhi: Full Circle, 2004.

Pechilis, Karen. "Introduction: Hindu Female Gurus in Historical and Philosophical Context." In *The Graceful Guru: Hindu Female Gurus in India and the United States*, edited by Karen Pechilis, 3–50. New York: Oxford University Press, 2004.

Pintchman, Tracy. *Guests at God's Wedding: Celebrating Kartik among the Women of Benares*. Albany: State University of New York Press, 2005.

Raheja, Gloria Goodwin and Ann Grodzins Gold. *Listen to the Heron's Words: Reimagining Gender and Kinship in North India*. Berkeley: University of California Press, 1994.

Ramanujan, A. K. "Toward a Counter-System: Women's Tales." In *Gender, Genre, and Power in South Asian Expressive Traditions*, edited by Arjun Appadurai, 33–55. Philadelphia: University of Pennsylvania Press, 1991.

Rudert, Angela. "A Sufi, Sikh, Hindu, Buddhist, TV Guru: Anandmurti Gurumaa." In *Religious Pluralism, State and Society in Asia*, edited by Chiara

Formichi. Series Editor, Bryan Turner. Routledge Religion in Contemporary Asia Series, 236–257. New York: Abingdon, 2014.

Sahajobai. *Sahaj Prakash: The Brightness of Simplicity*. Translated by Harry Aveling and Sudha Joshi. Delhi: Motilal Banarsidass Publishers, 2001.

Sangari, Kumkum. "Consent, Agency and Rhetorics of Incitement." *Economic and Political Weekly* May 1, 1993: 867–882.

Sarkar, Tanika. "Heroic Women, Mother Goddesses: Family and Organisation in Hindutva Politics." In *Women and the Hindu Right: A Collection of Essays*, edited by Tanika Sarkar, Urvashi Butalia, and Kali for Women (Organization), 181–215. New Delhi: Kali for Women, 1995.

Wadley, Susan S. *Wife, Mother, Widow: Exploring Women's Lives in Northern India*. New Delhi: Chronicle Books, 2008.

Wadley, Susan S. "Women and the Hindu Tradition." In *Women in India: Two Perspectives*, edited by Doranne Jacobson and Susan S. Wadley, 111–136. New Delhi: Manohar, 1977.

Yogananda, Paramahansa. *Autobiography of a Yogi*. Los Angeles, CA: Self-Realization Fellowship, 1947.

CHAPTER 11

"Chakravarthy, Pritham Blog." Accessed May 4, 2011. http://prithamkchakravarthy.blogspot.com/2009/12/theatricals.html.

Chakravarthy, Pritham K. "Road with No End." *The Journal of National Folklore*. Accessed May 3, 2011. http://prithamkchakravarthy.blogspot.com/search/label/Articles.

Ganz, Marshall. "Motivation, Story and Celebration." 43–63. Accessed March 22, 2017. https://annastarrrose.files.wordpress.com/2011/06/ganz-course-notes.pdf.

Mangai, A. *Acting Up: Gender and Theatre in India, 1979 Onwards*. New Delhi: LeftWord, 2015.

Mason, Elizabeth. "American Masculinities in Crisis: Trauma and Super Hero Blockbusters." MA Thesis, Bowling Green State University, 2010.

Monteiro, Anjali and K.P. Jayasankar, directors. *Our Family*. Mumbai: Centre for Media and Cultural Studies at the Tata Institute of Social Sciences, 2007.

Nicholson, Helen. *Applied Drama: The Gift of Theatre*. New York: Palgrave Macmillan, 2005.

Prentki, Tim and Sheila Preston (eds.) *The Applied Theatre Reader*. New York: Routledge, 2009.

Root, Maria P. "Reconstructing the Impact of Trauma on Personality." In *Personality and Psychopathology Feminist Reappraisals*, edited by Laura S. Brown and Mary Ballou, 229–265. New York: Guilford Press, 1994.

Rudisill, Kristen D. "Pritham Chakravarthy: Performing Aravani Life Stories." *Asian Theatre Journal*, special issue on *Women in Asian Theatre* 32, no. 2 (Fall 2015): 535–554.

Santhanam, Kausalya. "Communication is the Key." *The Hindu,* June 20, 2008.

Sircar, Badal. *The Third Theatre*. Calcutta: Sri Aurobindo Press, 1978.

Subramanian, Lakshmi. *From the Tanjore Court to the Madras Music Academy: A Social History of Music in South India*. New Delhi: Oxford University Press, 2006.

Taylor, Philip. *Applied Theatre: Creating Transformative Encounters in the Community*. Portsmouth, NH: Heinemann, 2003.

Wilkinson, Sue and Celia Kitzinger, "Representing the Other." In *The Applied Theatre Reader,* edited by Tim Prentki and Sheila Preston, 86–93. New York: Routledge, 2009.

CHAPTER 12

Anālayo. "The Bahudhātuka-sutta and its Parallels on Women's Inabilities." *Journal of Buddhist Ethics*, 16 (2009): 135–190.

Cabezón, José Ignacio. *Buddhism, Sexuality, and Gender*. New York: State University of New York Press, 1992.

Causton, Richard. *Nichiren Shoshu Buddhism: An Introduction*. London: Rider, 1988.

Faure, Bernard. *The Power of Denial: Buddhism, Purity and Gender*. Princeton, NJ: Princeton University Press, 2003.

Gross, Rita M. "Buddhism." In *Women in Religion,* edited by Jean Holm and John Bowker, 1–29. New York: Pinter Publishers, 1996.

Kubo. Tsungunari and Yuyama Akira (trans). *The Lotus Sutra*. Berkeley, CA: Numata Center for Buddhist Translation and Research, 2007.

Minichiello, V. and R. Aroni. *In-Depth Interviewing: Researching People*. Melbourne: Longman Cheshire, 1990.

Powers, John. *Introduction to Tibetan Buddhism*. Ithaca, NY: Snow Lion, 2007.

Romberg, Claudia. "Women in Engaged Buddhism." *Contemporary Buddhism* 3, no. 2 (2002): 161–170.

Schedneck, Brooke. "Buddhist Life Stories." *Contemporary Buddhism* 8, no. 1 (2007): 57–68.

Shaw, Miranda. *Passionate Enlightenment: Women in Tantric Buddhism*. Princeton, NJ: Princeton University Press, 1994.

Stone, Jacqueline I. "Chanting the August title of the Lotus Sutra: Daimoku Practices in Classical and Medieval Japan." In *Re-Visioning "Kamakura" Buddhism*, edited by Richard K. Payne, 116–166. Honolulu: Kuroda Institute, University of Hawaii Press, 1998.

CHAPTER 13

Anagol, Padma. "Agency, Periodisation and Change in the Gender and Women's History of Colonial India." *Gender & History* 20, no. 3 (2008): 603–627.

Anagol, Padma. *The Emergence of Feminism in India, 1850–1920*. Aldershot, England: Ashgate, 2005.

Bor, Joep. "Mamia, Ammani and Other Bayadères: Europe's Portrayal of India's Temple Dancers." In *Music and Orientalism in the British Empire,*

1780s–1940s: Portrayal of the East, edited by Martin Clayton and Bennett Zon, 39–70. Aldershot, England: Ashgate, 2007.

Chatterjee, Partha. *The Nation and Its Fragments: Colonial and Postcolonial Histories*. Princeton, NJ: Princeton University Press, 1993.

Chinmayee Manjunath. "Reluctant inheritors of a tainted legacy?" July 17, 2004. Accessed September 13, 2013. http://archive.tehelka.com/story_main4.asp?filename=Ne071704Reluctant.asp.

Datar, Chhaya. "Reform or New Form of Patriarchy? Devadasis in the Border Region of Maharashtra and Karnataka." *The Indian Journal of Social Work* LIII, no. 1 (1992): 81–91.

Dubois, Jean Antoine. *Hindu Manners, Customs and Ceremonies*. Translated by Henry K. Beauchamp. Oxford: Clarendon Press, 1906.

Epp, Lynda. *Violating the Sacred? The Social Reform of Devadasis among Dalits in Karnataka, India*. Unpublished PhD Thesis, York University, 1996.

Gangoli, Geetanjali. "Immortality, Hurt or Choice: Indian Feminists and Prostitution." In *Prostitution and Beyond: An Analysis of Sex Work in India*, edited by Rohini Sahni, V. Kalyan Shankar, and Hemant Apte, 21–39. New Delhi: Sage, 2007.

Hubel, Teresa. "The High Cost of Dancing: When the Indian Women's Movement Went After the Devadasis." In *Bharatanatyam: A Reader*, edited by Davesh Soneji, 160-181. New Delhi: Oxford University Press, 2010. Originally appeared in *Intercultural Communications and Creative Practice: Dance, Music and Women's Cultural Identity*, edited by Laura B. Lengel, 121–140. Westport, CT: Praeger, 2005.

Jordan, Kay. *From Sacred Servant to Profane Prostitute: A History of the Changing Legal Status of the Devadasis in India 1857–1947*. New Delhi: Manohar Publishers, 2003.

Mosse, G. Lachmann. *Nationalism and Sexuality*. Madison: The University of Wisconsin Press, 1985.

Nair, Janaki. "The Devadasi, Dharma and the State." *Economic and Political Weekly* 29, no. 50 (1994): 3157–3166.

Nair, Janaki and Mary John. *A Question of Silence: The Sexual Economies of Modern India*. New Delhi: Kali for Women, 1998.

Natarajan, Srividya. *Another Stage in the Life of the Nation: Sadir, Bharatanatyam, Feminist Theory*. Unpublished PhD Thesis, University of Hyderabad, 1997.

Orchard, Treena. *A Painful Power: Coming of Age, Sexuality and Relationships, Social Reform, and HIV/AIDS among Devadasi Sex Workers in Rural Karnataka, India*. Unpublished PhD Dissertation, University of Manitoba, 2004.

Orr, Leslie. *Donors, Devotees and Daughters of God: Temple Women in Medieval Tamil Nadu*. Oxford: Oxford University Press, 2000.

Parasher, Aloka and Usha Naik. "Temple Girls of Medieval Karnataka." *Indian Economic and Social History Review* 23, no. 63 (1986): 63–78.

Ramberg, Lucinda. *Given to the Goddess: South Indian Devadasis, Ethics, Kinship*. Unpublished PhD Thesis, University of California, 2006.

Reddy, Muthulakshmi. *Autobiography of Mrs. S. Muthulakshmi Reddy*. Madras: M.L.J. Press, 1964.

Shankar, Jogan. *Devadasi Cult: A Sociological Analysis*. New Delhi: Ashish Publishing House, 1990.

Shortt, John. "The Bayadere; or, Dancing Girls of Southern India." *Memoirs Read Before the Anthropological Society of London* 3 (1870): 182–194.

Tarachand, K. C. *Devadasi Custom: Rural Social Structures and Flesh Markets*. New Delhi: Efficient Offset Printers, 1991.

Thurston, Edgar. *Ethnographic Notes in Southern India*, Vols. I and II. Madras: Government Press, 1906.

Chapter 14

Ammerman, Nancy T. "Religious Identities and Religious Institutions." In *Handbook of the Sociology of Religion*, edited by M. Dillon, 207–224. Cambridge: Cambridge University Press, 2003.

Bae, Geung-chan. "Global Changes and North–South Korean Relations in the Early 1970s." In *The Socio-Political Change of Republic of Korea in the Early 1970s*, edited by the Academy of Korean Studies, 11–66. Seoul: Bae-san Suh-dang, 1999. (Korean)

Brock, Rita Nakashima and Susan Thistlethwaite. *Casting Stones: Prostitution and Liberation in Asia and in the United States*. Minneapolis, MN: Augsburg Fortress, 1996.

Cho, Grace. *Haunting the Korean Diaspora: Shame, Secrecy, and the Forgotten War*. Minneapolis: University of Minnesota Press, 2008.

Cockburn, Cynthia. *From Where We Stand: War, Women's Activism and Feminist Analysis*. New York: Zed Books, 2007.

DuRaeBang, A. *2007 Report on the Foreign Victims of Prostitution in Gyeong-Ghi Province*. (Korean)

Edwards, Paul. *Korean War Almanac*. New York: Facts on File, 2006.

Enloe, Cynthia. *The Curious Feminist: Searching for Women in the Age of Empire*. Berkeley: University of California Press, 2004.

Gang, Joon-man. *Buying and Selling Sex, Strip Korea: How Has the State Power Controlled Sex?* Seoul: Inmul and Sasang, 2012. (Korean)

Gang, Yi-Soo. "Prohibition of Public Prostitution and Women's Movements during the American Military Occupation." In *Social Changes and History of Korea during American Military Occupation*, Vol. II, 261–292. Choonchun, South Korea: Hanrim University, 1999. (Korean)

Hohn, Maria and Seungsook Moon. "Introduction: Politics of Gender, Sexuality, Race, and Class in the U.S. Military Empire." In *Over There: Living with the U.S. Military Empire from World War II and the Present*, edited by Maria Hohn and Seungsook Moon, 1–38. Durham, NC: Duke University Press, 2010.

Hong, Sung Chul. *The History of Brothels* [Yu-Kwak]. Seoul: Paper Road, 2007. (Korean)

Jung, Hee-jin. "Human Rights of the Women Who Should Die in order to Live." In *The History of Korean Women's Human Rights Activism*, edited by Korean Women's Hotline, 300–358. Seoul: Hanul, 2005. (Korean)

Kim, Elli. "Women's Disarmament and Anti-War Movements." In *Korean Women's Peace Movement: Its Unfolding and Issues*, edited by Young Hee Shim and Elli Kim, 139–201. Seoul: Han Wool Academy, 2005.

Kim, Yon-Ja. *A Big Sister in Americatown*. Seoul: Samin, 2005. (Korean)

Lee, Na Young. "The Construction of Camptown [*kijichon*] Prostitution and Women's Resistance." In *Women and Peace*, edited by Peace Institute of Korean Women and Peace, 170–197. Seoul: Hanul, 2010. (Korean)

Moon, Katherine. *Sex among Allies: Military Prostitution in U.S.–Korean Relations*. New York: Columbia University, 1997.

Naikakufu, Danjō kyōdōsankaku kyoku [Cabinet Office, Government of Japan, Gender Equality Bureau] 2010. Danjō kyōdōsankaku Hakusho [White Paper on Gender Equality 2010]. Accessed March 15, 2017. http://www.gender.go.jp/whitepaper/h22/zentai/pdf/index.html. (Korean)

Naikakufu, Danjō kyōdōsankaku kyoku [Cabinet Office, Government of Japan, Gender Equality Bureau] 2008. Heisei 20 nenpan Danjō kyōdōsankaku shakai no keisei no jōkyō [2008 White paper on Gender Equality]. Accessed March 15, 2017. http://www.gender.go.jp/about_danjo/whitepaper/h20/gaiyou/index.html. (Korean)

National Campaign for Eradication of Crimes by U.S. Troops in Korea. "The Fifteen Year History of National Campaign for Eradication of Crimes by the U.S. Troops in Korea, GI Crimes and the Korean–U.S. SOFA." In *Revise the SOFA!*, edited by National Campaign for Eradication of Crimes by U.S. Troops in Korea, 16–53. Seoul: Yin Publishing, 2008. (Korean)

Soelle, Dorothee. *The Silent Cry: Mysticism and Resistance*. Minneapolis, MN: Fortress Press, 2001.

Soelle, Dorothee. *Suffering*. Minneapolis, MN: Fortress Press, 1984.

Takeda, Hiroko. "All the Japan State Wants is Shining Women (and Their Families): Tatemae and Honne of AbeWomenomics." Conference Paper (2015). Accessed March 15, 2017. https://www.psa.ac.uk/sites/default/files/conference/papers/2015/Abe-Womenomics_R_0.pdf.

Yi, Yim-hwa. *Korean War and Gender: Women Stood up over the War*. Seoul: Seohae Moonjip, 2004. (Korean)

Yuh, Ji-yeon. *Beyond the Shadow of Camptown: Korean Military Brides in America*. New York: University Press, 2004.

Chapter 15

Begum, Khani. "The Dialogics of the New Orientalist Discourse: Telling Tales of Iranian Womanhood." In *Women and Islam (Women and Religion Series)*, edited by Zayn R. Kassam, 263–288. Santa Barbara, CA: Praeger ABC-CLIO, 2010.

Chakravarty, Sumita S. "Fragmenting the Nation: Images of Terrorism in Indian Popular Cinema." In *Terrorism, Media, Liberation*, edited by J. David Slocum, 232–247. New Brunswick, NJ: Rutgers University Press, 2006.

"Does Zero Dark Thirty endorse Torture" December 10, 2012. Accessed August 28, 2015. http://ohnotheydidnt.livejournal.com/74089779.html.

Engle, Karen. *Seeing Ghosts: 9/11 and the Visual Imagination*. Montreal: McGill Queen's University Press, 2009.

Foster, Kathleen. *Afghan Women: A History of Struggle*. The Cinema Guild DVD, 2007. 69 mins.

Greenwald, Glenn. "Zero Dark Thirty: CIA Hagiography, Pernicious Propaganda." Accessed August 28, 2015. http://www.theguardian.com/commentis free/2012/dec/14/zero-dark-thirty-cia-propaganda.

Hirsi Ali, Ayaan. *Nomad: From Islam to America a Personal Journey through the Clash of Civilizations*. New York: Free Press, 2010.

Hoberman, J. *Film After Film: Or What Became of 21st Century Cinema*. New York: Verso Books, 2013.

Kassam, Zayn R., ed. *Women and Islam (Women and Religion Series)*. Santa Barbara, CA: Praeger, 2010.

Merrill, Robert. "Simulations and Terrors of Our Times." In *Terrorism, Media, Liberation,* edited by David Slocum, 171–184. New Brunswick, NJ: Rutgers University Press, 2005.

Morris, Rosalind C. "Theses on the Question of War: History, Media, Terror." In *Terrorism, Media, Liberation,* edited by David Slocum, 297–320. New Brunswick, NJ: Rutgers University Press, 2005.

"Nobel Winner Malala Opens School for Syrian Refugee Girls." *The World Post*, December 7, 2015. Accessed September 30, 2016. http://www.huffington post.com/2015/07/12/malala-refugee-school_n_7779388.html.

Novak, Marcos. "Speciation, Transvergence, Allogenesis: Notes on the Production of an Alien." *Architectural Design* 72, no. 3 (2002): 4–7.

Razack, Sherene H. *Casting Out: The Eviction of Muslims from Western Law and Politics*. Toronto: University of Toronto Press, 2008.

Sarker, Bhaskar. *Mourning the Nation*. Durham, NC: Duke University Press, 2009.

Satrapi, Marjane, Azar Nafisi, Farzaneh Milani, Persis Karim, and Ayaan Hirsi Ali. *Nomad: From Islam to America a Personal Journey through the Clash of Civilizations*. New York: Free Press, 2010.

Spivak, Gayatri Chakravarty. *An Aesthetic Education in the Era of Globalization*. Boston: Harvard University Press, 2013.

Spivak, Gayatri Chakravarty. "Can the Subaltern Speak?" In *Colonial Discourse and Postcolonial Theory: A Reader,* edited by Patrick Williams and Laura Chrisman, 66–111. New York: Columbia University Press, 1994.

Zizek, Slavoj. *Welcome to the Desert of the Real: Five Essays on September 11 and Related Dates*. New York: Radical Thinkers (Verso 1st Edition) 2013.

CHAPTER 16

Chandhasrisalai, C. and P. Boonsuk. *Khun Yai: The founder of wat phra dhammakaya*. Bangkok: Fongthong Enterprise, 1998.

Dattajeevo Bhikkhu, P., *Telling Khun Yai's Story*. Bangkok: Pradhiphat, 1997.

Dhammakaya Foundation. *The Full Moon*. Bangkok: Watchara Offset, 2001.

Phrabhavanaviriyakhun. *Do Good Deeds Must Get Merits*. Bangkok: Rungsilpa (1977), 2004.

Phrabhavanaviriyakhun. *Precepts, Meditation, Wisdom: The Moral Principle of khun yai*. Bangkok: Nuruemit Soul, 2003.

Phrabhavanaviriyakhun, interview by P. Lovichakorntikul. *The Vice Abbot of Wat Phra Dhammakaya* (November 29, 2012).

Rangsisakorn, S. *The Moon at the Center of Mind*. 2nd edition. Bangkok: S.P.K. Paper and Form, 2005.

Trianusorn, A. *The Waning Moon Night,* 3. Bangkok: Siriwatthana Interprint Co., Ltd., 2001.

Vorasubin, V., S. Vorasubin, P. Tisuthiwongse, C. Kanhalikham, B. Intakanok, and D. Jung. *Khun Yai's Teachings: Wisdom from an enlightened mind*. Pathumthani: Dhammakaya Foundation, 2012.

CHAPTER 17

Becker, Peggy and Pawan Dhingra. "Religious involvement and Volunteering: Implications for Civil Society." *Sociology of Religion*, 62 (2001): 316–335.

Bourdieu, Pierre. *The Logic of Practice*. Cambridge: Polity, [1980] 1990.

Brown, Phil and Faith Ferguson. "'Making a Big Stink': Women's Work, Women's Relationships, and Toxic Waste Activism." *Gender and Society* 9 (1995): 145–172.

Bunkachō [Japanese Agency for Cultural Affairs]. *Shūkyō nenkan* [Religions Yearbook]. Tokyo: Gyōsei, 2009.

Catholic Bishops' Conference of Japan. *Statistics of the Catholic Church of Japan 2010*, 2010. Accessed July 7, 2016. http://www.cbcj.catholic.jp/jpn/data/st10/statistics2010.pdf.

Chaves, Mark. "Secularization as Declining Religious Authority." *Social Forces* 72 (1994): 794–775.

Fujita, Makiko. "'It's all Mother's Fault': Childcare and the Socialization of Working Mothers in Japan." *Journal of Japanese Studies* 15, no. 1 (1989): 67–91.

Fujiyama, Midori. "Genpatsu ni taisuru shūkyōkai no kenkai" [The position of religious organization vis-à-vis nuclear power], *Shūkyō jōhō* [Religious Information], January, 30, 2012. Accessed July 7, 2016. http://www.circam.jp/reports/02/detail/id=2012.

Granovetter, Mark S. "The Strength of Weak Ties." *The American Journal of Sociology* 78, no. 6 (1973): 1360–1380.

Gutierrez, Lorraine M., Ruth J. Parsons, and Enid Opal Cox, eds. *Empowerment in Social Work Practice: A Sourcebook*. Pacific Grove: Brooks/Cole Publishing Company, 1998.

Kanbayashi, Chieko and Naoko Miura. "Sei, kekkon to josei: seikihan kekkon, shufuyakuwari kara no jiritsu" [Sexuality, marriage and women: autonomy from the normative married and housewife model]. In *Gendai Nihonjin no sei no yukue—Tsunagari to jiritsu*. [The direction of contemporary Japanese lives: relatedness and independency], edited by T. Miyajima and S. Shima-zono, 97–142. Tokyo: Fujihara shoten, 2003. (Japanese)

Kawahashi, Noriko. "Gender Issues in Japanese Religions." In *The Nanzan Guide to Japanese Religions*, edited by P. Swanson and C. Clark, 323–335. Honolulu: University of Hawaii Press, 2006.

Keishin, Inaba. "Religion's Response to the Earthquake and Tsunami in Northeastern Japan." *Bulletin of the Graduate School of Human Sciences* 42 (2016): 43–59.

Naikakufu, Danjō kyōdō sankaku kyoku [Cabinet Office, Government of Japan, Gender Equality Bureau] *Heisei 28 Danjō kyōdōsankaku Hakusho* [White Paper on Gender Equality 2016]. Accessed July 7, 2016. http://www.gender .go.jp/english_contents/about_danjo/whitepaper/pdf/ewp2016.pdf.

O'Connor, Mary Katherine and F. Ellen Netting, eds. *Organization Practice: A Guide to Understanding Human Service Organizations*. Hoboken, NJ: Wiley & Sons, 2009.

Putnam, Robert. *Bowling Alone: The Collapse and Revival of American Community*. New York: Simon and Schuster, 2000.

Takeda, Hiroko. *The Political Economy of Reproduction in Japan: Between Nation-State and Everyday Life*. New York: Routledge Curzon, 2005.

Takeda, Hiroko. "Reforming Families in Japan: Family Policy in the Era of Structural Reform." In *Home and Family in Japan: Continuity and Transformation*, edited by R. Ronald and A. Alexy, 46–64. New York: Routledge, 2011.

Taniguchi, Hiromi. "Men's and Women's Volunteering: Gender Differences in the Effects of Employment and Family Characteristics." *Nonprofit and Voluntary Sector Quarterly* 35, no. 1 (2006): 83–101.

Wilson, James Q. *Political Organizations*. New York: Basic Books, 1974.

Wilson, John and Thomas Janoski. "The Contribution of Religion to Volunteer Work." *Sociology of Religion* 56, no. 2 (1995): 137–152.

CHAPTER 18

Chaudhuri, A. B. *The Santals: Religion and Rituals*. New Delhi: Ashish Publishing House, 1987.

Chaudhuri, Nanimadhab. "Cult of the Old Lady." *Journal of the Royal Asiatic Society of Bengal* Letters, V (1939): 417–418.

Kularnava Tantra, edited by Upendrakumar Das. Calcutta: Nababharat [Navbharat] Publishers, 1383/1976.

McDaniel, June. *The Madness of the Saints: Ecstatic Religion in Bengal*. Chicago: University of Chicago Press, 1989.

McDaniel, June. *Offering Flowers Feeding Skulls: Popular Goddess Worship in West Bengal*. New York: Oxford University Press, 2004.

Troisi, J. *The Santals: Readings in Tribal Life*. New Delhi: Indian Social Institute, 1979.

Chapter 19

Batchelor, Martine. "Achaan Ranjuan: A Thai Lay Woman as Master Teacher." In *Women's Buddhism, Buddhism's Women: Tradition, Revision, Renewal*, edited by Ellison Banks Findly, 156–158. Somerville, MA: Wisdom Publications, 2000.

Berkwitz, Stephen, Juliane Schober, and Claudia Brown. "Introduction: Rethinking Buddhist Manuscript Cultures." In *Buddhist Manuscript Cultures: Knowledge, Ritual, and Art*, edited by Stephen Berkwitz, Juliane Schober, and Claudia Brown, 1–16. New York: Routledge, 2009.

Bond, George. *The Buddhist Revival in Sri Lanka: Religious Tradition, Reinterpretation, and Response*. Columbia: University of South Carolina Press, 1988.

Braun, Erik. *The Birth of Insight: Meditation, Modern Buddhism, and the Burmese Monk Ledi Sayadaw*. Chicago: Chicago University Press, 2013.

Carrithers, Michael. *The Forest Monks of Sri Lanka: An Anthropological and Historical Study*. New Delhi: Oxford University Press, 1983.

Collins, Steven. "Pāli Practices of the Self." Keynote Address of the Theravāda Civilizations Project. March 10, 2012.

Collins, Steven and Justin McDaniel. "Buddhist 'nuns' (*mae chi*) and the teaching of Pali in contemporary Thailand." *Modern Asian Studies* 44, no. 6 (2010): 1373–1408.

Cook, Joanna. *Meditation in Modern Buddhism: Renunciation and Change in Thai Monastic Life*. Cambridge: Cambridge University Press, 2010.

Falk, Monica Lindberg. *Making Fields of Merit: Buddhist Ascetics and Gendered Orders in Thailand*. Copenhagen: NIAS Press, 2007.

Foucault, Michel. *The History of Sexuality*. Translated by Robert Hurley. New York: Pantheon Books, 1976.

Foucault, Michel. "Technologies of the Self." In *Technologies of the Self: A Seminar with Michel Foucault*, edited and translated by Luther Martin, Huck Gutman and Patrick Hutton, 16–49. Amherst, MA: University of Massachusetts Press, 1988.

Gombrich, Richard and Gananath Obeyesekere. *Buddhism Transformed: Religious Changes in Sri Lanka*. Princeton, NJ: Princeton University Press, 1988.

Houtman, Gustaaf. "Traditions of Buddhist Practice in Myanmar." PhD Dissertation, School of Oriental and African Studies, London University, 1990.

Irons, Edward. "Naeb Mahaniranonda, Ajahn." *Encyclopedia of Buddhism*, 354. New York: Facts on File, 2008.

Ito, Tomomi. "Questions of Ordination Legitimacy for Newly Ordained Theravāda *bhikkhunī* in Thailand." *Journal of Southeast Asian Studies* 43, no. 1 (2012): 55–76.

Jacobsen, Trude. "In Search of the Khmer *Bhikkhunī*: Reading Between the Lines in Late Classical and Early Middle Cambodia (13th–18th Centuries)." *Journal of the Oxford Centre for Buddhist Studies* 4 (2013): 75–87.

Jordt, Ingrid. *Myanmar's Mass Lay Meditation Movement: Buddhism and the Cultural Construction on Power*. Athens: Ohio University Press, 2007.

Jordt, Ingrid. "Women's Practices of Renunciation in the Age of *Sāsana* Revival." In *Myanmar at the Turn of the 21st Century*, edited by Monique Skidmore, 41–64. Honolulu: University of Hawaii Press, 2005.

Kawanami, Hiroko. "Patterns of Renunciation: The Changing World of Burmese Nuns." In *Women's Buddhism, Buddhism's Women: Tradition, Revision, Renewal*, edited by Ellison Banks Findly, 159–171. Somerville, MA: Wisdom Publications, 2000.

Kawanami, Hiroko. *Renunciation and Empowerment of Buddhist Nuns in Myanmar-Myanmar: Building a Community of Female Faithful*. Boston: Brill, 2013.

Kee Nanayon, Upasika. *Pure & Simple*. Translated by Thanissaro Bhikkhu. *Access to Insight Website*, June 7, 2010. Accessed December 4, 2012. http://www.accesstoinsight.org/lib/thai/kee/pureandsimple.html.

King, Sallie. *Socially Engaged Buddhism*. Honolulu: University of Hawaii Press, 2009.

Kornfield, Jack. *Living Dharma: Teachings and Meditation Instructions from Twelve Theravada Masters*. London: Shambhala Publications, 2010.

Löschmann, Heike. "The Revival of the *Don Chee* Movement in Cambodia." In *Innovative Buddhist Women: Swimming Against the Stream*, edited by Karma Lekshe Tsosmo, 91–95. Richmond, Surrey: Curzon Press, 2000.

Meister, Kelly. "Burmese Monks in Bangkok: Opening an Abhidhamma School and Creating a Lineage." *Religion Compass* 3, no. 4 (2009): 549–565.

Mendelson, Michael, E. *Sangha and State in Myanmar: A Study of Monastic Sectarianism and Leadership*. Ithaca, NY: Cornell University Press, 1975.

Mrozik, Susanne. "A Robed Revolution: The Contemporary Buddhist Nun's (*Bhiksuni*) Movement." *Religion Compass* 3/3 (2009): 360–378.

Naeb, Mahaniranonda. *The Development of Insight*. Bangkok: Abhidhamma Foundation, 1982.

Nyanaponika Thera. *The Heart of Buddhist Meditation*. Kandy, Sri Lanka: Buddhist Publication Society, 1996 [1954].

Ray, Reginald. *Buddhist Saints in India: A Study in Buddhist Values and Orientations*. New York: Oxford University Press, 1994.

Rozenberg, Guilliame. *Renunciation and Power: The Quest for Sainthood in Contemporary Myanmar*. New Haven, CT: Yale University Southeast Asia Studies, 2010.

Schedneck, Brooke. *Constructing Religious Modernities: Hybridity, Reinterpretation and Adaptation in Thailand's International Meditation Centers*. PhD Dissertation, Arizona State University, 2012.

Schedneck, Brooke. "Enacting Female Buddhist Roles Through *Vipassanā* Meditation Centers." 13th Sakyadhita Conference. Vaishali, India, January 8, 2013.

Schedneck, Brooke. "Western Buddhist Perceptions of Monasticism." *Buddhist Studies Review* 26, no. 2 (2009): 229–246.

Scott, Rachelle, M. "Buddhism, Miraculous Powers, and Gender: Rethinking the Stories of Theravāda Nuns." *Journal of the International Association of Buddhist Studies* 33, no. 1–2 (2011): 489–511.

Seeger, Martin. "'Against the Stream': The Thai Female Buddhist Saint Mae Chi Kaew Sianglam (1901–1991)." *South East Asia Research* 18, no. 3 (2010): 555–595.

Seeger, Martin. "The *Bhikkhunī*-Ordination Controversy in Thailand." *Journal of the International Association of Buddhist Studies* 29, no. 1 (2006): 155–183.

Seeger, Martin. "Reversal of Female Power, Transcendentality, and Gender in Thai Buddhism: The Thai Buddhist female saint Khun Mae Bunruean Tongbuntowm (1895–1964)." *Modern Asian Studies* 47, no. 5 (2013): 1488–1519.

Shankman, Richard. *The Experience of Samadhi: An In-depth Exploration of Buddhist Meditation*. London: Shambhala Publications, 2008.

Sharf, Robert. "Buddhist Modernism and the Rhetoric of Meditative Experience." *Numen* 42, no. 3 (1995): 228–283.

Silaratano, Bhikkhu. *Mae Chee Kaew: Her Journey to Spiritual Awakening and Enlightenment*. Udon Thani, Thailand: Forest Dhamma Publications, 2012.

Tambiah, Stanley J. *The Buddhist Saints of the Forest and the Cult of Amulets: A Study in Charisma, Hagiography, Sectarianism, and Millenial Buddhism*. New York: Cambridge University Press, 1984.

Thanissaro, Bhikkhu. "Upasika Kee Nanayon and the Social Dynamic of Theravadin Buddhist Practice." Access to Insight Website. 2010. Accessed April 26, 2012. http://www.accesstoinsight.org/lib/thai/kee/dynamic.html.

Tiyavanich, Kamala. *Forest Recollections: Wandering Monks in Twentieth-Century Thailand*. Honolulu: University of Hawaii Press, 1997.

Van Esterik, John. "Cultural Interpretation of Canonical Paradox: Lay Meditation in a Central Thai Village." PhD Dissertation, University of Illinois at Urbana-Champaign, 1977.

Index

Note: Page numbers in *italics* indicate illustrations.

About the Editor and Contributors

Editor

Zayn R. Kassam is the John Knox McLean Professor of Religious Studies at Pomona College in Claremont, California. The winner of three Wig Awards for Distinguished Teaching, she has also won the national American Academy of Religion award for Excellence in Teaching. Kassam has authored a volume on Islam (Greenwood Press, 2005) and has also edited the volume in this series titled *Women and Islam* (2010). She has published articles on religion and migration, on pedagogy, feminist Muslim hermeneutics, and Muslim women and globalization. Her current research investigates contemporary challenges facing Muslim women and issues pertaining to migration.

Contributors

Nicole Aaron has a PhD in geography and religious studies from the University of Otago in New Zealand and a joint master of arts in religion and development from the University of Leeds, United Kingdom. Her research interests encompass the relationships between gender, religion, and development in postcolonial India.

Vivienne SM Angeles is associate professor of Religion at La Salle University in Philadelphia, with research interests in Islam, women and gender in Southeast Asia, religion and migration, and visual expressions of Islam. The author of several articles on Muslims in the Philippines, her coedited volume titled *Gender, Religion and Migration: Pathways to Integration* was published in 2010. She is cochair of the Religion in Southeast group of the American Academy of Religion.

Khani Begum teaches modern and contemporary literature; feminist, postcolonial, and film theory; and contemporary global cinemas at Bowling Green State University. Her research and writing ranges from feminist and postcolonial analyses of male modernists to exploring gender issues in cinemas from Iran and South East Asia. Her most current work on global cinematic perspectives explores the effects of the tragedy of 9/11 and the U.S. war on terror on non-Western cultures both outside and within the United States.

Paola Cavaliere is an assistant professor of Japanese studies at Osaka University, Japan. She received her double PhD degree in East Asian studies from the University of Sheffield, United Kingdom, and law from Tohoku University, Japan. Her recent publications include *Promising Practices: Women Volunteers in Japanese Religious Civil Society* (2015). Her research interests include Japanese women's activism in religious civil society and its implications for participatory democracy.

Keun-Joo Christine Pae is associate professor of religion/ethics at the Departments of Religion and Women and Gender Studies at Denison University, Ohio. Taking Christian social ethics as a discipline, she has published many articles, including some that examine the intersection of race, gender/sexuality, and militarism from a transnational feminist perspective, others on feminist spiritual activism, and some dealing with Asian and Asian American ethics.

Leesa S. Davis is a lecturer of philosophy at Deakin University, Australia. She is the author of *Advaita Vedanta and Zen Buddhism: Deconstructive Modes of Spiritual Inquiry* (2010) and is currently working on a book on the use of paradox in Zen Buddhism.

Antoinette E. DeNapoli is an associate professor of South Asian religions at Texas Christian University in Fort Worth, Texas, where she teaches courses on Hinduism, Buddhism, Indian, and Tibetan mystical traditions of yoga and tantra, goddesses of South Asia, the divine personality in Eastern religions, gender and religion, and theories of religion. Prior to this she was at the University of Wyoming where she also taught a study abroad course in India on religion and globalization. She received her PhD in West and South Asian religions from Emory University. She is the author of a number of articles and book chapters. Her first book titled *Real Sadhus Sing to God: Gender, Asceticism, and Vernacular Religion in Rajasthan* was published in 2014. She is currently working on her second book project titled *Religion at the Crossroads: Experimental Hinduism in Twenty-First Century India*.

William Harman has written extensively about Hindu goddesses, Tamil temples, rituals, and violence in religious movements. He studied at Oberlin College, the University of Chicago, L'Université d'Aix-Marseille, and Madurai University and has taught at DePauw University and the University of Tennessee. He is now retired and divides his time between Pittsburgh and southern France.

Jae Woo Jang is an undergraduate student at Stanford University majoring in mathematical computational science and minoring in anthropology. His notable works have been published in the Stanford undergraduate economics journal and other peer-reviewed journals. He hopes to continue to integrate engineering in the academia of humanities.

Anru Lee is a faculty member at the Department of Anthropology, John Jay College of Criminal Justice, at the City University of New York. She is the author of *In the Name of Harmony and Prosperity: Labor and Gender Politics in Taiwan's Economic Restructuring* (2004) and is the coeditor of *Women in the New Taiwan: Gender Roles and Gender Consciousness in a Changing Society* (2004). Her current project investigates mass rapid transit systems as related to issues of technology, governance, and citizenship. Her most recent fieldwork looks at the urban mass transit systems in Taiwan in the context of the country's struggle for cultural and national identity.

Petcharat Lovichakorntikul teaches at Stamford University in Bangkok, Thailand, after serving as a lecturer at the School of Management, Shinawatra International University (SIU), where she obtained her PhD in management. Her dissertation is titled "Buddhist Principle Model towards the Human Resource Development of Professionals in the Healthcare Business in Thailand." She earned a BA in marketing from Chulalongkorn University and in liberal arts from Ramkhamkhaeng University, Thailand, and an MS in leadership and management from the United States. Her interests and publications are in management, human resource development, self-development, spiritual development, and applied Buddhist teachings. A peer reviewer for *SIU Journal* and the Emerald Market Case Studies, she has also worked in public enterprise, the private sector, and nonprofit organizations both in Thailand and abroad. Since 2011 she has been on the executive committee for the Traimbuddhasart school for young Buddhist novices. She has been practicing meditation since she was in high school and loves to learn new things from all aspects.

June McDaniel is professor of history of religions at the Department of Religious Studies, College of Charleston. She teaches courses in world religions, religions of India, women and religion, goddesses in world religions, mysticism, myth, ritual and symbol, and psychology of religion, as well as other courses. Her MTS in theology was from Emory University, and her PhD in the history of religions was from the University of Chicago. She spent two years doing field research in India, on grants from Fulbright and the American Institute of Indian Studies. She has three books published on Indian religions: one on religious ecstasy in West Bengal, another on women's rituals, and a third on popular goddess worship. She has recently coedited a volume on the spiritual senses. She has chaired three groups at the American Academy of Religion: on mysticism, on ritual studies, and on anthropology of religion (for which she was the founding chair).

Visisya Pinthongvijayakul received his BA in English and MA in comparative literature from Chulalongkorn University, Thailand. He teaches at the Faculty of Humanities and Social Sciences, Chandrakasem Rajabhat University, Bangkok. Visisya is currently a PhD candidate at the Department of Anthropology, the Australian National University. His research focuses on the practice of spirit mediums in northeast Thailand. He conducted fieldwork in Chaiyaphum Province from April 2012 to March 2013.

Phramaha Min Putthithanasombat is a doctoral candidate at the School of Management, Shinawatra University, Thailand, where his research focuses on the role of Buddhist philosophy in the management of educational institutions. His research interests lie in Theravāda, socially engaged Buddhism and Educational Management. Additionally, since 2009, he has held an administrative post at Traimbuddhasart school, Prachin Buri province, Thailand, at which young novice Buddhist monks are trained. He has been a practicing Theravāda Buddhist monk for 17 years.

Angela Rudert has a PhD in religion from Syracuse University and is lecturer at the Department of Philosophy and Religion at Ithaca College, where she teaches courses related to religion and gender in South Asia. Her current book project, developed from her doctoral thesis, examines tradition and innovation in 21st-century guru devotion through a study of Anandmurti Gurumaa, a young, yet prominent and globetrotting north Indian female guru. A Doctoral Dissertation Research Award from Fulbright-Hays and a dissertation research award from FLAS supported her fieldwork research in India in 2008 and 2009.

Kristen Rudisill is an associate professor and chair at the Department of Popular Culture at Bowling Green State University. Her PhD is in Asian studies from the University of Texas at Austin and she specializes in Tamil theater and dance. She has published on this topic in venues such as *South Asian Popular Culture*, *The Asian Theatre Journal*, *Studies in Musical Theatre*, and *Text and Presentation*.

Brooke Schedneck is a lecturer of Buddhist studies at the Institute of Southeast Asian Affairs at Chiangmai University, Thailand. She holds a PhD in Asian religions from Arizona State University. The title of her monograph through Routledge's series Contemporary Asian Religions is *Thailand's International Meditation Centers: Tourism and the Global Commodification of Religious Practices*. She has been published in *The Buddhist Studies Review*, *The Pacific World Journal*, *The Journal of Contemporary Religion*, and *Contemporary Buddhism*.

Narasingha P. Sil obtained his PhD in the history of Tudor England from the University of Oregon. He is currently professor emeritus of history at Western Oregon University. Dr. Sil's other area of interest lies in the history of late colonial Bengal. Sil has published critical biographies of Sri Ramakrishna and Swami Vivekananda (in 2009 and 1997, respectively). His *Swami Vivekananda: A Reassessment* was selected by *Choice* as an outstanding academic book in religion in 1997. He has contributed articles (under the category of "Other Considerations") to the *Encyclopedia of Religion* (2nd ed.) and published a bibliographical essay on Ramakrishna in Oxford Bibliography Online (OBO). Additionally, he has published numerous scholarly articles and book reviews with academic presses and in journals around the world.

Maria Talamantes is a scholar and dance practitioner whose research on the region of Bali, Indonesia, brings together the fields of dance, anthropology, religion, and gender. She holds a PhD degree in Dance History and Theory from the University of California, Riverside, and a Master of Fine Arts degree from CAL ARTS. She has taught at the University of Minnesota, Scripps College, Cal State Long Beach, and the University of Texas, among others. Her article, "Performance of Identity: The *Pelegongan Andir* of Tista, Bali," *Asian Theatre Journal* (Fall 2006), is based on her dissertation fieldwork.

Wen-hui Anna Tang is a professor at the Center for General Education and the Department of Sociology at the National Sun Yat-sen University, Kaohsiung, Taiwan. Her major research interests are gender, migration, and parenting in East Asia and America.

Lavanya Vemsani is distinguished professor of history at the Department of Social Sciences at Shawnee State University. She is the author of *Hindu and Jain Mythology of Balarama* and a number of articles on the history and religions of India. She is the editor of *International Journal of Dharma and Hindu Studies* and an associate editor of the *Journal of South Asian Religious History*.

John Walsh is assistant professor at the School of Management, Shinawatra International University (SIU). He is responsible for supervising PhD and graduate students in addition to teaching Greater Mekong subregion studies at the undergraduate level. He is the director of the SIU Research Centre, editor of the *SIU Journal of Management* and *Nepalese Journal of Management Science and Research*, and regional editor (Southeast Asia) for Emerald's Emerging Markets Case Studies Collection. He received his doctorate from the University of Oxford for a thesis concerning international management in the East Asian region. His research mainly focuses on the social and economic development of the Greater Mekong subregion.